LEVEL UP YOUR LEGAL WRITING

ASPEN COURSEBOOK SERIES

LEVEL UP YOUR LEGAL WRITING

TECHNIQUES AND TECHNOLOGY TO SUPERCHARGE YOUR SKILLS

Joe Regalia

Associate Professor of Law
William S. Boyd School of Law, UNLV

Co-Founder, Write.law

ASPEN PUBLISHING

To contact Customer Service, e-mail customer.service@aspenpublishing.com, call 1-800-950-5259, or mail correspondence to:

Aspen Publishing
Attn: Order Department
1 Wall Street
Burlington, MA 01803

Printed in the United States of America.

2 3 4 5 6 7 8 9 0

ISBN 979-8-8890-6111-3

Library of Congress Cataloging-in-Publication Data

Names: Regalia, Joe, author.
Title: Level up your legal writing: techniques and technology to supercharge your skills / Joe Regalia, Associate Professor of Law, William S. Boyd School of Law, UNLV; Co-Founder, Write.law.
Description: First edition. | Burlington, MA: Aspen Publishing, 2024. | Series: Aspen Coursebook Series | Includes bibliographical references and index. | Summary: "Primary text for law school courses on Persuasive or Advanced Legal Writing, and a handbook for lawyers who want to advance their legal writing skills."—Provided by publisher.
Identifiers: LCCN 2024029853 (print) | LCCN 2024029854 (ebook) | ISBN 9798889061113 (paperback) | ISBN 9798889061137 (ebook)
Subjects: LCSH: Legal composition. | Legal composition—Technological innovations. | LCGFT: Textbooks.
Classification: LCC KF250.R425 2024 (print) | LCC KF250 (ebook) | DDC 808.06/34—dc23/eng/20240709
LC record available at https://lccn.loc.gov/2024029853
LC ebook record available at https://lccn.loc.gov/2024029854

ABOUT ASPEN PUBLISHING

Aspen Publishing is a leading provider of legal education content and digital learning solutions in the United States and globally. Our innovative products and platforms—designed based on best practices in learning science—engage students and enhance outcomes. From textbooks and audiobooks authored by renowned experts to digital platforms and products like LEAF, Connected eBooks, Connected Quizzing, PracticePerfect, and JD-Next, we empower the next generation of legal professionals with innovative, trusted, and accessible resources.

The Aspen Casebook Series, affectionately known as the "red and black" casebooks among law faculty and students, includes hundreds of highly regarded textbooks across more than 80 disciplines. These range from foundational courses like Torts and Contracts to emerging electives such as Sustainability and the Law of Policing. Our study aids, including the popular *Examples & Explanations* series, help law students master complex topics with clarity and confidence.

Aspen's expertise extends to undergraduate education with our Paralegal, Criminal Justice, and Business Law series, offering the same hallmark quality to a broader audience. JD-Next, our groundbreaking online law school prep course and admissions test, provides a realistic preview of law school, equips students with essential skills for academic success, and evaluates their readiness for legal studies.

Aspen Publishing Is Proud to Be a UWorld Company

Since 2003, UWorld has been a global leader in developing high-quality learning tools for students preparing for high-stakes exams. With a commitment to excellence, UWorld has helped millions of students in undergraduate, graduate, and professional programs in fields such as medicine, nursing, finance, and law achieve their academic and career goals.

Founded by Chandra S. Pemmasani, M.D., during his medical residency, UWorld began focusing on medical education and has since expanded into various academic fields, including law. In 2020, UWorld launched its Legal vertical, starting with its comprehensive Multistate Bar Exam (MBE®) Question Bank, followed by the acquisition of Themis Bar Review, which integrated resources to provide a complete bar exam preparation experience. In 2024, UWorld expanded its offerings by acquiring Aspen Publishing, enhancing its suite of legal education products.

Today, UWorld offers an unparalleled range of study materials that blend active learning methods with expert content, ensuring students and educators can access the most effective resources. From bar preparation to law school success, UWorld is committed to supporting the next generation of legal professionals. Learn more at uworld.com.

First, for my wife, Susie. I don't always get why you believe in me so much, but I'm glad you do. Like so many wonderful things in my life, this book wouldn't be here without you.

Second, for every law student or lawyer ever told, "You're just not a good writer." Don't believe them.

ABOUT THE AUTHOR

A leading expert in legal writing and technology, Joe Regalia is a law professor at the William S. Boyd School of Law at the University of Las Vegas, where the legal writing program ranks among the top in the nation. The author's academic research and teaching focus on legal writing, legal technology, and the science of persuasion.

The author's passion for revolutionizing legal writing led him to co-found Write.law, a premier global company that dramatically advances legal writing skills through an innovative approach that combines interactive courses, AI-fueled learning apps, and live training.

Write.law has worked with more than 200,000 practitioners on legal teams from every corner of the industry, including AmLaw firms, small firms, regional firms, federal courts, state courts, Fortune 500 in-house legal teams, legislative professionals, contract teams, nonprofits, and legal aid organizations. Not to mention the thousands of people who seek out Write.law every month because they want to learn how to level up their legal writing.

Write.law partners with law professors and trainers across the country to integrate innovative teaching methods and interactive tools into their courses and programs. Tens of thousands of law students rely on Write.law to guide them through the complexities of legal writing with confidence.

Prior to joining the faculty at UNLV, Joe Regalia honed his skills at three global AmLaw firms, clerked for the U.S. District Courts and the U.S. Court of Appeals for the Ninth Circuit, and graduated first in his class at the University of Michigan Law School.

SUMMARY OF CONTENTS

CONTENTS

Why I Wrote This Book

> "The best legal writers are not born; they are made."[1]

When I was a law student, legal writing was simultaneously new and frustratingly familiar. Sometimes it felt like college essays and high school reports. Sometimes it felt like I was learning a new language, and a weird one at that. Many of my fellow law students felt the same.

And it's not just law students. When I became a lawyer, I constantly heard others complain, law school long behind them, that they "didn't know how to write." They stared at a blank page for hours, or put off their important writing until the last minute. Some dreaded writing more than anything—more than demanding clients, harsh judges, or endless billable-hour tracking.

How could this be? Most lawyering really is about the writing. The writing is how legal business gets done. The writing is how cases are argued, clients are advised, and colleagues are communicated with. The writing is how the decisions that change people's lives are made.

Shouldn't writing be what lawyers love most—their chance to put into words all the work they devote to their clients' cases? But no, it wasn't. And it isn't.

Legal writing is easily the biggest roadblock faced by law students and lawyers alike. In my work at the training company I helped found, Write.law, and as a law professor, I've supported quite a few in improving their writing craft. Some were starting their careers; others had been practicing for decades. And I hear the same things:

"I still don't really understand how to write."

"Writing takes me forever."

"I dread getting words on the page."

[1] I riffed off a Stephen King quote here. His original was "I think that writers are made, not born . . . becoming a writer . . . is a direct result of conscious will." Which is even more true for us writers of the legal persuasion.

There is a better way. I know, because at Write.law, we've helped tens of thousands of lawyers learn to love their legal writing. Assisting folks on this journey has become our mission.

Let me explain why finding a way to love your legal writing matters so much. Research paints a clear picture: the best predictors of job satisfaction and success are whether you enjoy your day-to-day work and have the skills to excel at it. Enjoying your everyday tasks at work[2] and getting good at the skills you need for those tasks[3] makes you more productive, more creative, and influences how much you'll make and how successful you'll be.[4]

Most lawyers spend most of their time writing, whether a contract for a client or a brief for a court. So if you learn to love your legal writing and become excellent at it, you will invest more in your long-term success and happiness than just about anything else you could do.

Easier said than done, right? After all, becoming a great legal writer is hard, or at least that's what we are told. Many lawyers still struggle with basic writing principles years into their practice. Many others declare that the best legal writers are a talented few — the rare lawyer born with an ear for great prose. Troves of books are written on how to merely write competently, full of strict rules to be memorized.

But there's another path. You can improve your legal writing in weeks or months. You can become confident and no longer a victim of confusing grammar rules or arbitrary writing advice. Most importantly, you can develop your own authentic voice that connects with audiences.

I've seen it happen for lawyers around the world. After empowering them to be in the driver's seat of their legal writing, rather than a passenger, their feelings toward legal writing shift. One of my favorite clients put it simply: "For the first time, I enjoy sitting down to work on my briefs."

This book is dedicated to supporting you on that same journey. Whether you already love legal writing and want to love it even more, or you loathe putting pen to paper. This book will be a guide to enjoying your writing and a step-by-step manual for getting better at it.

[2] S. N. de Jesus, C. L. Rus, W. Lens, & S. Imaginário, Intrinsic Motivation and Creativity Related to Product: A Meta-analysis of the Studies Published Between 1990–2010, 25 Creativity Res. J. 80 (2013) (loving your work improves creative performance at work by as much as 9%).

[3] Tomas Chamorro-Premuzic, The Talent Delusion: Why Data, Not Intuition, Is the Key to Unlocking Human Potential (Piatkus, 2017).

[4] Ackerman PL, *Intelligence, personality, and interests: evidence for overlapping traits*, Psychol Bull. (1997).

ACKNOWLEDGMENTS

I want to first thank the legal writers whose examples are featured in this book. I've learned so much from each of you, and I'm glad your work will now help others.

Thanks to the many mentors who helped me love legal writing so much—especially the three judges I somehow convinced to hire me as their clerk. Thanks also to the many law students and practitioners I've had the honor of teaching. I've learned more from you than you have from me! Thank you for letting me be part of your journey.

I'm grateful to the entire Aspen crew, especially Jess Barmack and Denise Clinton. Jess, those red lines were exactly what I needed. Thanks also to the many practitioners and professors who read drafts of this book and offered much-needed feedback.

Thanks next to my Write.law co-founder, Jory Hoffman. As Marcus Aurelius said, "A friend is our chosen reflection." Thank you for reflecting the qualities to which I aspire. Speaking of Write.law, this book would not be possible without the entire Write.law team. Yaqui de Andrade, Jess Hernández—and everyone else—you have made Write.law what it is today.

Finally, my family. All those books you bought me and the nerdy discussions you endured have paid off. Your unwavering support made this possible. Thank you for always being there.

INTRODUCTION

Consider this legal writing:

> In accordance with established procedures, algorithms have been implemented to facilitate the dissemination of a wide array of information. This encompasses a spectrum ranging from critical instructional content to commonplace inquiries. The algorithms employed in search engines are designed to optimize the relevance and ranking of queried data. Similarly, video sharing platforms utilize algorithms systems to curate and present a diverse range of visual content, which includes, but is not limited to, educational material, entertainment media, and instructional guides.

If you were thinking, "That isn't the most exciting legal writing. I guess it's competent, but it's not motivating me to keep reading"—you'd be right. That paragraph was serviceable but not winning any hearts and minds.

It was also written by a robot.

Popular generative AI tool ChatGPT wrote that paragraph after I gave it several pages of background information from a real case about algorithms used by the popular video-sharing website YouTube. For a first draft, it's not bad. It summarized the key points about why algorithms are good. It would probably save us some reading and thinking time if we were writing the brief.

But it isn't this:

> The result of these algorithms is unprecedented access to knowledge, from the lifesaving ('how to perform CPR') to the mundane ('best pizza near me'). Google Search uses algorithms to recommend top search results. YouTube uses algorithms to share everything from cat videos to Heimlich-maneuver tutorials, algebra problem-solving guides, and opera performances.[5]

This version makes you *feel*. It leverages specifics to connect with your experiences. It may even persuade you that these algorithms are important enough to need protecting.

And humans wrote it.

So, yes, good human writing still matters. Even in the law. But you'd be better off spending your time honing the first version into the second, rather than starting from scratch on your own. And that's what this book is about. Using all your tools to level up your legal writing. Human and machine.

This book is a step-by-step guide for leveling up every dimension of your legal writing. From capturing your readers' attention to leveraging the latest generative AI, we'll explore decades of research on how to do legal writing better.

[5] Unless noted otherwise, all examples in this book are taken from public filings.

But before starting that journey, let me offer a few principles this book rests on. Each will help set the stage for everything to come. And each is derived from real research and experience.

Take the Reins of Your Writing

Understand that no book, including this one, can tell you what legal writer you should be. What this book can do is more exciting—provide you with the tools to find that answer for yourself. To that end, this book is not intended as a list of strict rules to follow. Nearly every rule should be broken if the time is right and your message warrants it.

This book is instead about empowering you to take control of your writing and start choosing how you do what you do. To make the writing your own.

Why must you be in the driver's seat of your writing decisions? Just ask Stephen King. In his book *On Writing* (an excellent book for us legal writers, too), King explains that even great writers like him usually "don't understand very much about what they do—not why it works when it's good, not why it doesn't when it's bad." He also points out that "most books about writing are filled with [useless fluff]," which is another pitfall this book aims to avoid.[6]

This book is about giving you tools with instruction manuals for using them. And examples from top legal writers to take the mystery out of how to do it yourself.

Then the magic happens. By focusing on your writing's machinery and learning new tools for everything you do, you take control. Many of us try to fix our writing without knowing the tools we're using. You can't fix a car without understanding what a wrench does. And you can't write well without understanding what sentences do.

It's these tools that will make great legal writing possible. Not talent. Not years of devotion to the craft. A set of tools. Learn to use them, regularly practice with them, and your prose will transform.

What will that transformation look like? Let's see the results in practice.

A team of crack-shot legal writers had a thorny case on their hands. They represented small fishing companies that troll the seas off Cape May in New Jersey. Their clients were sympathetic, everyday families. But the legal landscape was torrid. The case turned on how much deference the courts should give a federal agency, the infamous *Chevron* doctrine. And getting judges to change their minds about this long-entrenched rule wouldn't be easy.

So with their first words, the lawyers put off the legal fight. Instead, they tell a story. They pick you up and drop you into their clients' fishing boats.

> Operating fishing vessels in the Atlantic is **hard work**. The vessel operators **tend to be small, family-owned enterprises**. The profit margins are **tight, and the quarters onboard are tighter still.** The typical vessel has **room for only five or six individuals**. Nonetheless, the Magnuson-Stevens Act requires petitioners and other vessel owners to **make room** onboard for federal observers who can oversee operations to ensure compliance with a slew of federal regulations. **That is an extraordinary imposition that few would tolerate on dry land.** But without any express statutory authorization, the National Marine Fisheries Service has decided to go one very large step further and

[6] Stephen King, On Writing: A Memoir of the Craft (New York, NY: Scribner, 2010). I substituted "useless fluff" for King's more provocative word choice.

> **require petitioners to pay the salaries of government-mandated monitors who take up valuable space** on their vessels and oversee their operations.

The legal writers begin with familiar, simple language that tells a relatable tale. The story anchors your perspective with the clients — hard working folks trying to scrape by. This setup is no accident. Telling us only five or six people fit in the cabin paints a picture that characterizations couldn't. Overall, the lawyers used several tools that you could start deploying today without much difficulty:

- familiar words ("hard work" instead of formal language like "a difficult enterprise").
- simple sentence structures (no sentence requires more than two groups of words, and some make do with one);
- active verbs ("make room" and other simple verbs like "decide");
- a focus on choice details (setting the stage with the hard work the fishers do, conveying the cramped quarters, and then weaving in the law as a burden on these everyday people); and
- a little advanced style (like the "tight. . . .tighter still" echo).

You'll find that the more you fill your writing toolbox with tools like these, the more exciting the writing gets. You'll receive a project, and instead of fearing that blank page, you'll be thinking about which tool is the right fit. Clunky sentences become opportunities.

Small Steps Mean Giant Leaps in Legal Writing

You need to invest a little to transform your legal writing. Just writing more isn't enough. Indeed, some folks who have been writing the longest are the worst at it.

Nor is reading this book (or any other) enough. You must put your new tools to use. The good news is that breaking down your legal writing into discrete tools is also the fastest and most effective way to improve. Learning new skills doesn't require hours of agony each day. Instead, science says you are better off *leveling up a little at a time*. As habit expert James Clear explains, "If you can get 1% better each day for one year, you'll end up 37 times better by the time you're done."[7]

Get 1% better each day at your legal writing, and you'll level up weekly. You don't need to overwhelm yourself with the other 99%. It's about consistently investing in a few writing tools at a time so that you build better writing habits and eliminate poor ones. So that you know why you're doing what you're doing and can make choices about your writing, instead of being a victim to the words you spew on the page.

This book is organized to make that investment easy. Every chapter is a collection of related techniques. If you're looking for strategies to level up just one area of your writing, go there. If you want to overhaul your entire writing tool chest, start at Chapter 1 and work through each collection. Wherever you start, you'll find concrete explanations and examples from top writers so you can start using the techniques today.

But learning new writing techniques in theory can be difficult to implement in practice. That's why you'll find sample documents in Chapter 11. And then in Chapter 12, you'll find tips for bringing your techniques together into a process you can make your

---

[7] James Clear, Atomic Habits: An Easy & Proven Way to Build Good Habits & Break Bad Ones (Avery, 2018).

own. Finally, in Chapter 14, you'll find concrete tools for learning writing techniques faster and easier over time.

Rewire Your Legal Writing with Technology

One of the best tools in your arsenal isn't writing at all, but *writing technology*. By many accounts, we sit on the edge of a legal writing revolution, driven by exciting new technologies like natural language processing and generative AI that can already outwrite many lawyers.

Technology can slash the time you spend on routine writing tasks like checking cite formatting, incorporating legal research, and even improving your style. New tools promise to do more, like penning the first draft of a motion or putting together the bones of a complicated contract. While the pen-and-paper writing tools in this book remain relevant, you would be crazy to ignore all the benefits technology can bring to your writing projects.

In Chapter 1, we'll explore tactics for harnessing the power of technology in your everyday legal writing. In Chapter 13, we'll learn about the pitfalls and possibilities of generative AI for legal writers. And spread throughout all the chapters you'll find tips for weaving technology into your writing projects at each step.

In the end, you'll have picked up enough tools—writing and machine—for your transformation to begin. You'll see writing as a chance to try new techniques. You'll be confident enough to weave your own voice into your advocacy. And the more you level up your legal writing, the more you'll learn to love it.

For Legal Readers, Average Writing Won't Do

One thing you'll notice about all the techniques in this book is that they are built for the *legal reader,* not just *any reader*.

Yes, many writing principles are a good fit for any audience. But *legal readers* are special. They don't read our writing to learn something for fun (although, if you can manage to make your writing fun, that is great). Legal readers have a goal. They read our writing for insight they can act on. Many legal readers don't read linearly, either. They flip to the sections that interest them. They refer to parts later when writing a decision or deciding what advice to give a client.

Legal writing is functional writing, and functional writers serve a different master than other writers do. Other writers have the luxury of readers who take their time reading. Readers who read from start to finish because they enjoy the experience.

Our legal readers aren't so patient:

- Science shows that most will read only a tiny fraction of the words on our pages. Many words you write will never be read.
- Eye-tracking studies reveal that our readers often skim and skip around our documents, consuming more information from certain places like introductions and less from everywhere else.
- Our readers are so busy and distracted that the moment we are not proving useful in our document, chances are they will put it down and do something else (perhaps never to come back again).

- Our readers are not great at multitasking, including within our document. The more we make them remember or think about at once, the harder it is for them to follow.
- Legal audiences are often physically and mentally taxed when they read our documents, which research shows drains their focus even more.

The animating principle behind this book's techniques is *how can you make your writing valuable to today's legal readers*? Readers who are busy, harried, and may not have time to read your document from word to word. Readers who need the details that matter, and fast. Readers who want answers delivered to them precisely and plainly so that they can move on to the next item on their ever-growing to-do list.

We know that legal readers have less focus and pay less attention than ever before. But with that knowledge comes opportunity. Powered by the latest reader science, the techniques in this book can make you the one legal writer that readers listen to. That's why entire chapters are devoted to skills like distilling quick takeaways from dense background information (Chapter 2) and organizing legal documents so they are easy to navigate and self-explanatory (Chapter 6).

And you can trust the techniques. They were developed from years of research and work collecting the most effective, data-backed writing tools and principles. I stood on the shoulders of giants, and shamelessly so. Because no single person should be telling you how to write.

My goal in assembling these techniques is simple. Gather the great writing and technology tools so you don't have to. Many of us don't improve our craft because it feels too overwhelming. With books, courses, columns, and research piling up each day—where do you even start?

Lucky for me, I had the benefit of working with my team at Write.law for over a decade to distill insights from hundreds of books, thousands of practitioner documents, and the latest reader science. And that goes for the latest legal writing technologies, too.

Now, let's get leveling up.

1

Level Up Your Writing Perspective

> "The fight is won or lost far away from witnesses—behind the lines, in the gym, and out there on the road, long before I dance under those lights."—Muhammad Ali

When you *think* about writing a sentence—and when you *write* that sentence—two different regions of your brain fire.[1] That's because good writing is a mix of theory and technique. You need an array of techniques, like approaches to writing a sentence, organizing a fact section, or explaining a rule. But you need some theory, too.

Before getting to the techniques that make up most of this book, we'll explore a theoretical framework to guide your writing decisions. I've collected the ten most potent writing principles supported by decades of experience and research in the field. Legal writing will throw a lot at you. And these foundational principles will help you make the best decisions in hard situations.

I'm going to brag here. The principles are transformative. Your writing may never be the same. Each appears in some form in nearly every leading book, resource, or research on legal writing and persuasion. By incorporating them into their writing, thousands of lawyers have reached new writing heights they never thought possible.

When you aren't sure how to approach a legal writing challenge—whether it's the words to use, the order to put them in, or something else entirely—refer to the principles.

[1] J. Tracy et al., *Regional Brain Activation Associated with Different Performance Patterns During Learning of a Complex Motor Skill*, Cereb. Cortex, vol. 13, no. 9, 904–910 (2003).

Let's start with a brief overview of each. Then we will dig in with examples.

Write Fluently: Craft clear, accessible writing that requires minimal mental effort for readers.

Cut Clutter: Eliminate unnecessary information to emphasize important content and reduce your reader's cognitive load.

Engage: Use specific details, active verbs, and other style tools to engage readers and keep them reading.

Frame and Prime: Influence readers' perceptions by strategically ordering and describing information.

Guide: Lay out the breadcrumbs. Use hand-holding tools and a trustworthy tone to guide readers to your goals.

Explain: Provide practical context like background information or lay definitions so readers can grasp meaning instantly.

Distill: Package key takeaways up front with enough specifics for readers to understand what matters without reading all the details after.

Tell Stories: Weave a narrative to make dry points memorable and moving.

Teach the Rules: Simplify and clarify legalese to make it easily usable in your case.

Leverage Technology: Get on the technology train, because it's time. Look for tools to incorporate in every step of your writing process.

Now, let's learn more about each principle and how to start using them.

1.1 Write Fluently

Clear, easy-to-understand writing has a name: fluency. Fluency is a cognitive science term for measuring how much mental energy readers must exert to understand you. The more fluent our writing, the easier for readers to understand it with little effort.[2] When it comes to legal readers, fluency is even more important than usual. Because our readers are so distracted and time-pressed, they need to instantly understand what they read.

What makes writing not so fluent? First, too many ideas thrown at readers at the same time. Studies show that the more ideas readers need to juggle in the same sentence or paragraph, the harder it is for them to follow along.

Then we have other fluency-busters. Complex words, complex sentence structures, and complex organization. Too many long sentences. Too many esoteric words that

[2] Daniel M. Oppenheimer, *The Secret Life of Fluency*, Trends in Cognitive Sciences, vol. 12 no. 6, 237–241 (2008).

readers must rack their brains (or a dictionary) to decipher. Disjointed ideas or details that aren't grouped together meaningfully.

Your job, then, is to do all the hard work for readers so that they can enjoy the ride. Spoon-feed points one at a time (called *chunking* by cognitive scientists), use simpler words, use simpler sentence structure—and leverage other proven tactics to create writing that is as simple as distracted readers' attention spans can handle.[3]

What does fluent writing look like? Well, not like this.

> Patents provide an entitlement to the rights holder that allow for certain broad actions, however, said rights are of a strictly limited nature.

Instead, very fluent writer Justice Elena Kagan conveyed the same idea in half as many words and double the clarity.

> Patents endow their holders with certain superpowers, but only for a limited time.

Fresh words like "superpowers" make the prose accessible with even a quick skim. Look how hard it is to read this next passage full of long, formal words and ideas jammed in together.

> If the Company registers any shares of its common stock under the Securities Act of 1933, or any successor statute, or the regulations promulgated by the Securities and Exchange Commission (or any successor body) thereunder, as then in effect, the Stockholder may, in its sole discretion, at any time and from time to time, request the Company to register not less than 250,000 of the Shares under such Act, and the Company shall promptly comply with each such request.[4]

Wouldn't you rather read this much-more-fluent version?

> If the company decides to register any of its common stock under the Securities Act, the company's shareholders can force it to register at least 250,000 shares.

We'll explore several fluency boosters throughout this book, especially in Chapters 6, 7, and 8. To start you out, here are some first principles:

- Use simpler sentence structures. Deliver the main point of each sentence by starting with the subject, immediately moving to the verb, and then finishing with the result. "The lawyer filed the motion" may seem elementary, but if the backbone of your prose is sentences as simple as this, your readers will thank you. You can then build on this simple structure purposely—like using a list, dropping a modifying phrase after your base, or combining two main points with a semicolon.
- Focus on the specifics that readers care about. If you rely on conclusory language and characterizations—like urging that your client was "seriously"

[3] Fernand Gobet, *Chunking Mechanisms in Human Learning*, Trends in Cognitive Sciences, vol. 5, no. 6, 236–243 (2001).

[4] Howard Darmstadter, Hereof, Thereof, and Everywhereof: A Contrarian Guide to Legal Drafting (2002).

injured—readers wonder what specifics led you to those beliefs. Don't make readers wait.

- Choose nouns familiar to every reader. Fresh, familiar nouns (those people, places, and things) are how we all think and speak. Why let dense legalese and formalisms cloud your prose? Use simple, concrete nouns that anchor your sentences in easy-to-visualize terms.
- Choose vivid verbs. Actions rev up legal sentences. The action animates the points you're trying to convey. Replace weak verbs (like *is, was, has, have*, and so on) with active ones.
- Format for easy reading. Chop your content into shorter paragraphs, use bullet points, and add subheadings to increase readability. This allows even busy readers to navigate efficiently.
- Chunk out your points. Whether talking about the law, the facts, or something else, break up your ideas into the smallest parts that will make sense to readers. Then deliver each part, one at a time, keeping clear how each relates to the other.
- Handhold constantly. Map out where you are going. Recap anything helpful to readers that you delivered before (or will deliver later) if it will help them understand what you're conveying now.

1.2 Cut Clutter

Our second principle is cutting clutter. Lawyers love loading up their writing with every detail they can scavenge. But all that does is hide the crucial points in a sea of mediocrity. Every extraneous word or sentence or point drains the power out of what you care about most.

The more words in a section, the less likely your readers will read it. The more words in a sentence, the more likely readers will skip it. We legal writers often forget the sheer time legal reading takes. Extra words and sentences spread throughout your document equate to hours of extra reading time, and readers won't stick around for that.

Cutting clutter starts with the big picture. What major arguments, sections, or paragraphs are not pulling their weight? If a big group of words isn't immediately important to you as the writer, then it will be even less relevant to your readers.

Cutting clutter is also about the small picture: your sentences and words.

As famous grammarians Strunk and White wrote, "Omit needless words."[5] If a word isn't contributing to what you're conveying in the sentence, snip it.

Even though many lawyers have repeatedly been told to cut the clutter, most legal writing overflows with it. Like this:

> The judge made numerous errors in ruling on the case, but one of the most significant was wrongly interpreting and erroneously applying the legal precedent.

This sentence could easily be rewritten without the clutter:

> The judge misinterpreted the precedent.

[5] William Strunk, Jr. & E.B. White, The Elements of Style (4th ed. 2000).

We'll explore techniques for cutting clutter in several chapters, especially Chapters 2, 7, and 8. To get you started, here are the principles to remember:

- Savagely cut sections, points, and paragraphs that are not building toward your document's central takeaways.
- Edit paragraph by paragraph, cutting any sentence that doesn't support the paragraph's focus.
- Strip out any words in each sentence that are not helping convey the important content.
- Cut or rewrite common words and phrases that make your prose messy. Eliminate doublets and triplets (groups of words that can be replaced with a single, simple word), weak verb phrases, and formalisms or legalese that your readers don't need.

1.3 Engage

Don't discount the power of engaging your reader. Legal folks want to get invested. They read and read every day, and it's nearly always dry details and lazy legalese. Do something different. Spark your readers' senses by employing vibrant language. Help them *feel* what you write and *see* what you describe.

Even your sentence structure can engage. Using pleasing syntax, sometimes surprising readers, harnessing pithy language—all can draw readers in and make them pay attention. Most legal writers conveying that a CFO committed financial crimes would deliver that information something like this:

> The Defendant's CFO engaged in criminal activity including but not limited to embezzlement, evading taxes, and illicit trading.

But look at what happens when we switch up the sentence structure to focus on the crimes and the harm:

> **Embezzlement, insider trading, tax evasion**—these financial crimes, perpetrated by the CFO, led to the downfall of a once-thriving business and hundreds of people losing their jobs.

When Justice Ketanji Brown Jackson wanted to grab readers in her writing debut on the Supreme Court, she packed the style in. The **bolded** language highlights many of the style decisions this writer used to make the language engaging. Note that I use **bold** throughout this book to help you focus on the words or sentences most important to the concept we're talking about:

> **Gulf-sized** race-based gaps exist with respect to the **health, wealth, and well-being** of American citizens. . . . **Every moment** these gaps persist **is a moment** in which this great country falls short of **actualizing** one of its foundational principles—the **'self-evident' truth that all of us are created equal.**

The Justice's opening words leverage fresh descriptors (like "gulf-sized"), a balanced trio ("health, wealth, and well-being"), echo words ("moment" and "moment"), active verbs ("persist," "actualize," "created"), and a riff off the Constitution's language—all techniques we'll explore in this book.

We'll revisit how to craft engaging writing especially in Chapters 3, 4, 7, and 9. But let's start with some foundational style principles:

- Use active, vivid verbs so that most of your sentences convey ideas through action rather than abstractions readers must struggle to imagine.
- Choose concrete nouns and details so readers can wrap their minds around the information.
- Amp up your style when delivering crucial sentences and paragraphs. Advanced style tools will burn what matters into readers' minds. Techniques like echo words, inverted sentences, alliteration, and other easy-to-copy structures will make your writing memorable.
- Highlight crucial details by placing them at the beginnings and ends of your document, your sections, and your paragraphs.
- Leverage detail quantity. Emphasize the favorable points by including more supporting details; deemphasize by including fewer specifics and skimming (but not skipping) the less favorable.

1.4 Frame and Prime

Mountains of research leave no doubt: We increase our persuasiveness by making good first impressions and priming readers to see the law and facts in the right hue.[6]

How you prime readers—everything from your word choice to what details you lead with—can transform how your readers view the sentences that follow. Slow down and craft your beginnings strategically. This includes your introductions, headings, section starts, and the first sentences of your paragraphs. By wording points in a purposeful way early, you can control how readers see what follows.

The beginnings matter for another reason: your credibility. First impressions matter as much in writing as they do in speaking. The moment your reader picks up your document, they start judging you (especially judges, who can be *very* judgy). Some snap judgments are conscious and some are not. But these opening perceptions are hard to shake. The research is full of studies showing that even when faced with proof that we were wrong, we humans have a real problem changing our first impressions.[7]

Getting more granular, *priming* is about inserting choice details as you lead into a topic so that you shape how readers feel later in your writing. *Framing*, on the other hand, is about more directly changing your readers' perspective in the beginning to achieve a similar result—a more favorable lens for readers to see the details you dish up later in your writing. Experts often say that priming is about *what you say*; framing is about *how you say it*. The two go hand in hand, and you'll usually use both strategies when you craft beginnings like introductions, headings, and the first sentences of sections or paragraphs.[8]

[6] Kathryn Stanchi, *The Power of Priming in Legal Advocacy: Using the Science of First Impressions to Persuade the Reader,* 89 Or. L. Rev. 305 (2010-2011).

[7] Matthew Rabin & Joel L. Schrag, *First Impressions Matter: A Model of Confirmatory Bias,* The Quarterly Journal of Economics, vol. 114, 37–82 (1999).

[8] David H. Weaver, *Thoughts on Agenda Setting, Framing, and Priming,* Journal of Communication 57, 142–147 (2007).

Let's say you're representing Mr. Smith for unlawful termination based on his age. You'll eventually need to make your legal arguments that Mr. Smith's employer fired him for being too old. But let's set that aside for now. Many lawyers would stick to a dry factual recitation like this when introducing their client:

> Mr. Smith was unlawfully terminated from his job due to his manager discriminating against elderly individuals.

But don't rush. Use this introduction to Mr. Smith as a chance for readers to relate to him. All you need is a few details that will prime and frame readers' perspective.

> **Despite 20 years of not missing a single day of work and being awarded employee of the year twice,** Mr. Smith was fired **without warning or explanation.**

We inserted three priming details here: (1) not missing a day of work, (2) receiving an award for great work, and (3) being fired without notice. Now our readers are ready for our arguments.

A fantastic example of priming and framing is given by a brief written by lawyers representing YouTube in a charged case about inappropriate videos that slipped through the company's sensitivity filters. The legal writers began not by introducing the statutory provisions being fought over, but by laying out a narrative of priming details and framing perspectives. The writers get you thinking about the challenge companies like YouTube face when trying to monitor all the content users share online.

> In the mid-1990s, the growing number of people uploading and sharing abundant third-party content also created a serious legal challenge. . . . **Everyone online was a potential defendant any time they disseminated someone else's content. Anyone with an internet connection could become liable** for publishing or republishing others' speech **in all fifty States.** 1990s chat room websites faced potentially ruinous lawsuits for displaying others' speech, while **users faced liability for merely reposting articles.**

Of course, YouTube isn't just "anyone with an internet connection." But everyone will agree with the modest premise that online services can't be liable every time someone posts or clicks *Share*. And that was progress.

We'll explore techniques for priming and framing in several chapters, including Chapters 2, 5, and 6. But let's start with a few principles.

- At each major beginning (your document introduction, headings, section starts), brainstorm which choice details you can include to trigger favorable emotions. Consider what you want readers to feel and which details you can prime them with to get there.
- Likewise, consider how you can frame the major issues, legal arguments, and events as favorably as you can. Consider what challenges your reader is facing, like biases or arguments raised by opposing parties. Then consider what framing best counters these forces.
- Beginnings are where you make impressions. So craft beginnings with the best style. The crispest language. The fewest distractions. Your first impressions set the tone for whatever comes after.

1.5 Guide

Readers don't like being told what to think. Showing and guiding instead of telling and demanding will always work better. Your readers are smart. They can reach the conclusions you want if you guide them on a clear path. But if you force your points, they will fight you every step.

This is another principle fueled by science. When someone feels like they're being forced to agree, it triggers skepticism. *Reactance* is what persuasion experts call this response to being pushed into a decision.[9] By showing rather than telling, you avoid this. You give readers a sense of control over their opinions and decisions.

The most effective legal writers avoid relying on characterizations and conclusory statements like "the company **breached the contract *repeatedly*** and ***without cause***." Instead, they lay out the details in a line so that readers reach an inescapable conclusion all on their own.

> Despite agreeing to deliver the goods in writing, the company left the client empty-handed for months.

When lawyers representing Disney in a feud with Florida's governor wanted to convey that Disney was a powerful ally for the state, they didn't merely tell readers that the company was an "unparalleled engine for economic growth," as many would. They marched out the details that would walk readers to that conclusion.

> Fast forward five decades, and Disney today is an unparalleled engine for economic growth in the State. Among other distinctions, **Disney is one of Central Florida's largest taxpayers, with more than $1.1 billion paid in state and local taxes last year. Disney is also one of the largest employers in the State, with more than 75,000 cast members.**

We'll explore tools for guiding in Chapters 2, 3, 4, and 5. But a few principles will get you on track:

- Choose specifics to make your main points rather than relying on subjective characterizations. If a word embodies your opinion (like "significant," "egregious," or "substantial"), ask whether you can insert specific details instead.
- Lead readers one step at a time. Plan the steps that your readers will need to agree with to reach your desired goal. Then deliver those steps one at a time so that it's easy for readers to grasp your points without working for it.
- Use supporting authority or facts to make points. It's like social proof. You want readers to feel like it's not only you cheerleading for a result but that many others agree, too.
- Use hand-holding devices like roadmaps, recaps, and orientation to keep readers on task.

[9] Sharon S. Brehm & Jack W. Brehm, Psychological Reactance: A Theory of Freedom and Control (1966).

1.6 Explain

Today's legal readers are too busy to deal with confusing and convoluted writing. The best writers don't assume readers will remember a detail shared three pages ago. They don't assume readers will understand an esoteric word or acronym or legal term of art. The best legal writers provide what's needed for understanding *at the moment of delivery*. Modern-day legal readers skim and skip around. If you can create documents that make it possible for them to jump in anywhere and instantly understand, you're weaving legal writing gold.

But making your writing self-explanatory can be hard because you need to get out of your own head and into a fresh reader's perspective. Someone who doesn't know all that you know—and doesn't read all that carefully in the first place. Most legal writers, for example, will assume readers remember some detail or fact delivered earlier in a document. So when the same information comes up again, they refer to it in generic terms, thinking that, like them, the readers know what they're referring to.

> John, who is an independent contractor, claims that ABC Company breached the contract. The **relevant terms** were **clearly established in Section IV** of the agreement, as explained above.

Writers striving for the self-explanatory will instead remind readers of whatever specifics they need in the moment—that is, every time those facts, terms, or details come back into play. That way, if your reader wasn't paying attention earlier, things still make sense.

> John, an independent contractor, claims that ABC Company breached Section IV of the contract. **As a reminder, Section IV required payment within 30 days—which never happened.**

Self-explanatory writers offer simple breakdowns so readers instantly get it. Justice Kagan was relaying a complex tax equation (math!) to readers in an important opinion. The Justice wanted to include the somewhat confusing statutory language for readers' reference:

> A fraction (expressed as a percentage), the numerator of which is the number of [a] hospital's patient days for [the fiscal year] which were made up of patients who (for such days) were entitled to benefits under part A of [Medicare] and were entitled to [SSI] benefits[], and the denominator of. . . .

But she also knew that busy legal readers would have trouble absorbing all that. So she took a moment to break things down in simpler terms.

> That is a mouthful.[10] So again, in general terms: **The numerator is the number of patient days attributable to Medicare patients who are poor. The denominator is the number of patient days attributable to all Medicare patients. Divide the former by the latter to get the fraction "expressed as a percentage."**

[10] Dialogue like this engages you as a reader. It makes the writing accessible—perhaps even fun.

Another way to make writing self-explanatory is to ensure readers have a frame of reference before diving into the denseness. Federal Judge Jennifer Dorsey is a pro at this sort of orientation. Most lawyers would dive directly into the weeds when analyzing a legal issue, writing something like this:

> Defendant Country Mutual Insurance Co., moves for summary judgment on the grounds of breach of contract and lack of evidence to support bad faith claims. . . .

But Judge Dorsey instead orients readers with the simple, familiar background of a person buying a home and buying insurance for it. Then she guides us to what matters: the insurance clause everyone was fighting over.

> **When Teresa Sivil purchased her Eagle River, Alaska, home in 2014, she entered into an insurance agreement with Country Mutual Insurance Company[].** That policy covered the peril of sudden and accidental water damage. When Sivil moved to Nevada three years later, she contacted a[] representative to remove personal-property coverage from the home policy. **Allegedly without Sivil's knowledge or consent, the representative also removed coverage for sudden and accidental water damage.**
>
> **When a pipe broke at Sivil's Alaska home the following winter, she submitted the claim to Country Mutual, who quickly denied it,** citing the modification of the policy to remove coverage for water damage. Sivil sues Country Mutual for breach of contract. . . .

Giving readers the right background information like this is a skill. Self-explanatory writing requires thoughtful organization, sentence structure, and more — concepts we'll explore in Chapters 2, 3, 4, and 6. But here are some initial principles:

- Provide any context that readers need every time they need it. You can't assume readers will remember what you told them ten pages ago (heck, they may not have read it the first time). So give readers a reminder.
- Explain terms whenever helpful. If you're using a word that you aren't sure every legal reader will instantly recognize, define it. This is as true for legal terms as it is for factual ones. Jargon, terms of art, and any long or unfamiliar word can often use a quick definition. Of course, if you can cut these esoteric terms, all the better.
- Offer brief recaps after you've journeyed through a lot of complexity. When you've forced readers through some dense concepts, it helps to give a reminder to keep readers up to speed.
- Orient readers whenever helpful. Start by orienting readers at the most basic level. In your introduction and the first pages of your document, that means addressing "why the heck are we here?" When you get to sections, including your facts, take the same approach. Start by orienting readers to each situation or issue from the highest level. Then lead them to what matters.

1.7 Distill

As soon as your reader's expected value of the next second of reading is less than the value of doing other things on their plate, they stop reading. Think about that for a minute. Your legal readers are looking for an answer. The moment they decide you can't give it to them, they are done with you and your document.

On the flip side, if you are the rare lawyer who can connect the dots of a complex case or legal issue in the first few minutes of reading, you *will* persuade. Because you'll be giving readers what they care about before they can decide to look elsewhere.

In this book, I refer to this skill as *distilling the takeaways*. Figure out what you're trying to convey with your document, in each section, and even in each paragraph. Then distill those points as simply and directly as you can at the outset. Leave the heavy details for after your readers understand, so they never need to work hard on their own.

Your readers want the meat. They want to know what's behind your conclusions. Yet, most legal writers begin with the superficial and bury readers in a heap of minutiae after. Like this next lawyer, who tells you the conclusion they wish you'd reach but gives no specifics that might help you reach it.

> In this motion for summary judgment, we will argue that Barry Jackson's **wrongful termination claim must be dismissed. Substantial evidence confirms this.**

If you distill the specifics that matter, your readers' experience is transformed:

> Barry Jackson's wrongful termination claim falls flat. Here's why: **Jackson failed to show up to work more than a dozen times, he screamed at coworkers more than once, and he didn't complete the basic work he was assigned—any of which was justification for firing him under California law.**

What does distilling takeaways look like in the hands of a legal writing maven? In this next example, an introduction to a lengthy document, the less important details are skimmed over and the specifics readers need are front and center. Readers didn't need exact dates, so we are only told that "eight years" passed. Readers don't need to meet every character to get the gist, so we are introduced only to the players that matter (skimming past those "romantic partners and companies").

> **For eight years**, Robert Williamson, Victoria "Vicki" Gunvalson, Michael Nicholson, and **their respective romantic partners and companies** have battled over the fallout of failed spirits company **Vicki's Vodka, LLC**. By the start of the bench trial[], the case had distilled down to Williamson's and Vicki's Vodka's claims against Gunvalson and Nicholson for breach of contract, misrepresentation, promissory estoppel, and breach of the implied covenant of good faith and fair dealing. While the procedural vagaries of the case are complex, the substantive issues are straightforward: **Williamson claims that he was wronged after he invested in a reality-television star's alcohol company because his business partners inadequately promoted the product and unlawfully kept him from realizing the millions of dollars he was promised to reap. But based on five days of testimony and the parties' exhibits and briefing**. . . .

Chapter 2 is devoted to distilling takeaways, although we will revisit this technique in other chapters, like Chapters 3 and 4. To get started, here are some first principles:

- Constantly ask how you can wrap details into simple packages that readers can take away from your writing. How can you summarize what readers should remember after reading a section or paragraph in a way that they will remember?
- Distill with enough specifics that readers can be persuaded on their own by relying on the evidence you give them rather than on your word.

- Choose takeaways that align with your goals. If you want readers to see your document or a section or a paragraph in a certain light, summarize with specifics that will create the best lens.
- Use elevated style to drive home memorable takeaways. Use your best prose to persuasively deliver those imperative packages.

1.8 Tell Stories

By putting your legal messages into a story-like form, you increase your power to persuade.[11] And you can harness stories in every page of legal writing: the facts and the law and everything in between. Storytelling is about settings, characters, actions, and consequences. In short, things you already know a lot about. You just need to tap into that storytelling knowledge and leverage it in your legal writing.

The best legal storytellers use tools like pacing and perspective to immerse readers. This next example puts you into officers' perspective as they approach a traffic stop—quite different from the dry recitation of facts most legal writers would have given us.

> **While patrolling** South Las Vegas Boulevard **around midnight**, []officer Lukas Turley **noticed a sedan stopped in a no-parking zone** on Agate Avenue. []Agate Avenue is situated between an apartment complex known **to house sex workers and pimps, and a hotel frequented by narcotics traffickers**. When the officer **pulled up behind the car, which had no lights on and showed no signs of distress**, it began to drive away, so he initiated a traffic stop. Though the area and vehicle's location were suspicious to Turley, he testified that the only basis he had to pull the car over was the parking violation.

The author gives us the setting so the movie can start playing. We see Las Vegas Boulevard around midnight. Then we meet the main character and join him as events unfold.

One of my favorite examples of legal storytelling was penned by Chief Justice John Roberts in the "Bong Hits for Jesus" case (named for the First Amendment story the case addressed).

> On January 24, 2002, **the Olympic Torch Relay passed through Juneau, Alaska, on its way to the winter games in Salt Lake City, Utah**. . . . Petitioner Deborah Morse, the school principal, **decided to permit staff and students to participate** in the Torch Relay as an approved social event or class trip. **Students were allowed to leave class** to observe the relay from either side of the street. **Teachers and administrative officials monitored the students' actions.**
>
> Respondent Joseph Frederick, a senior, **was late to school that day**. When he arrived, he joined his friends (all but one of whom were [] students) across the street from the school to watch the event. Not all the students waited patiently. **Some became rambunctious, throwing plastic cola bottles and snowballs and scuffling with their classmates.**

[11] Herbert A. Eastman, *Speaking Truth to Power: The Language of Civil Rights Litigators*, Yale L.J. vol. 763, 813 (1995) (quoting Justice James Boyd White on the persuasiveness of stories).

> As the torchbearers and camera crews passed by, Frederick and his friends unfurled a 14-foot banner bearing the phrase: "BONG HiTS 4 JESUS." The large banner was easily readable by the students on the other side of the street.

A slew of storytelling tools is at work here. The characters are developed to be either sympathetic or not so much (the principal was nice enough to let students out of school; the "rambunctious" student at the heart of the case, on the other hand, is introduced as "late for school that day"). We start with the setting (a national spectacle traveling across the country) and then zoom into the event, with time slowing down until we can feel the seconds passing as the offending banner is unfurled.

Chapter 3 is devoted to telling legal stories like this, but here a few narrative foundations:

- Develop your storyline. What setting should you lay out for readers? How will you orient them? How do you want to zoom readers in and slow down key events so they can experience each one?
- Develop your characters. Consider whose perspective you want readers to follow (usually, these will be the folks you put in the subject position in each sentence). Weave in favorable or unfavorable details to build characters into how you want them to be perceived.
- Use details to bring the story to life. Choose specific details when they will help play the movie for readers; use summarizing language to convey less important parts of the narrative and shuffle readers by.

1.9 Teach the Rules

Most lawyers fall short on the rules—the standards, explanations, and other discussions about the law that we legal writers constantly write. This is surprising, because the lawyer who convinces the judge on the right way to look at the rule often wins.

Teaching readers the rules is about leveraging principles we've already covered: distilling what matters from dense authority, using simpler words and sentences to break down complexity one step at a time, and guiding readers to the conclusions you want them to make rather than forcing them.

Don't be the legal writer telling readers:

> Per the stipulations delineated under the statute, the court maintains the discretion to institute monetary penalties and remediation for any violation incurred hereto.

Be the legal writer that teaches:

> The statute instructs that the court may fine you for any violation.

Take this next example. The lawyers dropped a pile of details from a case but forgot to distill the takeaway for readers first (feel free to skim here, as most legal readers would).

> [The] "agitated state" theory derives from the Supreme Court's language in *DeShaney v. Winnebago County Dep't of Soc. Servs.*, which held that a plaintiff must allege facts showing that the police placed him in a "worse position than that in which he would have been had [the police] not acted at all." 489 U.S. 189, 201 (1989). Where the police leave a third party "in an agitated state" (and therefore more likely to cause harm), so the theory goes, the plaintiff is in the type of "worse position" *DeShaney* requires. And where the police then "leav[e] the scene without taking any preventative action whatsoever". . . .

Do you have a concrete sense of what the rule requires? Probably not. All that changes if we distill first, using specifics to show readers how the law works before asking them to wade through the muck.

> Federal courts have held that officers who agitate a suspect, reasonably should have known he was a danger to others, and then leave him to do harm are liable under Section 1983.

Or take this example breaking down a complex legal landscape in easy terms.

> This case is controlled by a simple rule: Because this Court rendered judgment and its mandate is silent as to any award of prejudgment interest, the district court lacked authority to award it. That simple rule follows directly from the Supreme Court's decision in *Briggs* and this Court's decisions applying it, as well as Federal Rule of Appellate Procedure 37(b).

We'll tackle many tools for crafting winning rules in Chapter 4. Here are first principles to start with:

- Distill what matters from the rules before forcing readers through authority details or legalese. Package the principles that matter from the rules so that readers can easily use them to get the answers they need.
- Give some thought to your rule strategies. Rules are often the most complex things in your documents. As with stories, consider how to orient readers to what matters, break up rules into smaller points readers can tackle one at a time, and then take readers by the hand and guide them along the way.
- Don't let the law get in your readers' way. Minimize how citations, legalese, and other legal denseness clutter up your sentence and your message.

1.10 Leverage Technology

The last principle is different from the others because it's not about the what, but the how. The digital metamorphosis of legal writing is upon us, and it's time to embrace its many perks. Simple technology can automate the error-prone steps in your legal writing. AI-driven platforms, advanced research tools, and generative AI (GAI) can do more, completely redefining how you approach legal writing.

To get the most out of legal writing technology, you need to develop your legal writing *tech stack*—the tools, and features in those tools, you use when working on your legal writing. Building your tech stack takes two steps: (1) choosing the right technology, and (2) investing in your technology the right way.

Choosing the Right Legal Writing Technology

You can't use every app out there. Not only would that take too much time and money, but you would find that many apps don't work all that well. To decide what technologies, and which features in those technologies, are worth investing in, you first need a good sense of the options.

If you don't understand how a technology tool (or feature) can add value to your everyday writing, you can't make an informed decision about whether to use it. This is often the biggest problem for lawyers. Many don't understand how different their work lives would be if they used the right technology set up in the right ways.

An easy way to learn about what is possible with technology is to use GAI. We will dig into GAI more in Chapter 13, which is devoted to that topic. But this technology can collaborate with you on any project, including educating yourself about what technology is out there and what it can do for your practice.

Sometimes technology is more hassle than it's worth. Not every writing task is cut out for technology. Ask yourself some questions when considering new tech tools or learning new features:

- What is the bottom line for you? What value does this technology add? How much is it? Will it make your work faster or better? How?
- Will this technology save you more time than you put into learning it? How much?
- Will you use this technology often or just sometimes?
- Are there any risks in using this technology (like confidentiality or privacy challenges)? Can you avoid or mitigate those risks?

Also consider what tools can smoothly integrate into your current workflow (the way you work on projects now). Sometimes technology conflicts with other technology. Sometimes a tool won't have the data privacy protections your organization or clients require.

But make no mistake: Investing in legal technology is crucial for making you efficient and better at what you do. So let's look at a quick rundown of key categories to keep on your radar in legal writing:[12]

- **Research technologies:** Legal research tech has made a quantum leap in the past few years, drastically reducing the time needed to research case law, statutes, regulations, and legal journals. Traditional databases like Westlaw and LexisNexis have been enhanced by features like the ability to analyze a brief or memo for weaknesses. Innovative research platforms like Fastcase are using data visualization to enhance the process of legal research. And legal research companies release new features all the time.
- **Outlining and organizing tools:** Tools like Cogli, Miro, Microsoft OneNote, Evernote, and MindNode have emerged as great tools for taking notes, tagging them so you can find them in the future, and visually organizing information as you are planning out a document.

[12] To stay up to date, you can also check out legal technology directories like the LawNext Tech Directory.

- **Editing software:** Platforms like BriefCatch, Grammarly, Word Rake, and Hemingway App employ AI to not only check grammar and spelling but also improve style, tone, clarity, and conciseness.
- **Document management and knowledge management systems:** Platforms like iManage, Dropbox, Clio, and NetDocuments allow you to securely store, share, and find your documents (or your team's documents) in the cloud so you never lose your work. Many also integrate with other tools that handle documents, including Microsoft Word and Microsoft Outlook.
- **Citation software:** These tools automate references and ensure they adhere to the citation rules. BriefCatch, Clearbrief, and Citeright are options for automatically formatting your legal or factual citations.
- **Time management and task management:** Apps like Toggl and RescueTime help you keep track of what you spend your time on, providing insights into productivity patterns. Project management tools like Asana and Todoist can help you organize your daily and weekly tasks and set deadlines.
- **Legal analytics tools:** Platforms like Lex Machina and Ravel Law extract data from past court cases and provide analytics that can help users predict outcomes, understand judicial trends, and formulate case strategies.
- **Collaboration and communication tools:** Tools like Microsoft Teams, Slack, and Zoom have made it easier to work with others, discuss ideas in real time, and facilitate virtual meetings.
- **Cybersecurity tools:** Cybersecurity tools protect the integrity and confidentiality of legal documents and client information. Solutions like Norton, McAfee, and Avast offer virus protection, while virtual private networks (VPNs) provide secure, safe remote access. Tools like Mimecast and Proofpoint provide email security, and password managers like LastPass or Dashlane offer secure password management.
- **Speech recognition software:** Software like Dragon NaturallySpeaking allows you to dictate with natural speech. AI-powered tools are improving speech-to-text capabilities and the ability to do things like take automated notes during a meeting.
- **Document automation tools:** Many apps can help automate parts of your legal documents. Even technology you use daily, like Microsoft Word, can save useful text snippets that you use often. Tools like Gavel and Smokeball use preset templates and customizable fields to generate documents quickly.
- **E-discovery tools:** E-discovery tools like Relativity and DISCO help with the identification, collection, and production of factual information. These tools offer keyword searches, tagging, redaction, exhibit labeling, and emerging features like visual searches to help you quickly zero in on the factual information you need for a brief or motion.
- **Legal calendaring software:** This software helps keep track of deadlines, court dates, and appointments, ensuring you don't miss any critical dates as you juggle different writing projects. Mastering calendaring tools will help in planning and managing timelines for drafting, reviewing, and finalizing your documents.
- **Focus and wellness apps:** This one isn't about your writing exactly, but it's important enough to mention. Wellness apps, like Headspace or Calm, can aid in stress management, offering guided meditations, mindfulness exercises, and

relaxation techniques. Focus apps like Zero can help reduce digital distractions, freeing you up to get your writing projects to the finish line.

Investing in Your Technology the Right Way

Let's say you've started using a new tech tool. Great. But make sure you use it properly.

Lawyers constantly complain about technology. But it's often operator error. Lawyers don't learn the basics of their tools. They don't set up basic preferences and defaults so that the tools work as they should. In other words, they don't invest enough in learning how and when to use their technology.

Setting aside time to figure out what you don't know about each of your writing technologies is hard for busy lawyers and law students. But the investment is necessary. If you don't learn enough about how your tools work, how to set them up, and how to use them, you're destined for late-night panic when those tools don't do what you need them to.

For example, there's no reason to ever lose a Microsoft Word document, yet lawyers lose their work every day. Even if your computer melted down, it shouldn't affect your documents. But that's true only if you know how to set up a cloud backup the right way. You can't blame Microsoft Word for losing your document when it offered you a simple way to prevent that.

Dedicate time to mastering your key technologies and their functions. Investing in setting up and learning your tools well will save you hundreds of hours a year. Not to mention the angst you'll save in not having to figure it out on the fly when you're under pressure. Even if it's 20 minutes a week, get in the habit of investing a little in setting up, learning, and reevaluating your tools.

Here are a few final tips about investing smartly. First, rather than learn every feature of a tool, focus instead on the features most useful for your practice. You don't need to be a power user. But you do need to spend the time learning the core features and *relevant* advanced features that will boost your practice.

Second, get help when you need it. GAI can be a fantastic collaborator here, explaining what an app does, how to set it up, and how to use it. You can even take a screenshot of an app's interface and ask GAI for step-by-step instructions for using it properly, given your goals. Technology vendors also offer a slew of learning resources, including live help to walk you through a new technology or function.

Third, invest in making your tools easier to use, features easier to find, and helpful resources easy to refer to. Put useful links on your desktop or in your browser favorites and use dashboards to make finding your key tech easy on all your devices. Understand each tool's settings and what you can customize and what you can't. Often you can link different tools to keep them updated and synchronized. Keep a list of helpful instructions or guides for each tool in a tech journal (yes, that sounds nerdy, but you will thank yourself later). When you learn how to do something complicated, jot down a reminder so you won't forget next time.

Fourth, figure out the risks of technology tools relevant to your practice. Data security poses risk to everyone. Mistakes in emails, in video conferencing setups, in formatting—the sky is the limit for how technology can go wrong. By developing a sense of the risks and weaknesses of different technologies, you can better insulate yourself and your clients from problems.

We'll return to your technology at the end of nearly every chapter. But whatever tools you use, consider some best practices:

- Choose which technologies and features of technologies to invest in with care. Inventory your current technology and your biggest challenges, and then learn what technology options are out there so you are well-informed before investing.
- Invest in your technology. You don't need to be a power user of every technology tool. But you do need to invest time in learning how to use each tool well. Also set aside time to streamline your technology tools and manage them.
- Stay abreast of how relevant technology is evolving. As we will explore in Chapter 13, technology like GAI is transforming the legal industry, especially when it comes to legal writing. By staying up to date on what is possible (and impossible) with technology, you are ensuring you will be empowered (and not replaced) with tech.

If you stopped reading here, these ten principles would take you a long way toward joining the best legal writers in the world. But why stop? These animating principles, combined with the techniques in the rest of this book, will turn you into a legal writing superstar.

Practice these techniques and technologies with Write.law's exercises and checklists, plus other resources at www.levelupyourlegalwriting.com

ASPEN PUBLISHING | write.law

2

Level Up Your Legal Message

> If you can say it in a paragraph, don't write a book."—Frank Sonnenberg

Legal writers love writing books instead of paragraphs. Our pages of background details finally give way to the bottom-line points that legal readers want.

I hear it all the time from lawyers, from judges, from clients: The hallmark of the best legal writers is that they *cut to the chase*. And they are right. Cutting to the chase is the most powerful skill in your legal writing arsenal. Figure out which ideas your readers need to make decisions. Then deliver those ideas at the outset, saving readers a winding journey through details and denseness.

I call this skill *distilling the takeaways*. You are doing the hard work for readers, *distilling* what matters from your writing into short *takeaways* that busy readers can use. This is the work of homing in on the precise information that will be most useful for readers first, and then following those crucial points with all the citations and authorities and minutiae that legal writing requires. After all, no one will remember most of what you write. To control what readers *do* remember, tackle the hard part for them by distilling what matters most, right from the start.

Let's look at a quick example. Say you're writing a brief and trying to convey one central point to the judge: A statute of limitations was blown because the plaintiff didn't file his complaint before the deadline. Most lawyers would start with a heading that delivers nothing more than the general conclusion they wish readers would reach:

> The plaintiff violated the applicable statute of limitations.

Then they would dive into the details: the cases, the dates, the citations, and all the other things that come along with briefs.

Why would the lawyer even bother with that general conclusion at all? Because no one will agree that there was a violation just because the writer said so. Readers need the takeaway, the specific details that connect the dots for them right now. With only this generic conclusion to start things off, readers will need to read the section on their own to understand why the writer is so convinced the statute of limitations was violated. So, really, that conclusion at the start was a waste.

Distilling takeaways requires you to highlight the details that will empower readers to reach a favorable conclusion without filtering through all the details on their own. Note the takeaway language in this example:

> The plaintiff's battery claim **triggered California's five-year statute of limitations ending in September 2022**—and the complaint was filed in November 2022.

In short, the takeaways I want you to distill for readers at the outset *are the specifics that readers need to understand and agree with you.*

Let's look at a smaller scale example. In this paragraph, the first sentence is a conclusion—the sort of superficial opening that lawyers love. But this sentence tells us what the lawyer thinks, not what the reader needs to draw the same conclusion.

> Mr. Parson clearly intended to defraud the government. Over a period of two years, he moved money around dozens of times. Some of those transactions were legitimate, but it appears that many were not. Many of these transactions appear suspect. Thousands of dollars were moved around in various months in 2019 and 2020. As well, many suspicious transactions occurred in 2018. Mr. Parsons also failed to adequately explain purchases in 2018. At the least, Mr. Parson doesn't explain virtually any of these movements.

Some important specifics lie buried in the paragraph above. But busy legal readers may never find them. To distill the takeaway, we capture those specifics in the initial sentence. In so doing, we create an anchor for readers that the rest of the paragraph can latch on to.

> **Mr. Parson moved money between several different accounts—dozens of times over two years—and failed to explain why.** In 2019, he moved money around 16 times and gave one-word descriptions that were unhelpful, like simply stating "transfer."[1] In 2020, he continued moving money around and continued to fail to explain why. For example, in March 2020, he moved $6,000 from one personal checking account to another, describing the transfer as "personal."

Distilling takeaways is about going to your writing cupboard and selecting enough ingredients so your readers get a nuanced flavor of the meal to come. Choose what specifics to include with care, and package them so that they make sense to a reader who hasn't tasted the dish yet.

In this chapter, we'll explore the three main places you need to distill the takeaways: the beginning of your document, the beginning of your sections, and the beginning of your paragraphs. At each juncture, your goal is to (1) sift through dense concepts, language, and legalese to figure out which specifics matter; and (2) package those specifics in a few short sentences that readers can readily understand without additional explanation or information.

---

[1] This targeted quote conveys more than merely suggesting that the descriptions were "unhelpful."

As a preview of this chapter, we'll work through techniques to:

- **Distill your document:** The best thing you can do for busy legal readers is to distill what matters from your document into a quick "cheat sheet" they can wrap their heads around in a few brief moments. Developing this skill will not only help you craft effective document summaries, like an introduction, but articulating the central takeaways will also keep you focused as you work through your draft.
- **Distill your sections:** Read your sections and ask, *What are the specific points my readers should get out of all this?* Then feed those points to your readers at the outset, so they don't need to labor through the whole section searching for them.
- **Distill your paragraphs:** If you distill the specifics your readers need from each paragraph into a brief sentence at the outset, your readers no longer need to read paragraphs carefully to find what matters. And they will love that.

Before diving in, let's look at an example from practice. This legal writer introduces their document with a long summary of basic, superficial conclusions. Any lawyer representing this client would make the same assertions about burdens and that the government violated a rule. You could find all this on Google in about a minute.

> **I. Introduction**
>
> The burden to prove that a traffic stop was lawful rests on the government. *Sanderson v. James*, 329 U.S. 87, 93 (2012). This burden is squarely on the government's shoulders, and it must be met before suppression is denied. *United States v. Roberson*, 90 F.3d 75 (3d Cir. 1996); *United States v. Garcia*, 205 F.3d 1182, 1186 (9th Cir. 2000) (citations omitted). Here, the police exceeded the mission of the traffic stop. The state has not met its burden to show that the traffic stop was lawful or that they did not exceed the mission of the traffic stop. And thus the evidence should be suppressed.

What is missing are the specifics so that you can figure out how to reach the conclusion on your own. As readers dig into the brief, they have no sense for what points matter. Here's a version that distills:

> **I. Introduction**
>
> The defendant moves to suppress firearms that police recovered during a routine traffic stop for driving 40 mph in a 35 mph zone.[2] **The State has the burden to prove that police did not spend even "seconds" exceeding the mission of their traffic stop. The Ninth Circuit emphasized last year in *United States v. Landeros* that "[a] demand for a passenger's identification is not part of the mission of a traffic stop." The court then explained that delaying for any measurable amount of time to demand identification—"even seconds"—is thus outside the mission.**[3]

[2] Weaving this detail into the first sentence— highlighting that this case stems from a modest 5 mph speeding ticket— primes readers to be less sympathetic to the state.

[3] Instead of including long, cumbersome quotes, the writer uses only short portions of the quote within a simple sentence structure.

> Here, **officers admit they spent "three minutes" demanding identification from the defendant and, during that delay, found contraband.** Officers thus exceeded the mission of the stop and the fruits of their search should be suppressed.[4]

Now we understand the key takeaways that help us understand how police violated the constitution here: (1) established law confirms that police exceed the mission of their traffic stop when they delay for "even seconds" to investigate a car's passenger, and (2) officers spent three minutes investigating the passenger in this case, so they exceeded the mission of the stop. The writers also included enough context so these points make sense and are trustworthy—by highlighting the appellate case the rule came from, for example.

Focusing on the crucial takeaways like this drives the best legal writing. Because it puts you in control of what readers take out of every part of your writing, rather than leaving it to chance. So let's start at the top, with your document as a whole.

2.1 Distill Your Document's Takeaways

Experienced attorneys will tell you that most disputes come down to just a few points of contention. That means a few sentences can usually capture the crux of the case.

Whether it's a brief, response, summary, report, or any other legal document, figure out what the heart of it is and distill those few points in a quick pitch that your readers can absorb without wading through a dense analysis. If you provide those takeaways up front, readers will be equipped to absorb your entire argument later because they'll have a roadmap of where you're taking them.

Below is an example of what *not* to do. The key takeaway readers need to agree with the conclusion in bold is nowhere to be found.

> Plaintiff moves this court respectfully to block the merger of Terrance Systems LLC and MGT Corporation. As extensively detailed below, **the merger between the two companies poses a significant threat to competition in the marketplace.** The defendant has failed to include the critical evidence required by controlling case law in this jurisdiction. Because of this failure, the court must halt the merger and provide any other relief it sees fit.

If you read the entire brief, the lawyer did have some specifics hiding away that could have convinced readers. Let's transform this introduction into one that focuses on those takeaways.

> Terrance Systems LLC and MGT Corporation want to merge their two already-massive companies so they can, in the words of MGT's CEO, "dominate the marketplace."[5] **The merger between Terrance Systems and MGT would result in a combined market share of over 60 percent, reducing competition by 20 percent, limiting consumer choice in a market that already has few options, and**

[4] Readers get all the context they need to understand the key points. The writers start with the traffic stop that led to this case, the key principles from the law, and then the key factual points— everything you need to understand.

[5] Using a quote here is more credible than paraphrasing what an opponent's intent may be.

> **increases the risk of monopolistic practices within the industry.[6] That 60 percent share passes the level set in at least four cases decided by this Court. The merger should thus be blocked.**

What's different? We gave readers the details and the perspective they need to understand why the merger should be blocked; we don't just hope they'll take our word for it. Even if readers are busy and not paying close attention, we can be sure that they will take away the key points.

Now let's see how master distillers do it. In these examples, tech conglomerates Microsoft and OpenAI were defending themselves in a lawsuit alleging that their use of copyrighted articles in training AI constitutes infringement. Microsoft boils down one of its key legal arguments with enough specificity that readers can understand *why* they should agree. Note how the writers package the takeaways with enough context that this point makes sense to the reader without needing to comb through the rest of the brief.

> The Times alleges that Microsoft is contributorily liable for *end-user* copyright infringement through use of GPT-based tools. **But it alleges no end-user infringement at all, and thus no knowledge on Microsoft's part that end-users are making infringing use of LLMs that have a universe of entirely lawful uses. The claim is therefore the exact one the Supreme Court rejected when it blessed the VCR.**

And here is some distilling from OpenAI's opening salvo in the same case. OpenAI distills a takeaway from the factual story, not the legal one. But again, the specifics make the story credible, and there's enough context that it makes sense without reading the rest of the brief.

> The allegations in the Times's Complaint do not meet its famously rigorous journalistic standards. The truth ... is that the Times paid someone to hack OpenAI's products. It took them tens of thousands of attempts to generate the highly anomalous results that make up Exhibit J to the Complaint. They were able to do so only by targeting and exploiting a bug (which OpenAI has committed to addressing) by using deceptive prompts that blatantly violate OpenAI's terms of use. And even then, they had to feed the tool portions of the very articles they sought to elicit verbatim passages of, virtually all of which already appear on multiple public websites. Normal people do not use OpenAI's products in this way.

Distilling the takeaways like this is so effective because readers now understand the document's points in a straightforward way—but on a nuanced enough level that they can start reaching a conclusion without working for it. And if there is anything busy legal readers appreciate, it's not having to work.

When readers pick up a legal document, especially when they're busy, it's easy to feel dread. The thought of trudging through pages of citations and cases and statutory analysis is enough to deflate anyone. And who knows what points those busy, skimming readers will even pay attention to among the morass. But if you can instead dish up your

[6] Specifics engage readers and make them pay attention. But too many details will drown out key details. By focusing on these key percentages (and not including various other details the writers could have), readers focus on what the writer wants.

document's key points in a commonsense way at the start, suddenly reading the rest isn't such a chore—and your readers will take away exactly what you want them to.

A Quick Summary

Develop your document's takeaways. **Discern up to four points that are critical for your document. If you have more than four, cut or combine points until you have four or fewer.**[7]

Make your takeaways stick. **Add enough specifics to your takeaways so that readers can use them as anchors throughout your document.**

Use your takeaways. **Use your takeaways to keep your draft focused and connected.**

2.1.1. Develop Your Document's Takeaways

When you strip away all the details, it's nearly impossible to make a persuasive pitch with a document that packs in more than a few basic takeaways. These points are the specific reasons that you should win (or the reasons your analysis is worth adopting). Even if your document contains dozens of issues, readers won't be able to manage all that. So you'll need to distill it all down into a few main takeaways.

Picking those takeaways is where most of your prewriting work lies. To be effective, the takeaways need to be nuanced, address any counterpoints, and package enough detail so that readers understand what they mean. In other words, you're looking for takeaways that will convince readers on their face.

So after you've researched and worked to develop the raw material for your document, craft the takeaways you want readers to remember. Turn each into a sentence or two that makes sense even for readers new to the matter. Then write them down as bullet points or in an outline (or even on a sticky note). That way you can use them to guide you as you write.

But how do you figure out your document's takeaways? Start at the start. What questions does your document seek to answer? Lawyers often get distracted by details that have little to do with the relief they are arguing for, the governing rules that will get them there, or even the facts that will aid their cause. They get caught in the fluff.

To figure out these key points, a simple brainstorming tool can help. Try answering the following questions:

1. Start with the relief or result you're looking to get with this document. Who is asking for what, exactly?

[7] The goal is to condense to a manageable number of points for readers. You may technically have several more subpoints, but in the end, strive to condense the takeaways to four or fewer.

2. Apply the procedural standard. How do any procedural standards change what you or the other side have to show to get that relief? For example, if you are writing a motion to dismiss, allegations are all that's needed.
3. Apply your understanding of the rules. What does the substantive law require? What elements or factors do you or the other side need to meet?
4. What do the parties dispute? Everyone always agrees on some things, so what do you disagree on (and need to persuade readers about)?

What you are left with after applying this process should be the main questions your document answers. And your takeaways should offer those answers. So, for example:

1. **What's the relief requested?** The defendant wants to dismiss the complaint.
2. **What's the procedural standard?** The plaintiff must have specific facts that plausibly entitle it to relief.
3. **What are the substantive rules?** The plaintiff is suing for breach of contract, so must allege specific facts about (1) existence of contract, (2) breach of contract, and (3) actual financial damage.
4. **What's actually in dispute?** The parties don't dispute a contract existed or that it was breached, but they do dispute whether Plaintiff alleged actual financial damage.

The result: The question that matters is *whether the Plaintiff alleged enough specific facts about the damages it suffered so that a reasonable jury could find for it.* Your readers will need specific takeaways that will get them to the answer.

Now the fun part comes. Once you've researched an answer, ask yourself what points will get readers to a place where they understand that answer. In this case, perhaps one of your key takeaways is:

> **The plaintiff alleged how much she spent to replace the machine, how many customers she lost, and other concrete financial losses that courts have held are sufficient to file a claim—which is all the law requires.**

This takeaway is concrete and useful. It gives readers enough information that they can understand, and perhaps even agree, with your answer.

2.1.2. Make Your Takeaways Stick

When distilling your document takeaways for readers, be specific. And make sure readers won't need too much context or nuanced background to understand them. You're aiming for something like a slogan: a sentence or two for each point that persuades on its own because it's self-contained.

Your goal is to equip readers with the knowledge they need to leverage the good and deal with the bad. In other words, your takeaways must deal with any facts or authorities or arguments that undermine you. One-sided takeaways don't help readers make hard decisions.

Each takeaway should deal with any counterarguments, undermining facts, or unfavorable law that detracts from your point. Your goal is for these takeaways to guide your reader through the gauntlet to reach your goal. So you'll need to research and think quite a bit until you've found a path for readers to follow. The more time you take to craft these cornerstone takeaways, the easier persuading your reader will be.

Let's say in our damaged machinery example an unfavorable fact is that our client doesn't have receipts for any of the repairs she's suing for. You'll need to find authority or facts to counter that point. Once you do, incorporate them into your takeaway.

> The plaintiff alleged how much she spent to replace the machine, how many customers she lost, and other concrete financial losses that courts have held are sufficient to file a claim—**and all the law requires is allegations, receipts or other evidence aren't required at this stage.**

Read this next effort by a lawyer to summarize the key takeaways for readers. But ask yourself if you understand exactly how the rule leads to the conclusion:

> The standard definition of gambling includes: (1) consideration paid, (2) an opportunity to win a particular prize, and (3) that the person wins or loses by chance. An opportunity to win the prize is the most important of the elements.
>
> . . .
>
> Here this key prong is not met because wagerers did not necessarily win the $100 prize but could also win a smaller one.

If you're like me, you were stumped. Why did this specific $100 prize matter? The problem is that the second element of the gambling definition requires a precise, predetermined prize. The word "particular" doesn't fully explain this crucial requirement. We could have distilled that specific information readers needed with a little bit more effort:

> The standard definition of gambling includes: (1) consideration paid, (2) an opportunity to win a particular prize **that the casino sets ahead of time**, and (3) that the person wins or loses by chance. An opportunity to win the prize is the most important of the elements—**and it requires that the casino set a dollar amount for a prize that doesn't change. . . .**

You'll find that if you work to craft specific takeaways for readers that plot a path to conclusions for readers—navigating around or through anything that undermines your position—you'll persuade audiences no matter what is thrown at them.

Let's take another example. You're writing a motion to dismiss a complaint. You've done your research and know the facts cold. When penning their argument, most lawyers will focus on abstract phrases like "the plaintiff failed to allege sufficient facts." But generic statements aren't convincing anyone. You need to dig deep to find the issue's crux.

Perhaps one argument you'd like to make is that a battery claim is not supported by sufficient allegations. You know the plaintiff will argue that she alleged who struck her and that this is enough to state a claim. But you've found a strong case, *Garrity*, suggesting the plaintiff must allege the date and location of the battery, as well as the perpetrator's identity. So your first takeaway might be this.

> **Plaintiff was required under *Garrity* to allege when and where she was struck, and she did not do so.**

With that specific path to victory plotted, you can now focus on arranging the cases, analysis, and facts you need to prop up that single point. This will also keep you, the writer, focused on what matters. It's much easier to avoid clutter and distractions when you have a single goal to reach. That done, craft your second point and repeat the process.[8]

In this next snippet, the legal writers offer just enough context for the takeaway to make sense.

> This appeal challenges the district court's dismissal of claims against a foreign automaker and denial of leave to amend, for lack of personal jurisdiction. **The district court applied a heightened standard for establishing specific jurisdiction against foreign entities that neither this Court nor the Supreme Court has endorsed.** The district court's decision finds no support in the text of the applicable long-arm statutes or the Constitution's Due Process Clause, none of which favor foreign over domestic defendants.

Check out this next example. A top federal litigator sums up the main takeaway from her document in two sentences. The case was complex but the point that carried the day was simple. A California law required an environmental study before a local agency approved a pipeline. That study never happened. So although the lawyer could say a lot about the complicated background in the case, she blew by all that and got to what mattered.

> **California law requires the Water Board conduct a "thorough" research study before approving a new pipeline that transports water across different states.** The Board admits **it didn't do a study** before approving the Diaz pipeline despite that it **moves water from Arizona and New Mexico.**[9]

In this next two-paragraph powerhouse, the attorneys manage to distill a complicated equal-protection case down to its bones. The case turned on whether same-sex couples could claim parental rights if one would have married in the past, but couldn't because, when they had their child, the Supreme Court had not yet recognized the right to same-sex marriage.

The writers take pages of argument (relying on a mix of facts and case law) and distill it into two takeaways. Now reading those two argument sections will be a breeze because you already know where the writers are aiming.

> The trial Court should have granted Ms. Edmonds' parentage claim for two reasons. **First, but for Ohio's[10] same-sex marriage ban, the parties would have married—and Ohio would recognize both as parents to their three children today.[11] By denying Ms. Edmonds parentage, the trial Court allowed an unconstitutional statute to control the outcome below.**

---

[8] Keep in mind we would, of course, support these takeaways with the proof—the authority illustrating that our takeaways are accurate.

[9] The writers give you the specifics you need to understand and agree with their conclusion. They don't merely say "and here the water was moved across states." They provide you with the specific states the water moved across.

[10] Anchoring sentences in concrete subjects makes sentences easier to understand. Instead of using an abstract principle like "Ohio law" in these sentences, the writers opt to personify Ohio throughout, keeping the subject consistent.

[11] This quick roadmap helps readers follow the two distinct points in this section.

> Second, the decision below violates Equal Protection because it **deprives the children of one of their parents simply because they were born to a same-sex couple. But for Ohio's same-sex marriage ban, these children would have two parents;[12] now, they suffer the stigma of knowing their family is "somehow lesser."**

In a few sentences, readers understand the point. The couple would have been married before if same-sex marriage were constitutionally protected in the past, and because the Supreme Court held that same-sex marriage is now and has always been a fundamental right enshrined in the Constitution, treating this couple as if they were unmarried in the past doesn't make sense. They were always married in the eyes of the Constitution.

Hopefully you see that this ability to distill what matters is profound. Whether it's explaining what matters to a judge, a client, or a colleague. Whether it's capturing your main points in a document's introduction or presenting your analysis to a senior partner. Distilling takeaways is a skill that will serve you now and forever.

Before digging more into how to use your document takeaways once you've developed them, one final suggestion on this step. You can often home in on what takeaways matter most by talking it out with others. There's a connection between speaking and writing. When we are forced to talk out our points, it's easier to focus on the gist.

> **We win here because, although we missed the deadline, that's allowed if we have good cause. Cases have held that good cause is met if notice was lost in the mail. And that is exactly what happened here. . . .**

Until you can explain your main points like this—in your own words and simply enough for someone to understand in a single telling—you're probably not ready to distill the takeaways.

2.1.3. Use Your Takeaways

You've crafted the specific points you want readers to remember after they turn the last page. Now what do you do with them?

First, use your document takeaways to focus your outlining and drafting. By keeping your end goals in view, you'll cut clutter and avoid tangents. Consider printing your takeaways and keeping them next to your screen. You won't believe what a difference it will make. If you're like most, the anxiety around writing will let up. You will have clear targets to aim readers at as you write.[13]

Second, your document takeaways should form the backbone of key sections like your introduction or summary of the argument. Your goal in these areas should be to package everything readers need to reach the correct conclusion.[14] Ultimately, your

[12] Semicolons highlight contrasts between two key ideas.

[13] And, as we'll explore shortly, you should use your document-level takeaways to help you craft your section-level ones, too.

[14] For more strategies on crafting excellent introductions, see Chapter 6.

document takeaways should be built to win. They should guide readers from where they are, through anything that undermines your goals, to the right conclusion.

But consider one final principle. If you deliver the main takeaways up front, with specifics, your readers won't have the benefit of much background and buildup. You'll need to convey your takeaways with enough context that the nuances will make sense. For example, let's say a takeaway from your document is this.

> The plaintiff presses a claim of monetary appropriation under Ca. Stat. § 8-1-46, so she cannot maintain a claim of nonmonetary appropriation under § 9-1-28, because the ladder statute says it's an exclusive remedy.

For this to make sense to readers, you'll need to give them a sentence or two of background. Because they are wondering:

- What is this legal mumbo jumbo: "Ca. Stat. § 8-1-46" and "§ 9-1-28"?
- What is "monetary appropriation"?
- What is "nonmonetary appropriation"?
- Why are they mutually exclusive?

So when delivering your takeaways to readers at the start (of a document, of a section, or of a paragraph), consider how you can package them so that they make sense to a *fresh* reader. That may mean simplifying and explaining more.

> The plaintiff first claims—under a California consumer fraud statute—that the defendant stole funds from her bank account. But she also presses a claim based on the same facts under a different statute, which regulates business reputation harms. The problem is this reputational-harm statute states it may be used only if the plaintiff concedes "no other statute applies to the factual claim asserted." In other words: Plaintiffs can sue under the reputational-harm statute only if they agree that no other statute applies to the facts used to underpin the claim. And plaintiff has not done so.

Yes, that takes some more words. But there is no value in presenting deeper points first if readers won't understand them. Check in with your imaginary readers and explain what needs to be explained—right now, as they need it.

Now let's zoom in to your sections and apply these distilling principles at a smaller scale.

2.2 Distill Your Sections

Distilling is a superpower for your sections, too. Readers can keep in their minds only a few takeaways from each major section. Your goal here should be to deliver a few major points that readers need to reach the document-level takeaways you set for them in the last stage.

You need to distill the takeaways from each major section in your document. And then within each of those major sections, distill the takeaways for each subsection, if you have them. Remember the goal is to extract the specifics readers need to be persuaded. This is quite the task when you're dealing with entire sections. But the payoff is worth it.

Look at this next example. In a single heading, you get enough of the section's gist that you may already be persuaded. How much more must you know before you accept the author's premise?

> I. The defendant had **no expectation of privacy in his bathroom** because he **"called police on the phone"** and **"asked them"** to come inside.

Great takeaways like this are self-explanatory. Readers instantly get a deep understanding. It's hard to imagine any definition of "privacy" that stands after you've called someone and "asked them" to come inside your bathroom.

You should be distilling takeaways for every part of your document, whatever the document. But to cement this skill, we'll look at strategies for distilling two of the most important sections: the facts and the analysis.

A Quick Summary

Distill your facts. **Distill a manageable few specific takeaways from your fact section. Use those takeaways to craft effective fact headings and paragraph openers.**

Distill your analysis. **Distill the key principles from your rules and application into a manageable set of takeaways. Use those takeaways to craft headings and paragraph openers in your analysis.**

2.2.1. Distill Your Facts

The facts are often as important, if not more important, than the law. Legal readers relish a good story. It's part of being human. Who are these parties? Why do they have so much invested in this dispute? How will the results affect them?

And if the facts are against you, it's even more important that you leverage strategies for rehabilitating or deemphasizing what's harmful. Because you can bet the other side will press the facts to their advantage.

When distilling your fact sections into takeaways, you're looking to turn that long list of details into a set of manageable takeaways readers can wrap their heads around. And persuasive ones at that. Your factual takeaways should either persuade readers through the power of story itself, or illustrate points readers need for the legal analysis later.

For example, let's say one of your document takeaways is that your client took exhaustive steps to notify another party that they were terminating a contract. In your fact section, you will probably drive home takeaways about all that your client did to notify the other side—those are the points readers will need for your legal analysis later.

> A. Mr. Jameson sent Ms. Patterson **dozens of emails, two letters, and left three voicemails—all notifying her that he wanted to terminate.**

The other factual takeaway is one that will move your readers for pure storytelling reasons. For example, this next writer didn't need to establish that the opposing party mistakenly sent some emails, only that she told people a concert was canceled. But the mistake related enough to the analysis—and was persuasive—so the lawyer weaved that detail into her takeaway.

> III. Park Corp. **mistakenly emails half of the attendees the wrong location,** then calls another group of attendees to tell them the concert is canceled.[15]

Crafting factual takeaways will also force you to refine your paragraphs and figure out why they are there. If you can't find an overarching takeaway from a group of paragraphs that you can use to stitch them together, that is a red flag that you haven't figured out what main factual points your need readers to know.

So work with your factual story and figure out how to categorize all those details into a set of overarching points. Then describe those points persuasively by packaging them for readers.

In this next example, a plaintiff's lawyer in a discrimination case included in his fact section all the details you'd expect: the alleged harassment, the company's response, and the procedural history. But what the lawyer did not do was distill the key factual takeaways.

First, the lawyers used generic headings instead of breaking up the facts into major takeaways. For readers to figure out what they needed from this fact section (which spanned several pages), they had to do all the work, reading through pages of details, then organizing it all into something manageable. The headings were not guiding them:

> **I. Statement of the Case**
>
> **A. Factual Background**
>
> **B. Procedural History**

Let's zoom in and take two paragraphs from the lawyer's facts. These two paragraphs were buried among many other paragraphs about different time periods and events. Consider how we could develop a takeaway from each, then use those takeaways to craft a heading that makes the points easy to grab.

> In 2020, Ms. Stook started a new position as a Senior Janitor at the company. The first day she showed up for work, a note waited taped to her desk that read "Welcome Bit$#." This note set the tone for the rest of the year. Ms. Stook faced harassment after harassment. Nearly every week some new insult was slung at her. Coworkers and supervisors used racial slurs when giving her tasks. They continued to leave racist notes on her desk. During one incident, Ms. Stook was walking to the bathroom when a coworker pushed her into a wall, telling her to "get out of the way idiot."
>
> There were numerous incidents of harassment all year. The harassment was carried out by at least three coworkers and two supervisors. One supervisor, James Terry, was Ms. Stook's direct report.

[15] Simple, familiar word choice like this makes this key heading easy to absorb. Most legal writers would have used formal language like "informed" or "stated."

> The other supervisor, Michael Patlov, was a general manager in the janitorial department. All three coworkers who carried out the harassment, Mary Holt, Sam Perrins, and Higgs Taylor, worked in Ms. Stook's division—so she was forced to see them each day.

Will readers remember every harassing incident? No. Will they remember the coworkers' names? Probably not. What takeaway *could* readers leave with? That various coworkers and supervisors inflicted a lot of deplorable things on Ms. Stook. If we do the work and show readers, that is. We can use a heading to dish up the most moving, useful information in a package that readers can take with them. Those specifics are what sell, like this.

> A. **In 2020, Ms. Stook endured[16] a string of harassment from three coworkers and two supervisors—including racial slurs, racist notes left on her desk, and being pushed against a wall.[17]**

With the main factual takeaways identified, we can use this point to refine the paragraphs, too, cutting out clutter and pulling in details from other sections that fit better here. Organizing our major factual points for readers is, again, also helpful for organizing us writers.

Here is a fun set of fact headings that distill a story for readers. The lawyers were suing a hog farm because "particulates" from the farm were spilling over onto homeowners' land (and other surfaces, as you'll see). First, you get a sense of the three main factual categories you need for the rest of the brief (facts about the farms, facts about how the waste is scattered around, and facts about how the waste is harming the plaintiffs). Second, you get the story in three sentences that make sense on their face.

> II. STATEMENT OF MATERIAL FACTS
>
> A. **Defendants Own Seventeen of Eighteen Hog Farms in the Neighborhood.**
>
> B. **Trouble on Highway 50**: A Special Delivery for Plaintiffs.
>
> C. "**I Can Take My Hand and Rub It**": When Defendants **Spray**, They **Cake**[18] Plaintiffs' **Yards**, **Homes**, and **Bodies** with **Hog Waste**.

Here's another example of headings that distill a story's takeaway, this time by listing the categories of facts the legal writers would march through:

> **A. Ms. Edmonds Raised Her Marriage-Based Arguments in Her Complaint, at Opening Statement, During Evidentiary Objections, in Her Written Closing, and in Her Objections to the Magistrate's Report.**

To keep clear: the power here is in identifying the factual takeaways themselves. With them in hand, you'll have a guide when crafting important real estate like headings

[16] Concrete, targeted verbs like this make the writing more gripping.
[17] This takeaway highlights moving details that will likely color the reader's perspective as they now enter the section.
[18] Quoting these factual details from the testimony brings the victims' perspective front and center. The concrete verbs and specific details paint a picture (and a disturbing one at that).

and deciding what details to include in your fact section in the first place. Distilling is as much for you as it is for readers. You're forcing yourself to articulate what really matters so that you can then craft the focused, powerful writing you need.

That's enough of the facts. Let's distill some analysis.

2.2.2 Distill Your Analysis

We next need to figure out what takeaways are lurking in our analysis sections. Then (like we did with our facts) we can work backward, building our headings and paragraphs and sentences to deliver those takeaways.

In big, complex matters, maybe you think your brief or motion must make dozens of legal points. But not so. Stripped bare, I dare you to find a great analysis that presses more than three or four main points. Beyond that readers get lost. So we might have smaller takeaways that build into a few bigger ones (in the form of subheadings and headings). But try to confine yourself (and your readers) to a few manageable points across your analysis.

Your guiding light here is *what specific points will convince readers to reach the legal conclusion you need them to*? Focus on the details that you used to convince yourself. Where in case law or policy or analysis do you think you have a winning perspective? A perspective that will get your readers past anything set out against you and your client?

We'll work on how to develop your takeaways about the rules more in Chapter 4. But as a quick preview, your goal is to create an easy-to-digest interpretation of the authority that will lead readers to the decisions you're aiming for. A rule takeaway. Like all good takeaways, your pitch must deal with the good and the bad. If you can give readers a view that will get them through any fact or authority or argument that undermines you, persuading becomes almost too easy.

This next heading from a legal analysis is poorly written. It's loaded with conclusions and generalizations, but light on the specifics readers need.

> **I. This Court Should Grant Certiorari Pursuant to Rule 39(a)(1)(D) Because the Court of Criminal Appeals' Decision Affirming Summary Dismissal of Mr. Hoffman's Claim That He Received Ineffective Assistance of Appellate Counsel Due to Appellant Counsel's Failure to Argue That Remand Was Necessary to Demonstrate That Mr. Hoffman Is Intellectually Disabled.**

When we focus on the persuasive takeaways from the lawyer's analysis and distill them into a heading, everything changes.

> I. Certiorari is warranted because trial counsel never so much as mentioned that Mr. Hoffman was intellectually **disabled—despite that he has an IQ of 50 and this Court has held that an IQ of 65 warrants relief.**

We've distilled the winning view of the law (that the court has held anything below an IQ of 65 makes us win) and the specific fact that gets readers to the conclusion (that our client has an IQ of 50).

In this next example, the lawyers were challenging New Jersey's practice of allowing political candidates to include a six-word slogan next to their name on a ballot—but prohibiting certain words, like references to another person or company. The authors address a point that undermines them (that the state could have prohibited all speech), while emphasizing their view of the law (that if a state allows these slogans at all, it can't regulate their content).

> A. Although candidates do not have an absolute constitutional right to extend the political debate onto the ballot, **states that allow such core political speech at the moment of decision must fully respect the First Amendment when it matters most.**

We'll return to more strategies for writing about the law in Chapter 4. For now, know that your most specific, precise, winning view of the law—and the facts that line up with that view—are what you want to distill for readers at the outset of your analysis sections.

Each of the following examples illustrates top-notch analysis distilling. Notice how each conveys key details in an accessible way that new readers can grasp—and with excellent style.

> I. The Supreme Court case law requires **alleging the date, time, and means of carrying out the conspiracy—none of which happened here.**

> I. This court has no jurisdiction because the deadline to file the complaint was **June 2017 and plaintiff filed in September of that year.**

> I. Plaintiffs press for an interpretation where they **can breach and buyout—but that has never been the parties' intent, they said so under oath, and their actions confirm it.**[19]

Distilling your analysis is about identifying a few powerful takeaways from the law and then aligning them with the most compelling facts of your case. Put these takeaways up in neon in your headings, in the beginning of sections—and use them as an anchor when deciding what to include in each section.

2.3 Distill Your Paragraphs

To wrap up distilling, let's talk paragraphs. Distill the point of each paragraph into an easy-to-digest takeaway at the outset (preferably, the first sentence). That way, readers can skim each paragraph and see what you want them to see. Perhaps most importantly, if you distill the takeaway from each paragraph at the outset, you'll be controlling what readers remember as they work through your document.

Paragraph takeaways can be simple and still convey the specifics that matter. In this next paragraph, the first sentence makes sense on its face and captures the gist of the sentences to come:

> **First, "dissemination of information" is plainly "speech within the meaning of the First Amendment."** [] After all, "if the acts of 'disclosing' and 'publishing' information do not constitute speech, it is hard to imagine what does." [] That is so even when the private party does not "generate, as an original matter, each item featured in the communication" or "isolate an exact message

[19] Alliteration (breach and buyout) makes the point memorable, as does the em dash that emphasizes the key points and the simple, familiar word choice.

> as the exclusive subject matter of the speech." [] The "presentation of an edited compilation of speech generated by other persons" falls "squarely within the core of First Amendment security."

One of the top legal writers in the nation, Deepak Gupta, is a maven at distilling what matters from paragraphs at the start. As you read this next paragraph about complex debt rules, this anchoring takeaway at the start makes it easier to track the dense details after. You focus precisely on the takeaway that the writer has in mind, leaving nothing to chance.

> **The ability to accurately price debts based on age and timeliness is critical to a debt buyer's success.** For example, Encore touts its "information advantage" and proprietary valuation models as two keys to its competitive advantage. To that end, Encore claims to "obtain detailed information regarding the portfolio's accounts," and it "continually monitor[s] applicable changes to laws governing statutes of limitations." Encore is not unique — the FTC concluded "that debt buyers usually are likely to know or be able to determine whether the debts on which they are collecting are beyond the statute of limitations."[20]

A Quick Summary

Distill your point first. Read each paragraph and ask yourself: What is the single idea that you want readers to remember? Deliver that takeaway in the first sentence or so. Leverage specifics, quotes, pithy language, or other details from the paragraph to capture the persuasive flavor.

Break up paragraphs. If you can't capture everything that matters in a single, specific sentence, that may mean there's too much crammed in. If so, break up the paragraph around the takeaways.

2.3.1. Distill the Point First

The first step to writing a good paragraph is to figure out why it's there. Why do readers need this group of sentences? Once you've figured out what matters from the paragraph, then it's time to craft an opener that readers will remember. Use specific details, quotes, or other gripping language to convey the gist.

In the end, the best legal writers convey the main takeaway in the first sentence of most paragraphs. If you read their paragraphs' first sentences, you don't need to read the rest of the writing all that carefully. You already understand enough. And who doesn't like to feel smart with barely any effort?

[20] Using a quote to convey this key policy point maintains the writer's credibility and allows readers to feel like they are getting the outside information they can rely on.

Let's go back to the discrimination case we looked at when trying to craft section takeaways.

> In 2020, Ms. Stook started a new position as a Senior Janitor at the company. The first day she showed up for work, a note waited taped to her desk that read "Welcome Bit$#." This note set the tone for the rest of the year. Ms. Stook faced harassment after harassment. Nearly every week some new insult was slung at her. Coworkers and supervisors used racial slurs when giving her tasks. They continued to leave racist notes on her desk. During one incident, Ms. Stook was walking to the bathroom when a coworker pushed her into a wall, telling her to "get out of the way idiot."
>
> There were numerous incidents of harassment all year. The harassment was carried out by at least three coworkers and two supervisors. One supervisor, James Terry, was Ms. Stook's direct report. The other supervisor, Michael Patlov, was a general manager in the janitorial department. All three coworkers who carried out the harassment, Mary Holt, Sam Perrins, and Higgs Taylor, worked in Ms. Stook's division—so she was forced to see them each day.

The details in the first paragraph depict the harassment. The second paragraph was all about the harassers. So we can craft first sentences that present those takeaways. We can also cut sentences that don't support our new takeaways now that we've found them.

> **Ms. Stook faced constant harassment throughout 2020: She was called racial slurs, left racist notes, shoved into a wall, and more.** The first day she showed up for work, a note waited taped to her desk that read "Welcome Bit$#."

> **The harassers included three coworkers Ms. Stook was forced to work with each day, as well as her direct supervisor and another senior manager in her department.** One supervisor, James Terry, was Ms. Stook's direct report. The other supervisor. . . .

For another example, look at this paragraph relating some facts without an anchoring takeaway at the start.

> Higgs Corp. filed its corporate paperwork the following day. Two days after that, the company's CEO called for a press briefing. He told reporters that Higgs planned to roll out a new process to ensure that no defective parts would be shipped again. This process involves 40 additional checkpoints on all products. He emphasized that this new program had a zero-tolerance policy for defects. Even one defect was too much.

Maybe you need all those details because you're going to analyze them later. But no one is remembering them all like that.[21] So let's capture the point that serves you and your reader.

> **Higgs Corp. implemented a new "zero-tolerance" process with 40 checkpoints—all to ensure no defective products will be shipped again. . . .**

[21] In situations like this where the point isn't packaged at the outset, busy readers skim the paragraph and remember something general like "the company took some actions to fix things." But it's not a specific detail that can stick with readers and convince them.

This single takeaway captures the paragraph's persuasive essence. It serves up key language and details, and now when readers finish the paragraph, they'll have a package to take with them.

In this next paragraph, the lawyer gives us only a topic sentence, forcing us to read the sentences that follow if we want to figure out why this *Park* case matters.

> The *Park* case is also key. The plaintiff there filed a complaint against the federal agency. The agency waited more than two months to respond, then when a default was entered, showed up and tried to set it aside. The court denied the agency's request, saying that "the deadline applies with as much force to agencies as it does to a company or individual."

By creating a takeaway from the paragraph's details, readers can grasp your persuasive point first, and the details will fit in after.

> **The deadline to file an answer "applies with as much force" to federal agencies—and missing it ends the case....**

These initial takeaways will force you to convey what is useful to readers in a single package. And that skill will transform your writing like nothing else. In this next paragraph, lawyers for OpenAI knew a key point for their argument was that The New York Times (who was suing OpenAI) waited too long before suing. So in their fact section, the lawyers for OpenAI distilled in this opening sentence of a paragraph the key factual takeaway readers would need later:

> **By July 2020, OpenAI had disclosed that Times articles were a tiny part of the diverse datasets that had been used to train these language models.** And according to the Complaint, by the time GPT-3 was released in mid-2020, OpenAI had already established itself as a commercial enterprise. The Times itself reported in 2020 that OpenAI plans to sell access to GPT-3 via the internet, turning it into a widely used commercial product.

Now readers will easily remember that OpenAI disclosed the relevant information back in 2020. When the legal argument comes later, it will be obvious that The Times missed the filing deadline.

In this next series of paragraphs, from Justice Elena Kagan, the first sentences do two things: (1) distill what matters from the paragraph with deep specificity, and (2) weave together each paragraph with the next.

> **With one exception,[22] PROMESA says nothing explicit about abrogating sovereign immunity.** The exception is for Title III cases, and comes via the Federal Bankruptcy Code. PROMESA incorporates, as part of its mechanism for restructuring debt, the Code's express abrogation of sovereign immunity.... But as to all other matters PROMESA addresses, Congress did not mention sovereign immunity. In particular, no provision states that it is abrogating any immunity the Board possesses from legal claims.

[22] The Justice likely didn't want to clutter her takeaway here with specifics about an exception that turned out to be irrelevant. So she used summary language (generally referring to an exception) and kept the specifics focused on her main point—the lack of any language about abrogating immunity.

> **At the same time,[23] several provisions of PROMESA contemplate that, even outside the Title III context, the Board may confront legal claims against it.** Most fundamentally, Section 2126(a), entitled "Jurisdiction," states that "any action against the Oversight Board, and any action otherwise arising out of" PROMESA, "shall be brought' in the Federal District Court sitting in Puerto Rico. And Section 2126(c) anticipates that those actions may lead to orders 'granting declaratory or injunctive relief against the Oversight Board";[24] under the provision, such orders cannot take effect until the litigation is over.
>
> **On the flip side, PROMESA sets certain limits on litigation targeting the Board.** Section 2125 forecloses monetary liability against the Board, its members, and its employees for "actions taken to carry out" the statute. And Section 2126(e) provides that no district court will have jurisdiction over challenges to the Board's "certification determinations"— mainly, decisions approving Puerto Rico's fiscal plans and budgets. See §§ 2141(e), 2142(e) (describing those determinations).

You get what matters from these opening sentences: (1) The statute does not verbatim abrogate sovereign immunity, (2) language contemplates the board will be sued, and (3) the statute even goes so far as to provide limitations for lawsuits (all of which suggests that lawsuits are not abrogated).

One final point about crafting your paragraph takeaways. You can often distill a paragraph into a single opening sentence. On the other hand, life isn't always so easy. More complicated paragraphs may require two sentences to convey what matters, depending on how many key points sit in the paragraph.

When more than one sentence is needed, it's often because readers will need a touch of context before consuming the takeaway. In this next example, the legal writer wanted to convey that no specific expert method was required to support an argument. But to get there, readers needed to understand why we were discussing the expert's method in the first place. These two sentences (complete with a pithy quote to distill the paragraph's persuasive point) give readers everything they need.

> **Thomson Reuters objects that Ross did not disclose its expert's methodology. But substantial similarity is not especially scientific: the question boils down to "good eyes and common sense."**

2.3.2. Break Up Paragraphs

You craft the perfect takeaway from a paragraph. But then you read it again and realize *it's really long*. To capture everything you think matters, your opening sentence became a little paragraph of its own.

This happens all the time. Too much is crammed into a paragraph. Idea lays atop idea. We just didn't notice when we were writing because we haven't tried to do what our readers must do. Distill what matters.

[23] Logical transitions like this stitch together the paragraphs, signaling to readers that this next paragraph will convey a point that fits alongside the first.

[24] This quote says exactly what the Justice wants to convey, so it's a great specific to include, rather than a paraphrase. But even better, the quote is short, making sure readers pay attention to the exact wording — many legal writers would have quoted a whole sentence, drowning the key language out.

So when you struggle to capture a paragraph in a single readable sentence, that's the best writing feedback you'll get. There's too much in the paragraph. If you can't articulate everything that matters in a smooth sentence, rest assured your busy reader won't be able to either. The answer? Break your takeaway, and your paragraph, into smaller pieces.

Take this final example. I warn you, it's dense. Feel free to skim past it (like most legal readers would) so we can do some distilling to pull out what readers care about.

> The Appellant contends that the lower court erred in its interpretation of Section 10(b) of the Securities Exchange Act of 1934 ("the Act"), 15 U.S.C. § 78j(b), and Rule 10b-5 promulgated thereunder by the Securities and Exchange Commission ("SEC"). Specifically, the court below failed to properly apply the well-established "scienter" requirement, which mandates that for a defendant to be held liable under Rule 10b-5, there must be a showing of intent to deceive, manipulate, or defraud. The evidence presented at trial, when viewed in the light most favorable to the Appellant, did not demonstrate the defendant knew any of the statements he made were false. . . .

To make it easier, we would normally start with a takeaway that distills the paragraph's main points.

> The lower Court misapplied the intent element because no evidence at trial suggests that the Defendant knew his statement was false—and the Court misapplied the causation element by requiring the Defendant to prove loss causation instead of transaction causation.

This takeaway is specific. But it's a lot. Readers would have an easier time if the paragraph (and takeaway) were broken into two so that they could tackle one point at a time—the intent element, then the causation element.

> **The lower Court misapplied the intent element because no evidence at trial suggests that the Defendant knew his statement was false.** . . . [Sentences supporting this single takeaway]

> **The Court misapplied the causation element by requiring the Defendant to prove loss causation instead of transaction causation.** . . . [Sentences supporting this single takeaway]

This example is why distilling takeaways is a game changer. Forcing yourself to articulate the key ideas in your paragraphs, your sections, and across your document will make it easy to provide one point at a time to readers. This will prevent important ideas from crowding one another and stealing the spotlight. And it will make you a legal writing superstar.

Level Up Your Legal Message with Technology

Distilling takeaways is about boiling complex information down to its essence. It's about extracting clear, accessible points from in-depth analysis. When thinking about the technology that can help you with these skills, consider tools that can help you summarize key ideas, refine the style of your key takeaway sentences, and help choose the details to highlight when distilling your points.

GAI tools: We'll return to GAI tools in nearly every chapter, and we'll explore these tools at length in Chapter 13. But GAI can be a fantastic collaborator when distilling takeaways.

As we'll learn later, GAI tools shine when working on defined text like a section of your document. By providing specific instructions about what you're looking for in a takeaway—perhaps an example or two of a good heading or first sentence of a paragraph, and a section of your text—GAI can help you brainstorm and then tweak that perfect takeaway. For example, you could instruct a GAI tool like this:

You're a professional legal writer. You're helping me come up with a single sentence that will capture the most important ideas in a section of my legal document. This sentence should convey important specific details that will help persuade readers. But the sentence should be easy to understand without reading the entire section. Provide at least four different options for me to choose from:

***

Here is an example of a good summary: "[insert an example of another takeaway you've drafted, like a heading]"

***

Here is the section of my document I'd like you to draft a summary sentence for:

"[insert a paragraph or section of your document that you want help distilling]"

***

Now provide at least four summaries for my text, recalling my original instructions.

You may need to follow up a few times, providing feedback about useful takeaways and what's not so useful. But GAI tools can be great collaborators here.

Text summarization tools: Summarization software employs algorithms to condense long documents into point summaries. By inputting lengthy rulings or your own legal analysis into these tools, you can get an automated quick summary that can help you nail down what readers should focus on. A slew of products use GAI to do this summarizing quicker and more thoroughly.

Concept mapping software: Concept mapping tools (like MindManager, Lucidchart, and Miro)[25] provide an interactive environment to visually organize your thoughts. You can plot out the logical flow of arguments and group similar points together, aiding in the identification of central themes for your key takeaways.

[25] When products are noted in this text, they are solely to offer an example so you can do a quick internet search and view demos or features yourself. I'm not endorsing any product (well, except my own, at Write.law).

Outlining apps: Designed for organizing the structure and logic of documents, these tools help legal writers build detailed and coherent outlines. They simplify the process of mapping arguments, reordering sections, and tracking key points, ensuring that the final written product is logically consistent and well-organized. Examples include OmniOutliner, Turtl, and Workflowy.

Distraction-free writing applications: Writing apps are designed to minimize distractions, offering a stripped-down, clean interface on your computer that encourages you to concentrate on the writing itself. These applications are ideal for distilling takeaways because they simplify your workspace, allowing you to focus on crafting precise, potent sentences without the clutter of toolbars or the temptation to multitask.

Collaborative document platforms: Platforms like Google Docs and Microsoft OneDrive facilitate real-time collaboration and provide an environment where multiple people can contribute to distilling what matters from a key document. Each person can suggest edits or highlight information they believe should be a key takeaway. The collaborative nature of these platforms also allows for instant feedback on the clarity and effectiveness of the distilled points, ensuring a broad perspective is considered.

Form and template libraries: Look for inspiration in crafting your takeaways in prior work product at your organization, references, or template documents. All these resources can help you brainstorm your big-picture organization.

Practice these techniques and technologies with Write.law's exercises and checklists, plus other resources at www.levelupyourlegalwriting.com

ASPEN PUBLISHING | write.law

3

Level Up Your Legal Stories

> “Those who tell the stories rule the world.” — Unknown

You've collected the details you need for the fact section of your document. Now, it's time to turn them into a story.

In recent years, neuroscientists discovered that when you deliver information in the form of a story, something special happens. Audiences' neural activity "synchronizes" across multiple regions of the brain, triggering emotional areas that would not be triggered if that same information were not delivered as a story. What researchers are finding is that stories trigger similar feelings and reactions in readers even when those readers have different perspectives, backgrounds, and biases.[1]

Good legal stories do more than inform — they reach audiences on a deeper level. An emotional one. Stories serve a purpose separate from the legal discussion that will come later. Stories help explain, teach, and sway judges and juries in a way that's different from the standard legal arguments most legal writers rely on.

We explored helpful storytelling tools in the prior chapter. Distilling takeaways from the facts will keep readers focused on what matters. Those takeaways will form the backbone of your fact section — and you should use them when doing things like crafting your headings and ordering your major factual points. But let's go one level deeper and dig into the details. Because that's where the story comes to life.

Here's what's ahead:

- Choose the pivotal facts. Start by identifying the pivotal analysis, context, emotional, and character facts that readers need to understand the legal analysis

[1] Wendy A. Suzuki, Mónica I. Feliú-Mójer, Uri Hasson, Rachel Yehuda & Jean Mary Zarate, *Dialogues: The Science and Power of Storytelling*, 38 J. Neurosci. 9468, 9468–9470 (2018) (collecting research and discussing the power of story on a neurological level).

and get invested in the story itself. Your underlying case likely has many facts to choose from, but your document can convey only a select few.

- Use tools to frame factual details convincingly. Even blockbuster stories can fall flat if the details aren't developed effectively. Fine-tune the details by using devices like location, quantity, and narration to enhance the story your readers see.
- Apply storytelling techniques to elevate your discussions about the law, too. Consider how you can frame court decisions and statutes in terms of the people involved and the events that unfolded.

Before diving into these tools, let's explore an example so you can feel some storytelling for yourself. You can learn a lot about telling good stories by spending time with this next passage. The writer is Judge Jennifer Dorsey, who we've heard from a few times now. And she knows her stories. She uses narrative devices that snap the story into focus like a movie. As you read, track the decisions Judge Dorsey makes about which characters to follow, which details to reveal, and in what order.

> Laid off and depressed, Juan Solis-Diaz put his kids to bed late one night,[2] took his contact lenses out, and retreated to his study to drink beer and blow off steam in an anger chatroom on his computer. When he heard noises outside, he feared that hippies[3] were trying to break into his SUV parked on his dark driveway, so he grabbed his AK-style rifle, pressed the button to open his automatic garage door, and "half sprinted" through the garage toward the driveway.[4]
>
> At the same time,[5] Las Vegas Metropolitan Police Officer Tompkins was walking up that driveway. He had cut short the traffic stop he was conducting on the street when he heard yelling coming from inside the Solis-Diaz home. Suspecting a domestic altercation, Tompkins called for back up, stepped away from his patrol car with its lights activated, and walked up the driveway toward the front door to check on the occupants. When the garage door began to open,[6] he saw the backlit silhouette of Solis-Diaz, armed and crouching below the door. As Solis-Diaz stood with the rising door, he pointed his gun toward Tompkins.
>
> Tipsy and without his prescription lenses, Solis-Diaz took several seconds to realize that the man in his driveway was a law enforcement officer. In that time, Tompkins drew his gun, ordered Solis-Diaz to drop his weapon, heard Solis-Diaz respond with an expletive, and then began shooting as he retreated toward his patrol car for cover.

The details engage you. You can see the events unfold in your mind's eye. Storytelling language like "at the same time" sets the pacing, and action-oriented sentences keep events moving forward.

[2] The writer doesn't tell us the exact time but conveys the facts she wants us to see (nighttime).

[3] This word choice keeps the perspective from the defendant's view.

[4] These sentences are examples of when a longer, more complex sentence does good work. We'll return to these sorts of action-unfolding sentences in Chapters 6 and 9.

[5] This is classic narrating and controlling the pace.

[6] Another fantastic timing device meant to help you experience the passing moments.

In the end, storytelling engages readers, burns details into their memories, and forges the sort of close bonds you need with your readers to persuade them. We understand the world through stories. We learn through stories. So let's tell stories.

3.1 Choose the Foundational Facts

Your task at this initial stage is to sketch out a storyline, mapping the major events and players essential for your reader to understand and, ultimately, to be convinced.

When drafting legal documents, we usually have a big pile of facts to pull from. Some will obviously be needed, like the core events leading to the dispute. If you're suing an insurance company over a car crash, you need to talk about the crash. But other facts might not be so obviously relevant, and you'll need to decide which to include and why.

Four types of facts animate the best legal stories. First, identify the *analytical* facts that form the backbone of your legal argument. These are the foundation of your narrative. Next, gather *contextual* facts to give depth to your analysis facts. Contextual facts paint the background against which your main story unfolds. Then, select *emotionally charged* facts that subtly bolster your narrative, striking a chord with the reader's sensibilities. Finally, incorporate *character* facts that portray key figures in a way that aligns with your goals.

Your goal is to tell a story, a narrative with a beginning, middle, and end. For example, lawyers representing Citibank had an unusual story on their hands. Their client accidentally wired nearly half a billion dollars to someone—and that someone refused to give it back. All agreed Citibank sent the money by mistake. But the legal writers knew that any person picking up this brief (judge or otherwise) would be curious: How could a major bank make such a colossal blunder? To prevent that nagging question from distracting from the narrative, the writers wove this scene into their narrative:

> Late afternoon on August 11, an analyst at Citibank's subcontractor Wipro prepped Revlon's wire transfer in "Flexcube," Citibank's loan-processing payment software. Executing a roll-up transaction in Flexcube was complicated: Citibank had to fictitiously "pay off" the original Revlon loan and create new versions of the loans in Flexcube accounting for the changes. To prevent actual principal payments from going to the lenders, the Wipro analyst was supposed to have Flexcube set the principal to an internal "wash account" that is not a real bank account and "does not contain any funds." This required inputting certain information in three boxes in Flexcube: one labeled "Principal," and two others labeled "Fund" and "Front," [which the analyst did not do].[7]

Why tell readers about the fateful mistake that led to the accidental wire if no one disputed that it was an accident? Because readers want the whole story.

So give readers what they want by developing the narrative from start to finish. Let's see how.

[7] This paragraph is also a great example of using details smartly, which we will return to in the next section. All the steps make you feel overwhelmed and perhaps a little sympathy for the analyst.

A Quick Summary

Choose the analytical facts. **Analytical facts are your anchors; they address the legal questions you analyze later.**

Choose the contextual facts. **Contextual facts provide the stage on which your analytical facts play out, ensuring they have relevance and weight.**

Choose the emotional facts. **Emotional facts bring persuasive power, nudging readers toward your ultimate goals.**

Choose the character facts. **Decide how you will develop your characters. Your client and related parties should be developed favorably. Opposing parties should be downplayed as much as you credibly can.**

3.1.1. Choose the Analysis Facts

Analysis facts are what your readers need to make sense of your legal analysis. Those are listed first here because they form the backbone of your fact section, and the contextual and emotional facts will flow from them.

Going back to our simple car accident, it's easy to determine that you'll need to include facts shedding light on who is liable and why. If you're representing the plaintiff, you'd include facts about the defendant speeding and failing to watch the road, for example.

Take time to ensure you've captured all these analysis facts. Your goal is to paint a vivid picture of the core—a narrative so clear that the later complexities of the legal analysis flow effortlessly. When choosing your analytical facts, consider:

- What facts are explicitly listed in your analysis?
- What facts must be established to succeed on your claims?
- What facts must be established to succeed on your defenses?
- What facts must be established to qualify for any other legal doctrine raised in your document?

3.1.2. Choose the Context Facts

With your analytical facts in hand, it's time to weave them into a story. Decide which contextual facts will help your analytical facts flow into a cohesive storyline. Is it strictly relevant that the defendant was distracted by a ringing phone during the crash? Perhaps all that is legally relevant is that the defendant was looking away from the road during the crash. But every human reader will be wondering: What was the defendant doing? Why were they looking away? Contextual facts turn a list of events into a story that makes sense to people.

When thinking about which contextual facts readers might want, borrow the framework used by the master storytellers at Pixar:

> Once upon a time there was _____. One day _____. Because of that _____.

First, "Once upon a time there was..." introduces your characters and sets your setting. Where do you want to start your story? How do you want your readers to feel leading up to the conflict? What do you want readers to see before learning about the core events relevant to the law?

Now to the "one day..."—the complicating facts that sparked the legal dispute. Readers will naturally be curious about what led to the key events, even if each step is not strictly relevant to the law.

"Because of that..." is about framing the harm or consequences flowing from the complicating events. Your readers might be wondering if anyone was injured in the car crash, regardless of whether that's a legally relevant fact in your case.

You don't need to address every element every time. But good legal storytellers (like all storytellers) usually address each, at least a little. Here's an example of a cohesive story following this framework:

> Defendant Oztark launched its company last year to help people who want to charter a private plane.[8] It filled out its corporate paperwork with the state of Delaware, but it forgot to send in a check to cover the corporate registration fee. Delaware, in turn, sent its request for payments to the wrong address—so Oztark never realized its mistake. Oztark then started providing services, not realizing that it was effectively not a legal corporation....

Try another example. The lawyers didn't give much thought to the context readers would want, simply listing the analytical facts.

> It is uncontroverted that Perry Corporation withheld from Terrance the software that it intends to use in support of its invalidity counterclaim and never produced during discovery. Perry objects to the consequence of its strategic decision to flout the discovery rules—paying the reasonable fees and costs for its blatant discovery violation. Perry does not object to the Order that permits Terrance's expert to inspect the software and supplement his report.

To share with readers that a party withheld something they were supposed to provide, it helps to first give context about why that was required. To tell readers that a party failed to pay fees, it helps to first explain why the party owed them. We can start assembling a real narrative by being mindful of what context readers need for each legally relevant fact.

> **The Court ordered[9] Perry Corporation to provide a copy of its software to Terrance's expert, because Perry planned to use the software to support its counterclaims. Perry Corporation never did so, and the Court sanctioned it.** Perry now objects to the consequence of its decision[10] to flout the discovery rules—the fines and costs it was sanctioned.

[8] Active verbs like "launched" make the sentence easy to read. Words like "help," "people," and "want" are all easier on readers than the more formal words most legal writers would use.

[9] We also used active, concrete verbs to improve the sentence style.

[10] Good legal writers can subtly narrate facts in a persuasive way without sounding like a pushy advocate.

When choosing your contextual facts, consider:

- What plot holes need to be filled so readers are not distracted? Readers want a complete story with a beginning, middle, and end. If your client was in a parking lot at 2 a.m., omitting why they found themselves there will make readers wonder.
- What background information will help readers understand each important factual event?
- Are there any factual concepts, jargon, or complexities that contextual explanations would make more accessible?

3.1.3. Choose the Emotional Facts

Emotional facts help prime readers, shift their perspective, or engage their feelings. But tread carefully. Legal readers are quick to dismiss facts that seem irrelevant to the legal issues at hand. Limit how many emotional facts you include and tuck them in subtly among the analytical and contextual details readers expect.

For example, consider this paragraph sharing the emotional fact that a plaintiff spent millions in legal fees in a legal fight over his home—even though this fact was irrelevant to the legal questions presented to the court. Because this fact was weaved into the relevant background, though, readers were unlikely to be turned off.

> After a decade of the Town's obstructionism, **Sherman had spent more than $5.5 million.** [] **And there was still "no end in sight."**[11] *Id.* Along the way, Sherman turned to Laroe. Laroe and Sherman signed two agreements regarding MareBrook, in 2003 and 2013. []. The combined effect of the two agreements was that Laroe purchased MareBrook from Sherman for $2.5 million, subject to a provision requiring Laroe to transfer some[12] lots back to Sherman depending on the number of lots the Town ultimately approved.

In this next example, a federal litigator wanted to build emotional support for his client's industry (nuclear energy). Weaving in a few facts about the money and resources nuclear energy creates for us does wonders.

> The commercial nuclear energy industry in the United States got its start **70 years ago,** and the benefits that it has provided in the decades since are undeniable. The industry is responsible for producing **nearly one-fifth**[13] **of the Nation's total electricity and nearly one-half of its carbon-free**[14] **electricity**; the industry generates **tens of thousands of high-paying jobs**; and the industry **adds billions of dollars** to the Nation's gross domestic product each year.

[11] Notice how short sentences like this emphasize a point by slowing down your reading pace. This quote (no end in sight) is made more striking at the end of this short sentence.

[12] Many legal writers would have listed out all the details here, but this writer smartly delivers specifics when they are persuasive (like the amounts of money spent) while skimming over less important facts like that "some lots" were given back—we are not given the number or identification of each lot.

[13] Specific numbers persuade readers.

[14] This is an example of a reputational character fact, too, which we explore more later in this chapter.

In the following case, a company faced criticism for a lax workplace alcohol policy. The attorney rebuilds the company's credibility with some strategic emotional facts, reframing a lazy-looking policy into a compassionate one.

> Exxon's . . . alcohol policy conformed to industry standards, **guaranteed that employees seeking treatment would not lose their jobs**, and rested on the **premise that without job security those needing treatment would hide their affliction.**

When wielding emotionally charged facts, finesse is crucial. Consider how former Judge Posner infuses emotion into a discussion about discrimination, weaving in striking facts about forsaken children and their guardians.

> The argument that the states press hardest in defense of their prohibition of same-sex marriage is that the only reason government encourages marriage is to induce heterosexuals to marry so that there will be fewer "accidental births," which when they occur outside of marriage often **lead to abandonment of the child** to the mother (unaided by the father) or to foster care. Overlooked by this argument is that many of those **abandoned children** are adopted by homosexual couples, and those children would be better off both emotionally and economically **if their adoptive parents were married.**

Notice how lawyers representing OpenAI point out that the plaintiff suing their client never tried to cooperate to fix the problems they complain about before rushing to the courthouse. These weren't relevant facts, but they are rousing ones:

> [T]he Times does not allege in the Complaint that it made any attempt to share these results with OpenAI (despite being asked to do so), or otherwise collaborate with ongoing efforts to prevent these kinds of outputs. Rather, the Times kept these results to itself, apparently[15] to set up this lawsuit.

When considering which emotional facts to include, consider:

- Where is your analytical or emotional position the weakest? Spend the most time hunting for rehabilitating facts here.
- Likewise, focus on hitting the other side's credibility where it will hurt most. Where are their weaknesses?
- Consider your feelings: What facts annoy you about the opposing party? What facts make you sympathize with your client?

3.1.4. Choose the Character Facts

You've selected and arranged the key events. Now consider your characters. Many legal writers don't consider how they want to introduce and build up each of their story's characters. You have many options in describing your client and everyone else involved in the case. And those perceptions matter.

[15] Telling readers that "apparently" the Times was setting up a lawsuit is unlikely to be very persuasive, though. The writers could have credibly made the same point by subtly leading readers to a conclusion instead of forcing it on them: "Rather, the Times kept these results to itself and filed a lawsuit."

Brainstorm all your story's characters, their importance, and your goals for each. For pivotal characters, we'll explore factors to consider like their motivations, interactions with others, how outside forces impact them, and other facts that will help develop the heroes, the villains, and the background players in your case.

Before diving into these tools, let's look at a quick example of character-driven writing in action. You can leverage the power of characters even if you don't have a human to focus on. Virtually anything can take on the role of a character in your case. In this next example, the story was about companies and states. But treating these actors as characters still works. You start to imagine websites as sympathetic figures and the state as a villain ignoring the First Amendment.

> Given the cacophony of voices on the Internet engaged in everything from incitement and obscenity to political discourse and friendly banter,[16] **websites like Facebook and YouTube have no realistic choice** but to *exercise* editorial discretion over the expression **they disseminate.** Their users and advertisers demand nothing less.[17] **Websites**, no less than traditional media, sometimes **face criticism for how they exercise that editorial discretion.** That is to be expected in a nation committed to the First Amendment.... But in 2021, **Florida took a different tack.** It **enacted** Senate Bill 7072, a law that seeks to punish[18] select private parties for exercising editorial discretion in ways the state disfavors.

> Florida **made no secret** of the law's motivation and aim:[19] The state enacted S.B.7072 **to combat** what **it perceived** to be a concerted effort by "big tech oligarchs in Silicon Valley" to silence "conservative" speech on their websites. To ensure that **the state's preferred messages** reach a broad audience, S.B.7072 singles out a handful of large websites and requires them to disseminate a wide range of third-party speech that they do not want to disseminate....

> While the **state is free to criticize** websites for their decisions about what content to display, disseminate, remove, or restrict, the First Amendment prohibits the state from countermanding those editorial decisions and substituting its own judgment. Just as **Florida may not tell** the New York Times what opinion pieces to publish or Fox News what interviews to air, **it may not tell** Facebook and YouTube what content to disseminate.

The lawyers could easily have done what most would, focusing on the abstract facts like this:

> User submissions to websites are reviewed and managed as needed to comply with various lawful policies. This management is needed to ensure accurate, safe information is provided to users.... Senate Bill 7072 states that certain speech may not be regulated by online service providers....

[16] The list (incitement, obscenity, political discourse, and friendly banter) is a simple use of examples to convey a point deeper than general descriptions would.

[17] A shorter, simple sentence like this stops readers and focuses them on a point.

[18] This strong verb delivers the thrust of the sentence.

[19] This sentence distills the paragraph's two main ideas: the reasons the statute was enacted and the conduct it targets.

Instead, the legal writers use concrete characters: "websites" and "Florida." The writers talk about websites making "choices," "facing" challenges, and taking out actions like a person would: "exercising editorial discretion" and "disseminating" things. Rather than simply describing what the relevant Florida statute does or says, the writers frame it as if Florida is sentient: It takes a "different tack," "ma[kes] no secret[s]" of its intentions, and "combat[s]" things, "perceive[s]," and seems to even talk, "telling" different companies what it can and cannot do.

Tell Your Story Using the Characters' Perspective: Readers are hardwired to identify with people and parties. We follow along better when facts relate to *someones* rather than *somethings*. So aim to deliver the key facts from a character's perspective. Readers most easily connect with people, and next best, companies or entities. It's better to talk about a "judge ruling" rather than the "ruling of the court." Instead of:

> **The defects have propagated throughout the defendant's vehicles.**

Focus on actors carrying out actions:

> ***Jumai Corp.* churned out vehicles with broken taillights in all three of its factories.**

Sticking with a character's perspective across several sentences helps readers see through their eyes. In this next example, the story is always told from Jones's perspective. The details (and subtle narrative) ensure the reader is drawn in and can start feeling what Jones felt.

> **Jones showed up** to work that morning **knowing he would be fired.** Two colleagues had already hinted[20] as much. **Jones had two kids and no other support or savings. Losing his job was not a matter of stress.**[21] Being unemployed made the difference between whether he could put food on the table.
>
> As Jones clocked in, his boss, **Terry Smith, yelled across the office, in front of all of Jones's co-workers,**[22] **"Guess we won't be seeing you anymore."**

Across your fact sections, consider how you can drive the story with characters. If you have an event to convey, consider how a character's story can convey it. In this next example, each paragraph controls your perspective by choosing which characters are in the driver's seat—first the victim, then the villain. You'll also notice the word choices shift to reflect each viewpoint.

> **Martinez-Agüero** and her aunt turned to leave, heading back toward Mexico. **Martinez-Agüero told** her aunt that she would call her husband to take them to a different bridge.

[20] Verbs can convey a lot of content.

[21] This technique, which we return to in Chapter 9, has you contrast two words or concepts to highlight the difference (here, "stress" and "put[ing] food on the table").

[22] Weaving in this emotional fact (even though it wasn't strictly relevant) creates sympathy for the client.

> Then **González yelled at them to "stop in the name of the law."**[23] **He grabbed Martinez-Agüero forcefully**, twisted her arms behind her back, and pushed her into a concrete barrier. **González then began to "hit her with his fists and knees,"**[24] kneeing her repeatedly in her lower back.

In this next snippet, the legal writers focus on the journalists that make up the New York Times's ranks rather than the more abstract company—even though it was the company, not the individuals, who were suing.

> **Times journalists go where the story is, often at great risk and cost,**[25] to inform the public about important and pressing issues. **They bear witness** to conflict and disasters, provide accountability for the use of power, and illuminate truths that would otherwise go unseen. **Their essential work** is made possible through the efforts of a large and expensive organization that provides legal, security, and operational support,[26] as well as **editors who ensure their journalism meets the highest standards** of accuracy and fairness.

And as we saw with Florida's attempts to regulate website speech earlier, you can turn abstract concepts or entities (like a state) into a character by using the same language you would use when telling a story about a person. Stick to verbs that convey movement and other personifying language.

> The **statute ignores** what matters, **pretending** that people of color do not exist. What the statute **should tell the world** is that the U.S. demands inclusive, fair representation at every stage of the process.[27]

Insert Reputation Facts Judiciously: Insert details that make the key characters look better or worse. In other words, include *reputational* facts. Inserting a line or two about the great things a company does for the world, or how critical a company's product is for everyday folks, can shift how your readers see your client. The same goes for characters you prefer to frame less favorably.

But sharing too many of these technically irrelevant facts will annoy busy legal readers. So keep reputation facts minimal and weave them into the relevant discussion. When lawyers at an elite law firm related the facts from a dry pharmaceutical case, like all good legal writers, they injected reputational facts that made their clients into heroes.

> Appellant eMed, LLC is a **healthcare and technology start-up**. At the **height of the COVID pandemic**, eMed1 approached Abbott Laboratories, one of the largest medical device manufacturers in the world, to propose a partnership to develop and launch **the United States' first COVID test that Americans could take at home**...

---

[23] This is a great example of using the smallest, most targeted portion of a quote to make a point. We'll revisit our quoting skills in Chapter 8.

[24] These specifics are much more compelling than describing the injuries as something generic like "severe."

[25] This emotional fact is weaved into the sentence using an interjecting clause so readers don't focus on it too hard, while still absorbing the point.

[26] Stacking examples together like this makes them feel weightier than sharing them piecemeal.

[27] Starting a sentence with "what" puts the emphasis on the end of the sentence, shifting the normal syntax.

Their client is a "start-up" helping the public during the "height of the COVID pandemic" with the "first COVID test that Americans could take at home." Who wouldn't sympathize?

Here, a lawyer attacks a party's credibility by emphasizing emotional facts about her being a serial plaintiff:

> Susanne Ball, the original plaintiff in this action ... was not and had never been a Cingular customer, and none of the challenged provisions had been enforced against her. **As she had done in many other lawsuits,** however, Ball allowed plaintiffs' counsel to sue in her name as a self-anointed[28] private attorney general ...

Consider another example.

> VOLT advertised its new products at the trade show prominently: hanging banners, displaying life-size cardboard cutouts, and handing out hundreds of flyers.[29] VOLT representatives had just finished discussing their **education products with a representative from a large charity organization who helps children access books for free at school** when the Defendant's representative cut in and demanded a personal meeting to discuss VOLT's signage. The Defendant's representative raised his voice several times, loudly proclaiming that VOLT was "violating the show's rules."

That VOLT works with charities had no relationship to anything relevant. The same goes for the Defendant's tantrum. This case was about a licensing agreement and all the writer *technically* needed to convey was that the Defendant objected to VOLT being at the trade show. But slyly insert some good details about your client and some bad details about an opposing party, and you could start shaping your reader's view.

In this next passage, the writers wanted to build up the opposing party, Georgia-Pacific, as a mega-wealthy company that could afford some litigation it was trying to escape through clever bankruptcy proceedings. You can see how effective the reputational details are:

> Georgia-Pacific is a **thriving business worth tens of billions of dollars. Founded nearly a century ago, it sells familiar paper goods, like Brawny, Angel Soft, and Dixie.** For decades, Georgia-Pacific also sold products containing asbestos, including products widely used in residential and commercial construction....

In this final example, Google's lawyers manage to put some unfavorable character facts into context while rehabilitating their client's image.

> In this case, petitioners contend that YouTube violated the Anti-Terrorism Act by displaying ISIS videos[30] to users watching similar videos. **YouTube abhors terrorism and over the years has taken increasingly effective actions to remove terrorist and other potentially harmful content.** But Section 230(c)(1) forecloses petitioners' claims.

---

[28] Tread lightly when using characterizations about individuals like this.

[29] Another example of, well, examples. Listing out specific samples like this is more persuasive than the generic summaries most legal writers use (like stopping at the fact that VOLT advertised "prominently").

[30] Hiding from adverse facts only draws more attention to them. These lawyers take the bad fact head on, drawing its sting.

These legal writers slipped favorable details into the narrative that made YouTube sounds less guilty, even though YouTube's views on terrorism were not questioned by anyone.

Develop Characters' Motivations: Motivations matter. Why did your client cancel the shipment? Or show up late? Or back out of the deal? There's usually motivational context that will clarify what led the characters to act like they did. Check out this example:

> When Mr. Samps showed up to sign the license, **he did not know that Terry Corp. had already entered into three nearly identical licenses with other artists. Mr. Samps had been negotiating in good faith** with Terry Corp. for more than nine months at this point and **no one had ever mentioned other licensees.**

These motivational details about what Mr. Samps knew (or didn't know) help us understand his intentions—good faith ones. Shine a light on motivation by sharing details that unveil a character's inner thoughts. Let's say we want to suggest our client meant well even though she ended up breaching a contract. We can share facts to help readers see that her motivations were pure:

> Ms. Terry was in a pickle:[31] If she went forward with the concert, **she would be contributing to a health crisis that was all too personal for her. She had lost her mother weeks before to COVID.** With the rising rates in Dallas at the time, **Ms. Terry genuinely worried what would happen at a large gathering.** On the other hand, Ms. Terry had committed to putting on the concert, and **she knew that canceling would affect some vendors and promoters.** So she did what she had to, **coming down on the side of promoting the health and safety of everyone.**

These details about the dangers of COVID help readers sympathize with the character's motivations.

Take this next passage from lawyers representing OpenAI. They smartly point out the timing of the lawsuit against them to suggest the plaintiff had impure motivations:

> It was only after this rapid adoption, along with reports of the value unlocked by these new technologies, that the Times claimed that OpenAI had infringed its copyright[s] and reached out to demand commercial terms. After months of discussions, the Times filed suit two days after Christmas,[32] demanding billions of dollars.

Refer to Outside Events, Experiences, and Interactions: Another way to develop your characters is by sharing details about what they've experienced. In most stories, we get to know characters not only by what they do and say, but also by what happens to them. This legal writer knew this lesson well, sharing details about their client's experiences to help shape our perception of them in a particular moment.

---

[31] Usually clichés and trite language like "being in a pickle" don't elevate your prose.

[32] This is an emotional detail not relevant to anything, but it sure puts you in a favorable headspace.

> Ms. Johnson had been rear-ended in a car accident the prior day. She had been accosted by insurance claim adjusters all day. She had meetings at work starting at 5 a.m. and continuing until she drove home after 7 p.m. Then she arrived home to find a letter in the mail demanding that she "pay her bill or lose her house to foreclosure."

Showing all that had happened and been done to this character can't help but build some sympathy with readers. We can also illustrate a character through their interactions with others. Even showing that your client was courteous and respectful in dealing with an opponent can go a long way.

> Ms. Park gave Mr. Terry several days more notice than the rules required, because Ms. Park knew how busy Mr. Terry was and that he would likely need to arrange his schedule. . . .

A final note on characters: You should use characters when discussing the law, too. But here, judges and lawmakers are the stars. Build up the credibility of a court or judge to lend additional weight to their word in an opinion. Downplay one of these characters to suggest that authority isn't all that important. And the players in past decisions can also be characters. Consider developing a party that is sympathetic to your own. Or point out a bad actor that has parallels with the opposing party in your case.

3.2 Frame the Details

You've designed the story's arc, selecting the animating events and how all the key characters fit in. Now it's time to get granular and harness the supporting details that will convey all those facts persuasively.

Don't make the mistake of thinking the small details don't matter. The best legal writers know that how many details you share about a point, the order of those details, how often you repeat them, and whether you quickly gloss over them or plunge into every nuance all transform readers' perceptions.[33]

Look at what power a single detail placed in the right place can wield. As you're reading this next passage, consider why the writer mentioned that the law was a "century-old" one.

> [The patent assignor-estoppel] doctrine, rooted in an idea of fair dealing,[34] limits an inventor's ability to assign a patent to another for value and later contend in litigation that the patent is invalid. The question presented here is whether to discard this century-old form of estoppel.

Inserting that small, unassuming detail about the rule's age adds gravity. We imagine an ancient, immovable pillar. Without those two words, the sentence would convey something less.

Several strategies will help you tune the details like this.

[33] Don't ignore negative facts. This is about leaving out *unnecessary* facts, not *unfavorable* facts for your side. A judge should never be surprised by the important facts, good or bad, after they read your brief.

[34] This is a reputational fact for a rule: The writer shares the favorable animating policy to promote the rule.

A Quick Summary

Harness specifics. **Well-selected details grab your reader's attention. But use summary language to skip readers past less helpful facts.**

Adapt detail quantity. **Provide more details for important events that you want readers to experience. Skirt past details you don't want readers to dwell on.**

Put details in the right place. **Strategic positioning matters with details. Anchor your good details at the beginning and close of paragraphs, sections, and sentences; drop fewer compelling facts in the middle.**

Collect details. **Collect disparate details together when their sum will make a bigger impression than the parts.**

Style your details. **Elevate your details by using style tools to enhance them. Important details should get dressed up with the best writing.**

Narrate your details. **Narrators aren't just for fiction. Good legal writers guide the reader's factual journey by providing context and signposts, too.**

3.2.1. Harness Specifics

Which details you share to convey a factual point can change how that fact hits readers. Let's say you want to establish the fact that a home is "valuable." Different details can deliver that fact in different ways. You might offer the fair market value—cold, hard numbers. Or you could share anecdotes about renovations the owners made with their own hands. Maybe you'd rather evoke the laughter and tears that echoed in the rooms during family gatherings.

The right specifics can stick with readers. But so can the wrong ones. Legal writers are often too specific about points that don't matter, while generalizing when they do. Lawyers love listing every tangential date and time and formal document label, but then rely on bare conclusions that their client was "egregiously injured."

A key point for the lawyers in this next appellate brief was that the trial court was "very thorough" and that the trial record was "extensive." Most lawyers would have used these bare characterizations to make their point. But great legal writers use details to do the persuasive lifting.

> He does not show why **the detailed 150 paragraphs of trial court factual findings** were somehow clear error.... [Among the witnesses] were **police officers, members of Congress, a chief of staff to another Congressman, a former member of the [] administration, Ellipse rally organizers, an Ellipse rally attendee who then went to the Capitol, four expert witnesses, and a representative from the Secretary's office.**

This next example is from an introduction to a plaintiff's brief that pitted consumers against pharmaceutical giant GlaxoSmithKline. The writers insert details that resonate with readers — who doesn't relate to eating tacos and pizza or a pastrami on rye?

> GlaxoSmithKline LLC **taught** two generations of **Nevadans** to take Zantac with **heartburn-inducing** foods like **tacos** and **pizza**. For almost forty years,[35] GSK's television ads made Zantac the household name in heartburn relief. If you want a "safe" drug doctors trust, take Zantac.[36] When **that pastrami on rye catches up with you**, take Zantac. [] **But two years before the first commercial aired, GSK knew that Zantac causes cancer.**[37]

When some of the nation's top legal writers were hired to represent Google in the fight about YouTube accidentally displaying inappropriate videos to users, the specifics were the stars. The lawyers share details about how much information the internet creates and the near-impossible challenge companies like YouTube face trying to wrangle it all.

> The internet lets **billions of people** instantaneously **access, share, and contribute** to a vast and ever-growing universe of information. Each day users worldwide generate **over 500 million tweets, 294 billion emails, 4 million gigabytes of Facebook data**, and **720,000 hours of new YouTube content**. To make this mountain of third-party data usable, **websites must filter, sort, and organize it.**

For more examples of how details can transform the story, take the below snippets peppered throughout the brief about hog waste we looked at in Chapter 2. Each leverages specifics to paint an image (almost literally).

> They see liquid or **"juice"** coming out of **Defendants' trucks** off Highway 50 and Paul Ed Dail Rd.

> The **tons of feces** they produce are dangerous. Not only do hog feces carry **bacteria** into the **water**, but they also **kill fish, feed algae, and cause toxic outbreaks.**

> She finds patterns of droplets on the driveway **"just like when it rain[s]"** — and she has learned the hard way where she can or can't park on her own property if she wants to avoid Defendants' splatter. Once, when Ms. McCullen was outside playing with her son in the yard, **a truck went by and the liquid "flew and hit me in my face."**

On the other hand, every extra detail is something that readers must try to remember. So cut dates, numbers, names, and any other specifics that won't help you

---

[35] Often intro phrases needlessly slow down sentences. But here, anchoring the sentence in the 40-year history makes the main clause after hit harder.

[36] Dialogue with readers like this engages you and all it took was inserting "you" a few times.

[37] This paragraph builds to land on the most powerful sentence, as should often be the case. Notice also how the ending independent clause is set off with a comma so it's short and punchy.

convey the meat of your points. To see why specifics are so useful (but also so dangerous), look at this next example, full of indiscriminate details.

> On December 12, 2020, attorney Denton Jackson filed a Chapter 13 bankruptcy case for debtor Sarah O'Neill. On December 15, 2020, Jackson filed a fee application 32112-2311, the form application every attorney uses. This application included five sections, one of which is entitled "Use of Model Retention Agreement." Jackson checked the box indicating: "The attorney and the debtor(s) have entered into the Court's Model Retention Agreement." On March 12, 2021, the Trustee, Mrs. Sally Smith, objected to Jackson's application because Jackson attached an addendum to his retention agreement that included $210.23 on top of the flat fee Jackson was entitled to.

Do you need to know the date the case was filed? The date a particular application was filed? The form number used and its description? It turns out even the amount of fees was irrelevant here. Here's how the legal writer wrote that same paragraph—summarizing with storytelling language the dates, names, numbers, and other specifics that didn't help her tell the story and using specifics to highlight the essential facts:

> **Late last year**[38] attorney Denton Jackson filed a Chapter 13 bankruptcy case [] for debtor Sarah O'Neill. **Shortly after** filing the case, Jackson filed **a form fee application. In the portion of the application** entitled "Use of Model Retention Agreement," Jackson checked the box indicating: "The attorney and the debtor(s) have entered into the Court's Model Retention Agreement." **Some months later**, the Chapter 13 **trustee** objected to Jackson's application because the [Model Retention Agreement] between Jackson and the debtor... attached an "addendum" that prescribed **fees in addition to the flat fee** to which Jackson was entitled.

The specific number of documents referenced didn't matter in this next example. Nor did the formats or contents. So the judge didn't drown you in digits and descriptions. Instead, she opted for a quick summary of the less important facts so she could spend more time on the details she wanted noticed.

> Metro's file[39] contained the same Football Leaks documents attached to Mayorga's response and disclosed in initial disclosures, **plus approximately 400 additional documents that also appear to be from Football Leaks. About half** of those additional documents are duplicates of the original Football Leaks documents but in a different format; **the other 200** documents did not appear in the set that the plaintiff disclosed to the defense in this litigation but **contain similar communications** between Ronaldo's and Mayorga's former lawyers and the mediator.

Once you've chosen your specifics, make sure you emphasize them within your sentences and paragraphs. You'll often need to restructure sentences to spotlight memorable points with specific details. For example, this sentence uses generic summary language to convey how often and extreme the breaches were:

---

[38] Conveying the passage of time using narrative language like this helps tell a story.

[39] This familiar language conveys a story—would most legal writers talk about "Metro file" or instead something formal and abstract like "records."

> The breaches continued and became more extreme.

If the persistence of the breaches is key, you might inject specifics to emphasize that point:

> **The breaches piled up for months,** increasing in severity.

Alternatively, if the severity of the breach is the focus, use specifics to emphasize that:

> More breaches followed, **leading to Acme failing to deliver three of the four shipments in the order.**

Put the favorable specifics where readers will notice them — in the strong parts of your sentences and at the beginning and end of paragraphs. Save the summary language for the background.

3.2.2. Adapt Detail Quantity

There's a link between detail *quantity* and *perception*. The more details you share about an event or fact, the more readers will focus on it. On the other hand, the quicker you move past the details, the quicker your readers will move past the fact they support.

Say you need to relay that a fight broke out at a prison on June 1 and one person, the defendant, was seriously injured. Those are the facts you must include for the analysis to make sense. You can think of detail depth as a spectrum ranging from conveying the fewest details to support those facts to the most.

First, you can summarize the supporting details in one sentence. This is the right tactic if you need to convey some facts but don't want readers dwelling on them:

> Defendant was seriously injured in a fight at the prison on June 1.

Next, you can share some additional details to add color and emphasize the event but keep it to a few short sentences that won't slow readers down too much. This would be a smart tactic to convey a fact favorable to your position, but not so central that you can take your reader on an entire journey.

> On June 1, a fight broke out in the Defendant's block at the prison. **The defendant was walking past the fight on his way to the cafeteria**, and someone punched him in the face. The defendant fell to the ground and **broke his arm, requiring medical attention**.

Finally, you can immerse your readers in the events, adding extensive details to set the scene and control the pacing. Use this approach when the facts are central and favorable, and you want readers to experience, remember, and feel.

> On June 1, a Friday,[40] Defendant spent the morning in his cell finishing math homework for the prison's GED program.[41] The lunch bell rang, and Defendant walked out of his cell and down the hall, toward the cafeteria. As he was leaving the block, he heard some commotion ahead of him.
>
> Because there was no other path to the cafeteria,[42] and because inmates are not allowed to return to their cells after leaving for lunch, Defendant had no choice but to keep walking. He came upon a scuffle among at least four men, each trading blows. Defendant saw that one had a knife, he saw blood on the ground around the men, and he quickly looked for an escape route. Before he could think to get out of the way, one of the men lunged for him, punching him in the nose and instantly breaking it.[43]

Which option you should use depends on the point you are trying to make. If you want readers to fully experience an event, or fully understand the nuances of a set of facts, go deep with the details. Start with the strictly needed, then expand based on your goals.

Let's wrap up with another example demonstrating how specifics and quantity work together. The legal writer gathers a slew of specifics to illustrate why a dispute should be moved to another country:

> Plaintiff, an Angolan corporation, has again sued the Angolan Defendants for allegedly breaching 13 contracts to provide power plant equipment and services in Angola. Each contract was negotiated, executed, performed and terminated in Angola. Each contract requires application of Angolan law and chose an Angolan forum and venue for the resolution of any disputes.[44]

Adjust your details to taste. Too much or too little will ruin the dish.

3.2.3. Put Details in the Right Place

Another detail tool is location. Where do you put the good and the bad? This one is easier. Put the details you want readers to remember at the beginning and ending of your document, your sections, and your paragraphs. Bury what you don't want readers to focus on in the middles.[45]

Say you want readers to pay attention to the date the plaintiff filed a motion, and you want them to quickly move past the unfavorable detail that the plaintiff failed to include a certification in that filing. You can't leave out the bad—that will only

[40] Every detail is serving a purpose here. Everyone can sympathize with someone enjoying a Friday, even if they are in prison.
[41] This is also a great example of a character fact that builds the defendant's reputation.
[42] This is an example of narration, which we return to later in this chapter. The author is guiding our understanding and helping us understand motivations without forcing it on us.
[43] But keep in mind that readers can only handle depth so often. You can only go really deep for one or two factual points in most documents, lest readers get bogged down. If you share too many details about too many things, your writing becomes taxing and readers won't know what matters.
[44] Thanks to professor and lawyer Kiran Nasir Gore for submitting this sample, taken from her excellent brief, as part of Write.law's Level Up Your Legal Writing competition!
[45] Also called *internment* by rhetoricians.

draw more attention. But you can deemphasize by haloing the less favorable with the more so.

> Plaintiff filed its motion two weeks before the deadline. The motion was 25 pages and included extensive citations to authority. **Although Plaintiff left out the compliance certification**, Plaintiff shared the full draft motion with the Defendant weeks before it was filed. Plaintiff filed early to ensure there were no surprises or problems with the filing.

Here is another example of deemphasizing the less favorable (that the nurse shoved a patient) by tucking it behind the more favorable. The lead-in sentences and finishing sentence both emphasize favorable details.

> Defendant is a nurse. He has never been accused of any violence. He was being punched by the two patients he was trying to hold down and—to protect himself and other patients around him—**was forced to push back against one of the patients**. There were no injuries.

In this next example, the lawyer knew his client would take heat because of his decision not to disclose information. So he put that decision into context, helping readers sympathize.

> The undisputed facts unique to Mr. Lewis show that he did precisely what the CEO of a large enterprise should have done when faced with the prospect of large interim and forecasted losses at Merrill: **he engaged on the question of disclosure[46] with [the other] CFO and received reports . . . that the question of disclosure had been vetted proactively with expert counsel on two occasions and that counsel had concluded that disclosure was not warranted**.

This last legal writer smartly places a favorable detail about missing registration and a license plate in a short, punchy sentence at the end of the paragraph:

> While returning to Pahrump that afternoon, Andreaccio noticed that Nye County police deputy Joshua Weaver began following his car for about three miles before pulling him over. **Andreaccio's vehicle had no license plates**[.]

You can manufacture prime document real estate, too. Simply remind readers of favorable details whenever it's been a while since you shared them and it will help readers understand the points you are conveying now. In setting up the new point, you can reinforce a prior point as background. For example, in the next snippet, an appellate attorney reinforced some details for readers in simple terms that are easy to understand.

> Visa uses the FANF structure to drive up the price merchants must pay to process debit transactions, while using its market power to insulate itself from the usual consequences of raising prices.

[46] In this example, the writer turns a bad fact— failing to disclose financials to shareholders— into a good one by telling the reader that Mr. Lewis did "precisely" what he was supposed to do in this situation. There is often a second way to look at facts if you frame it the right way.

> **Simply put, Visa charges merchants an upfront fee for the privilege of accepting Visa products, which merchants cannot refuse, and then uses that upfront fee to keep its per-transaction fees artificially low.**

Or look at this snippet of a complaint from *The New York Times v. OpenAI.* The legal writers use the opening sentence of a new section to reinforce the persuasive point from the last one (that OpenAI was a for-profit company):

> **With the transition to for-profit status came another change**: OpenAI also ended its commitment to openness. . . .

Location and repetition are the best highlighters; wield them to guide your reader's attention at every step.

3.2.4. Collect Details

Another location tactic is to collect details together when the sum will be more than the parts. Legal disputes often concern many little details that, taken alone, seem minor—but gathered together, take a different shape. When trying to highlight how overwhelmingly strong the evidence of wrongdoing was in a bank fraud case, these next legal writers used a bulleted list to collect the best details in one spot.

> After a month-long trial, a jury found BMO aided and abetted PCI insiders' breaches of fiduciary duty while perpetrating one of history's biggest money-laundering schemes and awarded \$484,219,716 in damages. The evidence was so strong the jury added \$79,533,394 in punitive damages . . .[47]
>
> The record abounds with evidence proving BMO's knowledge and substantial assistance of fiduciary-duty breaches, including that BMO:
>
> - **intentionally closed 39 months of anti-money laundering ("AML") alarms flagging billions of dollars of suspicious transactions that required action;**
> - **knew billions of wrong-direction wires came in from two sham wholesalers PCI should have been paying, not receiving money from;**
> - **knew retailers like Costco and Walmart were supposed to wire money into the account to buy the products but never did;**
> - **knowingly processed tens of millions in payments to insiders that had no legitimate business purpose;**
> - **executed sham agreements to legitimize Petters' business and appease PCI's creditors, without intending to honor them;**
> - **implemented special overdraft policies for PCI to avoid detection;**
> - **let insiders ghost-write letters on BMO's letterhead; and**
> - **refused to file a single Suspicious Activity Report, as required by law, which would have stopped the scheme.**

[47] This is an example of an advanced style move we will explore in Chapter 9, setting up what something is *not* to highlight what it *is*.

Or take this next passage from a plaintiffs' brief. The lawyers used this collection technique on their first page to give readers a sense of the cumulative gravity of harms that, taken on their own, might not have been as compelling.

> Plaintiffs have the uncontroverted testimony of sixteen witnesses, who together can:
>
> - **Watch the sprayfield mist settle on their yards and houses;**
> - **Feel[48] the mist dampen their clothes and skin when Defendants spray;**
> - **See the dingy film that builds up on their homes;**
> - **Watch waste leaking from Defendants' trucks leave a pattern like muddy rain on their driveways and vehicles;**
> - **Touch and smear the feces on their homes and cars;**
> - **Smell that fecal residue on their homes, cars, and hands; and**
> - **Experience a reprieve only after hiring cleaners.**

Another way to collect details is to create a *movie trailer* for your fact section, a preview of the narrative that puts readers in the right headspace. Movie trailers allow you to prime readers with key details or some context before getting to the technical facts legal writing requires.

After you've assembled your factual background, go back to the start and play a preview of the best scenes. You will not only engage readers, but you'll lay out the basic storyline so they can better follow the details as they go.

The two steps here are to (1) roadmap the overarching plot points, and (2) show a highlight reel of some of your best facts. A good movie trailer can take a few paragraphs or a few sentences. Here's an example that highlights a key persuasive detail and lays out the major segments of the facts (the lead-up to the harassment, the harassment, and the resolution):

> The thrust of the complaint is that plaintiff has **worked at the defendant's store for several years and repeatedly complained about racial harassment**. For example, **he complained that his supervisor allegedly made comments about his "weird accent." Months in, the defendant finally acted, but by then, plaintiff had already been harassed so much that he quit.**

Here's an example of a movie trailer that offers a simple set of three categories that will be covered in the story to follow:

> **Three periods in plaintiff's employment are relevant here.** First, plaintiff offers allegations about when he was interviewed and how the defendant made promises to him then, like that he would be a foreman within six months. Second, plaintiff alleges that over the next six months, his job turned out to be a "**glorified secretary. . . .** "

Finally, these next legal writers had a story to tell about bringing a new railroad to an isolated basin in northern Utah. Their movie trailer sums up the thrust of the story in two sentences.

[48] Using verbs to start each item connects the details together even more.

> Infrastructure is perpetually in the news, for good reason. Without strong infrastructure—highways, train tracks, transmission lines, water lines, and much more—the whole economy slows. This case involves a new piece of infrastructure in a part of Utah that has long lacked it: the Uinta Basin.[49]

Strategically group details and spin a compelling movie trailer, and your readers will make it through even the densest stories.

3.2.5. Style Your Details

You can also control how your details land with readers by using style. Vivid verbs, engaging descriptors, and other techniques can highlight specifics so they stand out from the noise. We won't go through the hundreds of style tools at your disposal here (check out Chapter 9 for a full menu) but using exceptional style to relay important details will emphasize them.

In the next example, the factual details remain bland and unemphasized, emblematic of mediocre legal writing.

> The victim eventually learned that her debit-card number had been fraudulently obtained by a criminal using a skimmer. A skimmer is a device that is used to electronically download sensitive financial information from a credit card so that it can be utilized for criminal purposes.

Now here is a version with improved storytelling style, including vivid verbs, a focus on the subjects, the use of pacing, and well-placed em dashes for emphasis.

> **Imagine** that a decade ago,[50] a Las Vegas tourist is **feeling lucky** but just **spent her last dollar early in the night**. Out of cash, **she heads** for the nearest ATM with her debit card in hand, **swipes the card**, and withdraws $500. After the machine **spits**[51] out **a stack of twenties,** she walks into the nearest casino, hoping that **her jackpot is minutes away**. Days later, she learns that a fraudster had **purloined** her debit-card number **using a skimmer surreptitiously installed** on the machine—a device that criminals attach to ATMs to **steal** the information on a card's magnetic stripe—and **emptied** her bank account.

Vivid verbs and descriptors similarly emphasize the details in this next snippet from an introduction.

> Initially brought in an attempt to *unwind* a 2010 confidential settlement agreement, this case has **devolved into a clash** over the plaintiff's [] use of the defendant's **cyber-hacked** attorney-client privileged documents to **revive** long-since-released claims.

[49] Thanks to attorney Jay Johnson for submitting this example as part of Write.law's Level Up Your Legal Writing competition.

[50] Directly speaking to readers through dialogue is an advanced style tool we return to in Chapter 9. This is also a great example of how an occasional hypothetical can immerse readers in a story or concept, which is a technique we also return to in future chapters.

[51] Verbs spin stories from abstract legal details.

In this next example—from Google's lawyers in the YouTube case about the video-sharing company showing users terrorist videos—look at how the writers use verbs that inject connotations when describing what the plaintiffs are doing, alongside other concrete actions and targeted specifics.

> Petitioners and the government would **gerrymander** YouTube's display of additional video recommendations out of Section 230(c)(1)'s scope. But the **sorting** and **grouping** of videos is quintessential publishing. Every website that **displays** third-party content must **select** and **organize** that content.[52] If Section 230(c)(1) does not apply to how YouTube organizes third-party videos, petitioners and the government have no coherent theory that would save search recommendations and other **basic software tools that organize an otherwise unnavigable flood of websites, videos, comments, messages, product listings, files, and other information.**[53]

Craft the style of your details wisely, and you'll shape what readers remember.

3.2.6. Narrate Your Details

You've assembled your supporting details. Now consider how you can guide readers by being a narrator. Narrating is about considering all the details your readers are given—and then asking if there is any guidance, context, signposting, or other help you can offer.

You can think of this as breaking the fourth wall: You're directly communicating with your reader, offering asides or information so the details flow more easily. Although you'd be smart to avoid talking to readers as an obvious *advocate* when spinning your factual story, that doesn't mean you can't *guide.*

- After relaying your factual story, consider whether there are gaps, important facts, confusing facts, or other details that you can help guide your readers through so they aren't distracted.
- Ask whether you can help narrate key logistics like your reader's sense of time to help make it easy to digest the facts.
- Ask whether you can narrate for readers by highlighting important factual points or telling readers why those facts will matter later.
- Consider whether you can help readers understand the facts better with some extra explanation or guidance, like a quick definition or lay explanation.

Look at how Justice Kagan narrates by highlighting why a part of her factual story will matter to her later analysis, making it easy for readers to take note.

> When a Commission elects the latter option—**as in these two cases**—it typically delegates the initial adjudication to an ALJ.

In this next example, the author narrates by letting us know that two devices are similar because that will be relevant later.

---

[52]The legal writers are using character techniques here, personifying "websites" to make them the stars of the show.

[53]Listing the flood of "unnavigable" websites and files that would "flood" the internet is a great use of policy supporting the legal argument—as well as a great use of stacked examples to make a point.

> Called the Minerva Endometrial Ablation System, the device **(like the NovaSure System)** uses an applicator head to remove cells in the uterine lining.

Although we've been talking about facts, narration is helpful for the law, too. This next legal writer mentions that the statute she's referring to is the "core federal trademark statute." You realize this is a key statute without fluff.

> The Lanham Act, **the core federal trademark statute,** defines a trademark as follows: "[A]ny word, name, symbol, or device, or any combination thereof" that a person uses "to identify and distinguish his or her goods . . . from those manufactured or sold by others and to indicate the source of the goods."

In this next example, the legal writer uses parentheses to add helpful examples as context so readers instantly understand the ideas in familiar terms.

> But whatever else it may do, a trademark is not a trademark unless it identifies a product's source ***(this is a Nike)*** and distinguishes that source from others **(not any other sneaker brand).**

Sometimes it helps to narrate by pointing out gaps in the facts. For example, this next legal writer knew readers would be wondering why there was no mention of the defendant's motive:[54]

> The defendant **didn't pay any of the three times he entered the facility.** To this day, **he has never offered a reason why.** Indeed, the defendant has **never explained — in any filing or otherwise — why he decided not to pay** after entering.

Sometimes it helps to simply point out important factual points (without advocating) so that readers will remember these points later in the document. For example, Chief Justice John Roberts wanted to ensure readers paid attention to a particular event early in an opinion because it would later matter in the analysis. So he took the direct route, telling readers precisely what they should remember for later.

> **Then came the incident we are concerned with here.** As the torchbearers and camera crews passed by, Frederick and his friends unfurled a 14-foot banner bearing the phrase: "BONG HiTS 4 JESUS." The large banner was easily readable by the students on the other side of the street.[55]

Sometimes you can help readers understand concepts with a longer narration, perhaps a quick hypothetical or example. In this next passage, a pro Supreme Court advocate offers some samples of legislation to illustrate a concept.

---

[54] And the detail brought the bonus of making this opposing party look bad.

[55] Telling you that you could "easily" read the banner from the other side of the street creates an image that "14 feet" doesn't.

> For example, Missouri recently considered tax credits for businesses that were shut down by local government orders over the past year. New Mexico recently passed a bill establishing a gross receipts tax deduction for food and beverage establishments, which were hit particularly hard by pandemic-related closures and restrictions. Maryland recently passed its own sweeping COVID-19 relief bill that, among other things, supports small businesses with a sales tax credit of up to $3,000 per month—a nearly $200 million commitment.

You can play the narrator from many angles. Maybe you want to tell readers that they shouldn't worry about a set of facts because they won't matter later in the analysis. Or maybe you want to suggest that one set of facts is more important than another. Or you might want to define or explain a term you'll use in your document, like industry jargon. In this final snippet, the legal writer explains a concept in concrete terms before giving us the needed jargon she would use throughout the document.

> [The defendant] bills itself as a hub connecting requests from people like our tourist with a national processor. According to its founder and CEO . . . [the defendant] provides its clients with both hardware—such as ATMs, the point-of-sale (POS) terminals that shoppers insert their card into or tap their card against, or kiosks to get cash or casino chips—and the software that powers consumers' interactions with the hardware and its ability to communicate with a national processor. **[The defendant] calls its proprietary combination of hardware and software "Multi-Choice Cash."**[56]

Narration allows you to shape readers' understanding, ensuring the facts hit as you want them to.

3.3 Tell Stories About the Law

Now that you've learned how to tell a story in your fact section, many of the same tools will help you explain the law better, too. The law is, after all, a story. Where did a rule come from? How have courts interpreted it over time? What situations do the rules apply to? Maybe you want to tell a story about a statute that has evolved over time—or a story about why it's essential that a rule sticks to its roots, unchanging.

There's often a broader narrative to be told about the legal principles and procedural history involved in your matter. And these stories can persuade. Supreme Court Justice Elena Kagan can weave a story about even the most abstract legal concepts. Look in the next example how she tells a story about a law to help you understand why you should care about it.

> Courts have long applied the doctrine of assignor estoppel to deal with inconsistent representations about a patent's validity. **The classic case[] begins with an inventor who both applies for and obtains a patent, then assigns it to a company for value. Later, the inventor[] joins a competitor business, where he develops a similar—and possibly infringing—product. When**

[56] This narration is also an example of defining or explaining terms for readers so they never need to look them up themselves. We return to this skill in Chapter 6.

> the assignee company sues for infringement, the [inventor] tries to argue—contrary to the (explicit or implicit) assurance given in assigning the patent—that the invention was never patentable, so the patent was never valid.[57] That kind of about-face is what assignor estoppel operates to prevent.

Like any good story, we get context then dive into the events unfolding, following hypothetical characters along the way.

A Quick Summary

Highlight favorable procedure. Highlight the good facts from the procedural history to bolster your client's position and build goodwill.

Tell a crucial law's story. Consider whether there's a story to tell about the law. This can help prime readers without cluttering up your analysis section later.

3.3.1. Highlight Favorable Procedure

The procedural history is whatever happened in the courts (or other legal proceedings) before the current matter you're working on. This history can be a goldmine for highlighting favorable details, like useful cases or quotes. Point your reader to the specific record cites (or provide copies of them) so that they can instantly find the good fodder.

Obviously, any helpful language in prior decisions should be invoked. Even if it's only dicta and even if it's your own judge's past orders.

> This court has rejected Plaintiff's attempts to file his complaint three times now. Each time, the court told Plaintiff that without meaningful amendment this case was "going nowhere. . . ."

In this next example, look how the lawyer front loads the lower court's rejection of her client's arguments—but in doing so, highlights the best facts from it.

> The [lower court] rejected respondents' showing that the searches uncovered gang activity and potential health problems because, in its view, such searches are not the least intrusive means for achieving these goals.

Likewise, here the lawyer inserts an even more obvious highlight, bolstering key evidence with a cite to a case.

[57] Hypotheticals like this can immerse readers in abstract concepts, pulling on the power of story.

> The court noted that Essex submitted an expert report by George M. Camp, **whose studies this Court credited in *Turner v. Safley*, 482 U.S. 78.**

Notice how this next lawyer emphasizes favorable procedural facts and quotes.

> In a 3-2 decision, the court reversed **the $50 million verdict** against Masset and dismissed the case with prejudice—while **"making perfectly clear that the facts of this case demonstrate Masset's conduct warranted the type of judgment rendered."**

Jumping on a lower court's dissents, caveats, and other instructive language can also help you make your points.

> Justice Albright and Starcher filed dissents. Both expressed alarm at the **"result-driven effort"** of the majority to relieve Massey of liability. . . .

> [The court] did so despite acknowledging that *Wolfish* states that **evidence of a smuggling problem is "of little import" to the analysis.**

Finally, there are often helpful atmospherics you can weave in that will shape how your readers see the current dispute. In this next passage, the writer knew that a counterargument would be raised that claims under the relevant statute, the Clean Water Act, were waived. So they weaved in atmospherics from the procedural history to show that the statute was squarely raised.

> The Ninth Circuit issued its first opinion in November 2001. The court rejected Exxon's arguments that no punitive damages were authorized, but added a number of significant caveats. Addressing whether the judge-made maritime punitive damages remedies could expand the penalties already provided in the CWA, **the court acknowledged that the question was "serious," "not without doubt," and "close."**

Beyond the atmospherics, weave helpful authority into your procedural history by using your court's, or a lower court's, references:

> In its last order, **the Court discussed *Exelco* at length.** That case held that a defendant should be shielded from claims brought against its subsidiary unless the corporate veil is pierced. **The Court noted that *Exelco* had been upheld repeatedly. . . .**[58]

Dissents and any other helpful language are ripe for highlighting in the procedure:

> **Judge King dissented in part. He explained** that Georgia-Pacific had "improperly or collusively" "manufactured the jurisdiction of the bankruptcy court . . . in an unmistakable effort to gain leverage over future asbestos claims against New GP." [] **Judge King further opined** that the

[58] Judges care what other judges think, even lower court ones, and even when the standard of review doesn't require deference.

> **"creative"** use of the so-called **"Texas divisional merger"** and the creation of unorthodox contractual relationships between Bestwall and New GP . . . **ran afoul of the foundational principle** that parties may not artificially construct a federal court's jurisdiction — especially that of a federal bankruptcy court, which possesses particularly limited jurisdiction.

Don't just summarize the procedural history, weaponize it. Highlight favorable decisions, include persuasive dissents, and bolster your strongest arguments.

3.3.2. Tell a Crucial Law's Story

There's a final sort of legal story you can tell. The story of a law itself; that is, the background of a statute, regulation, or other legal doctrine that is central to your document. For example:

- Stories about how statutes or cases or rules came to be;
- How they changed over time;
- How other courts have treated them;
- How a law has worked in the real world; and
- How a complicated legal process works.

Most legal writers include lengthy legal stories in the fact section, lest it bog down the analysis. That's probably smart, given that your analysis should usually provide decision-makers with a concrete, focused legal framework for reaching a final decision. Nestling lengthy legal background in your fact section keeps all the background resources in one place.

Telling a background story about the relevant law is especially helpful when some of your points rely on deep, fundamental understanding of how a statute or doctrine works, how an agency operates, or any other complicated legal principles. This legal story should be that: a story. A background journey to put your reader in the right mindset to digest the surgical analysis later.

Most legal writers would introduce this rule:

> The Free Exercise Clause does not exempt religious persons from laws of general applicability. *Employment Division v. Smith*, 494 U.S. 872 (1990).

Look how much you care when the rule is a story first. The rule becomes more than a plain legal standard. You see the people and understand the ideas that built it.

> **Our story starts with *Smith*.** In *Employment Division v. Smith*, 494 U.S. 872, 110 S.Ct. 1595, 108 L.Ed.2d 876 (1990), the Supreme Court held that the Constitution's Free Exercise Clause does not exempt religious persons from the dictates of neutral laws of general applicability. **The devout must obey the law even if doing so violates every article of their faith.** When *Smith* was handed down, **some worried that it upset existing free exercise doctrine dating back to *Sherbert v. Verner*, 374 U.S. 398, 83 S.Ct.**

This next snippet is part of a brief's fact section. It deals with legal stuff, but it's a story. It's not yet setting up a specific rule to apply to specific facts, but it's offering context that will lead readers subtly toward a sense about the law.

> **The damages provision of the Copyright Act has existed in the same basic form since 1976,** subject only to amendments to increase both the minimum and maximum amount of statutory damages available. . . . Because the Copyright Act's statutory damages provisions refer to the court, **statutory damages were typically awarded by the judge, rather than[59] the jury. . . .**

Dense regulatory or statutory documents are often ripe for a law story. In this next passage from an appellate brief, the paragraphs convey the relevant statute's climate-protection story and the regulations that followed.

> On December 11, 2000, **Congress enacted the WRDA 2000 . . . to restore, preserve, and protect the South Florida ecosystem while providing for other water-related needs of the region, including water supply and flood protection. . . .**
>
> To ensure that the [] projects don't adversely affect the many people who rely on water from Lake Okeechobee, including the Cooperative and its members, **WRDA 2000 includes a Savings Clause. . . .**

Another power of the law story is that it gives you flexibility. Root around long enough in any rule's past, and you'll find some skeletons. Perhaps a shoddy case that twisted the law in a way it shouldn't have. Or some assumptions or factual circumstances that suggest an entirely different purpose animated the rule than what you might expect.

Telling a story about the two paths the Securities and Exchange Commission can take in this next example turns bland legalese into a story that encourages you to think of the agency like a character.

> The SEC **generally has two routes** by which to enforce the federal securities laws in a civil proceeding. The agency can bring a civil action against the alleged violator in federal district court, or it can initiate an administrative enforcement proceeding. **At one time,[60]** the remedies the SEC could seek against respondents in administrative proceedings were relatively limited. **In 2010, however,** Congress enacted the Dodd-Frank Wall Street Reform and Consumer Protection Act, which expanded the remedies available to the SEC in administrative proceedings.

This next example tells a compelling story about the history of a U.S. Constitutional provision at the core of the case (the "insurrection" clause). Notice how a legal story gave the writers a chance to guide readers to a deep understanding of this law, which shapes how readers will approach the analysis later.

> Section 3 has been applied sparingly for the last 150 years because insurrection against the Constitution has been mercifully rare. . . .
>
> First, Section 3 was a "measure of self-defense." . . .

[59] "Rather than" is a smoother transition than the "instead of" most legal writers tend to use.

[60] The writers don't bore us with precise years that statutes were enacted because that wouldn't help the story.

> Second, Section 3's oath requirement meant it would target insurrectionist leaders—"those who have heretofore held high official position, and who therefore may be presumed to have acted intelligently." . . .
>
> Third, Section 3 imposed no "punishment mean[t] to take away life, liberty, or property," but merely "fix[ed] a qualification for office."

Stories sell legal readers. So whenever you need to relate some dry information to legal readers, consider whether there's a story to tell.

Level Up Your Stories with Technology

Technology is a great coauthor in your storytelling. Generative AI (GAI) is a groundbreaking collaborator, offering avenues to brainstorm, organize, draft, and experiment with storytelling styles tailored to your case.

GAI: GAI will really shine here in helping you come up with a more compelling narrative.

- **Idea generation:** Use GAI prompts to brainstorm different ways to present a fact set, exploring various angles and perspectives. For example, "I have these facts about a breach of contract dispute: [List facts]. Generate 5 different overarching themes I could use to frame the story in my fact section."
- **Narrative experimentation:** GAI can draft multiple versions of a story, testing different narrative voices and structures to see which most effectively conveys the desired message. For example, "Rewrite this fact section excerpt in the style of a [choose a genre: hard-boiled detective novel, journalistic exposé, etc.]. Maintain the core legal arguments but transform the voice and tone."
- **Style and tone adjustments:** GAI can adjust the writing style and tone to match the brief's requirements, whether it's authoritative, explanatory, or aimed at evoking empathy. Perhaps: "Make this paragraph of my fact section more persuasive. Incorporate vivid imagery and language that evokes a sense of [emotion: outrage, urgency, etc.] without being hyperbolic."
- **Outlining and structuring:** These tools can suggest an outline based on the facts provided, ensuring all relevant points are covered logically. Maybe: "Analyze the facts in this section. Create 3 different outlines for how to present them, each emphasizing a different issue: (1) chronological order, (2) priority of legal significance, (3) escalating severity of damages."

E-discovery technology: These tools assist in the process of identifying, collecting, and producing electronically stored information in response to a request for production in a lawsuit or investigation. These tools can handle vast amounts of data and provide functionalities for data sorting, tagging, and reviewing—as well as visualizing your facts and finding the perfect fact for your argument.

Factual research tools: For investigation reports and public records, platforms provide comprehensive information. News archives allow attorneys to explore relevant news articles, tracing events and opinions tied to their cases.

Timeline apps: These tools help you quickly put together timelines or interactive lists of events so that you can refer to them (or even incorporate them into your writing). Examples include simple tools you already have like Microsoft PowerPoint.

Outlining tools: The structured precision required in factual storytelling is adeptly managed by digital outlining tools. Applications like Workflowy, OmniOutliner and Scrivener offer environments rich with features such as hierarchical structuring, which is key in plotting the factual landscape of a case.

Visualization software: The factual story can also be illustrated through visuals. Apps like Tableau and Microsoft Visio can help create timelines and relational charts, offering support to the written narrative. Other apps designed for creative writers, like Coggle, can help you brainstorm or organize your stories.

Narrative construction aids: Beyond conventional writing tools, narrative construction aids can enhance the drafting process. Leveraging the techniques of scriptwriters and game designers with tools like Scriptwriting and Storyboarding can help you structure the factual narrative and bring the facts to life in a powerful, visually engaging manner.

Document automation and workflow: With automation apps, you can ensure that repetitive elements in fact sections are consistently executed, allowing you to focus on your story's substance. You can save fact templates that you can use in future documents, create a checklist of storytelling techniques to keep you focused as you draft, and more.

Online source verification: In an age of misinformation, ensuring your facts are unimpeachable is crucial. Tools like FactCheck.org or Snopes specialize in debunking myths and scrutinizing sources. For more niche areas, explore fact-checking databases related to your practice area (medical, scientific, financial, etc.).

Deep search engines: Go beyond Google with tools like Pipl, designed to uncover information hidden in the less indexed corners of the Web. This can reveal witness backgrounds, prior statements, or even inconsistencies in the opposition's version of events.

Image and video authentication: As multimedia evidence grows, its authenticity must be verified. Tools like InVID or FotoForensics aid in analyzing metadata and identifying potential manipulation or deepfakes.

Practice these techniques and technologies with Write.law's exercises and checklists, plus other resources at www.levelupyourlegalwriting.com

4

Level Up Your Law

> Know the rules well, so you can break them effectively." —Dalai Lama XIV

You've turned your bland list of facts into a compelling story. You're ready to guide readers to the final answers. And that means explaining the rules that will take them there.

You will need to tread with care. Even seasoned legal writers struggle to lay out the governing rules persuasively. After all, rule sections are hard. They combine cryptic authorities, convoluted legal language, and the complicated interplay of cases, statutes, and policies.

That is why many legal writers take the easy path. They offer readers little more than a generic rule standard—often one copy-and-pasted from a court decision. These legal writers then sprinkle in some quotes and facts from precedent cases to add an air of authority. They then jump into applying these surface rules to their case. And to be fair, if you explain only that a rule requires something general like "good cause," it's easy to find facts that sound like they hit such a wide target.

The problem is, if you don't explain how the rules work on a deeper level, then you can't predict how decision-makers will apply the rules to your case. Broad rules are easy to hit for your opponents, too. You will assemble a list of facts that sound like "good cause." Your opposing party will assemble a list that sounds like "bad cause." Now your decision-maker must sift through all those facts and decide which one sounds more convincing.

Instead, the best legal writers teach readers how the rules work on a deeper level that will aim readers at a favorable end. These writers offer a perspective that will suggest how to apply the rules favorably, so readers don't stumble through on their own (and possibly reach an unfavorable conclusion on top of it).

But rule-teaching is hard work. The rules are usually the densest parts of our documents. How do you (1) teach readers enough about the rules so that they can understand on their own how to reach a conclusion, and (2) explain all this so easily that readers don't need to work for that understanding?

Four techniques will turn you into a professional rule teacher, and we'll explore each in this chapter:

- **Teach the law to readers:** Explaining complex rules so that they easily apply to your factual situation is tough, so use a consistent step-by-step process to break down the rules in a concrete way that readers can use to reach a conclusion in your case.
- **Teach text-based rules:** Rules that come from statutes, regulations, and other codified sources lend themselves to several unique tools. Use trusted interpretation principles—like canons of construction and statutory structure—to help readers understand what the text means.
- **Link your rules to your facts:** Once you've taught readers how to view the rules, make that application easy by clearly linking your rules with your facts.
- **Make citations useful:** Citations and parentheticals slow down legal writing because they interrupt your prose. Use simple tools to increase citation fluency, like moving citations to the ends of sentences and highlighting important citation information in your own text.

Before diving into specific techniques, let's see the difference that this rule-teaching makes. Imagine you're reading a rule discussion in a brief and stumble onto this next paragraph. How the rule works is never explained. You first read about a general legal concept (prejudgment interest) and then are besieged with details from the decision.

> This case is controlled by *Briggs v. Terry*, 314 F.3d 241, 213 (9th Cir. 2020), which addresses the prejudgment interest rule. That case involved two shipping companies, one of which challenged a contract it had entered into with the other. The plaintiff ultimately succeeded at trial, and was affirmed on appeal. However, on appeal, the court did not include the prejudgment issue in its mandate....

Now watch a legal writer teach us how to understand the rules first. For context, the lawyer's ultimate argument will be that prejudgment interest should not be given to the other side because the appellate court's mandate was silent about the interest. The lawyer teaches a rule that leads straight to a favorable ending.

> When a Court **renders judgment and its mandate is silent about any award of prejudgment interest, the district court lacks authority to award it.** That rule follows directly from the Supreme Court's decision in *Briggs* and this Court's decisions applying it, as well as Federal Rule of Appellate Procedure 37(b)....

Later in the analysis, it will be easy to agree no interest is warranted because the mandate was silent about it—and the lawyer knew that when she taught us the law in the way that she did.

Now check out a rule maven, Judge Andrew Gordon. Watch as he breaks down three rule concepts from three lines of cases so readers never need to work for understanding. The authority and supporting details never jump ahead of simple explanations about how each part of the rule works.

> **There are at least three separate lines of cases that provide guidance about whether consent by deception comports with the Fourth Amendment's requirements.**
>
> **One line of cases involves law enforcement agents who pose as criminals, or friends or acquaintances of criminals, and use deception to "catch those engaged in criminal enterprises."** For example, in *United States v. Bramble*, the defendant invited undercover police officers into his home to negotiate the sale of illegal sea otter pelts. . . .
>
> **A second line of consent by deception cases involves government agents who deceive the occupants into believing that an emergency or life-threatening situation exists.** For example, in *United States v. Giraldo*, a police officer pretended to work for the gas company and told the defendant she was checking for a gas leak. . . .
>
> **A third line of consent by deception cases involves law enforcement officers who conceal their identity and purpose to gain entry for a legitimate or lawful purpose, such as to buy a home, rent an apartment, or to provide a good or service. . .**

Many lawyers rely on generic conclusions and superficial summaries when relating the rules. If you can instead explain the rules enough so that the application later will feel simple and intuitive, you will be in the best legal writing company.[1]

4.1 Teach the Law

Explaining how the rules work can be overwhelming. You're juggling all the authority, all the legalese, and must somehow make sense of it all for readers who don't want to be there in the first place. Like any overwhelming task, a step-by-step framework will make all the difference. Just take each step, one at a time.

Because rules have many moving parts, the framework we will work through breaks down the rule-teaching process into three steps. This framework is based on the most effective and well-regarded legal writing. It's also informed by cognitive science research on how readers process complex information. The framework is called the *PPP*: the prep, the pitch, and the proof. Each step is based on goals for teaching your readers a winning view of the rules.

This framework is all about your reader. First, prepare readers by orienting them to the general area of law and the parts of the rule that you'll be explaining in more depth. Second, deliver your simple, specific pitch for how the rule works in a way that readers can practically use to reach answers. That means distilling the rule into a manageable set of concrete principles that readers can use to tackle the facts (and opposing arguments) that

[1] In multiple surveys and studies, legal writers come up short on the rules. In one study, researchers looked at the "stickiness" of lawyer citations— in other words, how often the judge analyzes the cases cited by the lawyers, and how often the judge instead cites and analyzes entirely new cases on their own. The authors point out examples like a Tenth Circuit decision in which the judges cited 33 cases— 31 of which did not appear in either of the parties' briefing. Kevin Bennardo & Alexa Z. Chew, *Citation Stickiness*, 20 J. App. Prac. & Process 61, 64 (2019).

will come later. Finally, prove your pitch by showing how the authority supports the rule principles you explained—convincing readers that your pitch is the right one to adopt.

One of my favorite judges, Judge Andrew Gordon, shows us in this next example how helpful it is to break down the rules by starting with some background and guiding readers to the parts that matter. He avoids rule principles we don't need and delivers the rules that do matter in plain language that readers can instantly follow:

> **With a few exceptions that are irrelevant for this case,** "any civil action brought in a State court of which the district courts of the United States have original jurisdiction, may be removed by the defendant . . . to the district court of the United States for the district and division embracing the place where such action is pending." **In other words, if the federal district court has subject matter jurisdiction over the case, it may be removed from state court to federal court. . . .**
>
> **Koslow raises only diversity jurisdiction as a basis for removal.** Diversity jurisdiction requires that all plaintiffs be "citizens of different states" from all defendants . . . and that the amount in controversy exceeds $75,000.

This simple prep got us ready for one of the specific rule principles that would make all the difference:

> [A]n LLC is a citizen of every state of which its owners/members are citizens. . . .

That understanding makes it easy for readers to apply to the facts that come later:

> Koslow does not provide the citizenship of the members of Silver State, **which he must do because the citizenship of an LLC is based upon its members' citizenship.**

Legal readers are desperate for a lifeline when it comes to the rules. Give it to them by guiding them each step of the way.

A Quick Summary

Prepare readers for the rule. **Welcome readers into your rule discussion by orienting them to the big picture. Guide readers from the general legal universe down to the legal neighborhood where you'll do the hard work.**

Pitch your rule. **Don't make readers untangle how the law works on their own. Take a few sentences to distill the rules into a simple pitch that readers can use later to navigate the analysis. Your goal is to use your distilling skills to produce three or fewer concrete principles that readers can easily apply to the facts of your case later.**

Prove your rule. **March out your supporting authority and reasoning from more angles. Leverage multiple types of authority and reasoning in different forms to make your pitch undeniable.**

4.1.1. Prepare Readers for the Rule

The preparation step is about welcoming readers into your rule discussion by orienting them to the major area of law and preparing them for the specific parts of the rule that matter most in your case. Don't shirk this step. If you dive straight into the nuances without laying out the big picture, readers will be overwhelmed.

You have two main goals during the prep: (1) welcome readers to the area of law, and (2) narrow in on the parts of the rule you'll explain more in your pitch. Start your rule section at the highest level: the black-letter law or the basic elements you (or another party) must meet for the rule to apply. Then shepherd readers to the parts of the rule you will develop in your pitch.

Your goal is to get readers prepared as quickly as you can to avoid wasting their time. After all, it's your rule pitch where you will teach them about the parts of the rule that will answer your document's ultimate questions. Keep citations and discussion to a minimum in this prep stage. You are not winning or losing in the high-level background.

Let's say we will eventually ask readers to understand a specific element of a rule under the Americans with Disabilities Act. To get readers ready for what matters, we start by orienting them to the general elements and then quickly zoom in to the part of the doctrine that matters. We cite only one or two authorities here:

> Under the Americans with Disabilities Act (ADA), employers must provide reasonable accommodations to employees with a qualified disability. [1 cite]. **The ADA states that one way employers "may"[2] provide accommodations is by reassigning an employee to a different job.** [1 cite].

We started at the highest level. What is the ADA about and what are the general requirements? Then we quickly home in on the one disputed element (what qualifies as reasonable accommodations), and then we narrow in more to the relevant reassignment accommodation.

Let's see some legal writing mavens do this preparation work for readers. Justice Kagan first shows us how to break up rules in the prep.

> [This type of] violation has two necessary elements. **First, the government must take the property. Second, it must deny the property owner just compensation.**

We're now ready to tackle one element at a time. Or take this next example, which uses a numbered list to break up the big-picture law into a few smaller concepts.

> The Court's precedent can be summarized into two factors: **(1) how informal the interrogation was, and (2) whether police said anything during the interaction that suggested the witness would be arrested if they didn't cooperate.**

Now with the precedent neatly chopped into two subparts, you can further refine one concept at a time (What does *informal* look like? What sort of remarks *suggest a*

[2]The legal writers use the statute's language to start priming you for their argument (which will be that reassignment is optional).

witness will be arrested?). And you can apply both rule subparts separately, so readers never get lost.

Other than orienting readers to the legal universe and breaking up the law into smaller parts that are easier to work with, another key tactic in the prep is to be sure you explain how the subparts of your rule interact. Should they all be satisfied? Only one? For example, this next legal writer talks about three relevant steps, each of which must be met.

> The case law in this area can be distilled into a series of three simple steps the court must follow: **(1) find the allegations about exhaustion in the complaint, (2) test those allegations against those in the agency letter, and (3) if there are differences, decide whether they are misleading.**

Now that readers have a lay of the land, they are ready to forge ahead into new territory.

4.1.2. Pitch Your Rule

Your pitch is about distilling the legalese into concrete principles for how the rules work in your case. Rather than make your reader wade through the dense authority and legal mumbo jumbo, do the work for them at the outset of your rule discussion. Give readers concrete tools they can use. Like the distilling technique we started with in Chapter 2, this is about giving readers understanding before asking them to do hard work.

For each legal question or issue in your document, your goal should be to give readers one to three concrete rule principles that are specific and will guide them through all the favorable and unfavorable facts and law. Keeping your pitch to three or fewer principles for each issue will keep these principles manageable so readers can easily keep them in mind when they need to use them later. If you can't distill a rule's inner workings into three or fewer concrete principles, that usually means your issues are too complicated and you should break them into smaller sections.

Ultimately, your pitch is a set of tools for readers to take with them into the application. Take that ADA case we looked at when exploring the rule preparation step. We introduced readers to the general elements of a disability claim and the accommodation element that matters. In other words, we took readers from the universe of ADA law and walked them to the neighborhood where we'll be doing the real work. Now readers are ready for a pitch that will answer the hard question: whether employees must provide a reassignment accommodation at the employee's election.

> "May" in the statute simply means that employers *may* choose between reassignment and other reasonable accommodations when they are available. "May" does not mean that reassignment is "mandatory."

Many lawyers are lazy with their pitch. They cite a generic rule (often one they found and pasted from another case) and then they urge the court that the standard is satisfied by heaping up the facts. Here is a rule like that from a motion:

> False imprisonment requires (1) intentional, (2), confinement, (3) against another's will. [Citation]. Use of "legal authority" meets the confinement element. For example, in *Chart v. Turtle*, 314 F.3d

> 315 (N.D. Ill. 2012), an off-duty police officer took the plaintiff's purse and told her to stay where she was "or she would be arrested." *Id.* The court focused on the fact that the officer told the plaintiff explicitly that she would be arrested and that he took her personal item to discourage her from leaving.
>
> Here, legal authority was used because . . .

What's missing are concrete principles at the outset that are easy to memorize and apply. What is legal authority? How do we know when it's present? What is useful from this case that will help readers get to answers? Let's distill a specific rule principle that would have won the day, designed for the facts of the case:

> When a defendant **uses words suggesting they have legal authority to hold a plaintiff and seizes a personal item from them to support that authority**—this Court has held that confinement is met.

The principles you need to distill turn on what your readers need to understand about the law to reach a decision on this particular issue. For example, say your general rule standard for an issue is this:

> Attorney fees are available to a "prevailing party." CITE. In particular, "attorney fees are proper if the court's action in granting a preliminary injunction is governed by its assessment of the merits." CITE.

To actually use this legal-speak in a real situation, readers will first need to know what a "prevailing party" is. Do you need to win your whole case? Only part of it? Something else? And then they'll probably need to know what "assessment on the merits" means. Again, that legal language isn't intuitive and easy to apply to the facts.

> **Attorney fees are available to a "prevailing party"—which simply means that a party won on at least one claim in some way, even in an injunction. CITE. For an injunction to qualify, the court merely needed to have "assessed the merits" in reaching its decision. CITE. In other words, the court considered some evidence and found that injunctive relief was warranted.**

Your touchstone in the pitch is to distill what readers need from all those authority details. So rather than delivering a stack of events from a case like this:

> In *Jasperson*, a fuel tanker was carrying supplies to another carrier and hit a reef, damaging the tanker. The insurance companies for the tanker and the shipping company both denied coverage because another carrier was arguably in coverage. . . .

Explain the principle readers can use from the authority first. Once they understand how the authority is useful to them, they might actually read more about the cases and statutes and regulations and everything else we legal folks throw at them.

> **Two insurers cannot both refuse coverage merely because the other could also be liable.** In *Jasperson*, a fuel tanker hit a reef and the owner submitted a claim to his two insurers, one that

> covered the tanker and one that covered his company. The court held that it was wrong for both insurers to rely on this potentially overlapping coverage as a reason to deny payments.

Here's another great example of how a great rule pitch can make the law easy to apply for readers. The writer articulates two concrete rule principles: (1) you can copyright the things within a collection, not just the collection as a whole, and (2) authority suggesting otherwise is limited to situations where there is no copyright in the individual parts—only in the collection. With these rule principles in hand, readers can reach their own answer, even when the opposing party marches out their authorities or arguments.

> Ross's theory is this: Because Westlaw has just one copyright registration, comprising hundreds of thousands of headnotes and key numbers, copying a mere few thousand is not enough for infringement....
>
> **[But] [a] copyright in a compilation extends to the copyrightable pieces of that compilation....**
>
> **[The cases suggesting otherwise] are the exceptions that prove the rule.[3] In those cases, the copyright holder owned only the compilation...** the plaintiffs owned "thin" copyrights: other than their selection and arrangement choices, none of their compilations' components were protectable.

Check out this next rule pitch from a case we looked at earlier (about hog farms spewing waste on people's yards).

> **Something "flowing" onto Plaintiffs' land satisfies the "unauthorized entry" element.** *Shadow Grp.*, 579 S.E.2d at 287 (collecting cases). Dirt that passes through public land—such as a river—first, and is only then deposited on Plaintiffs' land, is still a trespass.[4] *Phillips v. Hassett Mining Co.*, 92 S.E.2d 429, 433 (N.C. 1956) (permitting trespass action against mine operator by downstream landowner for dirt dumped in a river).

This pitch is specific and concrete. If liquid flows onto someone's property, it meets the rule. Period. That principle is clear enough that you can apply it to new facts and understand whether the rule is satisfied or not. And that is the goal. Notice how in this next pitch the rule's line is similarly drawn, but then the legal writer draws it even darker for good measure.

> **A director's conflict with a transactional counterparty[5] is material information** that should be disclosed. In fact, a director's ***potential*** **conflict with a transactional counterparty is material information** that should be disclosed.

Try out one more excellent rule pitch that empowers readers to reach conclusions on their own. The defendant was accused of using Jack Daniels's trademark within the

[3] You often don't need to call out opposing arguments on their face, but instead can walk readers through any authority that appears unhelpful (which you know the other side will rely on) and show how they support your pitch.

[4] This proof illustrating the principle immediately snaps the concept into place.

[5] This is a bright-line rule that makes the best pitch. If the fact was present, the rule was met.

defendant's own logo, "Bad Spaniels"—not in general expression like a creative advertisement. The writer's rule pitch equips us to deal with situations like this. When we later discover the facts of the case—that the trademark was used to designate a source logo and not as expression—it will be easy for us to conclude how the rules should apply.

> Over the decades, the lower courts adopting ***Rogers* have confined it to similar cases, in which a trademark is used not to designate a work's source, but solely to perform some other expressive function.** So, for example, when the toymaker Mattel sued a band over the song "Barbie Girl"—with lyrics including "Life in plastic, it's fantastic" and "I'm a blond bimbo girl, in a fantasy world"—the Ninth Circuit applied *Rogers*.[6] *Mattel, Inc. v. MCA Records, Inc.*, 296 F. 3d 894, 901 (2002)....
>
> **The same courts, though, routinely conduct likelihood-of confusion analysis, without mentioning *Rogers*, when trademarks are used as trademarks—i.e., to designate source.**[7] ... For example, that court held that an offshoot political group's use of the trademark "United We Stand America" got no *Rogers* help because the use was as a source identifier.

This same document gives us a world-class rule pitch explained with hypothetical examples (a tool we return to later). These examples give you an instant understanding of how the rule works.

> The first part of that [trademark] definition, identifying the kind of things covered, is broad: **It encompasses of the Court words (think "Google"), graphic designs (Nike's swoosh), and so-called trade dress, the overall appearance of a product and its packaging (a Hershey's Kiss, in its silver wrapper).**

Good rule pitching is all about asking yourself this question: *Will my reader understand enough of how the rules work from the outset and without extensive work so that they can navigate the dispute's waters and reach an answer?*

A rule-pitch walkthrough

Because creating your pitch is such an important skill, let's dig into a longer hypothetical and walk through the main factors you'll want to consider as you design yours.

Let's say we are arguing that the excited utterance exception to hearsay should apply to a statement. The general rule allows hearsay statements (statements made out of court) to be admitted into evidence. The rule requires that the statement be made "under the stress of a startling event." In other words, although hearsay statements are usually excluded, if the statement was made by someone under severe stress caused by a startling event, courts will assume the statement is credible and admit it.

As is usually the case, there are nuances in the law and facts that our pitch must account for. Let's start with the facts. In our case, the statement was made at work by an employee who was assaulted by another employee. The victim who made the statement, however, waited two hours before giving his statement. That said, the victim was clearly still stressed

---

[6]This is a brilliant rule proof. The example from *Mattel* illustrates the source vs. expression distinction so that readers will instantly accept it. A song is different from a logo.

[7]The author is reminding us of the source distinction so we don't have to remember it on our own.

when his statement was taken, even shaking as he related the details. After all, he'd been the victim of an assault. And there was no real reason for him to make up anything. This was a statement about a coworker, and the victim wasn't in trouble for anything.

Now to the law we'll need to wrangle in our pitch. A slew of cases suggest that only a "slight delay" is allowed between the startling event and the statement. These courts theorize that, otherwise, the person making the statement will have time to fabricate a story. Some cases have rejected the excited utterance exception when only minutes pass between the event and the statement.

On the other hand, as is usually true, there are good points for us in the law, too. Many cases that talk about this short-delay requirement address situations when the statement maker has an incentive to lie—like a criminal defendant trying to implicate someone else in a crime. Courts have also allowed longer delays, up to even a day, when the person making the statement was under visible duress or experienced some sort of violence.

So now we have some favorable facts and some unfavorable ones, as is usually the case:

- Our victim was clearly under physical duress.
- Our victim experienced violence.
- Our victim had no real incentive to change his statement during the period between the assault and the statement.
- But there was a two-hour delay between the event and the statement, which is far longer than most courts have allowed.

We also have some good and bad law to untangle, as is usually so:

- Most decisions require a very short delay, perhaps only minutes, between a startling event and the statement.
- On the other hand, those decisions often involve situations where the person has an incentive to lie.
- Courts have allowed longer delays when the victim experiences physical stress or violence.

This hypothetical is true to life. A mix of helpful and the not so much. Our job in designing the pitch is to create concise, specific principles out of the authority that will lead readers through the morass. We want to help our readers deal with those pesky cases that require a "short" delay—that some courts have allowed only minutes to pass, when our case involves hours, will not go over well with decision-makers. We can distinguish those cases because, here, the person making the statement had no incentive to lie.

> The cases requiring only a "slight delay" nearly always involve witnesses who had some incentive to lie—like criminals trying to get out of trouble.

Next, we want to leverage those good facts about the victim's assault and physical duress with another concrete principle.

> Courts have allowed much longer delays—even up to a day—when the statement-maker was the victim of violence and under physical duress.[8]

[8] If you have the authority to explain what sorts of violence would qualify, and what sort of physical duress is enough, all the better. The more specific, the better for readers to apply later.

Now we have two concrete principles—a winning pitch. It's specific and deals with the unfavorable facts and authorities. It leverages our case's favorable facts by suggesting that they matter more than the unfavorable ones. And readers can easily apply it later.[9]

When readers finish reading your pitch, they should understand not only what the legal standards are but when they are met. If the rule you're explaining is that a defendant must take "reasonable steps" to protect a trade secret, then your job is to convey enough information so that your readers understand what "reasonable steps" looks like in a case like yours. It's not even enough to suggest that defendants should do things like "ensure trade secret information is not *excessively* shared with the public"—readers need to understand what "excessive" looks like in real life. How much information must be shared before someone is doing so excessively? Your pitch must drill down into each generic term that matters until readers are educated enough to get real answers.

Structuring your pitch

What you're developing in your pitch is often called *rule synthesis* in other corners. It's where you bring together the strands of cases and other authorities into a message that makes sense. Thinking of this goal as a *rule pitch* is about taking rule synthesis further, refining all those legal points into a concise package that will be easy for readers to hold in their minds as they march to the finish line.

To make it easier to do this packaging, let's look at some common rule structures great legal writers use. The more structures you have in your toolbox, the more angles you can take when synthesizing all the rule stuff into a tight pitch.

Sometimes the authority is strong enough to create a clear bright-line rule. If a fact exists, the rule applies. That's great. Legal readers love the simplicity of bright-line rules. It will be clear to them what sort of facts will meet the rule, and that makes this rule pitch the most powerful of them all. For example:

> This Court's cases have instructed that everything turns on whether the objector remains in the building after objecting. If so, the objection is still effective and police can't come in. There are no exceptions.[10]

Was the objector still in the building when the police entered? Yes? Great, case closed. Here's another example using this bright-line rule principle. The legal writer pitches you that the law does not *ever* apply to past acts (knowing that if readers are convinced of that, the writer wins).

> [The law] is intended to help protect the public from future harm by collecting truthful information and making it available to those who choose to access it. It is not a penal law intended to punish people for past acts and never applies retroactively."

[9] Of course, we will need to support each of these principles with authority, but we'll get to that in the proof section later.

[10] Clarifying that there are no exceptions prevents readers from wondering if this rule is as clear as it sounds.

Next is another example of bright-line drawing, but this time, in describing an opponent's version of a rule. These legal writers framed their rule persuasively by emphasizing that an opposing rule would sweep in "all" facilities.

> Petitioners would have this Court declare **all** private, away-from-reactor storage facilities unlawful because the Fifth Circuit recently issued an outlier[11] decision holding that the NRC lacks authority to license such facilities under either the Atomic Energy Act (AEA) or the Nuclear Waste Policy Act (NWPA).

But sometimes you can't manage to draw the rule's line that cleanly, and you need to settle for a fuzzier one—albeit one that nudges readers in the right direction. You can think of these rule principles as *narrowing your reader's discretion*, even if they don't eliminate it altogether. You are making an outcome more or less likely.

You can narrow your reader's discretion by identifying factors, facts, or any other yardsticks by which your reader can measure whether your facts are within or outside a rule's reach. Let's look at some rule pitches that push the line instead of drawing a straight one.

> Courts have held that the **touchstone** of the test is how much economic injury is inflicted on the plaintiff.

By narrowing in on one factor that is favorable to your case and bolstering its importance (economic injury), you inch the rule's line in a favorable direction. Another common narrowing principle is to use burdens—burdens of persuasion or procedural burdens—to move your reader to one side or the other of a dispute. If the burden is in your favor, emphasize it heavily. If it doesn't favor you, it's the sort of opposing legal point you probably need to put into context.

> Plaintiffs have the **"strong burden"** of pointing the court to each detail supporting their motion to compel....

We are using the burden to create a rule principle in our pitch so that the plaintiffs' job feels harder. We can then stack on more rule principles to finish our pitch.

> Plaintiffs have the "strong burden" of pointing the court to each detail supporting their motion to compel....
>
> **Courts have held that details like those Plaintiffs pointed to here—ignorance of the law and avoidable mistakes—[12] are not enough to warrant pushing back a filing deadline.**

Another great rule pitch structure stems from presumptions or default perspectives in the law. For example, if you're aiming to go to trial and want a reader to believe that

[11] Better yet to explain how it's an outlier.

[12] This is a well-placed em dash that highlights the two most important points in the brief.

there are too many factual disputes on an element of a claim, then you can emphasize that presumption in your rule pitch as one tool.

> **Substantial similarity "is usually an extremely[13] close question of fact, which is why ... summary judgment has traditionally been disfavored in copyright litigation."**

You can also craft your rule principles to operate like elements:

> Marks must include specific facts in his complaint about **(1) what was said, (2) who said it, and (3) how the statement was misleading. If he falls short on any of these, his complaint is infirm.**

What if you face a discretionary rule or a factor-based one? Can you still develop a winning pitch to guide readers? Very much so. One option is to suggest that a certain factual situation is likely to satisfy all factors.

> Courts have **mostly looked to two factors** when deciding whether to allow these sorts of claims to avoid summary judgment: (1) whether the defendant kept anything hidden from the purchaser during the negotiation process and (2) whether there is any evidence the defendant knew it was hiding something. **Every relevant case in this district has granted summary judgment when neither of these two factors are present.**

Here are some other examples that make even a flexible rule sound more outcome-determinative:

> **Every case that has considered** allowing a parent company to use the *Malcolm-Forsent* defense has said no.

> When companies take extra efforts to test their products, beyond industry norms, **courts nearly always find their duty to make safe is satisfied.**

Consider using common rule pitch structures

To help fill your rule-pitch toolbox, consider the common rule structures when designing your pitches. It turns out that when you dissect the best legal writing, you find the same rule structures again and again. Why? Because they work. Each embeds a deeper sense of structure for readers. After all, research suggests that legal readers are more convinced by arguments that *sound* logical (whether they are logical or not). Simply by breaking down an argument into pieces and putting it into a logical structure, your chances of persuading rise.

This next appellate team gives us a prime example. Merely converting an argument into a logical structure (here, an obvious A to B) can be persuasive.

[13] When a source you're citing uses an intensifier like this, it's more persuasive than when you use it.

> **Simple logic dictates that if A can be "converted" to B, then A is not B.**[14] Hence the need for conversion. And what is true generally is true of frames and receivers under the plain text of the Gun Control Act. . . .
>
> **According to ATF's new rule, "partially complete, disassembled, or nonfunctional frame[s] or receiver[s]," . . . are already "frames or receivers."**[15]

And one final example of putting an argument into a clear logical framework, here, that because *A and B are different*, the FDA cannot interpret *A to be B*. Once the logic snaps into place, it's hard to shake.

> FDA's interpretation — that to be *analogous* to a protein a product must *be* a protein — is contrary to the statutory text. FDA . . . cannot define a product as "analogous" to a "protein" to the exclusion of everything *except* proteins.

Let's explore some more simple structures you can use as inspiration for your rule-pitch toolbox. This is the simplest of them all:

> **You cannot meet [the rule standard] by doing [insert facts].**

Framing your rule principle in terms this simple can often cut out the fluff. But you must be specific so your readers understand the disconnect:

> Plaintiffs cannot overcome the jurisdictional and justiciability concerns [] by naming only phantom "Doe" defendants.

Another simple rule principle structure looks like this:

> **The [insert authority or legal principle] generally requires [insert generic principle or spirit of the law] and that principle requires [insert your favorable conclusion.]"**

And here is an example:

> Accepting the Plaintiff's argument and siding with the courts he cites would mean that supply costs are ignored in the damages calculation. The *Daubert* expert standard requires accuracy, and to accurately value the damages requires adding what consumers would pay and subtracting what the product costs. Plaintiff and his cases require this Court to ignore half of that equation.[16]

[14] This is also an example of a common hypothetical structure great legal writers use.

[15] This example highlights a contradiction in language, which is a great tool for analyzing text or an opponent's words.

[16] This final short sentence punches.

Another great structure that leverages the quality of authority is:

There is no mandatory authority on point because [make clear no binding authority answers your legal question]. And the best persuasive authority teaches [insert your preferred rule or principle].

Another structure that highlights the different perspectives between you and another is this:

The law addresses [insert explanation of what a law affirmatively covers]. But the law does not govern [insert facts that feel very different and are not included in the first explanation].

This is a great structure for helping readers understand the boundaries around a law (and thus better understand where your own situation fits). Let's look at an example:

> The Lanham Act's injunctive-relief provision gives courts the power to grant injunctions "according to the principles of equity and upon such terms as the court may deem reasonable, to prevent the violation of any right of the registrant" of a registered trademark. But nowhere in that provision does it grant courts the power to impose such injunctions on unidentified . . . persons. . . .

Like many great rule structures, this next one works because it juxtaposes two points:

The party did not [insert what they failed to do]. But the party wants [insert request or argument that hinges on that failed action].

Notice how this next example is so powerful because it leverages an obvious hypocrisy:

> [Plaintiffs] have not named a single defendant whom they expect to sell counterfeit merchandise while BTS is performing in Las Vegas, but they seek to enjoin anyone who may do so.

Here is another structure that highlights the disparity between two actions. It's another simple structure to get readers on your side.

The party has not done [insert facts that would have satisfied the rule], instead the party did [insert the actual facts which are very different].

This structure works well because you give readers a sense of what a good case looks like, and then immediately compare the less compelling thing that an opposing party did:

> Here, by contrast, the statement at issue relates to Moreira-Brown's performance not as an attorney—let alone his "courtroom conduct"—but as a would-be political figure 16 years earlier in a Congressional district thousands of miles from Nevada.

The general rule is [define the law broadly enough to encompass your facts with as specific examples as possible].

In this next example, the legal writer uses key language (any) and an example to make a rule sound broad enough to easily encompass the case's facts.

> This Court has emphasized that "any" damage is enough to warrant relief. Even harm that costs a victim as little as "ten dollars" is enough. Plaintiffs have shown that each class member has lost at least $100 after the Defendant ignored the SEC's new rule.

Sometimes we need to bring readers on a journey that requires a few stops. It could be that satisfying one rule or standard is likely to satisfy a second. Or it might be that you must satisfy a threshold issue to get to a second rule:

> **[Insert facts] meet the legal standard of [insert the first rule]. Courts (or some other authority) have instructed that [the first rule] satisfies [insert second rule or concept].**

This next snippet connects the dots on the journey:

> Courts have held that a "gross deprivation" of rights is enough to grant standing. And once standing is present, no case has ever found a claim to fail the Rule 8 standard. The Alaska court here has already held, as a matter of res judicata, that the Plaintiff suffered a gross deprivation. So Rule 8 is surely met.

Categorical structures are great. They start by explaining what a category encompasses, either through clear language or examples. Then it's easy to show why your situation falls in or out of the category. This next structure is about narrowing the category a rule encompasses to make it obvious why your facts don't fit inside.

> **[Insert narrow explanation of the law or examples of what it covers] does not extend to [facts or situation that you prefer to not be covered by this law].**

In this next example, all the effort to narrow the rule's category sets you up to understand why the facts can't possibly fit in.

> Courts have held that **only "the rarest of cases"** justify setting aside a maritime tribunal's judgment in admiralty cases. That's because certainty and consistency are paramount in this area of law, which often touches on relations with foreign governments. **The cases that have set aside a judgment include acts like "outright fraud" and "gross dereliction of duty." The classic case is mutiny, where a ship's crew steals the ship.** This case involves a minor disagreement between the captain and bridge, nothing more.

Another form of rule categorization is to suggest what the typical case looks like to highlight why your situation either fits, or doesn't fit, the bill.

> **Most [insert common examples that sound like your situation] fail to meet the relevant legal standard. This case is one of those situations.**

Here's a great example of this structure, which is about playing to majority rule:

> Like most motions [to set aside judgments], the City's motion here should be denied: It fails to meet the demanding standards imposed by the Rule, and so the interests of justice favor finality over perfection.

Rule structures are everywhere. Keep developing this toolbox and you'll be equipped to teach readers a favorable view of the law in every situation you can imagine. Here are some more structures to draw from:

> **The legal standard requires [insert explanation of the standard in a single sentence]. Here, [insert the single most powerful detail that obviously lines up, or doesn't line up, with your explanation of the standard].**

> The City must show "mistake, inadvertence, surprise, [or] excusable neglect." Civ.R. 60(B)(1). Here, the City waited until after the First District ruled in Rick's favor to correct the record—even though two judges on the First District panel read the City's mistake aloud, line by line, in front of two City attorneys at oral argument.

> **The [insert extremely authoritative or trustworthy source] agrees that [rule or fact that you want to establish beyond a doubt].**

> As the First District noted, the City could have "sought leave to correct the record" while the appeal was pending, but it sat on its hands for a month.

> **Not until [some obvious fact that anyone would respond to] happened, did the party do [insert what they eventually did, but that obviously they should have done earlier.]**

> Not until it suffered an adverse ruling did the City attempt to fix the record.

> **If [insert opposing argument] is accepted, then [insert bad things that will happen].**

> If the City—through its errors—can prevent Rick from having the First District (and higher Courts) hear his appeal, this raises serious Due Process and Equal Protection concerns.

> **Courts often [insert action you want the court to take on facts similar to yours]. So here the court should feel comfortable doing that.**

> A party cannot use [identify the legal rule you don't want to apply] by doing [identify facts].

> **The party does not argue [insert obvious or emotional points that are related but not at issue], but only argues [narrow the dispute to what you are countering]."**

Normally, [insert the traditional story or norms your reader may be familiar with and think should apply here from experience]. But here [explain how this case is different from the norm].

Battery normally requires that a defendant actually touch the plaintiff, but if the defendant causes something else to contact the victim, that counts, too, because the plaintiff suffers the same harm and the defendant is just as blameworthy.

More rule pitch structures are hiding in cases and briefs all around you. Just watch for them and keep filling your toolbox.

Styling your pitch

Your rule pitch must be memorable. Pull out all the stops on these sentences. Rule pitches should be specific and usable, yes. But also consider using rhetorical techniques, word choice, sentence structure—everything in your arsenal to make your reader notice, remember, and adopt your pitch.[17] Look at these next examples. Each makes the rules memorable and pithy.

Courts commonly sanction parties for failing to comply with their automatic discovery obligations *for months*—and here, Smith failed to fulfill its obligations *for years*.[18]

No money, no standing—that has been California law for four decades.[19]

Neither bare allegations nor sparsely clothed[20] ones can survive a motion to dismiss under Rule 9 when fraud is alleged.

[A search can be] reasonable even though there was no concern about the loss of evidence[] and the arresting officer had no concern that [a defendant] might be armed.[21] ... [For example, the] Court did not draw a line between a search of Robinson's person and a further examination of the cigarette pack found during that search. It merely noted that, "[h]aving in the course of a lawful search come upon the crumpled[22] package of cigarettes, [the officer] was entitled to inspect it."

Contrary to *Williamson County*, a property owner has a claim for a violation of the Takings Clause as soon as a government takes his property for public use without paying for it. The Clause provides: "[N]or shall private property be taken for public use, without just compensation." It does not say: "Nor shall private property be taken for public use, without an available procedure that will result in compensation."

---

[17] For more inspiration on elevating your style, you can also check out Chapter 9, which covers dozens of the major rhetorical structures in legal writing.

[18] A simple rhetorical move we'll return to is to contrast words or concepts to make a bigger point about the gap between them.

[19] The two identical phrases at the start of this sentence create a rhetorical flourish we look at again in Chapter 9.

[20] This example combines the figurative language and playing off other words in the sentence.

[21] Notice the balance between the first two "no concern" clauses. Balancing phrases or echoing words like this is a powerful style technique.

[22] This is a rare example of a descriptor adding value to a noun.

> The well-pleaded complaint rule means that a case may not be removed to federal court on the basis of a federal defense, including the defense of pre-emption, even if[23] the defense is anticipated in the plaintiff's complaint, and even if both parties concede that the federal defense is the only question truly at issue.

As we will explore more in Chapter 9, rhetorical style is about learning how different structures work and when to use them. For example, one common way to amp up your rule pitch's style is to use rhetorical questions. You can turn nearly every rule into a simple question that makes it clear for your reader where your facts fall. For example, look at Justice Ginsburg doing exactly that.

> The [question] in this case is not whether the Constitution compels [a] University to adopt a special admission program for minorities, but only whether the Constitution permits [a] University to pursue that course.

The underlying rule that Justice Ginsburg is trying to set up is that the Constitution treats *permission* and *compulsion* differently, and she sets up that rule by framing it as a question. Here's another example. The original rule looked like this:

> Companies need only have a legal right to collect on a debt to avoid liability, they need not actually intend to collect on it.

Turning this into a question is easy.

> The question under California law is whether a company has a legal right to collect on a debt. Nothing more.

And here are a couple more examples of this move at work.

> **What is the real issue?** Whether INS agents . . . can, within the bounds of the Constitution, attack a non-resident alien on U.S. soil, arrest her without reason or provocation, and use excessive force in doing so.

> **The narrow question** raised by this pretrial motion is whether, if Antoine Watts is convicted of possessing with intent to distribute five grams or more of crack cocaine, the court will be compelled to impose a minimum. . . . **The broader question** is whether federal courts will be required, for the next five years, to perpetuate a congressionally recognized injustice. . . .

Judge Patricia Wald is a master of setting up carefully constructed, nuanced legal questions that will guide her reader to the answer she wants.

> This case presents a straightforward, but nonetheless hard, question of law: **Has the United States waived sovereign immunity for a back pay award to an individual denied federal employment in violation of his constitutional rights?**

[23] Echoing words (the "even if" leading into two parallel clauses) makes the sentence memorable.

Perhaps the best example of how a simple question can frame an entire way of looking at a rule is from Kathleen Sullivan's brief in *SEC v. Siebel Sys.*

> Is someone riding around[24] a golf course from shot to shot really a golfer?

Include the why behind your pitch

Finally, consider incorporating the *why* behind your rule pitch. Two *whys* often matter. *Why* does the law work the way you say it does? *Why* would following your view of the law outshine the alternatives?

This next legal writer explains his position on the law by connecting it to background context that aligns with his position. Congress wants to protect fishers, and when it wants to allow them to be charged money by the government, it says so explicitly.

> **Space onboard a commercial fishing vessel is a scarce and precious resource. Thus, displacing someone engaged in active fishing to make way for a federal observer tasked with overseeing regulatory compliance is already an enormous imposition.** Making the fishing vessels foot the bill for that imposition adds insult to injury. **In light of that reality, when Congress wanted the fishing industry to cover the cost of federal observers, it has said so expressly.** For example, the MSA expressly provides that the North Pacific Council—whose jurisdiction encompasses Alaska, Washington, and Oregon and some of the largest and most commercially successful enterprises, § 1852(a)(1)(G)—"may . . . require that observers be stationed on fishing vessels . . . for the purpose of collecting data necessary for the conservation, management, and scientific understanding of any fisheries under the Council's jurisdiction," and **"to pay for the cost of implementing the plan," the Council "may . . . establish a system . . . of fees."** § 1862(a).

Now to prove our pitch by showing readers all the great work we did in coming up with it.

4.1.3. Prove Your Rule

You've delivered your winning pitch. Readers understand how you view the rules and how they should, too. That's most of the battle. But there is one last hurdle between your reader and the conclusion you want them to reach: convincing them your pitch is worth following. You prove this by pointing to evidence. Not factual evidence, but evidence from the authority. And when you dig deep, you will find a lot of authority evidence to point to.

The best legal writers are those with the biggest boxes of authority evidence. They can look at a case and develop compelling perspectives that others won't. Even when a precedent first seems like it binds the result, these attorneys can work creatively to make readers question. Because you can distinguish any case; you need only find the right fact or comment or contradiction that will change what readers see on the page.

You can think about these tactics as *authority evidence*. The reasons readers should view an authority in the way you suggest is the evidence that proves your view (and ultimately, your rule pitch).

---

[24] This is purposely familiar language. What stuffy legal writer would describe operating a golf cart as "riding around"?

While your factual evidence is what it is, you can *create* authority evidence. You can use what is said and what is not said in cases, the facts, interactions with other cases, interactions with statutes, analogous laws that seem to work similarly, and so much more, to develop the proof you need. So take your rule discussions beyond the simple fact-to-fact comparisons most legal writers rely on.

Before moving further, one practice pointer: Developing your pitch and working with your authority is a symbiotic enterprise. The more angles you can take with authority, the more options you'll have to develop a winning pitch. The more authorities you pull evidence from, the further you can push your pitch. So while we're talking about pitches and proof separately (and they should be distinct for your readers in the final product), the two are part of a single process for you as the writer.

Here's the running example we looked at in the prep and the pitch, with some proof now included. Notice how we use multiple different details from the authority, each helping confirm our pitch for the law that came first. We combine facts from authority, key quotes, distinguishing facts, and more.

> Plaintiff brings a single claim for battery, and Defendant moves to dismiss. Battery includes four elements: an (1) intentional (2) contact (3) with another that is (4) harmful or offensive. [Cite.] There is no dispute that the defendant acted intentionally or that Plaintiff was harmed.
>
> Contact does not merely include touching someone with your hand, it also includes both (1) contacting something the plaintiff is carrying, and (2) putting something into motion that makes contact.
>
> Defendants need not contact the plaintiff's skin to carry out a battery. Contacting something on the plaintiff's body is enough. **True, the only Supreme Court case on point involved someone "punching" another, but that case is 40 years old. [Cite.] And there is no language in that case suggesting that other sorts of contacts do not qualify. [Cite.] Other district courts facing this same issue have held that "contact within anything the plaintiff is holding is enough." [Cite.] In *Park v. Hoffman*, for example, the defendant was found liable for battery after ripping a plate from the plaintiff's hands. [Cite.]**

These next legal writers use quotes, paraphrasing, and multiple authorities to support their pitch.

> In *Barnett*, this issue of permissibility **was never raised** so the Court never considered it. *Barnett*, instead, held that **"employees remain free to show . . . that the requested accommodation is reasonable"** even if a company's policy needs to be violated. **Other courts have treated the "may include" language as simply reflecting an example**, not a suggestion that reassignment is not somehow mandatory. [Five cases with details from these authorities].

Notice in this next example how the writer uses a combination of proof to convince the reader that their pitch is accurate—including a quote, paraphrasing authority language, arguing the quality of the authority, pointing out omissions in the authority, and distinguishing facts in the authority.

> If the defendant is still in the home after he objects to a search, police **cannot cure that objection by getting consent from someone else in the home**. In *Hoffman*, the court explained, **"whether**

the defendant is in the boundaries of the home is what matters." The case mustered by the other side, *Park*, was **decided in the 60's and never considered this same issue**. There, the **defendant had left the home before police searched**....

The following legal writers show off several rule pitch designs with surgical quotes and authority to support each. You'll find a modifier rule principle ("only in exceptional circumstances" does the opposing law ever apply, and "far more rarely" in cases like this one), a typical-case rule principle, and other language meant to stack the deck for the writers. What you won't find is a string cite or empty recitation of facts from precedent.

Courts may surrender their jurisdiction **only in "exceptional" circumstances.** *Colorado River Water Conserv. Dist. v. United States*, 424 U.S. 800, 813 (1976). **Some courts** have held that perceived international-comity concerns can present such a circumstance. *Id.* at 44-48. Those concerns **typically arise when** "courts consider whether to respect the judgment of a foreign tribunal or to defer to parallel foreign proceedings." *GDG Acquisitions, LLC v. Government of Belize*, 749 F.3d 1024, 1030 (11th Cir. 2014). **When, unlike here,** such "parallel proceedings" exist abroad, U.S. courts often afford respect for those proceedings by abstaining from hearing the same claims in the United States. *Royal & Sun All. Ins. Co. of Canada v. Century Int'l Arms, Inc.*, 466 F.3d 88, 93 (2d Cir. 2006).

"Far more rarely"—in fact, almost never—some courts have applied international-comity abstention without any "conflicting past or present foreign proceeding." [] **The few courts to entertain** this brand of abstention have done so only in "rare (indeed often calamitous) cases in which powerful diplomatic interests of the United States and foreign sovereigns align[] in supporting dismissal." *Id.*

This next example is a master class in attacking the credibility of an opposing case through different types of authority evidence: using distinguishing facts, faulty reasoning in the precedent, contradicting language within the opinion, pointing out dicta, and more.

First, *Griffin* does not speak to the power of states like Colorado to enforce Section 3 under their own law....

Second, [*Griffin's*] reasoning glossed over the mandatory language of Section 3, and [its] suggestion that Section 5 gives Congress exclusive power to enforce the Fourteenth Amendment does not survive this Court's controlling precedent in cases like *City of Boerne*....

Third, [*Griffin*] later took a contradictory position in the treason prosecution of Jefferson Davis....

Fourth, [*Griffin*] rested [its] opinion mainly on the supposed "inconveniences" and "mischief" that would result from collateral challenges to convictions by sitting Confederate judges....

Finally, [*Griffin*] worried about declaring an official disqualified "without trial" in a collateral habeas challenge to which the official was not a party.

A few tips on your authority evidence. First, keep your supporting authority focused on your rule pitches. Tangential authority discussions will confuse readers. If you decide that your initial rule pitch—your initial explanation of how the law works—isn't broad or effective enough, go back and adjust it. But if you can't explain how authority should be used to understand and apply the law, why would your much busier and less invested reader want to figure it out for you?

You don't always need a dozen authorities to prove a pitch (despite what many legal writers believe by the looks of their briefs). Authority is where quality exceeds quantity. The right case or two will be more useful to a decision-maker trying to get to an answer than hundreds of generic cases ever could be.

That said, you can adjust how much authority you include depending on how important the rule is and how hard the question is for your decision-maker. If you're proving the single most important rule principle in your document, marshal more authority. And more reasoning, or evidence, from the authority. If you're supporting a straightforward rule with a case that undeniably shows you're in the right, then perhaps you need nothing more than that.

Tools for supporting your proof

Finally, let's start filling your authority-evidence toolbox. What follows are some of the best ways to pull evidence from authority and support your pitch on the law. These tools will help you push, bend, expand, narrow, and otherwise interpret the law for your audiences. But these tools are not exhaustive. Good legal writers are constantly on the hunt for new types of authority evidence.

1. **Use multiple types of authority evidence for key points.** Often it's more persuasive to combine multiple types of authority evidence—a quote, a comparable fact, and so on—rather than relying on only one dimension of an authority. Collecting compelling points from authority together, in different forms, is persuasive proof.

> Petitioner relies on a handful of cases but ignores *the cases that have explicitly ruled against his position as well as the text of the statute*. . . .

2. **Quote authority**. Use quotes to illustrate how rules work. As with all quotes, use the smallest portion of text that will illustrate the most useful information.

> This Court has said "the touchstone is the burden of proof."

3. **Compare language from different sources.** When courts use different language to talk about a rule, and you think those contradictions or contrasts will help you illustrate the rule, show readers.

> While this court said the touchstone was "burden of proof" in *Sybeck*, it did an about-face in *Perelis*, stating that from now on "intent" is what courts should "focus on most."

> The court mentioned that specific intent may be required, but then finished its opinion by saying "never before have we required plaintiffs to show precisely what the defendant intended."

4. Compare facts. Compare specific facts from prior cases to your case—the similarities for favorable points and the differences to distinguish. Often, it's best to compare an actor in an authority to an actor in your case. There are two sorts of factual comparisons: silent fact comparisons and reasoned fact comparisons. *Silent* fact comparisons are when the precedent opinion never mentioned the fact in its reasoning, but the facts were in the opinion's background somewhere. *Reasoned* facts are more persuasive because the precedent case said that the fact was important to the rule.

> *Jones* turned on several facts, all of which suggested that the prejudice was so severe that money could not make the party whole. **The company had been slaughtered in the stock market**, plummeting so much each day that analysts questioned whether it could ever recover. **Not to mention the company's pure loss of liquid funds**, which nearly put it out of operation. The **court highlighted both of these facts** in granting preliminary injunctive relief. . . .[25]

> ***Calico* did not deal with companies at all**: it was a case about a mother asking for custody of her child.[26]

> Plaintiffs urge that their corporate walls shield them from a suit. **But not in a single one of their cited decisions did the court mention piercing the corporate veil. That is so despite that *each* involved a parent and child company waging the same battle that the parties are waging here. The court's silence matters. . . .**

> **Farmer Filburn was not an organic home baker who had decided to raise wheat for a few loaves of bread. Rather he "raised wheat commercially and regularly sold a portion of his crop on the open market."**

5. Analyze the quality of cases. All sources are not created equal. Consider leveraging the age of the case, the thoroughness of its reasoning, what court it came from (mandatory? reputable?), who wrote it, the level of the court, how other authorities have treated it, publication status, and how many judges signed on.

> The other case that mentioned this rule, *Samar Trusts*, **was decided 30 years ago and gave it only three lines of analysis. . . .**[27]

6. Identify a line of cases and address it together. Whenever a string of cases has addressed a rule, look for weaknesses in one of the chains in the link, or use the chain as further evidence that the rule is trustworthy, depending on your goal. Courts often rely on prior cases without looking too deeply into why they held what they held. And this can be an angle for suggesting that later cases were wrong because they relied on shaky footings.

---

[25] This is an example of a reasoned fact: The court explicitly reasoned that the fact mattered to the rule.

[26] This is an example of a silent fact. The court didn't emphasize how it related to the rule, but it's still a fact that can help shape readers' understanding.

[27] This is a great example of guiding readers, too. No need to tell your readers to "ignore this case" or that it is a "horrible" and "unhelpful" case. Just show your readers and let them reach the inevitable conclusion.

This requirement of pleading the relief down to the penny comes from a single line of cases — **but the original cases that created this rule were about forfeiture, a context that involves different considerations than garden variety tort claims like the court is facing here. . . .**

Lynch has been relied on recently by, among others, **the Third Circuit in *Chi Thon Ngo*, the Sixth Circuit in *Rosales-Garcia*, and the Ninth Circuit in *Kwai Fun Wong v. United States*. It has been continuously cited by this Court as well.**

Jerico Systems Inc. states that it applies the no-flunking rule, but its reasoning and analysis tell a different story. **Before *Jerico*, never had a court suggested that flunking was even part of the analysis. That goes for all 14 cases that had taken on this same issue before. But *Jerico* not only considered flunking — the court said that this was the "touchstone" of the case. . . .**

7. Point out which facts or concepts a case emphasized most, emphasized least, or ignored. Often courts give you some idea about which facts or legal concepts were most important. You can use this focus to argue that those things should be weighted more heavily, or less heavily, than others when applying a rule.

The court brushed aside Ace's harms, giving it barely two sentences of consideration. The thrust of the question, instead, was whether Ace had laid out a plausible legal claim in the first place.

8. Point out dicta. Showing that language in a case is not binding because it did not address the facts before the court is always a key tool when it serves your goals.

González turns to dicta from a single case — dicta seemingly endorsed by only a plurality of the Supreme Court in *United States v. Verdugo-Urquidez*. **Relying on this dicta,** González argues that aliens have no Fourth Amendment rights even when they step onto U.S. territory.

9. Point out a rule's broadness or narrowness. Did a case narrow its holding to certain facts or suggest broader principles? Look for any language in the case that narrows or broadens. And then, of course, you can always use the facts to narrow or broaden, as well.

The High Court **made sure lawyers would not use its holding in the future, saying: "if [it] were a different plaintiff and different defendant, the rule would likely come out differently."**

That case addressed a unicorn — a company that had never even sold a product much less practiced its claims invention. *Perry* says nothing about a blanket rule requiring every company in the nation to support its practice with admissible evidence.

Home Depot v. Grumpk is about the right to a fair hearing, **not the right to preferred evidence. . . .**

10. Explain where the rule came from to inform your pitch. Legal readers are persuaded by the "why." Why does this rule exist? Is someone trying to twist it in a direction that doesn't bear any resemblance to its original purpose? The purpose behind rules can be authority evidence to support a rule interpretation.

> The exhaustion requirement is about efficiency and expertise. The rule was borne in *Tyrion*. The court there made clear that if efficiency and expertise are not on the table, exhaustion makes little sense....

11. Look for ways an opponent's case supports your pitch. If you can pull this off, the case will move from your opponent's column to neutral—or maybe even to your side. Look for language, facts, or reasoning that can align with how you're framing your rule pitch.

> Viacom ignores *Grokster's* actual holding. Instead, it tries to shift the legal playing field, disavowing the term "inducement" and contending that liability "rests on the existence of the unlawful purpose itself." The murky standard Viacom proposes diverges from *Grokster* in two critical respects.... Viacom glosses over the point, repeatedly emphasized by the Supreme Court, that inducement liability is not based on some amorphous bad purpose, but instead requires that the defendant have the specific objective of "promoting" the use of its service....

12. Use similar statutes or laws to shed light on your rule pitch. Comparing one rule to another can clarify how the rule should be viewed in your case.

> A private individual's surreptitious installation of a GPS tracker onto the property of another to monitor the owner's movement is not only a trespass to chattels... but can form the basis for criminal liability under the laws of various states.

> Although plaintiff sued under Title VII, courts have often looked to case law interpreting Title IX for guidance.

> Courts have addressed this same question in the nearby context of debt collection. And not one of those cases requires that a company actually collect on a debt before a plaintiff can sue them.

13. Point out how fundamental principles support your pitch. Principles like equity and fairness can nudge readers toward viewing a rule in a favorable way. The same goes for emotional details from your case.

> The court has a novel legal question on its hands: interpret the doctrine as applying to companies only, or also to individuals. But applying this rule to individuals will irretrievably change the dynamic of this market, preventing many small businesses from even entering it.

> To require companies to file a form every time they want to sell a device to a patient would shut down [the company] overnight. The FDA takes an average of three months to process a single form. How long will it take them to process 12,000 this month alone?

14. Point out novelty (when helpful). Judges especially don't like going in new directions. So framing an opposing view as creating new rules, new standards, or new consequences is a useful way to support your rule pitch. The same goes for reassuring audiences that the rule you're urging is a trustworthy, well-trodden path.

> González proposes to apply the rule of *Mezei*—**for the first time in its fifty-year history**—outside the context of immigration and deportation proceedings, outside the arena of immigration law, and outside the bounds of Congress's plenary power over immigration matters, the power that forms the rule's basis and rationale.

And that is the PPP. Prepare your readers for the hard rule work. Make that work easier by pitching the complexity in a few concrete principles. And prove your work by digging deep into your authority evidence.

4.2 Teach Text-Based Rules

Textual laws like statutes, regulations, constitutions, rules, and other enacted or passed laws require special care. These rules bring with them an even larger toolbox of specialized ways you can develop pitches and perspectives for readers.

Of course, often the easiest way to teach readers about how a statute or other codified rule works is to use cases that have already done that interpreting. But the best legal writers have several other tools in their textual toolbox. For example, you can use the principle that the legislature is consistent in the words it uses to convey similar things across a statute. If Congress uses certain words to carry out a goal in one section, we can assume it means those same words carry out that same goal in another section. This sort of common-sense interpretation principle can mean everything when explaining the import of a text.

To see why these text tools are so powerful, let's look at another top legal writer using them.

> As the government itself emphasizes, Congress has made clear beyond cavil that some incomplete "firearms" do count as "firearms" under the GCA and related laws. **But Congress did so by using language that is conspicuously absent from the "frame or receiver" provision. Congress' choice to use those words elsewhere must be respected. So must its decision not to use those words to modify "frame or receiver."**

A Quick Summary

To weave together the most compelling statutory narrative, consider a few tactics.

Use the canons and the text. Canons of construction are principles that many legal audiences use to interpret the text of statutes and other codified laws. Text is about language. Consider what language will help focus readers on the value.

Use structure and history. Often the text's structure (like a statutory section's title and the surrounding text and sections) and atmospherics can help develop your pitch. Many audiences are also receptive to legislative history: how the statute or codified law was enacted and anything said by its creators during the lawmaking process.

4.2.1. Use the Canons and the Text

Over time, bedrock interpretive principles emerged that act as a compass through the labyrinthine world of legal language. There are many. And their persuasive force will vary, depending on your audience. Not every legal reader loves these principles (often called "the canons"), and even at their best, they are usually guiding principles, not unbending rules.

Before we get to the canons, though, interpreting text can be as straightforward as developing common-sense arguments for what words mean. For example, courts rely on dictionaries a lot, and looking at the technical definition of the text you care about is always a good place to start. Chief Justice Roberts wanted to illustrate that the adjective "personal" had taken on its own distinct meaning from "person." So he pulled out a hypothetical and walked through dictionary definitions of similar adjectives that had taken on different meanings:

> Adjectives typically reflect the meaning of corresponding nouns, but not always. Sometimes they acquire distinct meanings of their own. The noun "crab" refers variously to a crustacean and a type of apple, while the related adjective "crabbed" can refer to handwriting that is "difficult to read," Webster's Third New International Dictionary 527 (2002); "corny" can mean "using familiar and stereotyped formulas believed to appeal to the unsophisticated," *id.*, at 509, which has little to do with "corn," *id.*, at 507 ("the seeds of any of the cereal grasses used for food"); and while "crank" is "a part of an axis bent at right angles," "cranky" can mean "given to fretful fussiness."

When working with language directly like this, pay particular attention to key operative words that often change the meaning of the text. Words like "must," "may," "shall," and "should" often suggest obligations, for example. Look for modifying words and any other language you can use to narrow in on the meaning.

Also pay attention to punctuation. What points are put together in a sentence and how the points are punctuated within the sentence can change the meaning (and some canons address this, too).

Perhaps the most common punctuation principle is the serial comma (also known as the Oxford comma). This refers to using a comma before the last item in a list. For example, in one famous case, a Maine statute exempted certain employees from overtime laws if they were involved with "the canning, processing, preserving, freezing, drying, marketing, storing, packing for shipment or distribution of [various foods.]" The problem was that because no comma was used before the final list item (distribution), it was unclear whether "packing" modified "distribution"—or whether distribution was a separate list item. When a dairy company tried to stop paying their delivery drivers overtime because they worked in "distribution," the drivers sued. The Maine courts eventually held that it wasn't clear whether "distribution" workers were exempt, or only workers who "packed for distribution." The drivers used the lack of a comma to successfully argue that they did not fall under the statute.

But let's dig in more to the canons themselves. The first step to wrangling with legal text is to find canons that support your position. When analyzing statutory or regulatory language, start with the canons that courts have turned to for centuries.

These next legal writers used several of these traditional interpretive principles in a case about the SEC seeking to claw back millions from companies.

> Congress has never given the SEC authority to seek and obtain an order of disgorgement from a district court. As a matter of ordinary statutory construction, that conclusion is inescapable. **It is shown by the absence of "disgorgement" from the detailed system of penalties and other relief that the SEC may seek in court; by the contrast with administrative proceedings, where statutory text authorizes "accounting and disgorgement"; and by comparing the SEC's authorities to those of other agencies, to which Congress made court-ordered "disgorgement" available.** . . . A statute must say it, and here no statute does.

Here are some of the most common canons, which can be used for any textual argument, really. Even those involving contracts.

1. **Supremacy-of-text principle**. The words of text should generally govern the interpretation.
2. **Presumption against ineffectiveness.** A textually permissible interpretation that furthers rather than obstructs the document's purpose should be favored.
3. **Presumption of validity.** An interpretation that validates outweighs one that invalidates.
4. **Ordinary-meaning canon**. Words are to be understood in their ordinary, everyday meanings—unless the context indicates that they bear a technical sense.
5. **Fixed-meaning canon**. Words must be given the meaning they had when the text was adopted.
6. **Omitted-case canon**. Nothing is to be added to what the text states or reasonably implies. That is, a matter not covered is to be treated as not covered.
7. **Negative-implication canon**. Expressing one thing means excluding others.
8. **Mandatory/permissive canon**. Mandatory words impose a duty; permissive words grant discretion.[28]

These principles help you untangle the complex threads of technical language and weave them into coherent arguments. Although not all audiences are equally persuaded by the canons (particularly the more obscure ones), you'll find that some of the basic principles will persuade nearly anyone.

For example, the supremacy-of-text principle is where most legal folks will start when analyzing a text-based law. Like these writers did:

> The law means what it says: "No person may file a claim without first exhausting the remedies provided in Section 3.2." **The plain meaning of "exhausting the remedies" is that no claim may**

[28] I borrowed the naming of some of these traditional canons from Antonin Scalia & Bryan A. Garner, Reading Law: The Interpretation of Legal Texts (West 2012).

> **be filed "until the remedies or claims have been exhausted" in Section 3.2.** And the plaintiff here admits they have never once filed anything under Section 3.2's claim scheme.

In the end, canons of construction are general principles. Their mileage with legal audiences varies. You should always look for authority that makes clear a canon or interpretive principle is persuasive with your audience before relying on it too much.

These next legal writers use a less common canon to convincingly argue for a statutory interpretation, followed by a citation to authority that confirms this principle is relevant for the particular audience.

> [A] court should avoid interpretations of a statute that would facilitate "evasion of the law" or "enable offenders to elude its provisions in the most easy manner." . . . That principle [is] known as the "presumption against ineffectiveness". . . . **Three recent precedents . . . illustrate that principle.**

Understanding the canons is the beginning of a journey. Mastering legal interpretation requires both practice and an ongoing awareness of how courts apply these principles.

Use the text

When interpreting statutory language, most readers expect to see the language for themselves. Because with text, the particular words (and as we just saw, even the punctuation) can matter.

Scour statutes for the most compelling language to bolster your position. Quoting key language anchors your argument in the text and provides a foundation for your interpretation. But make sure to clean up the quote and deliver it as fluently as you can. Long, dense quotes tax readers, statute or not.

These next two snippets show off surgical statutory quoting. The author snipped out the key text and delivered it in their own precise prose. Smart quoting like this ensures readers never get lost.

> When the statute says, **"before 12 days have transpired,"** it means **"before 12 days have transpired after the court's own deadline."**

> The regulation requires only **"best efforts,"** which is defined. **"Best efforts"** means the **"most effective"** option **"regardless of cost."**

In this next example, Chief Justice John Roberts was untangling whether a statute's right to "personal privacy" extended to a *corporation's* privacy. AT&T argued that "personal" should take its definition from "person"—a defined term in the statute that expressly included companies. The Federal Communications Commission disagreed, pointing out that adjectives like "personal" can carry meanings distinct from their root word (here, "person"). Chief Justice Roberts uses surgical quotes from neighboring sections to illustrate that "personal" means something different.

> The phrase **"personal privacy"** first appeared in the FOIA exemptions in Exemption 6, enacted in 1966. . . . Exemption 6 covers **"personnel and medical files and similar files the disclosure of which would constitute a clearly unwarranted invasion of personal privacy."** . . . [W]e have

> regularly referred to that exemption as involving an "individual's right of privacy." . . . AT&T does not dispute that "identical words and phrases within the same statute should normally be given the same meaning"[29]. . . .
>
> In drafting [the relevant language here], Congress did not, on the other hand, use language similar to that in Exemption 4. Exemption 4 pertains to "trade secrets and commercial or financial information obtained from a person and privileged or confidential." [] This clearly applies to corporations—it uses the defined term "person" to describe the source of the information—and we far more readily think of corporations as having "privileged or confidential" documents than personally private ones.

Quote statutory language selectively. Use it to solidify your interpretation and provide clear guidance for readers.

4.2.3. Use Structure and History

A statute's structure, title, definitions, and sibling sections often include evidence you can use to support your rule interpretations.

The structure of a statute, much like the blueprint of a building, can offer essential insights into the intent and interpretation of the law. The organization and presentation of its content—titles, definitions, and the relationship between its various sections—are not just stylistic choices, but strategic ones that can reflect legislative intent.

Consider the distribution of requirements throughout the statute. Is a requirement repeated across multiple sections? If so, its omission might not be accidental, but a conscious decision by the legislature. By noting these patterns and anomalies, you can make arguments about the intended scope and application of the statute.

For example, suppose an early-filing requirement appears in every section of a statute except for the one under which a plaintiff is suing. This omission could support a compelling argument:

> The legislature did not insert this requirement in nine out of ten sections and simply miss one. The omission in this section confirms the requirement does not apply here.

Likewise, statutory titles and definitions can provide context. Titles give a broad overview of a statute's purpose, and definitions govern how terms are to be understood within that particular legal framework. Ignoring these elements in your analysis can lead to shallow understanding.

And don't forget sibling sections within the statute or in other analogous laws. Other legal frameworks can share a common objective and provide supporting context for your arguments. For example, these next legal writers analogize their case (about a former U.S. official allegedly violating the Constitution's "insurrection" clause) to lines of cases about mob bosses inciting violence.

---

[29] This is one of those interpretive canons we looked at in the last section.

> For obvious reasons, the First Amendment does not protect mob bosses who deliberately incite violence through thinly veiled language they know their audience will understand. *See, e.g., United States v. White*, 610 F.3d 956, 960-961 (7th Cir. 2010). So too here.[30]

Later in this same case, the writers also analogize to outside language to draw inferences about how to interpret the relevant language:

> This plain meaning is confirmed by Section 3's symmetry in pairing barred offices with excluded individuals. For instance, "Senator or Representative in Congress" (barred position) corresponds to "member of Congress" (excluded individual). Similarly, "any office, civil or military, under the United States" (barred position) corresponds to "officer of the United States" (excluded individual).

In this next example, from a sensational trademark case, the legal writer used an analogy to another provision in the same statute to illustrate a point about a provision the parties disputed. The writer shows us that an exception in this other provision would make no sense if an opponent's interpretation of the relevant provision prevailed:

> However wide the scope of the "noncommercial use" exclusion, it cannot include, as the Ninth Circuit thought, every parody or humorous commentary. **To begin to see why, consider the scope of another of the Lanham Act's exclusions**—this one for "[a]ny fair use." As described earlier,[31] the "fair use" exclusion specifically covers uses "parodying, criticizing, or commenting upon" a famous mark owner... [b]ut not in every circumstance. **Critically, the fair-use exclusion has its own exclusion: It does not apply when the use is "as a designation of source for the person's own goods or services."**... In that event, no parody, criticism, or commentary will rescue the alleged dilutor. It will be subject to liability regardless....
>
> **Given the fair-use provision's carve-out, parody (and criticism and commentary, humorous or otherwise) is exempt from liability only if not used to designate source. Whereas on the Ninth Circuit's view, parody (and so forth) is exempt always—regardless whether it designates source.**

A statute's structure, titles, definitions, and sibling sections can all unlock a trove of insights that will bolster your pitch.

Legislative history

Finally legislative history can be persuasive, too. Legislative history holds a unique place in statutory interpretation. This history, comprising various documents created during the passage of a law, like committee reports, early draft versions of the statute, floor debates, and more, can provide valuable insights into the intended meaning and application of the text.

[30] This fragment sentence was likely made popular by Chief Justice John Roberts, who has used it several times now. It's an example of using a final, short punch to emphasize a point.

[31] An example of making your documents self-explanatory: The writer is reminding you of key information from before that you'll need to make sense of things here. No need to flip backward to refresh your recollection.

Legislative history is like a time machine, transporting us back to the enactment and allowing us to explore the reasoning, debates, and compromises that shaped the final statute. Judges differ on what weight to give legislative history, but most agree that it offers valuable context and color.

You may uncover discussions or amendments during the committee markup that clarify the statute's intended application. Or you can point out the general intent of the statute is being served (or not served) by a particular interpretation. Like these next attorneys:

> The history and purpose of the CWA provide further confirmation. Congress's express purpose was to control the discharge of pollutants "at the source." S. Rep. No. 92-414, at 7 (1971). Petitioner would transfer the focus of the statute away from the source to the means by which pollutants reach navigable waters, with absurd results. If the CWA covers only pollutants added "directly" from a point source to navigable waters, then a polluter could design a pipeline that dumped pollutants into groundwater 10 feet away from a lake and avoid all liability when those pollutants were added to the lake.[32]

Another useful aspect of the history is how a statute or regulation has been amended over time. When a legislature changes a statute's wording, adds language, or removes language, there's a reason. And that reason can suggest how courts should interpret the statute now. Amendments often reflect a legislative response to prior interpretations, ambiguities, or evolving societal needs.

In this next passage, the amendments to a statute are used to make a bigger point about how the text should be applied today:

> In the past, several circuits interpreted the Americans with Disabilities Act to exclude disabilities that were "episodic," reasoning that these were not a "substantial limitation on any major life activity." But in the 2008 Amendments to ADA, the legislature **explicitly changed the definition of "disability" to include any "impairment that is episodic or in remission . . . if it would substantially limit a major life activity when active."**

Ask: Why was the statute enacted? What is its purpose? What decisions or compromises or changes did legislators make? This is all helpful guidance when urging readers to read the text from a certain angle. Also find cases that rely on the same history to give your analysis the flavor of case law rather than forcing your judge to rely on the legislative history alone.

Finally, consider how relevant agencies have interpreted or applied the text. Agencies are usually charged with enforcing and implementing laws, and their view can offer valuable expertise. Although not always binding, what agencies do and say about a law can be highly persuasive, especially if the agency has taken a long-standing approach.

[32] A fantastic hypothetical that pulls in the power of persuasive policy, too.

> [T]he Attorney General issued a memorandum to executive departments and agencies explaining that "personal privacy" in that exemption "pertains to the privacy interests of individuals." ... The exemption, the Attorney General noted, "does not seem applicable to corporations or other entities."

Statutory interpretation is a cornerstone of effective legal writing. Use every element of a statute—from its text and structure to the legislative history—to prepare your textual pitch.

4.3 Link Rules to Facts

You've crafted winning rule pitches that are built for your case. You've set up the background of the rule and homed in on the most important pieces. You've added guidance about how to view the rules in a way that charts a course through all the bad facts and bad law for your position. And you've guided readers through your authority so that they are ready to agree with you.

Now all that's left is to take everything you've done and apply it to the facts. Just make it easy for readers to connect the work you did in your rules. Let's say you crafted a rule pitch like this:

> When law enforcement (1) creates a situation that would cause any reasonable person to invite them into their home and (2) officers used their authority to create that situation in a way a general member of the public could not—there is no consent for purposes of the Fourth Amendment. ...

The pitch narrows in on concrete principles that will help readers. But now you need to create a bridge between those principles and your facts. Do this by making it obvious which application paragraphs are addressing each of the rules you mapped out in the pitch. That sounds simple and, really, it is. Often it's as easy as using quotes from cases or statutes. If busy readers will see the links, your job is done.

This next lawyer was defending people being mistreated at the U.S. border. When he got to applying his rule pitch to his facts, the writer smartly weaved quotes from his rules into his application. Let's start with a snippet of the lawyer's rule pitch.

> In *Lynch*, the Court ... reason[ed], ... excludable aliens ... are entitled under the due process clauses of the fifth and fourteenth amendments to be free of **gross physical abuse** at the hands of **state or federal officials.**

When the lawyer got around to applying this rule pitch to his facts, he made it easy for readers to see.

> In this case, **"gross physical abuse"** is alleged by **"state and federal officials."**

Using quotes to weave your rules and facts together like this is simple. And a few other techniques will help you link all the great work you did in explaining the rules with your case's facts. Let's see how.

A Quick Summary

Link rules logically. **Make it instantly obvious to readers where you are applying each of your rule principles. Repeat similar language and use clear signposting.**

Link characters, quotes, or facts. **Connect relevant characters or language from the authority to your factual situation.**

Make applications intuitive. **Consider using headings, hypotheticals, or other techniques to finish your application.**

4.3.1. Link Rules Logically

Linking rule and application is usually easy: Use the same words or phrases that you used when explaining your rule, or directly tell your reader which rule is being applied where.

In this next example from litigation against Elon Musk over his compensation plan at Tesla, the legal writers use the key language to link their rule pitch with the application:

> To show that the stockholder vote was **fully informed**, Defendants must establish that "stockholders were apprised of 'all material information' related to that transaction." . . .
>
> Plaintiff [here] advanced many arguments for why the stockholder vote was **not fully informed.**

This next passage inserts the same buzzwords from the rule discussion into the first sentence of the application paragraphs to link everything up.

> The state is liable when officers (1) "used their authority" to bludgeon their way into a home without a warrant, or (2) "created a situation so dire that would make any reasonable person invite them in." [Cite.] . . .
>
> Police **"used their authority" here**: they brandished their badges and called out "police!" . . .
>
> Police **"created a situation so dire that would make any reasonable person invite them in"** by shutting off the water residents needed to carry out even the most basic life activities. . . .

This next Supreme Court Justice first explains a rule pitch in clear terms: There's no sovereign immunity.

> In *Heinrich* we decided that sovereign immunity does not prohibit suits brought to require **state officials to comply with statutory or constitutional provisions.**[33] . . . Thus, we concluded that suits

[33] A great rule pitch distilling the useful principle from the case for readers.

> complaining of ultra vires actions may not be brought against a governmental unit, but must be brought against the allegedly responsible government actor in his official capacity....
>
> In this case, the Threaders did not plead that the Department and Commission officials exceeded the authority granted to them; rather, they challenged the constitutionality of the cosmetology statutes....

Outside of echoing the same telltale language, another option is to simply tell your reader which rules you are applying where:

> The first part of the rule, which requires that police use their authority, is met here given that the police brandished their badges and called out "police."
>
> The second requirement, that police create a situation that would force any reasonable person to invite them in, is met, too.

Forge the links between the great rule crafting you've done and the facts that will get your readers answers.

4.3.2. Link Characters, Quotes, or Facts

To enhance the link between rule and facts, consider connecting characters—a technique that aligns individuals in your case with those in prior ones. You might associate your client with the victor in a court decision or draw parallels between the opposition and a defeated party. Like this:

> The Hospital in *Granger* took the same steps that the County did here: Both hospitals put harassment policies in place, they enforced those policies, and they even fired folks under the policies. The County even went further than what was held to be enough in *Granger*, creating a harassment committee to efficiently field complaints.

Or like this:

> Jameson, like the Defendant, ignored the red flags and allowed the conduct to proceed. Jameson, like the Defendant, failed to step in even when authorities got involved.

Next, consider weaving in quotes or references to the key authority you offered readers earlier. These reminders will add credence to the application.

> Four negative reviews about the plaintiff—following 16 positive reviews before those—passes the hurdle of "at least marginally suggestive" set by this Court. After all, as this Court highlighted last year, "posting even mildly suggestive comments prompted the statute's creation in the first place."

Check out this next example. The legal writers weave the statutory language seamlessly into the first sentence applying the text to the facts:

> A bump stock enables a semiautomatic rifle to fire multiple shots **"by a single function of the trigger."** The function of a trigger is to allow some act by the shooter to initiate a firing sequence.

Another way to connect rules with their application involves contrasting or comparing facts from precedent with those in your case. Direct fact-to-fact comparisons can be potent, provided they are neatly outlined in your rule discussion so they are easily compared in the application.

> **Unlike *McNary*,** this is not a case in which meaningful judicial review likely would be thwarted by an inadequate factual record [given how different the cases are]. . . .

By marshaling out key facts from precedent, alongside your facts, you can make a compelling pitch that your case should come out the same way:

> **In both *Lafayette* and here,** a national emergency created the need to breach a contract. **In both cases,** the emergency was catastrophic and no one disputed that the breach was necessary to ensure folks were safe. **If the emergency was sufficient in *Lafayette*, it was here, too.**

Aligning characters, weaving in authoritative language, and contrasting key facts will forge a connection between the rules of law and the facts of your case.

4.3.3. Make Applications Intuitive

Avoid the fact-dump-and-conclusion tactic that many lawyers use. In other words, don't drop a load of factual details on readers only to eventually explain how they meet (or don't meet) your rules. Show how each fact fits with the rule as you progress. Instead of:

> In *Melody Systems*, the court was faced with a tech company operating out of Dallas. The company made switchboards for consumer devices and had done so for many years. Defects started popping up in the boards, and Melody ignored them. It continued ignoring them even when customer complaints flooded in by the thousands. ***Melody Systems* is thus distinguishable.**

Aim for a version that explains how each relevant fact matters as you go:

> *Melody Systems* isn't helpful here because **the company there ignored thousands of complaints and failed to act**; **here, Trailblazer Corp. acted within days after receiving just one complaint.** Melody created computer software and first ignored internal defect reports and then ignored thousands of complaints made on the company's website—**unlike Trailblazer, who started working on a solution to its defect after receiving a single complaint.**

Concise headings or bullets can help organize longer application sections:

> *Barringer acted intentionally when it blew up the deal.* [analysis of these facts]
>
> *Barringer acted intentionally when it refused to negotiate a solution.* [analysis of these facts]

Storytelling tools we explored in Chapter 3 can be just as powerful here given that you're again talking about the factual story (albeit with the rules mixed in).

> The question thus comes down to whether Mr. Terry acted reasonably, and there is little guidance from the case law about what reasonable looks like in this context. But Mr. Terry's situation is about as reasonable as it gets. **He was beaten senseless and hospitalized the day before the incident. On the day of the incident, he woke up to a burglar in his home, rummaging through his effects. Mr. Terry feared for his life, and reasonably so.**

Hypotheticals or examples can also do wonders for making final application points. Short examples can make arguments hit home; longer hypotheticals can engage readers even more. We return to these skills in Chapters 5 and 9, but it's a smart move to check your application sections for places where a quick hypothetical could help readers understand.

> [The class] is more than 1.5 million women, **a group that outnumbers the active duty military personnel in the Army, Navy, Marine Corps, and Air Force combined. The size of the putative class exceeds the entire population of at least 12 of the 50 states.**

> Petitioner's argument that the word "from" in the CWA means "delivered by" is not supported by any of the dictionaries it cites. It is also contrary to common usage. **When you receive a birthday card from your mother, that card is "from" your mother even if it is delivered by the mailman. So, too, are the pollutants "from" petitioner's wells even if they are delivered to navigable waters by way of groundwater.**

The application is where everything comes together for readers. You're making your final pitch about why the facts line up with the law in the way you say they do. Don't shirk this step.

4.4 Make Citations Useful

Citations matter. Love them or hate them, legal readers want them and, to be fair, they need them. After all, citations are how readers verify what you tell them about the law. But citations are also one of the easiest ways to clutter your writing. Choose your cites with care and make it clear how each supports what you say.

To see why your citation style matters, look at this snippet of legal writing, drowned by cites:

> Defendants contend that the exclusion of evidence relating to the plaintiff's prior legal actions is appropriate pursuant to Rule of Evidence 403, quoting with approval a series of cases that address the question of prejudicial impact versus probative value, including *Mercer v. City of Cedar Rapids*, 308 F.3d 840, 845 (8th Cir. 2002); *Collins v. Kibort*, 274 F.3d 377, 385 (7th Cir. 2001); and *Springs v. First Nat'l Bank of Cut Bank*, 835 F.2d 1293, 1297 (10th Cir. 1988). Further complicating matters, the plaintiff cites to an entirely different set of authorities to counter defendants' argument and to present an antithetical view of the standard for probative value, including *Sprint/United Mgmt. Co. v. Mendelsohn*, 552 U.S. 379, 384 (2008); *Huddleston v. United States*, 485 U.S. 681, 688-89 (1988); and *L.B. Foster Co. v. America Piles, Inc.*, 138 F.3d 81, 89-90 (2d Cir. 1998). This Court's role is now to untangle the threads of these cases and form a coherent rule to apply here.

Did readers need all these citations? Likely not. Here's a rewrite without the legalese:

> Defendants argue for the exclusion of evidence, citing Rule 403 and cases like *Mercer v. City of Cedar Rapids*, 308 F.3d 840, 845 (8th Cir. 2002). The plaintiff, conversely, offers cases like *Sprint/United Mgmt. Co. v. Mendelsohn*, 552 U.S. 379, 384 (2008). This Court's role is now to untangle the threads of these cases and form a coherent rule to apply here.

Citations are double-edged. Use them well, and they help. Lean on them too heavily, and your writing loses its voice. Here's how to find the balance.

A Quick Summary

Use citations to support. **Be clear about what *you* are saying and what *citations* are saying—and don't rely on citations to do the work for you.**

Use parentheticals with purpose. **Use parentheticals to bolster arguments, choose the right leading participle, and make sure each parenthetical adds value.**

4.4.1. Use Citations to Support

Let's start with the basics many legal writers forget. If you cite authority, you should either quote the source or directly paraphrase it (saying precisely the same thing in slightly different words). But lawyers constantly drop citations on readers without explaining how those citations support their points. Talk about a credibility killer. If your readers need to go look up a case to figure out how it supports the sentence you're writing, you've likely lost them.

All that said, often the cite's relationship to your sentence is already clear. As you set up the prep for your rule, you might share general principles that require a quick cite and nothing more. "**Plaintiff has the burden here. [cite]**" might be an example. But that would still be true only if the case said that in so many words—no inference needed.

In any event, when you start explaining your rule, especially an important one, don't rely on empty citations. Do the inferential reasoning for your reader and put it on display. Link what matters from the source to your points so obviously that even the busiest readers can't miss it.

Say you write this:

> Defendants need not touch the plaintiff's skin to carry out a battery—touching something laying on the plaintiff's body is enough. *Park v. Hoffman*, 324 F.3d 42, 44 (9th Cir. 2018).

When your reader pulls up page 44 of *Park*, it should say something like:

> "**A defendant contacts another by touching any item on the plaintiff's body.**" Different words, but identical meaning.

If your reader must infer—say, you assume that this was the court's reasoning based on the facts in the case, or you're reading between the lines of some language and what the court *didn't* say—don't just cite the case for that general proposition. Walk readers through what in that case led to your reasoning. One option is to explain your inference directly:

> **Given that the court in *Park* addressed a defendant who ripped a plate from the plaintiff's hand**, contact with the plaintiff's skin is not needed. 324 F.3d 42, 44 (9th Cir. 2018).

Your citation is not misleading because you're telling your reader what inferences you relied on. You did the inferential work for them. You could also interpret the rule in your own words then explain the supporting facts or quotes with citations.

> Contact with the plaintiff's skin is not needed. **In *Park*, the court addressed a defendant who ripped a plate from the plaintiff's hand.** 324 F.3d 42, 44 (9th Cir. 2018)....

Now you made clear where the inference came from. Credibility managed. But when your reader will not instantly know what a case said or why you cited it, explain it. So again, avoid using cites like this:

> The rule of plevin requires courts to inquire further when parties dispute the terms of an agreement. *Park v. Hoffman*, 654 F.2d 578 (2012).

Instead, explain the citation's purpose and operation plainly. You could use a parenthetical:

> The rule of plevin requires courts to inquire further when parties dispute the terms of an agreement. *Park v. Hoffman*, 654 F.2d 578 (2012) **(considering a contract dispute and explaining courts cannot stop at plain language when interpreting).**

A quote:

> The rule of Plevin requires courts to **"inquire at length into the parties' dispute on the terms of an agreement."** *Park v. Hoffman*, 654 F.2d 578 (2012).

Or a direct explanation:

> **In *Park*, the court required further inquiry into the terms of the agreement because the rule of plevin was raised in the complaint.** *Park v. Hoffman*, 654 F.2d 578 (2012).

You might have noticed we skipped citation "signals" here: *see, see also, but see, contra,* and the like. Signals tell readers why you are citing a source or how readers should view a source. Some signals can help. For example (pun intended), "*e.g.,*" is a quick shorthand for readers that a source is an example of a proposition you just made. But in most cases, you can simply explain to readers in your own words what matters: "For example, in X case . . .," and make it even clearer.

Signals can sometimes help if you are using them to avoid confusing readers. But many signals effectively tell readers to go do work: "*See* [source] and read it and figure out how it supports my statement." Use signals sparingly and only if they won't require readers to do heavy lifting.

Before moving on from citations, a few more quick tips. First, consider moving citations to the end of sentences whenever you can. Or describe them first with a shorthand. Consider putting the court, year, and other quality information directly in the text, if it's helpful. Don't expect that readers will read the cite—because many don't.

So instead of:

> In *Gonzala Orzhina v. Paleot Systems and More Inc.*, 321 U.S. 141, 155 (2024), the court held....

Try cutting the burdensome citation information from your affirmative text:

> **The Supreme Court held just last year that...** ***Gonzala Orzhina v. Paleot Systems and More Inc.***, 321 U.S. 141, 155 (2012).

In this next snippet, the useful information is delivered in everyday language and the citations are kept in their place (after the sentences). Most legal writers would have quoted the statutory language and dropped the cites into the initial sentence, too (*Texas Occupation Code Section 1602.002(a)(8) requires "..."*). But not this Texas Supreme Court Justice:

> In 2011, commercial threading became regulated in Texas when the Legislature categorized it as a practice of "cosmetology." *See* Tex. Occ. Code §1602.002(a)(8).... In order to legally practice cosmetology in Texas a person must hold either a general operator's license or, in certain instances, a more limited but easier-to-obtain esthetician license. *Id.* §1602.251(a).... Licensing requirements for general operators include completing a minimum of 1,500 hours of instruction in a licensed beauty culture school and passing a state-mandated test. *Id.* §1602.254.

Using too many citations is like using too many quotes. The good ones get drowned out by the lackluster. And that's particularly true with string cites. These often clutter your writing with little payoff. That said, with a purpose and used sparingly, they can sometimes help. Use the *occasional* string cite to:

1. Drive home that a key point is beyond reproach.
2. Provide quick examples of how a rule has been used.
3. Illustrate other points, like which jurisdictions adopted a rule.

These next lawyers needed readers to believe that courts "around the nation" supported a rule. So a sampling of cases from different jurisdictions did the trick:

> Every court around the nation to consider this issue agrees with this approach. ***E.g., Verus v. Samtel,* 312 F.3d 221 (9th Cir. 2002); *Jerico Binding Co. v. Pontiac,* 312 F.3d 221 (4th Cir. 2002); *Namesta v. Purtel Corp.,* 312 F.3d 221 (7th Cir. 2002); *Jameson LLC v. Orangtan Corp.,* 312 F.3d 221 (8th Cir. 2002).**

By explaining how your sources support your points, you'll gain your reader's trust. And nothing will serve you better than that.

4.4.2. Use Parentheticals with Purpose

Parentheticals are words, phrases, or sentences sandwiched between parentheses at the end of a legal citation. They typically tell readers how the authority supports whatever you wrote before the citation, such as offering an example of a rule being applied.

Adding a tidbit of insight or explanation in a parenthetical after a citation can do wonders for readers. You can amplify a critical point. Or provide illuminating examples. But too many thoughtless parentheticals make this tool worthless.

Let's start with legal writers using parentheticals wrong. First, parentheticals are not the place to deliver crucial points for the first time. Parentheticals convey *an aside*, something inessential. They can bolster, support, or clarify. But they are not the place to make your main points. If you've never made the transferred intent point in this next example, then don't expect your reader to see it crammed inside a parenthetical.

> Battery requires intent. *Jeremey v. Terry*, 324 F.3d 24 (2004) **(explaining that transferred intent is appropriate only in cases involving purposeful contact).**

Second, don't use parentheticals for tangential points that won't help your reader understand the law, the facts, or your reasoning. In other words, don't use parentheticals to pad your legal writing so that it looks more "supported." Readers won't be impressed.

Third, avoid lengthy parentheticals. If you have a lot to say, and it matters so much that you want to use up real estate, again, it needs to be explained with ordinary sentences. And relatedly, avoid repetitive parentheticals. If one parenthetical delivers your point, don't add them to every other cite for fun.

So when should you use parentheticals? First, you want to offer examples from different authorities, and listing them in full sentences would be excessive. You've made the point in your sentence and the citations merely offer some examples that drive your point home. You'll often start the citation with an "e.g.," here.

> Courts have held a prima facie case is stated in only the rarest of cases, like when a medical doctor has left a device inside of a patient. *See, e.g., James v. Taylor*, 86 F.2d 310 (9th Cir. 2020) **(pliers left in patient's chest cavity);** *Sampo v. Medical Executives*, 192 Cal. 21 (2017) **(medical tape left under the skin during stomach surgery).**

The main point—that the cases are rare and involve things being left inside patients—sits in the main sentence. The parentheticals emphasize the point with vivid examples.

Second, use parentheticals when you have an unusually critical point to make, and you want to amplify your voice with quotes or holdings. Use this tool sparingly.

> No court has required a plaintiff to show actual harm before bringing this claim. *Belfi v. Hariton Homes LLC*, 134 U.S. 45 (2006) (holding that no actual harm has "ever been required").

Third, you might want to subtly add in the force of a speaker but not make it obvious. Or, similarly, you want to let an authority suggest something that you don't want to say yourself. You might want to add emotion or persuasive force, but coming right out with it would not strike the right tone.

No court has required a plaintiff to show actual harm before bringing this claim. *Belfi v. Hariton Homes LLC*, 134 U.S. 45 (2006) **(noting that the U.S. Supreme Court has sanctioned counsel for ignoring this rule).**

Under Rule 9(B) of the Local Rules of Appellate Procedure, an appellant's brief may not exceed 30 pages. *Jerry v. Tarkanian*, 29 U.S. 329 (2000) **(refusing to address nine claims because they were "contained in the portion of appellant's brief that exceeds the page limit under Loc. R. 9(B)").**[34]

Fourth, use parentheticals if you are citing authorities that readers otherwise won't instantly understand. If you cite a case or other authority and it won't be obvious how it supports your sentences, a parenthetical is always a safe bet. Because the last thing you want is to force readers to look up authorities for themselves.

But now let's assume you've decided you have a good reason to drop in a parenthetical. Let's finish with some final tips for crafting the perfect one.

If you'd like to use the traditional participle format (beginning the parenthetical with an "-ing" word) then choose one with a goal in mind. Each offers a different flavor. For example, (**holding** that the plaintiffs were in the wrong . . .) is not as strong as (**rebuking** plaintiffs for . . .).

You've got a long menu of participles to choose from, and each will focus your parenthetical points. Here is just a sampling that do more than the classic "stating" and "holding":

Admitting
Adopting
Affirming
Applying
Approving
Asserting
Authorizing
Awarding
Balancing
Broaching
Cautioning
Charging
Commending
Classifying
Collecting
Comparing
Conferring
Contrasting
Deferring
Declining
Differentiating
Dismissing
Defining
Denying
Dividing
Endorsing
Equating
Expanding
Excluding
Extending
Justifying
Highlighting
Illustrating
Interpreting
Insisting
Invalidating
Focusing
Listing
Negating
Paralleling
Prohibiting
Questioning
Reinforcing
Rebutting
Refusing
Refuting
Recalling
Rejecting
Reconciling
Renouncing
Redefining
Reversing
Reexamining
Resolving
Signaling
Synthesizing
Taking
Tracing
Uncovering
Underscoring
Upholding
Yielding

[34] The legal writers allude to cases that struck claims altogether to drill home their point.

Examples and full-sentence quotes don't require a participle. And these sorts of parentheticals can be a great way to bolster your main sentences.

> Courts have allowed delay only in extreme cases of neglect. *See, e.g., Terry v. Paralta*, 87 F.2d 370 (9th Cir. 2021) **(minor abandoned for three days);** *Sorrento v. Torolina*, 151 Cal. 56 (2019) **(minor left to supervise four other children for two weeks).**

> *James v. Morel Medical LLC*, 255 F. Supp. 2d 55 (Nev. 1999) **(holding that a golf cart is not a "vehicle" because it is not a "combustible-fuel" machine).**

A final point about citations. Do whatever you need to so that readers never feel you misrepresented a source. If you misrepresent facts or authority, good luck getting your reader to listen to you again.[35] Double-check for any citation or statement that could even be ambiguous. Don't even take the chance, like this next attorney did. The case he cited specifically said that it did not reach a jurisdictional issue but he suggested it did anyway.

> The *Borsick* court held there was clearly jurisdiction where a defendant resided in a different state.

The court later called out the attorney on it. Rest assured this credibility hit affected the case's outcome. Even if a court doesn't notice, you can bet your opponents will. Look at how these next legal writers used a convenient omission by an opposing party to bolster their argument.

> The SEC responds that "equitable remedies often have a deterrent effect, [but are not necessarily penalties]," quoting *Hecht Co. v. Bowles*, 321 U.S. 321, 329 (1944), as saying that "[t]he historic injunctive process was designed to deter." **But the SEC leaves out half the Court's sentence: "The historic injunctive process was designed to deter, *not to punish*."**[36]

Parentheticals should be deployed surgically. Use them to enhance crucial points, clarify complex rulings, and subtly shift the tone of your authority—without bloating your main arguments.

Level Up Your Law with Technology

Because the rules tend to be dense and complicated, technology can help in several ways here. It can help us organize all our authorities and research, it can help us quickly understand an area of law, and it can help outline and draft your explanations of the rules themselves.

[35] We will return to how important your tone and credibility is in Chapter 5. But in short: If your reader doesn't like you, you're not likely to persuade them of anything—regardless of what law or facts you give them.

[36] The legal writers figured out how to use an opposing case to their own advantage here. If you have enough authority evidence tools in your toolbelt, you can find an angle that will reframe just about any of your opponent's cases, at least somewhat.

GAI tools: This is another part of your writing process where GAI tools can make your life easier. Use GAI to:

- Brainstorm simpler ways to explain a rule. Feed a GAI tool your concepts about the law and ask it to help break it down for a sixth grader, step by step. Ask for ideas and inspiration in explaining a rule concept or case.
- Collaborate on better ways to organize your rule discussion. Ask a GAI tool for ideas in breaking down your rules into smaller parts or otherwise spoon-feeding complex concepts.
- Get help with editing complicated portions of your rule section to spot mistakes and remove unneeded legalese or clutter: "Edit my legal discussion in this brief to be easier for readers to understand." Or, "Highlight any legal jargon or overly technical terms in this paragraph of my rule section. Suggest simpler alternatives for each."
- Avoid using GAI to retrieve cases, rule statements, or similar information—without fully verifying it. And even then, you are better off using a GAI-powered research tool made for this sort of work, like Westlaw or Lexis.
- Ask to test your legal explanations: "Review my arguments about the law and provide at least five key reasons why I am wrong. Be specific."

Research and note management tools: Thorough research forms the backbone of any strong legal argument. But managing multiple sources can be a headache. Research management tools like Evernote, OneNote, and Mendeley provide a solution. They allow you to store, organize, and annotate cases, statutes, and other legal materials in one place. One powerful feature is tagging, which lets you label key sections of your research for easy retrieval later.

AI-powered legal research platforms: AI-powered legal research platforms like Westlaw AI and Lexis+ AI carve out a path to expedite the research and rule-writing process. Many legal research providers are now incorporating GAI so you can quickly get a summary of a key rule drafted for you—straight from the research. Advanced legal research tools also offer a host of visual and advanced features that could fill a book all on their own. Investing here is worth it, guaranteed.

Outlining and mind-mapping tools: Once the research is complete, figuring out how to structure all those thoughts can be challenging. This is where outlining and mind-mapping tools come into play. For instance, applications like XMind, MindMeister, and Microsoft Visio offer visual means to generate, visualize, structure, and classify ideas.

Organizational or individual knowledge management: These digital concierges curate, organize, and retrieve the troves of data, research, and precedent that your organization has created or assembled from prior matters. Use these to give yourself a jumpstart on similar analysis and argument structures.

Rule visualization software: This is a niche but powerful category. Tools like Neota Logic and BRYTER allow you to build decision trees or interactive rule explainers.

Practice these techniques and technologies with Write.law's exercises and checklists, plus other resources at www.levelupyourlegalwriting.com

5

Level Up Your Persuasion

> The best and most beautiful things in the world cannot be seen or even touched. They must be felt with the heart."—Helen Keller

We've already unpacked some potent tools. Distilling takeaways will create instant understanding for readers, and making sense quickly is persuasion gold. Storytelling will persuade. And designing your rule discussions to spoon-feed complicated ideas to busy readers will persuade, too.

The law is often framed as a bastion of logic and reason. We simply "call balls and strikes," Chief Justice John Roberts once famously said. But analyzing legal issues—and more important, making legal decisions—is as much about the heart as it is about the mind. In this chapter, we take persuasion head-on by engaging with your readers' hearts: their emotions, their values, and their beliefs.

Using brain scans, researchers revealed that thinking about legal questions first triggers the regions of our brains that process emotions—before we even turn on our rational-processing thinking centers. In other words, we apply emotions before we apply our lawyerly logic.[1] So consider how your writing will touch readers in the *feels*.

- **Frame and prime:** Several tools can help you make a point feel more favorable depending on how you frame it or whether you prime readers before.

[1] Catherine J. Cameron & Lance N. Long, The Science Behind the Art of Legal Writing, 2nd ed. (2019). Or consider the example of Elliot, a man who suffered damage to the emotion center of his brain. Elliot makes all his decisions based only on reason. But it turns out that being entirely rational is entirely useless. After the injury, Elliot was kind, smart, and articulate, but he could no longer make even the smallest decisions with his emotions out of reach. In short, emotions are an essential part of decision-making. Antonio R. Damasio, Descartes' Error: Emotion, Reason, and the Human Brain (Avon Books 1995).

- **Weave themes and policy:** Integrate meaningful themes that resonate with readers. And enhance your points with well-placed policy considerations that support your narrative.
- **Maintain a credible tone:** Cultivate a tone that builds rapport with your readers while gently guiding them to the favorable outcome.
- **Persuasively counter opposing views:** When addressing opposing points, do so sharply but respectfully, neutralizing biases and emotional reactions that could detract from your argument.

Before digging into these techniques, let's see an example of what this "emotional work" can do. In a sensational complaint Disney filed against Florida's governor over a governance dispute, the company weaved in a theme about vindicating rights for smaller companies and managed to pull in free speech, too.

> Disney finds itself in this regrettable position because it expressed a viewpoint the Governor and his allies did not like. Disney wishes that things could have been resolved a different way. **But Disney also knows that it is fortunate to have the resources to take a stand against the State's retaliation—a stand[2] smaller businesses and individuals might not be able to take when the State comes after them for expressing their own views. In America, the government cannot punish you for speaking your mind.**

Next, Disney triggers favorable emotions by tapping into the historical roots the company planted in the state over decades.

> The State of Florida has flourished in the years since **Walt Disney[3] himself surveyed many acres of swampland in 1963 and dreamed of the possibility of Walt Disney World**. Florida's elected officials have long understood how consequential Disney is to the State's economy and future, just as **Disney has sought to be a constructive, responsible, and charitable Florida resident."**

In this final snippet, Disney shared its planned future investments in the community. The reason was obvious. Disney wanted readers to feel aligned with the company going forward.

> **Disney plans to invest over $17 billion** in Walt Disney World[4] over the next decade. The Company estimates that those investments will **create 13,000 new Disney jobs in that same 10-year time period....**

You can tap into your readers' emotions and values like this, too. Let's see how.

[2] Echoing "stand" connects the two sentences and shows off a style tool we look at again in Chapter 9.
[3] A great use of characters to animate the story (pun intended).
[4] Why name where it will invest and not just "in the community"? Because this detail will gain sympathy points with readers. Who doesn't love Disney World?

5.1 Frame and Prime

Psychologist Elizabeth Loftus pioneered the study of framing in law. *Framing* means presenting information in a way that emphasizes certain aspects over others to change how readers understand content. Framing is about shaping details, language, and angles to influence what readers see.

One of Loftus's experiments showed that changing a single word when questioning eyewitnesses about a car accident changed how they perceived—and even remembered—the accident. If you ask witnesses "Did you see *the* broken headlight?" you'll get more witnesses to say *yes* than you would if you ask them "Did you see *a* broken headlight?" This difference in responses persists even in scenarios where no cars in the accident actually had a broken headlight.

For another example, more people will decide to have surgery if they are told that the "survival rate is 90 percent" than if told that the "mortality rate is 10 percent"—even though both mean the same thing. Likewise, telling people you'll institute a *surcharge* for late payments gets more people to pay than telling people they get a *discount* for paying early.

Priming involves sharing facts when you first introduce a topic that will put readers in a favorable headspace for when they read more about this same topic later. You subtly expose readers to stories that trigger thoughts or feelings that you think will make readers more receptive to your arguments. For example, you can prime in a heading by mentioning a fact that will build sympathy for your client as readers then enter into the section that follows.

> A. The plaintiff **lived in the home without water or heat for months** before filing the complaint seeking restitution.

Both techniques are game-changers for legal writers. Here is an example of framing a rule favorably to boost the plaintiff's perspective. The writers simply use a modifier to make the rule sound easier to meet:

> **So long as** the plaintiff includes allegations supporting the elements of her claim, she wins.

And here is a rule framed for the defendant on the same issue, using a different modifier to make the rule feel harder to meet:

> **If** the plaintiff fails to allege a **single** element of her claim, her claim must fail.

Now look at priming and framing in the hands of a persuasion expert. Nothing is pushy. But the details dropped along the way make you want to agree that the licensing requirements are unreasonable before you're even asked to.

> [S]everal ... commercial eyebrow thread[ers] ... assert that, as applied to them, Texas's licensing statutes and regulations[5] violate the Texas Constitution[]. **They claim that most of the 750 hours of training Texas requires** for a license to practice commercial eyebrow threading are not related to health and safety or what threaders actually do. The State concedes **that over 40% of the required hours are unrelated**, but maintains that the licensing requirements are **nevertheless constitutional**.

[5] Notice the writer didn't list all the statutory numbers and sections here. Readers don't need that yet. Those extraneous specifics would just clutter the writing.

Describing the training as an overwhelming "750 hours" stacks the odds against Texas, as does the state's admission that "over" 40 percent of the time is irrelevant to the job. Strategically placed modifiers, *most* and *nevertheless*, push the points in a favorable direction.

Luckily, framing and priming like this is easy with a few tools at your fingertips.

A Quick Summary

Play the angles. Use language to reframe how readers see the same fact or point. Choose whether the glass is half full or half empty.

Use modifiers to frame. Modifiers are words or phrases that add detail or descriptions to other words or phrases. Use modifiers to make a point feel more or less favorable.[6]

Use dependence and independence. Use main clauses to highlight main points. Put less favorable or subtle points into dependent clauses and phrases.

Narrow the field. Clear away undisputed points or distractions to focus readers on narrow questions or issues you care about.

Frame the negative. Draw a legal line in the sand by showing readers the opposite of your affirmative points.

Prime with specifics. Choose specific details that will put readers into a favorable headspace.

Prime with context. When helpful, rather than lead with your primary point, weave a tale first to give readers the right context for your main course.

5.1.1. Play the Angles

Maybe you've heard the adage about the glass being half full or half empty? You're either a glass-half-full person, or a glass-half-empty person.[7] The difference is all in your perspective.

The same is true for many facts and points we deal with as lawyers. The language you use to describe something can change how people perceive it. The best legal writers are those who can look at a scary-looking fact or quote from a case and come up with ways to see it from a not-so-scary angle.

[6] We revisit modifiers in Chapter 8 and cover the grammar pitfalls they sometimes create.

[7] There's no consensus on where this idiom comes from. But an early example is a speech by Ronald Reagan. The American Presidency Project, "The President's News Conference," February 21, 1985, accessed February 27, 2024, https://www.presidency.ucsb.edu/documents/the-presidents-news-conference-956.

Imagine you're suing a landlord for failing to keep an apartment maintained, which caused the place to collapse and injure your client. The landlord testifies that he has "extensive experience" as a contractor and uses that experience to ensure his apartments are in the best shape. What's another way we could frame the landlord's experience? Perhaps:

> Given the landlord's "extensive experience" as a contractor, the signs of wear in the complex should have been even more obvious.

Some context for this next example from a harassment case: An attorney pointed out in a motion that their client, a major corporation, enacted extensive anti-harassment policies the prior year. The opposing attorney took that seemingly favorable fact and reframed it:

> That Merrix enacted a new "industry-setting" harassment policy in June of 2023 confirms that management knew about the harassment being inflicted on workers like Ms. Stein up until then. Ms. Stein reported the most serious incident within weeks of this new policy being rolled out.[8] That a company instituted an expensive new policy after years of inaction leaves no doubt that Merrix knew how serious the harassment was.

You can't help but love this next lawyer's effort to reframe a late filing. Instead of laziness, it was hard work that led to the delay.

> Although the plaintiff's response missed the deadline by minutes, that was because plaintiff's counsel chose to review each of the thousands of pages of documents provided by the defendant's counsel only a week ago.

Or look at this next attorney, who reframes a company's high turnover into a positive.

> Although plaintiffs suggest that Delson has a high turnover rate because of mismanagement, it's actually because Delson actively works to support its people in lateraling to other companies.

Let's now look at some more targeted methods to frame and prime.

5.1.2. Use Modifiers to Frame

Use *modifiers* to change your reader's perspective. Simply choose a modifier that will focus readers on the part of the sentence or paragraph most favorable (or least favorable, depending on your goal). Modifiers that broaden or narrow, like "only" and "unless," are an easy place to start.

> The government need **only** show a single mistake to win.
>
> *becomes*
>
> **Unless** the government can show a bona fide mistake, it loses.

[8]The writer might have gotten more persuasion out of the sentence by focusing readers on Merrix carrying out actions: "Merrix rolled out its new policy weeks after Ms. Stein reported the harassment."

Different modifiers will help add weight to different concepts. Simply insert the modifier that will highlight the characteristic you want to emphasize. Some common modifiers include:

Narrow or isolate: only, unless, never, very rarely, nearly always, even if, always

Stress conditionality: except when, only if, in the event that, provided that, subject to

Show trends: increasing, growing, accelerating, escalating, ongoing, persistent

Highlight a lack of supervision: unchecked, unmonitored, unrestricted, unregulated, unsupervised

Create a sense of scope or certainty: widespread, pervasive, undeniable, clear, indisputable, certain

Convey urgency: immediate, urgent, critical, pressing, essential

Convey credibility: measurable, quantifiable, significant, documented, established

Convey context: recent, outdated, evolving, unprecedented, historical

Compare: greater, lesser, disproportionate, unequal, inconsistent

Emphasize probability: inevitably, probably, likely, almost certainly

Suggest necessity: necessarily, must, absolutely

Stress rarity: seldom, rarely, uncommonly

Emphasize practicality: practically, feasibly, logically, realistically, viably

Stress continuity: continuously, persistently, endlessly, increasingly, relentlessly

You can use modifiers to shift readers' perspective on the facts and on the law.

> Of the four elements, the **essential** one is irreparable harm.

> The defendant's **unmitigated** harm remains **unchecked** to this day.

> **Unrestricted** data collection practices threaten consumer privacy and should be halted under the Data Act.

5.1.3. Use Dependence and Independence

Put important information in independent clauses (the main clause in each sentence). Put points you want to deemphasize or be more subtle about in dependent clauses and phrases (groups of words that modify or rely on your main clause).

Readers are trained to focus on the main subject and action in each sentence. What you put in the dependent parts will be less on display.

> **Although the court never ruled on notice,** it stated that "notice was surely lacking in this case."

> **Although the court mentioned notice may be lacking,** the court never ruled on this issue at all.

What should go first, dependent or independent? Well, what do you want readers to know first? The important thing or the less so? If you're conceding something and then putting it into perspective, go with dependent first.

> **Although the defendant has two convictions,** he saved the prison guard from certain death.

If you prefer to lead with the thrust of your sentence and then offer less important or subtle coloring, start with the independent:

> **The court ruled every time for defendant,** although it never reached two tangential issues.

> **The jury found the defendant guilty beyond a reasonable doubt,** even if only on circumstantial evidence.

> The law clearly mandates a minimum sentence for this offense, **although the judge may consider mitigating circumstances.**

We return to sentence structure in Chapter 7. But don't forget the persuasiveness of placing the right information in the right place.

5.1.4. Narrow the Field

Discard points that you suspect will distract readers before getting to your important points. Maybe another party mentioned something that will bother your audience. Maybe unhelpful atmospherics are swirling around the case. Perhaps an opponent does not dispute some things, so you can clear the way for what matters.

This next lawyer clears away every piece of chaff to reveal the simple question at the bottom.

> The district court **did not dispute** the general rule under *Briggs* that when a federal court of appeals directs entry of judgment without providing instructions on prejudgment interest, the district court lacks the authority to award such interest. **Nor did it dispute** that this Court's mandate in this case never provided anything like the kind of explicit instructions that are required under *Briggs* to award prejudgment interest. **Instead, the district court gave only one reason for refusing to follow the clear teaching of *Briggs* and its progeny....**

Or check out how these next legal writers narrow the field by checking off a long list of actions not taken and issues not argued.

> Plaintiffs bring Missouri common-law claims in an American court against American companies responsible for the lead emissions that poisoned them. **The political branches have not barred those claims. Congress enacted no statute preempting them. Nor did it pass any law stripping[9] U.S. courts of jurisdiction over them. The Executive Branch negotiated no treaty blocking those claims. And the State Department repeatedly has declined to object to them.... So Defendants ask this Court to do what the political branches have not....**

[9]This visual verb creates a memorable image that bland options like "abrogated" wouldn't.

Finally, federal Judge Bibas shows how to narrow the field by taking every relevant argument out of the running, leaving a losing one behind.

> To start, note what it does not allege: fraud. Indeed, in oral argument before the District Court, Campaign lawyer Rudolph Giuliani conceded that the Campaign "doesn't plead fraud." [] He reiterated: "If we had alleged fraud, yes, but this is not a fraud case."[10]

By setting aside distractions, we pave the way for a persuasive argument built on the principles that truly govern our case.

5.1.5. Frame the Negative

With this tactic, you're drawing a line in the legal sand— explaining what a concept *is not* to clarify what it *is*. Great legal writers do it all the time. Look at how this next legal writer uses the first words of his brief to shift the legal horizon, allowing light to shine on what matters.[11]

> **This is not a telemarketing case.**[12] Telemarketers do not care who answers the phone, as long as someone answers the phone. They rely on random or sequential phone numbers to harvest their customers. **List-based calling**[13] **is [] different. It matters who answers the phone because the caller is looking for a specific person. . . .**
>
> **The economics of telemarketing depend on chance.**[14] Some percentage of people will succumb to the high-pressure sales pitch based on statistics. This model is successful so long as enough people (anyone)[15] are called. **In contrast, the economics of list-based calling depend on the successful location of a specific person.** Whether that person owes a debt, has engaged with customer service, or has used a particular product, there is information to be gained only by talking to the right person.

The following example similarly juxtaposes what a case does not involve to highlight what it does involve.

> **We are not dealing with property law, contract law, or other fields where stability and predictability may be crucial.** We are dealing with torts where there can be little, if any, justifiable reliance and where the rule of stare decisis is admittedly limited.

---

[10] The quotes allow the writer to emphasize the "fraud" again and again—the lack of which is a theme throughout the document.

[11] Thanks to lawyer Greg White for submitting this sample as part of Write.law's Level Up Your Writing competition!

[12] A short opening sentence projects confidence and sets the tone. This is an example of when distilling the paragraph's takeaway wouldn't have been as effective.

[13] A great use of characters and perspective. When talking about the unfavorable folks, they are "telemarketers." But when calling about the practices this writer is representing, we shift to the more abstract "list-based calling" or "callers."

[14] Ending the sentence on "chance" emphasizes this concrete word.

[15] Parentheses make this point more subtle.

This next legal writer makes clear that the sorts of facts in his case were far below the relevant defamation standard by starting with the negative side of the rule.

> But what exactly does Mr. Bustos have to do to show that the statement he challenges is "false"? Under Colorado law, much as elsewhere, **it is not enough for the plaintiff to show that the defendant got some innocuous detail wrong; the plaintiff must show that the challenged defamatory statement is but material.**

Framing the negative is a spotlight that can highlight the contours of your points. This tactic works at its best when a legal concept risks distortion, is hard to understand, or falls outside what readers might be used to.

5.1.6. Prime with Specifics

One of the best priming tools is to use the specific details that aim toward an emotional goal. Prime readers with more moving specifics to convey important points with emotional depth. Summarize or skim past less helpful points with few, if any, specifics. Remember, though, that avoiding unfavorable facts altogether is not advisable if opposing parties mention them—the tactic here is to briefly touch on them while spending more time on the favorable specifics.

In both these examples, the legal writers are conveying that an extension was asked for—but each use different specifics to lead into that point.

> **The plaintiff violated the deadline six times** before asking for an extension.
>
> *becomes*
>
> The plaintiff sought an extension to this deadline **weeks before it was due.**

Here's another example of selective specifics. The legal writers quote at length the portion of the statute beneficial to them (a safe harbor making service providers immune from lawsuits) while skimming over the portion that required companies like theirs to remove "objectionable" content.

> To address this dilemma, Congress enacted the Communications Decency Act [which states,] **"No provider or user of an interactive computer service shall be treated as the publisher or speaker of any information provided by another information content provider."** Section 230(c)(2) [also] **encourages the removal of "objectionable" content.**

The writers skim across the less favorable section (Section 230(c)(2)) that discusses when companies like YouTube should take down unlawful videos. This isn't an accident. Spending more time on the favorable specifics subtly suggests that readers should focus on these facts.

In this next example from litigation against Tesla founder Elon Musk, the legal writer describes Musk's compensation plan using specifics that shape the reader's perspective:

> **With a $55.8 billion maximum value and $2.6 billion grant date fair value,** the plan is the **largest potential compensation opportunity ever observed in public markets by multiple orders of magnitude—250 times larger** than the contemporaneous median peer compensation plan and **over 33 times larger than the plan's closest comparison, which was Musk's prior compensation plan....**
>
> The defendants were thus left with the unenviable task of proving the fairness of the **largest potential compensation plan in the history of public markets.**

Here are a few more excellent examples of framing points by leveraging specific details, particularly when contrasted with other specific details.

> The defendant ran up $80 in costs on a $200 job.[16]

> The defendant ran up a tab equal to 40 percent of the entire job's costs.

> USPS receives over 10,000 emails a week and it manages to answer nearly 99 percent of them, even though, like every company, mistakes happen.

5.1.7. Prime with Context

Finally, provide readers with context that will put them in a favorable mindset leading into your critical points. Sometimes it can help to lead with some priming details that will make readers more sympathetic to your main salvo.

These next legal writers share details about how small and understaffed a company is before getting to the relevant point that they made a mistake.

> **Westco is a small company and all its operations and personnel are within Nevada. It does not have the [human] power or ability to monitor companies operating on the other side of the country.** As soon as Westco's CFO noticed the defendant's product online, Westco took action.

Or take this following paragraph. Justice Kagan wanted to put readers in a headspace where they viewed a certain statute—the Armed Career Criminal Act—as only concerned about regulating people with guns. This primed them for her eventual point, which was that the statute should be read narrowly to avoid crimes when no weapons are involved.

> Congress enacted [the Armed Career Criminal Act], **as its full name makes clear,** to address the **"special danger"** associated with **"armed career criminals."** A **"small percentage of repeat offenders,"** Congress found, commit a "large percentage" of all violent crimes. And when a **habitual violent offender carries a gun,** he poses a serious risk of wreaking harm. As his prior convictions reveal, he is "the kind of person who," when armed, "might deliberately point the gun and pull the trigger."

[16] Whenever you mix different details in the same sentence or paragraph, ask whether they mix well. Some of the most poignant points are made by comparing or contrasting details like this.

These next legal writers built up how important and well-regarded an SEC enforcement mechanism was before delivering a pitch that the opposing party was trying to disarm it.

> For nearly a half-century, the Securities and Exchange Commission [] has enforced a requirement that a publicly traded company disclose management's analysis of important developments facing the company to investors. That narrative analysis (required by a regulation referred to as Item 303)[17] **supplies a vital tool investors use in assessing a company's financial results and business prospects. . . .**
>
> **Petitioners seek to negate that important enforcement tool. . . .**

Framing and priming are potent tools. With a little practice, they can become the secret weapons of your writing arsenal.

5.2 Weave Themes and Policy

Themes are broad, overarching concepts that resonate with readers on a personal level. *Policy* reflects your legal points' broader implications, appealing to values like fairness, efficiency, or public good.

The work you do weaving in themes and policy is never wasted. Your readers are human. They care about the real world. The real consequences—what this case is about beneath the citations and statutes. In *The New York Times v. OpenAI*, the Times wanted to make the case about more than seeking a paycheck from a big tech company (even though the Times admitted it tried to settle for cash before bringing the case). So the legal writers made it all about protecting the public's access to information.

> The Times **provides a service that has grown even more valuable to the public by supplying trustworthy information, news analysis, and commentary.**[18] Defendants' unlawful use of The Times's work to create artificial intelligence products that compete with it **threatens The Times's ability to provide that service.**

Or take the themes woven into the briefing by Microsoft and OpenAI in the same case. First, OpenAI uses its AI "transformer" structure as a theme in briefing about "transformative" fair use, a copyright doctrine.

> It is the essence of what copyright law considers **transformative**—and fair—use: A program called a **"transformer"** evaluates massive amounts of text, converts that text into trillions of constituent parts, discerns the relationships among all of them, and yields a natural language machine that can respond to human prompts.

OpenAI's brief also consistently weaves in a theme of beneficial, world-changing technology.

[17] The writers helpfully give readers the legal reference without distracting from the main sentence.

[18] A great use of examples to make a bigger point. Listing the different contributions the journalists make says more than a generic description like "valuable news" would.

> The artificial intelligence tool known as ChatGPT is many things: **a revolutionary technology with the potential to augment human capabilities, fostering our own productivity and efficiency; an accelerator for scientific and medical breakthroughs; a mechanism for making existing technologies accessible to more people; an aid to help the visually impaired navigate the world; a creative tool that can write sonnets, limericks, and haikus;[19] and a computational engine that reasonable estimates posit may add trillions of dollars of growth across the global economy**.

This next sample from Judge Andrew Gordon delivers a rousing policy call to support his analysis of why police can't be allowed to cut off internet access as part of a ruse to search someone's home without a warrant.

> [Policy] concerns also weigh against allowing the government to use a ruse of this type. Cable, telephone, and internet services are widely used in America. . . . Permitting the government to create the need for the occupant to invite a third party into [their] home would effectively allow the government to conduct warrantless searches of the vast majority of residences and hotel rooms in America. **The government need only disrupt the phone, cable, internet, or some other "nonessential" service, and reasonable people will opt to invite a third party onto their property to repair it, unwittingly allowing government agents into the most private spaces to view and record whatever and whomever they see.**

The law matters. But giving readers familiar themes and relevant policies will help them relate what you're conveying to their own life. If you frame your case as being about situations your readers recognize, they will get invested.

A Quick Summary

Use persuasive themes. **Themes animate your writing with a common thread, stitching ideas together. Determine the most compelling and powerful themes and incorporate them into documents.**

Use persuasive policy. **Policy includes all the reasons a decision-maker should side with you that don't sprout from the controlling law. Understand your policy options and choose policies to bolster your legal points.**

5.2.1. Use Persuasive Themes

If you've ever read (or watched the many movie adaptations of) *Frankenstein*, you probably spotted the theme without much effort. We can't judge someone by their looks or where they came from. Frankenstein turns out to be a sympathetic fellow rather than the monster he appears at first glance.

[19] This is also a great example of how choice details can convey powerful and complex points. The breadth of things covered here, from writing haikus to helping the visually impaired, conveys how wide-ranging the benefits are.

Or take a similar theme a bit closer to home for us legal lovers: Atticus Finch, the famous fictional lawyer representing the downtrodden. "You never really understand a person until you consider things from his point of view. . . . Until you climb inside of his skin and walk around in it."[20] On point, Atticus, especially for a legal writer who wants readers to see a client from a different angle.

Themes are simple concepts that resonate with people. They are moral, emotional, or practical principles that tie some or all of a document together. You might use small themes for an individual motion or document. Like that the opposing party is disingenuous and opposing your request only to delay. But you should also have a case-wide theme: a more overarching story you return to throughout your documents and presentations.

Your theme for a discrimination case might be "too greedy to care about employees" or "prioritizing money over people." It's not a whole story that settles the case, but an emotional pull that, regardless of the law, makes your audience *want* to rule for your client.

Often, a theme will become obvious after you've worked on a case long enough. In this next example, the legal writers weaved in a theme about "promises" throughout the brief. The theme is about sticking to your commitments—something we can all understand.

> **Promises are made to be kept.** That's especially so when Congress makes the *promise* through duly enacted legislation and the U.S. Army Corps of Engineers ("the Corps") doubles down on the *promise* through rulemaking. The **promise** here was that water sources that farmers in the Everglades Agricultural Area ("EAA") rely on to grow their crops can't be taken from them without first replacing those sources.
>
> Congress made the **promise** in the Water Resources Development Act of 2000. . . .
>
> The Corps **carried forward the promise** made in WRDA 2000 when. . . .

In this next example, the legal writer opened their brief by delivering the theme in no uncertain terms: Don't be fooled by the technical jargon; the legal issues are simple.

> **The science underlying this case may appear complex, but the rules of decision are Administrative Law 101.** Congress specified that proteins and analogous products must be regulated as biological products. FDA promulgated a definition of the term "protein" that it then refused to apply as written to Ipsen's product, Somatuline Depot. Had it done so, Somatuline Depot would be regulated as a biological product. FDA also refused to regulate Somatuline Depot as "analogous" to a protein by adopting an interpretation that read "analogous" out of the statute entirely.

Look at how this legal writer sets up the theme in a single sentence, from the briefing in a case against comedian John Oliver.

> **This case is about Plaintiff Robert E. [] Murray not liking a television program and somehow believing that is a legally actionable offense.**

[20] Harper Lee, To Kill a Mockingbird 33 (1960).

Here's a brilliant example from the *Facebook v. ConnectU* case.

> **The plotline of this controversy is all too familiar: Wunderkind entrepreneur conceives of a transformative business and propels it to meteoric success, but failed rivals insist they thought up the idea first and demand all the profits.**

This next example hearkens back to the SEC statute's roots in addressing the Great Depression as a theme for why the courts should strictly uphold the SEC's powers today.

> **Congress enacted the Securities Act of 1933 [] and the Securities Exchange Act of 1934 [] to counter "rampant abuses in the securities industry [that] led to the 1929 stock market crash and the Great Depression."**

The best advice for choosing a theme is to consider your audience and the atmospherics. Is there a particular counterargument to your position, a bias your decision-maker is likely to have, or some other obvious force working against you? That's where you push back. For example, in *The New York Times v. OpenAI*—where the publisher was suing the creator of AI sensation ChatGPT—the Times lawyers knew their audience might not like the idea of stifling these exciting innovations altogether. So they weaved a theme that suggested the Times actually supported this technology so long as everyone was fairly compensated:

> For months, The Times has attempted to reach a negotiated agreement with Defendants, in accordance with its history of working productively with large technology platforms to permit the use of its content in new digital products (including the news products developed by Google, Meta, and Apple).[21] The Times's goal during these negotiations was to ensure it received fair value for the use of its content, facilitate the continuation of a healthy news ecosystem, **and help develop GenAI technology in a responsible way that benefits society and supports a well-informed public.**

But what about when you need some inspiration to find the perfect theme? Three Oxford professors set out to identify the basic values that everyone shares across cultures and demographics. They found that six principles are consistent across people.[22] Tapping into these can help you identify the most gripping themes for any audience.

1. **Family values.** People care about anything that may affect their family. So if your audience can imagine a consequence that hits that close to home, they will pay attention. For example:

> Protecting schools' right to search lockers is about more than just catching minor mischief. It's about **protecting our children** from weapons and drugs that kill them.

2. **Group loyalty.** Next, people value anything that may affect the groups they identify with. Every judge (and other audiences) will slot themselves into groups. For judges an obvious one is, well, other judges. Touching on issues that implicate judges and courts is always a safe bet. The same goes for other groups a reader might identify with, like political parties or ideologies.

[21] This is a good example of inserting reputational facts subtly, as we saw in Chapter 3.

[22] Oliver Curry et al., *Is It Good to Cooperate? Testing the Theory of Morality-as-Cooperation in 60 Societies*, 60 Current Anthropology 47 (2019).

Americans have the right to choose how they live, how they work, and what they worship. Enforcing this injunction would force judges to split hairs between religious sects to determine what religion an American can worship in public buildings. That is un-American, and the courts' resources are better spent elsewhere.

3. **Effort and reciprocity.** People value those who work hard and give back for what they receive. The more you can frame a party as a freeloader, the less folks will sympathize. The more you can emphasize how hard a party has worked (or lawyers have worked), the more an audience will feel compassion.

Maria wakes up every day (except for Sundays)[23] at 3:30 a.m. She cooks breakfast and lunch for her three sons before she counts her change for the 5:15 a.m. bus fare. She transfers buses twice before she walks ten minutes from the bus stop to the warehouse, and then she works an eight-hour[24] shift lifting heavy cargo. She's never been late in her 8 years working for her employer. But when the new manager was hired—the cousin of the owner—she, and every other woman working at the warehouse, was fired within six months.

Defendant's attorney hired a summer law clerk who accidentally sent privileged information to Plaintiff. The Defendant followed the rules of civil procedure and combed through 42 gigabytes of documents within 48 hours and communicated which documents contained privileged information. Plaintiff has failed to respond and now seeks to subvert the discovery deadline by introducing this information as evidence.

4. **Justified confidence.** Research supports the power of confidence. Don't confuse that with bravado, arrogance, or a lack of humility. But legal audiences want to know that you believe what you're saying. Too much hedging and qualifying, and folks will wonder if what you've told them is worth following.

The First Amendment is clear. Giacomo did not make threats. He did not make false statements. He only stated his opinion on a public sidewalk, and law enforcement violated his rights when they ordered him to disperse.[25]

5. **Fairness.** When dividing money and resources, or making other decisions that affect multiple parties, people prefer equity. Whether the outcome is fair is one thing. But the more you can frame an outcome as fair and balanced, the better it will go over.

Mr. and Mrs. Kim missed the arbitration because the Hospital informed them, the night before, that the Hospital would not provide an interpreter. Now the Hospital claims a default victory. Although the Hospital is not legally obligated to provide an interpreter, the Kims relied on the entity's promise to provide "whatever [they] needed to understand the hearing."[26]

[23] Noting that Maria doesn't get up early on Sunday humanizes her (and perhaps nods to her devoutness, too).
[24] All these stacked details about time come together to persuade.
[25] Notice how the sentence lengths in this paragraph are used to make forceful points. Three short sentences punch you with the three background points, laying the groundwork for the final, longer finish.
[26] A great example of a quote doing more work than a paraphrase would.

> If courts apply this rule to the music market, **a lone clause on page 942 of the terms and conditions could expose the average consumer to thousands of dollars in liability for uploading their songs to a different device.**

6. **Possession and property.** People value property and what they view as theirs. That could be money, assets, or even ownership of an argument. This principle can also extend to rights that audiences view as fundamentally their own.

> Time and time again, the courts have made a distinction: Congress deals with political questions, but only the courts can establish civil rights. This law would strip the power of Judicial Review away from the courts and allow Congress to unilaterally alter the higher law of this land: the Constitution.

Here are a few more tips to consider when developing themes:

- Audiences will weigh losses twice as heavily as gains. Encouraging a reader to think about the negative effects of something will hit much harder than encouraging them to think of the positive gains for the court, for the public, or whatever else you're talking about.
- Audiences weigh something more heavily if they can imagine it happening to them or a loved one. The more relatable you can make points, legal or factual, the better. This is also why you should always consider policy, values, and other practical ramifications of your arguments. Your audience will.
- Audiences value simplicity and what makes sense. As we discussed in Chapter 2, the more an argument or explanation sounds logical and snaps into place, the more readers believe it.
- Another effective theme is novelty. When we believe that a question has no clear answer, we tend to be more open-minded about the resolution. Once you've shown it's clear that there are no easy answers in the authority, swoop in with your persuasive authority: "Bagel Mart marches out a litany of FCPA cases, but not a single one of those addressed the FCPA. **That's because no court has ever addressed the FCPA in this context.**"
- Procedural standards, burdens, and presumptions can all be useful backup themes. These themes focus on whatever the procedural standard, burden, presumption, or standard of review is—summary judgment, dismissal, and so on. They emphasize that a conclusion should be reached because a standard (often a hard-to-meet one like summary judgment) applies to the dispute.

Themes pull at our heartstrings and tap into our deepest values. You can't afford to ignore them.

5.2.2. Use Persuasive Policy

Policy is any reason a reader might side with you that doesn't stem from the governing law. And policy influences legal decisions. Your audiences won't ignore policy, at least subconsciously. You can't either.

That said, legal audiences want to focus on the law. So be subtle and aim policy where it matters: your opponent's strongest points and your greatest weaknesses. This next passage is a great example, taken from a fight over whether a company's shoes infringed a trademark. The legal writers urge the court to realize how the opponent's main argument—that no one but them can make entirely red shoes—would hamstring future designers.

> YSL would be prevented from executing one of its own venerable design traditions—monochrome shoes—[27] in a color that has long been an integral part of the brand's palette. . . . **Indeed, if Louboutin were to have its way, no other designee would ever again be permitted to make an all-red shoe.**

This next example highlights the hypocrisy of a party arguing there isn't enough evidence while refusing to turn over more.

> The government counters that "the court of appeals pointed to no evidence that law enforcement officers engage in GPS monitoring of vehicles without suspicion of criminal activity." . . . **It does not deny the misuse of GPS technology is occurring; it merely notes the absence of evidence in the court of appeal's opinions.[28] . . . More might be available if the government were more forthcoming in disclosing the scope and nature of its use of GPS. . . .**

Let's explore best practices when working with policy like this. First, start with the law. Because that's what your readers expect. The exception is when you know your audience is more receptive to policy-front arguments.[29] Otherwise, legal audiences want to first understand the law and what it requires. With that done, though, everyone wants to feel good about their choices. So follow important legal explanations with a good-feeling reason to agree.

In another example from a top appellate team, we first get the legal argument, which is all about precedent and authority. Then, we immediately feel better about it because we have a good-feeling reason to adopt the argument.

> As Judge Batchelder observed, that is "something that no other circuit court has . . . allowed." [discussing the rule pitch] . . .
>
> **That is for good reason: Applying preclusion to an entire MDL based on a handful of expressly non-binding bellwethers is fundamentally unfair. Initially, respondents have no answer to the palpable unfairness of treating trials as binding [after the fact] when the district court promised [beforehand] they would not be.**

Next, select from the spectrum. Policy arguments come in various flavors. Four classic categories are a good place to start. Most policies in legal writing fall into one of these buckets.

1. **Normative**: Policies about values and goals that the law should promote, like fairness to an individual person or future parties;

---

[27] The em dash ensures you won't miss the most moving fact in this case: The plaintiff is trying to assert trademark protection over any shoe that is a single color. But question whether the impact would have been greater by avoiding the esoteric reference.

[28] The writers are highlighting a gap and reframing it into a positive.

[29] We look at this exception when we work on our introductions in the next chapter.

2. **Economics**: Policies about the money or objective consequences of a rule or decision;[30]
3. **Institutional competence**: Policies about the proper relationship of courts to other courts and courts to other branches of government; and
4. **Judicial administration**: Policies about the practical effects on how courts will do business in the future.

Which policy (or policies) you weave into your document turns on your audience and the issues. Which policy is the best fit for your client and the points you're trying to make? Can you divine what policies your audience might be most receptive to — perhaps with some targeted research?

If you've nothing else to go on, another way to think about policy is a spectrum of objective to subjective. Objective policy might be the safest — and sometimes even welcome — form of policy. These include things like:

- Misunderstanding a rule (or case, or statute, or regulation)
- Court efficiency
- Creating a harsh rule for future litigants that has unintended consequences
- Clarity in the law
- Stare decisis/consistency
- Reducing costs
- Procedural fairness

Next on the spectrum, somewhat objective but not as much so as the last examples, are theoretical legal frameworks. These include concepts like:

- Natural law
- Formalism
- Legal realism
- Legal process
- Fundamental rights
- Law and economics/maximizing benefits
- Critical legal theory: political-based legal approach

Then we have pure subjective forms, where policy gets the riskiest. These are concepts like:

- Fairness in the result
- Protecting the innocent or sympathetic party
- Political and ideological values

Finally, when including policies, the more you relate the policy or value to the facts and law, the better they will work. So support policy points with citations from cases or other reputable sources, if you can.

[30] All these policies get varying mileage with different audiences. Some judges or other audiences are persuaded by economic policy arguments, like that companies will "lose millions." Other audiences might not be too sad if certain companies lost some money. Tailor your policies to your particular audience as much as you can.

5.3 Maintain a Credible Tone

Striking the right tone is tough for legal writers. Much of what we read in the legal world is either dry and boring, on the one hand, or over-the-top and downright scandalous on the other. But it turns out that the most persuasive tone in legal writing is, simply, a *likable* one. Big surprise. Audiences like agreeing with lawyers who are helpful and trustworthy—not people who sound like bullies and jerks.

How can we be likable in our legal writing? We use approachable language that doesn't talk down to readers. We avoid esoteric references that sound condescending. We use language that our readers will be familiar with. And we respect our readers' judgment by encouraging them to reach conclusions based on the law and the facts—not our bare opinions.

This last point is key. Readers trust conclusions more when they help connect the dots themselves. Some call this the *Ikea effect* from a study of the same name. Researchers found that people value furniture more—they found it sturdier and of higher quality—when they helped put it together.[31] When we contribute to the final product, we trust it.

So it's no surprise that the most effective tone will usually be one that guides readers to make their own decisions, highlighting the breadcrumbs for them to follow. The more our readers feel like they journeyed alongside us to reach a destination, the more we will persuade them.

In this next example, the legal writers achieve this sort of tone. They leverage pleasing style techniques without being annoying. And they avoid telling the court what it "must" do and instead *show* the judges why they should agree.

> **Lurking** beneath this **technical tax** dispute are important questions **about** the proper methodology for interpreting tax statutes and **about** the notice our Government owes members of the public before subjecting them to **ruinous**[32] **liability**. [] The question presented **is exceptionally important and this case is a good vehicle**. The Court **should** grant the petition.

Or take this next snippet from lawyers representing OpenAI. The tone is confident but it's not the lawyers pushing for a result, it's "established copyright doctrine" and Justice Brandeis:

> **Established copyright doctrine will dictate** that the Times cannot prevent models from acquiring knowledge about facts, any more than another news organization can prevent the Times itself from re-reporting stories it had no role in investigating. **As Justice Brandeis explained more than 100 years ago:** The general rule of law is that the noblest of human productions, knowledge, truths ascertained, conceptions, and ideas become, after voluntary communication to others, free as the air to common use.

[31] Michael I. Norton, Daniel Mochon, & Dan Ariely, *The 'IKEA Effect': When Labor Leads to Love*, HBS Working Knowledge (March 2011).

[32] A useful descriptor for once. The writers are making a general point, so they might not have specifics to convey how harmful the liability is. "Ruinous" is fresh and vivid enough to engage the reader.

A Quick Summary

Jump on trends with caution. We legal folks write for our audiences, not ourselves. Adopt new writing trends, but make sure they won't alienate readers.

Engage in wordplay carefully. Advanced rhetorical style can draw readers' attention, but use it too much, or too sloppily, and these tools do more bad than good.

Tailor your tone. Research the individual you're writing for and adjust your writing style to match theirs in useful ways. Readers love writing that sounds like they wrote it.

Avoid emotional, directive, or defensive language. Point readers to what matters without forcing your views on them. Obvious plays to emotion will usually backfire.

5.3.1. Jump on Trends with Caution

Language changes fast these days (to be fair, it always has). Word connotations shift, old words take on fresh meanings, and new words and phrases are born, getting added to our dictionaries each year. Ten years ago, most of us wouldn't know what to make of the phrase "hot mess." Today it's used in judicial opinions. A decade ago, using contractions in legal writing would have drawn raised eyebrows from most legal readers. These days, you'll find Supreme Court Justices and some of the world's top lawyers using them.

Should we jump on every new writing trend the moment it emerges? Some would say yes. After all, writing in the plain language that our readers speak and think makes the reading easy for them. But there is a rub. If we are too informal or change up our language too fast, some of our readers might judge us for it. New terms or changes to our syntax might feel off to some readers, even while others love it.

How do we balance our need to write in a way that feels familiar and modern while avoiding new trends that some readers hate? First, get comfortable with popular usage and style guides. Books like the *Chicago Manual of Style* (a popular choice for legal writers) give you a baseline of what the norm is in our field. But err on the side of conservative unless you're sure that your audience is receptive to trendy writing styles.

That doesn't mean you shouldn't adopt new approaches over time—just wait until acceptance is broad enough that you're unlikely to alienate legal audiences. And be sure that your team, your supervisors (if relevant), and anyone else with an interest in the document is okay with your approach.

All that said, some common writing trends that likely have reached the point of wide acceptance (if you use them sparingly and smartly) include:

- Ending sentences in a preposition when helpful. But the ends of sentences are emphasized, so you usually should end with a stronger punch.
- Splitting infinitives. This has been widely accepted in style guides for decades.

- Beginning sentences with conjunctions like "And" or "But."
- Using occasional contractions when helpful to construct a smoother sentence.
- Using single-sentence paragraphs to occasionally drive home a point.
- Using a sentence fragment as part of an obvious rhetorical move. Like this.
- Asking readers questions or dialoguing directly with them. Take this sentence; imagine you're talking to me directly.
- Cutting formalisms that have no direct legal effect (like "further affiant sayeth not" or "here comes now . . ." or typing out numbers in both letters and digits).
- Words and phrases that have reached such wide acceptance you see them often in judicial opinions and strong journalistic writing.

Acceptance of trends like this might be broad, but some audiences will still balk at even the occasional contraction — or a split infinitive, a sentence-ending preposition, or other grammar prohibitions that most legal writers have left behind. So always incorporate trends with care and consider whether your audience will be receptive.[33]

5.3.2. Engage in Wordplay Carefully

Legal writing doesn't require that you check your creativity at the door. Allusions, literary references, metaphors, hypotheticals, and other wordplay can enhance your writing when the time is right. We explore many of these tools in Chapter 9. But pushing the rhetorical envelope too far can backfire, killing your credibility. I could share many behind-the-scenes stories of judges being taken aback (or downright annoyed) by silly rhetorical attempts.

How should you decide when and how to go big on rhetoric? Consider a few guiding principles.

First, use bold style tools sparingly and only for important points. The best legal writers weave in some alliteration, or a quick hypothetical, or a metaphor, or even a literary reference. But they do so only with a goal — because the point they are making matters a lot. If you are being cute more than once on a page, that should be a red flag to tone it down.

For example, this lawyer used figurative language (that is, language that is not literal) to communicate a point that was so simple it required no fancy dressing.

> On the facts so far, Plaintiffs would still survive Defendant's Motion for Summary Judgment. What follows in Sections 11-D and 11-E is just extra icing on an already-frosted cake.

This lawyer could simply have said: **"Plaintiffs survive summary judgment on these facts alone,"** without wasting the readers' time. The rhetorical flare isn't adding value.

Make sure that references of any sort — whether rhetorical, historical, or popular — relate to the content you're writing about. Or at least ensure that the reference is so unique that it truly helps people understand something more. Dropping in a random reference to Harry Potter, as fun as it is, will annoy many.

---

[33] You might not always have time to do this. And you might not always know who your audience is in advance. But if you can look at writing penned by the judge, lawyer, or client you're writing to, that can give you insight into what writing trends they prefer.

In this next passage, Judge Andrew Gordon inserts some sly references that play on a defendant's request to exclude the plaintiff's use of "reptile" tactics.

> **Uncoiling** Costco's motion, it appears to ask that I order Aidini's counsel not to: (1) make any **venomous** remarks that might incite the jurors' "primal" instincts to protect their offspring (what Costco calls the "reptile theory" of advocacy), (2) suggest that Costco is **slinking** from its responsibility by defending this case, and (3) comment on the witnesses' credibility.
>
> **Once shed of its skin**, Costco's motion is little more than a request that I **monitor** Aidini's counsel to ensure they stay within the strictures of the federal evidentiary and procedural rules. . . . I will balance those **scales** when the time comes. But I will not issue a blanket pretrial ruling based on nothing more than **Costco's suspicion that there are snakes lurking in the grass**.

Still, avoid clichés like the plague. If you're pulling out an overused analogy like "this case is about having too many cooks in the kitchen" you are not elevating your writing. Clichés are impressive only if you make them novel and tightly linked to your points. So if you want to use any phrase that sounds like an overworn cliché, either take the time to make it new or cut the nonsense.

That does not mean you cannot use idioms or figurative language (words that don't literally mean what they say). For example, talking about the "nutshell" of a case is common, even if you are not talking about nuts. Same with figurative language like suggesting a party is being hypocritical with the phrase "in the same breath," like this Supreme Court Justice did:

> **In the same breath,** the district court said an Eleventh Amendment objection "is a challenge to a district court's subject matter jurisdiction" and yet "it does not implicate federal subject matter jurisdiction."

The difference between uses like these is that "in the same breath" communicates a complex and important concept—highlighting the inconsistencies between two concepts. It's also a novel writing structure that readers won't have seen a million times before.

Remember that we write for our clients, our colleagues, or judges. Not to entertain ourselves. So if cute wordplay is as likely to distract as to inform, cut it out.[34]

5.3.3. Tailor Your Tone

Another way to hone your tone is to tailor it to the individual you're writing to. What makes your writing easy for one reader won't make it work for every reader. Most techniques in this book rely on strategies that work no matter who you're writing for. But that doesn't mean you should ignore each reader's idiosyncrasies. Quite the opposite. The more tailor-made your writing, the more persuasive.

[34] For fans of the 1990s TV show *Full House*, this is a reference to character Joey Gladstone's frequent catchphrase. *Full House: The Origins of Joey's "Cut It Out" Catchphrase Explained*, ScreenRant, https://screenrant.com/full-house-joey-gladstone-cut-out-catchphrase-explained.

How can you tailor your legal documents to different folks? First, learn as much as you can about your readers and what they want. If it's a judge, read their past decisions. Read the briefs or motions written by attorneys who often win before that judge (the major legal research companies all offer these analytics). Ask around for insights from other advocates who have practiced before them.

In your research, look for preferences like tone, legal philosophy, policy priorities, organizational layout, and anything else you can glean. If your reader will be another attorney you work with, it's often easier to gather this information. Just ask other attorneys who regularly work with them. Better yet, ask the attorney directly. But critically, don't rely on what people tell you; ask for samples. People could have all sorts of perspectives about someone's preferences. Better to go to the source.

Your final product should look different depending on who is receiving it. If you're writing for a client, explain more of the basics. A client not only knows you less and will judge you more based on your writing skill, but they may be less equipped to process the legal and factual points you are throwing down. So more context, more defined terms, simpler writing.

In the end, the more you write like your reader, the more likely they are to agree with you. We like writing that looks like we wrote it. I would never suggest ignoring what your reader does or prefers (even if the research shows that *most* other readers like things a different way). If your reader is used to a convention, regardless of whether we might question its usefulness with the average reader, that convention is probably scoring you persuasion points.

So ask, does your reader like:

- Meaty headings or short ones?
- Traditional transitions (*moreovers* and *furthermores*)?
- Deep introductions?
- Extra-short sentences or paragraphs? (If not, they may be in the old-school camp that these are no-nos).
- Authority or legal background in the fact sections?
- Structural layout and white space?
- Fresh and vivid words? Other writing style quirks?
- Adherence to outdated grammar rules like never splitting an infinitive or starting sentences with conjunctions?
- Policy-forward discussion?
- Types of policy—slippery slope, ideological, etc.?
- Lengthy discussions of rules and authority?
- Approaches to interpreting case law (like full fact to fact exposition for every important case)?
- Textual interpretation—textualism? Results-oriented?
- Legislative history?
- Formal tone? Neutral? Pay particular attention to old-school legalese like "such as" and "furthermore."
- Legalese: Latin phrases, long formalisms at the start of the motion, etc.?
- Naming and definition conventions (ugh, acronyms)?
- Titles of documents?
- Anything else you notice in their writing?

5.3.4. Avoid Emotional, Directive, or Defensive Language

Research shows that *obvious* emotional language is more likely to harm than help. A team of researchers set out to test whether emotional language influences a brief's chances of success. The team used software to test 1,677 Supreme Court cases from 1984 to 2007. The software flagged emotionally charged words like "outrageous," "apprehensive," "wonderful," and "glorious."[35]

For petitioners, the impact was about 10 percent to the negative. Using this language reduces your chances of success by about one in ten. For respondents, the difference was even greater, coming in at a whopping 16 percent negative effect. The authors surmise that the harms are caused by attorneys losing credibility with their audience. Judges and lawyers want to view themselves as law followers. The more you come off as trying to ply a judge with emotion instead of logic, the less the judge will respect what you have to say.

The easiest way to avoid a blatantly emotional tone? Cut down on the lazy descriptors, which often contain our charged opinions about a fact or action. We legal writers love inserting adverbs (verb descriptors) and adjectives (noun descriptors) to manhandle our readers into feeling a certain way. For example:

> This was a **heinous** and **vicious** attack that caused **severe** and **permanent injuries** to plaintiff.

Instead, use choice details and clean prose to focus your reader's attention where the emotional response will build naturally.

> The defendant used **an aluminum baseball** bat to **beat plaintiff** until his **knee caved in**.

Next, try to remove yourself from the equation by avoiding opinion language. As a lawyer (this does not go so much for judges), there's rarely a reason to write in the first person, or to make a point based on your "belief" or "position." Make your arguments about what the facts say or what the authority illustrates. So not:

> Our **position** is that this discovery is too burdensome to be permitted.

But instead:

> This discovery **will burden defendant with an estimated $2 million in costs**, which is not warranted under the **Federal Rules given that much lower costs are routinely held to rise above the burdensome threshold**.

And when you use language that forcefully defends your position, you sound, well, defensive. The same goes for directive language that tells your readers what they "must" do. Take this example:

---

[35] Ryan C. Black, Matthew E. K. Hall, & Ryan J. Owens, *The Role of Emotional Language in Briefs before the US Supreme Court*, Journal of Law and Courts, vol. 4, no. 2, 377-407 (2016) ("Using an automated textual analysis program, we find that parties who employ less emotional language in their briefs are more likely to win a justice's vote, a result that holds even after controlling for other features correlated with success, such as case quality.").

> Should this Court decide to reach that issue in the first instance **it must conclude that the Agreement is unconscionable.**

Many judges' reaction will be, "Oh I must, must I? We will see about that!"

By demanding your legal reader "ignore" something, or insisting that something "doesn't matter," or that a position is "flat out wrong," science shows you could trigger the opposite reaction you hope for. One study showed that when people were told to "ignore" a fact, for example, that fact weighed more heavily in their decision.

A lot of that description and directive language is pure waste. Avoid telling your reader to do an "examination" or "review" of points—or telling the reader what courts will "look to" or that the court will "determine." Make your case and quietly slide out of your reader's DM.

But finally, none of that means you shouldn't be confident. Confidence is infectious. No, you should not misrepresent anything. And yes, exaggerating sinks your credibility. But you must find a winning position in your case. And then you must argue that position as if you believe it (because you do). If you don't sound like you trust yourself, why would a judge trust you? So cut words like these:

- maybe
- quite possibly
- at best
- at least
- might be
- seems to
- appears to
- perhaps
- so-called
- implicates
- probably
- tends to
- I believe
- my position

5.4 Persuasively Counter Opposing Views

It's hard enough to explain how the law works; it's even harder to respond to opponents trying to do the same thing. Penning responsive documents is tough. For one thing, you've probably read the other side's brief and spotted frustrating points you think are dead wrong. For another, it's hard to figure out which arguments you need to counter and how to do so without giving your opponent the floor.

In a joint response penned by powerhouse intellectual property writers at Wilson Sonsini and Wilmer Hale, what you won't find is a drawn-out regurgitation of their opponent's views. Nor will you find personal jabs like lashing out at the other side's "egregious misrepresentations of the record."

Instead, the legal writers focus on the questions before the court—which is not about whether the other party is wrong, but about what answer is right. The team leads with the affirmative pitch, focusing on the most trustworthy details and useful quotes that the judges could use in their decision.

> **Eight years ago,**[36] **this Court unanimously**[37] **held that** a "computer-implemented scheme for mitigating . . . the risk that only one party to a financial transaction will pay what it owes . . . by using a third-party intermediary" describes a "patent-ineligible abstract idea"[38]. . . .
>
> **[T]his Court has denied dozens of petitions for certiorari** asking [] to clarify, modify, or overturn the principles established in *Alice* . . ., **including in three of the cases that the court below cited in support of its decision.** . . .
>
> **As the unanimous panel below recognized**, these claims fall squarely under this Court's ruling in *Alice* . . .

Only after the court had the answers it needed did the lawyers turn to swiftly dismissing opposing views:

> USR contends that the Federal Circuit blurred the lines between *Alice's* first and second steps. . . .

In the end, countering an adversary's arguments is important. But we must do so carefully. Let's see how.

A Quick Summary

Take the affirmative stance (usually). In most documents, you're better off leading with your affirmative points rather than spending much time directly countering opposing views. Focus on the questions your audience must answer and guide them to answers.

Snip opposing points surgically. When you decide it's best to acknowledge an opposing point, do so one at a time and put it into context immediately.

Attack parties not people. Few legal audiences want to be distracted by drama about opposing parties. Focus on the facts.

[36] Storytelling language instead of dates no one will remember.

[37] Using the authority quality to help bolster the rule's credibility.

[38] This is a complicated quote, but it's actually surgical. It captures the precise invention at issue in this case and makes it easy for readers to see how the rule applies.

5.4.1. Take the Affirmative Stance (Usually)

Many legal writers are tempted to follow their opponent's structure, including the order that opponents analyze issues in and even how those issues are described. Sometimes it makes sense to approach things the same way your opponent did. But usually it doesn't.

The easiest way to counter opposing views is to start with what your reader needs: the legal questions they need answered, the rules that will guide them to answers, and, of course, the answers themselves. The back and forth between arguing parties is not something most decision-makers care about. Your affirmative story and rule pitch are usually the most useful things you have to offer.

If you need to *also* address counterpoints, do so quickly. After you tell your story about how a relevant rule works and map out a path to victory for your position—if needed—surgically cut your opponent's strongest arguments off. Weave this countering work among your own persuasive discussions as much as you can.

Counter others by giving your readers better answers than anything an opponent might raise (or has raised). Focus readers on the good and deemphasize the bad as you explain your view of things.

- Put the good authority and your own rule pitches in the spotlight—in the beginning of sections, paragraphs, and independent clauses. This also goes for compelling points about what your opponent missed, ignored, or is confused about.
- Put the unfavorable points that may cut against your positions into places of deemphasis—like in the middle of sections, paragraphs, and dependent clauses.
- Put the unfavorable facts or legal points into context right away. Don't do what many lawyers do and spend sentences or paragraphs re-creating your opponent's argument, only to then backtrack.

So not:

> **Plaintiff contends** that the entry-fiction doctrine requires only that the defendant be near the border. **He relies on** *Terry v. Conlin*, which stated that "this is not a precise test of measurement." **However, the Plaintiff is wrong because** *Terry* involved very different facts, such as that there the plaintiff was standing within steps of the border. . . .

Instead, lead with the question your reader needs to answer and a pitch that steers around any counters to your ultimate goal. Like this:

> The court must decide whether someone standing 40 feet from the border is "at" the border for purposes of legal entry. The Second Circuit in ***Terry* explained only how to categorize someone standing within inches of the border**—holding that, for practical reasons, people that close should be treated as if they never crossed. **But the court was careful to distinguish cases where the person is even fifteen feet farther away.** . . .

You would never know that these next legal writers were replying to an opponent's brief. They don't waste precious opening paragraphs with summaries of what the other side said. Rather, they explain how the judge can get to the right answer, giving opponents space only after the writer's answer snaps into view.

The whole case came down to whether a gun with a bump stock qualifies as a machine gun, defined as "any weapon which shoots . . . automatically more than one shot, without manual reloading, by a single function of the trigger." Do you even need to read more about the opposing view after this lawyer's pitch?

> A bump **stock transforms a semiautomatic rifle into a weapon that shoots hundreds of bullets per minute with a single pull of the trigger.**[39] Like a traditional machine gun, a rifle with a bump stock fires repeatedly without any further manipulation of the trigger by the shooter: **As long as the shooter leaves his finger on the bump stock's finger rest and maintains steady forward pressure on the front of the rifle, the gun keeps firing until it runs out of ammunition.** The only difference is that a traditional machine gun relies on the back-and-forth movement of the gun's internal parts whereas a bump stock relies on the back-and-forth movement of the entire forward portion of the rifle. Videos in the record vividly illustrate both how little input from the shooter is required and the rapid fire that bump stocks enable.[40]
>
> **Respondent nonetheless maintains that a bump stock is not a "machine gun" under the National Firearms Act.**

Or take this next pitch about a complicated case challenging the FDA's decision that a new drug doesn't qualify under a certain regulation. Again, the writers were on the responding end. But you'd never know it as they walk you step-by-step through how to qualify this new drug as a protein under the FDA's rules.

> The statute spells out that all proteins . . . are to be regulated as biological products. . . .
>
> [T]hat definition describes [this product] to a T. . . .
>
> **FDA must test its definition of protein against the finished [] form** of [this product]. . . .

With the judge now up to speed on how the law works from the lawyers' vantage, the writers can surgically cut down any counterpoints left over. Notice that the rule pitch above taught us all we need to know to dismiss the opponent's argument about testing "theoretical forms."

> The Government argues, however, that the protein test should be applied to some . . . theoretical form[] not actually present in Somatuline Depot as it is sold and administered.

In this next passage, writing maven Lisa Blatt leads by teaching us what the law requires (application of European Union law), which sets us up to easily dismiss the counterargument after (that non-EU law should apply).

[39] The style choices in this paragraph are worth learning from. The verbs target images. The specifics say more than characterizations could ("hundreds of bullets a minute" does a lot more than "rapidly" would).

[40] A fantastic example of a priming-first introduction opener, which we return to in the next chapter.

> **EU law—the product of treaties between sovereigns—is the specific international law that governs Spain's capacity to form arbitration agreements with EU members and their nationals like appellees.** EU law undisputedly deprives Spain of the ability to form such agreements, which violate the primacy of EU law and prevent the European Court of Justice from resolving EU-law issues.
>
> **Appellees instead invoke non-EU international law,** contending that the Energy Charter Treaty authorizes arbitration between signatory sovereigns and signatories' residents across the board. . . .

When you lead with your opponent's perspective, readers can see things from your opponent's perspective, regardless of your characterizations that those views are "flat wrong."

> Churchill County inexplicably spends much of its brief laboring on about standing. Churchill's flimsy theory is that the plaintiff was not harmed here because it never actually lost any money when the zoning plans were changed. Churchill points to cases that have held that financial loss is the primary way courts find standing. Churchill then notes the lack of evidence regarding any financial losses here in pages of affidavits, papering the court.
>
> **But Churchill is wrong. . . .**

Let me ask you: Are you sure Churchill County is wrong at this point? When I first read that brief, all I saw was an attorney desperate to avoid strong arguments raised by the other side.

Look what happens when we flip the narrative. We lead with the affirmative answer and only bring in our opponent's words and arguments surgically—immediately cutting them down before they gain momentum.

> This Court has held that standing exists when a plaintiff's legal position changed because of another's act. That includes when the government robs a plaintiff of her right to build on her own land. **Churchill does not dispute that Plaintiff lost her ability to build on her land because of the County's zoning decision.**[41] **Churchill mentions the lack of evidence about financial loss, but the law does not require that proof.**

In this next introduction to a reply, notice how a pro Supreme Court team not only leads with their affirmative points before disarming opposing ones, but they provide you with enough context so that you don't need to read the brief they are responding to.

> **The divided decision below eviscerates a key mechanism for resolving mass-tort litigation and undermines basic due process protections in cases that make up over 40% of the federal courts' civil caseload. The Sixth Circuit panel majority allowed the results of just three early trials to**

[41] A great example of narrowing the field. Establishing this fact anchors it in readers' minds.

> **preclude DuPont from litigating duty, breach, and foreseeability across an entire MDL**—even though all agreed the bellwether results would not bind future trials, and even though one of the tried cases was picked precisely because it was un-representative.[42] ... The decision below cries[43] out for this Court's review.
>
> **Respondents' attempts to defend the decision below, and to recast it as an unremarkable application of existing law, simply blink reality. . . .**[44]

Ultimately, the best counterarguments aren't arguments at all; they're just better answers than anyone else can offer.

5.4.2. Snip Opposing Points Surgically

When shouldn't you lead with an affirmative pitch? When it's easier for you to dismantle opposing views than to go straight to the answers. Perhaps the crux of the dispute is truly why your opponents are wrong—or perhaps the strongest rule pitches you have are about the opposition not meeting burdens or standards of review. Then, by all means, start on defense.

This next section opener lays out the three counters to be defeated, sweeps away what is undisputed, and primes you to view those counterpoints skeptically. So yes, a good legal defense can be the best legal offense.

> This case **attacks the Surface Transportation Board's discretion.**[45] Indeed, **Petitioners admit** that under the Administrative Procedure Act, **they must show that the Board acted arbitrarily and capriciously. They point to three main ways they think it did**: (1) by using its exemption procedures to authorize Seven County's new rail line; (2) by not labeling increased oil production and refining as an indirect effect of the new line; and (3) by not addressing the alleged effects of new traffic on other rail lines. **But on each of these fronts, Petitioners' arguments demand that the Board speculate about environmental effects, rather than study what is reasonably foreseeable. . . .**

Whenever you overtly counter others, give their arguments as little energy as possible. Take one opposing point at a time and disarm it immediately. Even a few intervening sentences can allow readers to start wondering if there's merit to their view.

> Respondent first tries to distinguish the cases that support the majority rule by arguing that those cases lack an appellate finding that officers did not have a reasonable fear of serious harm. **But the appellate court here did not make a ruling about reasonable fear either, which confirms the majority rule applies.**

[42] The parallel "even though" phrases create pleasing balance here. Notice also how the writer doesn't assume the reader knows all these facts but recaps all the key details from the original despite this being a reply. That makes this document self-explanatory and useful.

[43] This verb does a lot of work (and creates alliteration with "court").

[44] This example is a great use of distilling takeaways. Notice the first sentence captures key specifics that will persuade you, summarizing more of the brief in a single point. The authors continue leveraging specifics throughout.

[45] Your default goal should be to capture the paragraph's thrust in the first sentence or two, but there are exceptions. Complicated paragraphs sometimes require a slower build-up. This paragraph is going to overview quite a lot, so capturing the main takeaway isn't feasible.

When taking on counters directly like this, it's important to frame the issues favorably. That means accurately describing the opposing view but ensuring that the specifics you focus on or language you use tees it up for your swing right after. That said, I'll emphasize it again. When reframing an opponent's view, fairly set up their points—otherwise you may be accused of misrepresentation. Often a choice quote works best, followed by your counter or context.

> [The appellant] argues that the First Amendment's *Brandenburg* test protects him from disqualification **even if he "engaged in insurrection" in violation of the Fourteenth Amendment.** [] But the First Amendment does not somehow displace the disqualification rule in Section 3 of the Fourteenth Amendment—a constitutional provision of "equal validity."[46]

Highlighting that the opposing side argued he was immune even for "engaging in insurrection" is about as powerful framing as you can manage. In this next example, again, a surgical quote highlights the more favorable view of an opponent's point:

> The plaintiff argues for a standard requiring "little to no actual intent." **In other words, plaintiff seeks to flip a decade-old standard with no authority or other legal support for doing so.**

When countering like this, you can often riff off your opponent's words even more. Like by highlighting hypocrisy or contradictions:

> The government now contends that the evidence was "harmless beyond any shadow of doubt and under any standard of review." This is the same evidence that the government hailed at trial as "powerfully probative evidence" concerning the very "nub" of the case.

Countering others is like cross-examination. It's about keeping the focus on you and your affirmative points and preventing the witness from speaking as much as you can.

5.4.3. Attack Parties, Not People

No discussion of countering would be complete without an advisement against being a tattletale. That's right, I said it. A tattletale. Judge after judge will tell you that they detest lawyers who fill their briefs with personal jabs. And yet the first thing many lawyers do when sitting down to write a brief is start listing out all the annoying, petty things the opposing attorney did. "Just wait until the judge sees this!" they think to themselves.

But this tactic nearly always backfires, dirtying you with as much mud as you sling. Judges don't have time to listen in to your phone calls and read through hundreds of emails to figure out who called who a name first.

If there are bad facts about an opposing party or lawyer that you can subtly weave in, I'm not suggesting you don't try. Perhaps a party has filed a string of unsuccessful lawsuits against the same defendant—that is the sort of emotional fact that can turn heads if you reveal it subtly as part of relevant discussion.

---

[46] This well-placed em dash highlights the legal point that "equal" provisions must be given effect, and neither is superior to the other.

> **This Court is already familiar with the long and disturbing history of *Brady* violations in Orleans Parish during the tenure of district attorney Harry Connick. . . .**

Pointing out omissions, additions, hedging language, and revisionist histories can persuade. So long as you stick to the relevant missteps and avoid picking silly battles that amount to personal attacks. Here are a few great places to poke against opposing parties:

- Omitted facts that are relevant to the governing law, or failures to address important facts or rules;
- Additions to the record that are merely lawyer opinion, or additions to a reply or later briefing;
- Superficial analysis or spending little to no attention on an important issue;
- Revisions of the facts or law—including misrepresentations, misstatements, and so on.

Each is excellent fodder for hitting the other side's credibility while still maintaining a nondefensive tone. Like these lawyers did:

> **Apple's brief does not mention, much less offer a rationale,** for its three-year delay in bringing this suit.

> **Aurel does not once discuss the borrowed-employer line of cases**—a line that this court has applied to Aurel's claim more than once.

> **The city is unable to identify a single decision**—in this Court or elsewhere—in which a discriminatory ad valorem tax on vessels has been upheld. **And it is able to construct an argument only by omitting** from its quotation of this Court's opinions unfavorable language. . . .

Opposing other folks is tough. You might be tempted to focus on opposing counsel or opposing sides. But legal readers are busy and don't have time to sort out who's been naughty and who's been nice.[47] So stick to what your readers do care about: the facts.

Level Up Your Persuasion with Technology

Technology can help with several of your persuasive writing strategies. From brainstorming themes to subtly framing key sentences, let's look at ways to incorporate technology into this facet of your writing.

[47] Not to mention that you may be in the wrong. We are not good at objectively judging the merits of the other side's points—especially when we are firmly entrenched in our own arguments. The answer is to focus on the facts and the law, not the other side personally. If they left something out, misrepresented a case, or did something else annoying, show the reader.

GAI tools: GAI and tools that leverage it can be a great help with framing and priming. Simply enter a key sentence or paragraph and ask for ideas to make the language sound more favorable to one perspective or the other—without changing the underlying substance. For example:

- "How can I rephrase this paragraph to emphasize the benefits of my client's position: [insert some key points you want to emphasize and your original paragraph]."
- "What are some ideas for a theme based on this summary of my brief: [insert your introduction or have a GAI tool make a summary of your document first and insert it here]."
- "What are some policy reasons to support my legal analysis in this section: [insert the section and some guidance about policies you're interested, if you already have an idea]."
- "Read this section of my document and come up with the three most compelling counterarguments possible: [insert a section of your analysis]."

Tone tech: Tools like ProWritingAid or Grammarly's tone detector scrutinize your draft for thematic consistency and emotional resonance. They suggest language adjustments to maintain the chosen narrative frame, ensuring that each clause contributes to the thematic arc you've meticulously designed to captivate and persuade.

Document analyzers: Tools like Westlaw's QuickCheck harness the power of advanced algorithms to analyze legal documents and perform automated research. By scanning citations within a document and comparing them against a vast database of cases, statutes, and regulations, these analyzers identify potential weaknesses, overlooked authorities, and areas for improvement, ensuring that the legal argument is exhaustive.

Litigation analytics tools: These innovative platforms leverage data-driven insights to predict judicial behavior, analyze litigation trends, and examine the performance of opposing counsel or law firms. By incorporating historical litigation data and outcomes into your legal writing and strategy, you can craft more refined and persuasive arguments.

Practice these techniques and technologies with Write.law's exercises and checklists, plus other resources at www.levelupyourlegalwriting.com

ASPEN PUBLISHING | write.law

6

Level Up Your Organization

> Organize yourself before you try to organize anything else."—C. Jay

Great: You've locked down your key takeaways. You've spun a compelling story. You've designed a rule discussion that guides readers through the complexity. You've even chosen themes and policies to capture your readers' hearts.

Now make it effortless for readers to use all your great content. Craft an introduction that summarizes everything that matters in an easy-to-understand package. Ensure that all your major points connect with one another by inserting hand-holding tools like roadmaps, definitions, and signposts along the way. And finish your document by leaving readers with a lasting impression.

In other words: Begin strong; regularly guide; end decisively.

We'll often return to the first of those three goals: Begin strong. First impressions are everything in legal writing. If your readers finish the initial pages of your document thinking, "Wow, this lawyer is smart and detail-oriented; I'm impressed," you can't imagine what a difference that will make for the pages that follow. Readers who are won over at the start will overlook typos, poor writing, and even weak analysis buried later in your document.[1] That's the power of first impressions. We see what we expect to see.

But make a lackluster debut with readers, and they will notice every imperfection. Because they already expect you to disappoint. If you take nothing else out of this chapter, please, spend more time crafting the beginnings of your document, your sections, and even your paragraphs. Those first looks will change everything.

---

[1] Not that I am advocating any of these. But some insurance can't hurt. Even the best writers miss a thing or two every now and then.

To turn your document into a resource readers will come back to again and again, follow the techniques in this chapter for structuring legal documents so that readers can use them.

- **Craft introductions that prime and inform.** Collect all the most important takeaways in your document and package them in a quick page or two that readers can use to understand what matters. The best introductions are cheat sheets readers can use to make decisions.
- **Start sections with useful headings and roadmaps.** Providing self-contained, explanatory headings is a must. They should categorize, highlight, and summarize.
- **Order your points purposefully.** Legal writing is not a one-size-fits-all affair. In complex advocacy, a tailored approach to your document structure recognizes the reader's needs, preferences, and expectations. Deviate from traditional structures when the time is right.
- **Insert hand-holding devices throughout your documents.** Guide readers throughout your document. Like the narration tools we learned in Chapter 3, offer guidance like roadmaps, recaps of useful information, lay definitions, and other explanations where readers might need them.

Before diving into these techniques, look at what a difference purposeful organization can make. Here's an attorney mindlessly following an opposing party's order of issues in drafting a response.

A. Rico Corp. is wrong that courts have been clear about the deadline to file an answer.

B. Rico Corp. is wrong that the Primrose School's filing is deficient.

C. Rico Corp. cannot even make this argument because it lacks standing.

The narrative is all about how the other side is *wrong*—rather than what the judge really cares about. How do they get to an answer that feels *right*? That isn't to say you should never follow someone else's organization. But look at the same brief organized around the helpful answers:

A. Rico Corp. can't file a counterclaim in the first place because it was not injurred and thus has no standing.

B. Primrose filed its own claim before the September 2022 deadline set by Nevada's statute of limitations.

C. Rico Corp. suggests that Primrose was required to file a declaration to its motion, but this Court has held no declaration is required.

Beyond organizational decisions like this, this chapter is about how powerful the starts are, particularly introductions. A nice thing about introductions is that there aren't any technical requirements. You don't need to cite cases or include other formalities if you don't want to. It's your chance to speak freely and show readers you can help them.

Check out how this next legal writing team breaks down a complicated story that sets the stage for their arguments to come. You already want their opponents to lose after finishing the opening narrative.

> Wealthy manufacturing behemoth Georgia-Pacific hatched[2] this bankruptcy case to escape civil liability for poisoning people with asbestos.[3] It did so by pioneering a controversial scheme, now commonly called the "Texas Two-Step," that began with a divisional merger in 2017. The first step[4] was for Georgia-Pacific to separate into two new entities: Bestwall, which received the asbestos liabilities and minimal assets; and New GP, which received most[5] of the profitable assets and business operations. The second step was for Bestwall to declare bankruptcy and promptly obtain an injunction halting all asbestos lawsuits against not only itself, but also New GP and other affiliated companies it left outside bankruptcy. The bankruptcy court below blessed that maneuver. It gave Bestwall's non-debtor affiliates a core bankruptcy benefit—a reprieve from all civil litigation[6]—without asking them to shoulder any corresponding bankruptcy burden.

The key to creating useful documents is to be thoughtful about it. Don't mindlessly follow tradition or what everyone else is doing. Order and build every section for each issue and for each reader. And pay extra attention to the beginnings.

6.1 Craft Introductions That Prime and Inform

If we take what we know about good conversations and apply it to writing, the importance of introductions becomes obvious. Those first moments are everything when we meet a stranger. They shape how we perceive them, how we gauge their credibility, and, ultimately, whether we can trust them.

So use the introduction to let readers meet you. When Judge Don Willett needed to introduce readers to a dry statutory-interpretation analysis, he took time to craft an introduction that showed off his skill and style so effectively that you can't help but keep reading.

> The lion's share of modern appellate judging is reading legislative language and decoding what it means. On that score, our interpretive precedent favors bright lines and sharp corners. **If a case can be decided according to the statute itself, it must be decided according to the statute itself. This is a bedrock principle.**
>
> Today's case asks whether a notice provision in the Texas Premium Finance Act should be read as written, or instead whether the Court should adopt a "substantial compliance" approach that excuses slip-ups. **We opt for the former.** The Legislature has codified "substantial compliance" throughout Texas law—including in other Insurance Code notice provisions—forgiving

[2]Verbs can target emotional goals like this. "Hatched" connotes cunning. The same goes for the verbs animating the next sentence: "escape" and "poisoning."

[3]Ending the sentence on this word emphasizes it.

[4]Playing off the "Texas Two Step" label by referring to each "step" continuously reinforces this theme that the party was conniving.

[5]A deft use of details here. You aren't drowned in the exact percentages of ownership or particular assets. Those specifics wouldn't serve the story these writers are trying to tell right now.

[6]This em dash is used well to highlight the core message from the document.

less-than-strict conformity with various statutory commands. But it did not do so here. We decline to engraft what lawmakers declined to enact.

Not only do you get a deep sense of the document's takeaways, but the writer convinces us of his prowess by using:

- **Alliteration:** Using similar sounds to emphasize key words you want readers to notice ("Lion's share . . . legislative language"; "read . . . written"; "engraft . . . enact").
- **Targeted verbs:** Using verbs that aim at a purposeful emotional or imagery-laden goal for readers. The writer wanted to frame *substantial compliance* negatively, so he framed the question as one of "excusing slip-ups" to subtly cast an unfavorable light. The legislature "codifies" the statute (making the act sound authoritative) and the court is merely "decoding" it (making the act sound rote without room for creative departure).
- **Balanced words and phrases:** The author uses balanced phrases that create a melody by putting certain words in consistent positions ("bright lines and sharp corners"; "engraft what lawmakers declined to enact"; "read as written").
- **Short sentences:** One of the many simple ways you can emphasize a point, as we explore in Chapter 8, is to use extra-short sentences to halt readers and make them listen. The writer does this here. Again and again.

Crafting introductions that answer your readers' burning questions in the most memorable style will transform your legal writing. Let's see how.

A Quick Summary

Strike the right impression. **Introductions matter most because they set the stage and prime readers for the narrative that follows. The best ones provide a first impression that will convince readers to believe not just in the writing, but the writer.**

Craft your opening paragraphs. **An effective opener both situates and persuades; it guides the reader to the dispute's heart while embedding favorable details that subtly tilt the scales toward your client.**

Focus on your persuasive pitch. **Serving up crucial facts and distilling your key rule pitches early not only captures attention but aligns your reader's focus with the arguments you care about.**

Counter biases and leverage themes. **Anticipate potential preconceptions or biases by weaving in counternarratives and framing facts in a way that mitigates their impact.**

6.1.1 Strike the Right Impression

Above all, introductions create your readers' first impressions. And there's a lot to juggle in making that impression.

1. **Make your reader like you.** Use accessible language. Use familiar language. Use a direct, pleasing style that readers can consume easily. Avoid too many characterizations or empty conclusions. Don't focus on personal attacks or hyperbole.
2. **Show off.** The introduction is your chance to show your reader that you are an elite lawyer who has the chops to help the judge write a better opinion. Use your best style. Cut clutter ruthlessly.
3. **Emphasize what you add to the story.** Don't dwell on the mundane stories your reader already knows. Blandly reciting the basic elements of battery in your intro isn't helpful. Emphasize what is difficult or interesting about your case and the law you advocate for.
4. **Embrace the bad.** Embrace the bad facts and bad law and put them into context. Many legal writers run from the hard parts of their case, preferring to discuss (at length) the facts and law that support them. But this is the worst strategy. An audience should never discover a bad fact from opposing counsel.
5. **Include the entire elevator pitch.** Sometimes lawyers don't include their best stuff in their introductions, preferring to hold back some for the body. Maybe they want to tease the judge with some juicy details without putting all the pieces together yet. But judges, like most legal readers these days, are busy. Let's be honest, sometimes they can't do much more than skim. If you don't make your key points in your introduction, you might never get the chance again.

The best legal writers understand that introductions require balancing all these goals—striking a first impression that will convince readers you're worth listening to.[7] Look at how Chief Justice John Roberts engages readers by vividly introducing a case's main character—the dusky gopher frog. By the end of this opening paragraph, you can't help but care what happens to this little guy:

> The amphibian *Rana sevosa* is popularly known as the "dusky gopher frog"—"dusky" because of its dark coloring and "gopher" because it lives underground. The dusky gopher frog is about three inches long, with a large head, plump[8] body, and short legs. Warts dot[9] its back, and dark spots cover its entire body. It is noted for covering its eyes with its front legs when it feels threatened, peeking out periodically until danger passes. Less endearingly, it also secretes a bitter, milky substance to deter would-be diners.

The writing style harnesses storytelling tools we explored in Chapter 3 (developing characters, harnessing specific details, and detail quantity and location). And the

[7] A good introduction also forces you to distill your understanding of complex issues into simple prose. After all, until you can explain the key points in your document in a short, clear introduction, you probably don't understand them as deeply as you need to.

[8] Perhaps the best excuse to use a descriptor in this book. This "plump" frog with "short" legs creates an image in your head no noun alone would.

[9] Verbs, like nouns, can be used to convey images that play a movie for readers.

style leverages several tools we'll explore in future chapters (em dashes emphasizing important information, sentence structure drawing your attention to key images, and varied sentence types to keep you engaged).

Take Justice Elena Kagan's writing in the *Jack Daniels v. VIP Prods.* trademark case—a fight over a dog-toy-maker's "Bad Spaniels" chewie toy. The first sentence is about as engaging as you can get. How could you not continue reading with an opener like this? Then a couple of choice details give you a flavor of what's to come. Throw in some striking verbs and you have a first impression that makes people want to keep reading:

> **This case is about dog toys and whiskey,**[10] **two items seldom appearing in the same sentence.** Respondent VIP Products makes a **squeaky, chewable** dog toy designed to look like a bottle of Jack Daniel's whiskey. Though not entirely. On the toy, for example, the words "Jack Daniel's" **become "Bad Spaniels."** And the descriptive phrase "Old No. 7 Brand Tennessee Sour Mash Whiskey" **turns into "The Old No. 2 On Your Tennessee Carpet."**

Or take this example from an appellate brief introduction. You'll find a slew of style moves—echo words ("fight" and "fight," "each" and "each"), deft punctuation (a semicolon to contrast, an em dash to emphasize), parallel balance in the sentences, vivid verbs ("broken"), emphasized words at the end of sentences ("sit mute"), and more.

> This is a case about **a fight** between a prisoner and his guards, **a fight** which left the prisoner badly injured.[11] **No one denies that the fight happened;** the only question is **who started it and how much force was used. Barnett told one version of events, and his guards told another.**
>
> The key witnesses who might have **broken the tie**—the other prisoners who had seen what happened that day—were brought to trial. But when they were called to the stand, **each** refused to testify, **each** in nearly identical terms. And when they did, the district court permitted each of them to **sit mute.** And so Barnett, who never had the assistance of counsel but was at least counting on witnesses who could corroborate his story, **found himself in a gunfight without even the knife he had been promised.**

This next writer makes a striking first impression by leading off with direct dialogue and a hypothetical.

> **If, while walking down the street, you tap a jogger on the shoulder and the tap startles him, causing him to trip, hit his head, and suffer a concussion, have you committed a violent act?**

[10] Juxtaposing two details can create a powerful effect—a point the Justice calls out specifically here. But it would have been as effective without the narration. Simply pairing "dog toys" and "whiskey" in the same sentence conveys an image on its own.

[11] The familiar word choice throughout this passage is no accident. Words like "fight," "told," "tie," "mute," and "knife" are all terms we'd use when telling a compelling story.

Most would say no. But if you punch the jogger and the punch causes him to fall, hit his head, and suffer a concussion, you have undoubtedly committed a violent act. The difference between a non-violent and violent act, then, is the degree of force used. **Both a tap and a punch are capable of causing great bodily harm, but a tap involves a limited degree of force while a punch involves a substantial degree of force. Or, in the words of the Sentencing Guidelines, a punch involves "physical force."**

To make your readers like you even more, use your introduction to show that your document is user-friendly. In this next introduction, the legal writer signposts the document's two main issues for handy reference:

The infringement issue is the more substantial. In addressing it, we do not decide whether the threshold inquiry applied in the Court of Appeals is ever warranted. We hold only that it is not appropriate when the accused infringer has used a trademark to designate the source of its own goods—in other words, has used a trademark as a trademark. That kind of use falls within the heartland of trademark law, and does not receive special First Amendment protection.

The dilution issue is more simply addressed. The use of a mark does not count as noncommercial just because it parodies, or otherwise comments on, another's products.

Here's an introduction that delivers each of the key elements in order, making it easy for readers to see the document's organization. The two main issues are road mapped—and the key rules, facts, and conclusions are dished up for readers one after the next.

Plaintiff sues an officer for malicious prosecution and the police department for vicarious liability—stemming from the defendants' allegedly framing plaintiff for forging high school documents to help a friend get a scholarship.[12] That claim fails for two reasons. First: Qualified immunity. Under state law, a law enforcement official loses qualified immunity only if there was "no arguable basis for probable cause to arrest." And this Court's case law has held that forensic reports provide enough cause to meet this standard.[13] Here, a crime-lab report determined that the plaintiff signed a forged high school grade-change request. Relying on that report, Officer Ballard issued an arrest warrant.[14] Ballard is thus entitled to qualified immunity.

Second: Vicarious liability. Under state and federal law, municipal liability under Section 1983 requires proof of (1) a policymaker, (2) an official policy and (3) a violation of constitutional right whose moving force is that policy. Just last year, this Court held that a complaint must allege the policy and who made it. Here, the plaintiff alleges no policy and no policymaker. . .

This example shows how a good introduction is a cheat sheet for your document. And what legal reader wouldn't appreciate that?

[12]This sentence orients readers favorably by weaving in the plaintiff's bad act.

[13]This is a preview of the rule pitch. Notice readers are first prepped with the general qualified immunity standard followed by the specific principle that will answer readers' questions.

[14]This is the key fact that closes the first issue's case.

6.1.2 Develop Your Opening Paragraphs

Great introductions start with opening paragraphs that do two things at the same time: welcome readers into the document by orienting them to the crux of the dispute and subtly prime readers to see that dispute in a favorable light.

Check out this opener in a brief arguing that Citibank should get back $500 million it accidentally sent to lenders. Notice how you are invited into the dispute with background but also persuaded that Citibank is in the right with the use of favorable details (like that another company owed the money that Citibank wired).

> Last August, Citibank wired **over $500 million of its own money by mistake**. **Ordinarily, the recipient of such a mistaken transfer must return the money**. Yet the District Court held that, in this case, Citibank is not entitled to restitution **because another entity—Revlon Consumer Products Corporation—was supposed to pay the recipients the same sum of money three years later**—in 2023. That extraordinary result is as wrong as it sounds.

Or take this next introduction penned by a lawyer who wanted to tell a story about a community in desperate need of the economic growth his client would bring:

> The Uinta Basin is an **isolated empire**.[15] It is **surrounded . . . by mountain ranges and plateaus. No freeways go in or out, just two-lane roads** that were not built for freight. But the basin is rich in resources, including **phosphate, natural asphalt, and aggregate, as well as natural gas, coal, and oil.** The soil is **rich** too, **supporting alfalfa, corn, and cattle ranching.**
>
> The Uinta Basin Railway **aims**[16] **to end the basin's isolation and let the empire's economy grow**. While railroads of the past diverted around the basin's terrain, the Uinta Basin Railway will **link** the basin's **communities** to the national rail network. **Oil producers, farmers, ranchers, and miners**[17] **will all have more opportunities.** The goal is a more robust, more diverse economy for local communities in the basin.
>
> **That goal fits with the national rail transportation policy, which encourages new rail lines that create competition and strengthen the transportation system. . . .** [18]

This is a master class in many tools we've covered, all coming together to hook you from the first words. The "isolated empire" theme resonates with the legal argument. Choice storytelling details make you feel like you're flying over the basin, watching the natural landscape pass by. Priming details tug on some heartstrings by connecting the case to everyday farmers, ranchers, and miners in the region. The writer manages to make you care about what happens to these little communities—and there is no higher goal for an opening set of paragraphs.

Openers come in different flavors, depending on what matters most in your document. Three ingredients stand out in many cases: legal details, factual details,

[15] A slew of style techniques to note in this introduction: balanced phrases and words engage you (like "aims to end"), short sentences make punchy points (like the opening one), alliteration ("rich in resources"), concrete storytelling words (like "freeways go in or out"), and more.

[16] Active verbs propel the entire introduction forward.

[17] Characters make a story more real than anything else can.

[18] Thanks to lawyer Jay Johnson for submitting this example, taken from his excellent brief as part of Write.law's Level Up Your Writing competition.

and priming details. The amount of each that you include depends on your case. If one category is more compelling, include more. If one is less persuasive, trim or skip it.[19]

Let's see how to craft your openers like the greats.

Opening with the Law

This opener provides a snapshot of the legal issue that forms the crux of your document. Lead with this deeper legal discussion when the factual story isn't as helpful. In this next opener, the hard-hitting facts about the harassment are lightly touched while the legal issues are stressed.

> This case stems from a **pure question of law** that came up in a **garden-variety disability-harassment case**. Courts have now **ruled three different ways on a simple issue**: Does the Americans with Disabilities Act somehow create an implied requirement for employers to inform employees about the particular regulations relevant merely because the employee made a routine request for workplace accommodations?

Or take this next example from a U.S. Supreme Court Justice, who knew that readers wouldn't care about how the case got to the court (it was procedural and didn't matter). Instead, the focus is on the pure legal issues:

> This case presents a clash: **the plain English meaning of a statute versus a rigid rule that defies the ordinary tools of statutory construction and bears no relation to any interpretive technique this Court has ever applied**.

Opening with the Story

Emphasize the facts in your opener when the story is more compelling. Ensure there's a beginning, middle, and end—like any good narrative. If the import of your opening facts won't make obvious sense now, there's no use delivering them. So story openers should be reserved for times where the story speaks for itself.

In this next example, you can watch the case's story begin, unfold, and conclude, all in one paragraph. A persuasive detail about the harassment is weaved in to start persuading. And the worst fact for this lawyer (that the company eventually addressed the harassment complained of by his client) is put into context.

> Plaintiff worked at the defendant's store as a **star employee for a decade**, even receiving an **"employee of the region" award** twice. And for the past several years, he repeatedly complained about racial harassment at his job. **For example**, he reported that his supervisor made comments about his **"weird accent"** dozens of times. **Years into the abuse,** the defendant finally acted, but by then, the plaintiff had already been harassed so much that he was forced to quit.

[19] And don't forget to consider the general framing and priming tools we covered in Chapter 5, like using modifiers, using dependent clauses, narrowing the field, and other methods to shift your reader's perspective. You'll notice examples of many of those in the examples we explore in this section.

That doesn't mean you need to summarize the whole story in your opener. One gripping scene can set up your document and grab readers. Take this opener that tells a story you can't ignore.

> Richard Johnson wakes up every day in a prison cell about the **size of a parking space**. Most days, he spends **twenty-four hours in that cell** without any human interaction. On the rare occasions when he is permitted to leave his cell to shower or exercise alone, he is **strip searched and handcuffed**. And because he has no meaningful opportunity to challenge his continued detention in solitary confinement, Johnson does not know when, if ever, he will be permitted to return to the general population.

Finally, a sensational opener that again leverages the power of storytelling. The setting: the Kingdom of Saudi Arabia. The main character: a high-ranking minister. The intrigue: millions pilfered from the kingdom's coffers.

> This case concerns a dispute between current and former officials of the Kingdom of Saudi Arabia that allegedly led to a murder attempt in Canada.... Appellant Saad Aljabri was once a high-ranking official in the Kingdom of Saudi Arabia's Ministry of Interior. From 2001 to 2015, Saudi Arabia entrusted him with managing a counterterrorism fund created in the wake of the September 11, 2001 terrorist attacks. During that time, Saudi Arabia allocated $19.7 billion to finance anti-terrorism efforts. More than half—a staggering $11 billion—was misspent or outright stolen by Aljabri and his associates, causing incalculable harm to public safety and government integrity. Aljabri involved his adult children in the scheme, funneling vast amounts of money through their accounts and out of Saudi Arabia.

Opening with Priming or Contextual Details

Priming details emotionally charge readers and get them in a favorable headspace. Lead with these when you need to capture readers' attention to convince them to listen. Sometimes, the crux of your dispute is so complicated that readers need education before they can understand the main points. If so, give readers that background first.

These next legal writers knew their audience would be skeptical at first blush because the weight of authority was piled against them. They cut straight to that concern so readers would rethink their presumptions.

> **This case involves the critical element that was missing in earlier efforts to remove related suits: direct contracts with the federal government.** Shell USA, Inc. entered over 120 contracts to provide the federal government with aviation gasoline and other petroleum products that the U.S. military desperately needed to fight and win World War II.

In this next example, the legal team knew that the crux of their dispute involved complex regulatory schemes and esoteric energy pricing indexes. So before getting to the crux of the dispute, the writers taught readers how the system works. Eventually the writers would get into complicated calculations of energy rates, but first, we get a high-level overview.

> These consolidated cases concern Federal Energy Regulatory Commission orders relating to... energy sales... during an extreme weather event in the summer of 2020. Because of enormous demand generated by the weather event, these freely negotiated, arms-length transactions were made at sales prices above the so-called "soft cap" applicable in the market, triggering FERC review of those prices.

With all that background, readers could understand the team's real points.

But remember these are all ingredients, not the whole recipe. Often you'll want to mix and match, depending on your case. In this next opener, the legal writers weave together relevant factual details with priming details. The length of the family's quest to regain their lost art, among other historical details, was probably not relevant. But these persuasive nuggets are weaved amid the relevant story so readers don't mind.

> This appeal arises from **a two-decade quest**[20] by the **family of Holocaust survivor** Lilly Cassirer to recover a **family treasure**, Rue Saint-Honoré, Afternoon, Rain Effect, an 1897 oil painting by the renowned French impressionist Jacob Abraham Camille Pissarro (the "Painting"). . . . The Painting was **illegally smuggled** out of Germany, in 1951, **to a Beverly Hills art dealer.** The Painting was then sold twice in California. In 1976, Baron Hans Heinrich von Thyssen-Bornemisza, **a highly sophisticated collector** living in Switzerland, **bought the Painting at a New York gallery.**

With your introduction opened, it's time to dish up the key takeaways that will give readers what they came for.

6.1.3 Focus on Your Persuasive Pitch

The best introductions are a cheat sheet for readers—a resource that contains all the key information organized in a way that even new readers can instantly understand. The best legal writers are the ones who can capture 30 pages of briefing in three paragraphs of introduction. No mean feat.

First, teach your readers how the law works so that they'll be able to reach initial conclusions about your document. That means delivering the rule pitch that will win the day. The more specific the better. Because if you firmly embed your perspective on the law now, your reader will know how to make decisions without digging into the dense legal discussions in the body. Take this next introduction, which highlights the key view of the rules that will make this lawyer a winner:

> The district court repeatedly stated that there was no way for it to promote cooperation by the recalcitrant witnesses. That was error. The Federal Rules of Evidence give the district courts ample authority to exercise control over testimony and to question witnesses themselves. And several federal statutes authorize judges to penalize witnesses who refuse to cooperate without a good reason. **While it is true that all these powers are discretionary, failing to recognize their existence abuses that discretion.**

Next, identify the most persuasive facts that will trigger positive emotions in your reader, as well as those facts they'll need when applying the rules you just explained. Dish those up with enough context that they make sense without reading your whole document. Look at this example from a lawyer ignoring this advice:

> The Court of Criminal Appeals erred in affirming the denial of Mr. Hoffman's claim of ineffective assistance of counsel at the guilt phase of his trial. The record reflects numerous ways in which trial counsel were ineffective at the guilt phase, specifically by failing to advance a Batson jury

[20] This is an example of using storytelling language to describe a noun. Many legal writers would have simply stated, "This appeal stems from the plaintiff spending 20 years trying to recover stolen artwork."

> challenge and failing to address other issues relating to jury selection and various evidentiary and testimonial issues.

Now look at what he could have done with some of the key specifics from his brief, delivered in a narrative with enough background so we can understand off the bat.

> The Court of Criminal Appeals erred in affirming the denial of Mr. Hoffman's claim of ineffective assistance of counsel. For one example, **trial counsel did not attempt to object when the state introduced to the jury an hour-long video of the brutal murder scene, complete with a pentagram drawn in blood. For another, trial counsel did not attempt to object when the state eliminated each of the three African Americans from the jury.**

This next writer, Judge Andrew Gordon, delivers an entire story about a Las Vegas gambling bust in a few concise sentences.

> This case tests the boundaries of how far the government can go when creating a subterfuge to access a suspect's premises. Here, the government disrupted the internet service to the defendant's hotel room in order to generate a repair call. Government agents then posed as repairmen to gain access to the defendant's room and conduct a surreptitious search for evidence of an illegal sports betting operation. **By creating the need for a third party to enter defendant's premises and then posing as repairmen to gain entry, the government violated the defendant's Fourth Amendment rights.**

In this next example, a federal judge wanted to break down her analysis in a few quick paragraphs so that readers would get everything she cared about in 60 seconds. By the end, you don't just understand the writer's general conclusions—you understand *why* they believe what they do.

> This is a patent-infringement suit over LED lighting products. Plaintiff Signify alleges that defendant Lepro infringed seven of Signify's patents covering various LED technologies. **Signify moves to strike eight prior-art references from Lepro's amended invalidity claim charts, arguing that the court didn't authorize the addition of these "family references" when granting Lepro leave to amend. . . . I grant Signify's motion to strike because whether Lepro can use these uncharted references to directly support its invalidity contentions was never before the court, so this amendment was unauthorized. . . .**

You already understand why the prior-art references should be struck. The Defendants never mentioned them when seeking approval to amend their filing, so they were never properly authorized by the court.

6.1.4 Counter Biases and Leverage Themes

Your main goal for introductions should be to give readers answers. But this is also your first chance to start persuading. Confront possible reader biases and work to leverage those themes and policy points we covered in Chapter 5. Anticipate arguments against your position, understand your reader's potential preconceptions, and be aware of the emotionally charged facets of your case.

This requires you to do some hard thinking about (1) what persuasive points the other side might muster against you, (2) who your legal reader is (does this judge have known values or perspectives that might turn them against you at the outset?), and (3) any emotional facts about the underlying story or law that feel particularly important.

Take this next example. The writer takes your assumptions about what a "felony battery" sounds like and blasts them. And with fantastic style: a well-placed colon, two short transitions, a well-balanced trio of sentences, and a clear theme.

> No question about it: **a crime called "felony battery" sure sounds like a violent crime. But sometimes intuition can be wrong.** So we evaluate whether a crime qualifies as a crime of violence under the federal definition of that term of art by conducting legal analysis and applying Supreme Court precedent.

As we learned earlier, every good document has a theme and weaves in policies, too. The introduction is the place to start laying the groundwork for those elements. Look at how Justice Neil Gorsuch incorporates his theme about robocalls annoying everyday folks who are trying to enjoy their lives.

> **Disruptive dinnertime calls, downright deceit**, and more besides[21] drew Congress's eye to the debt collection industry. From that scrutiny emerged the Fair Debt Collection Practices Act, a statute that authorizes private lawsuits and weighty fines designed **to deter wayward collection practices. . . .**

Usually, you should start your introduction with an affirmative story that guides your audience in what they should do. But sometimes your audience has already been persuaded by an opposing point. Or the other side has done such a good job framing an issue or argument, you know your reader is already in that headspace. In that case, you might want to take on counters more forcefully.

Take this example. The attorney decided that she would have better traction taking the counterargument head-on. She starts her pitch by teeing up the argument made by the other side, though reframed and ripe for undermining.

> The State's argument boils down to this: **Why make them go refile this case in another court if this court already has jurisdiction? The answer is because the statute requires it.**[22] The State relies on a case that this Court has impliedly overturned.

If you think your audience might be distracted by a red herring—whether it be an opposing argument or something else—it can help to separate what matters from what doesn't right in the introduction (what I called *narrowing the field* in Chapter 5). Consider this tactic if you're worried your reader might be thinking about something

---

[21] Adding "besides" here is solely about creating pleasing balance. Stopping at "more" would have conveyed the same point. Read the sentence aloud both ways. It sounds better with the extra word, right? Part of the reason is that inserting a different grammatical structure in the third item within a trio of points like this is a well-known rhetorical improvement. Adding more words to that final item also emphasizes it, drawing out the "more" prominently.

[22] This question-and-answer format is a useful rhetorical move we look at again in Chapter 9.

they shouldn't be. This next attorney does this clarifying by drawing a line between what is and is not at issue.

> González cannot justify his attack on Martinez-Agüero. He does not even try. That's important here: **Nowhere in his brief does González attempt to meet the first prong of the test, requiring justifiable threats to his personal safety.** Instead, in an attempt to avoid liability, González asks the Court to create new law piecemeal out of dicta and doctrine borrowed from case law[23] that has nothing to do with this issue.

At bottom, your readers might not make it much farther than the introduction, so make every word count.

6.2 Start Sections with Snap

The entry point for individual sections also sets the tone for your reader's journey. Targeted headings coupled with strategic opening paragraphs will prime your reader, providing a clear map of the terrain ahead.

Let's revisit the hog case we looked at earlier (a lawsuit against farms for spraying waste onto lawns, cars, and people). The lawyers do a great job crafting headings that leverage vivid verbs (how can you not sympathize after thinking about waste being "smeared" on things?), and specific details. Perhaps most important, the headings link those facts to the law they satisfy — using terms from authority like "detect" and "invade" to make the connections clear. In short, the headings are snappy takeaways that will impress readers and help them get the gist of each section.

> Plaintiffs Establish Their Claims for Trespass.
>
> A. Defendants **Invaded** Plaintiffs' Land **by Spraying and Flinging Hog Waste Onto Plaintiffs' Yards and Houses.**
>
> B. Plaintiffs **"Detect"** the Hog Waste **By Smearing It, Seeing It, Feeling It Wet Their Clothes, and Getting Hit By It in the Face** — So They **Don't Need an Expert to Testify the Waste Is "Detectable."**[24]
>
> C. Plaintiffs Were **Injured** When They **Had to Pay Good Money to Clean Off Defendants' Hog Waste, When They Had to Stop Parking on Their Own Property Where They Liked**, and **When They Could No Longer Enjoy Their Yards and Porches as Before.**[25]

The heading is the first message your readers see when entering a section. It should be precise, engaging, and informative. But a heading's power is magnified when it acts in concert with the paragraphs that open your section. In other words, your heading and the initial paragraphs that follow should come together to provide a snapshot that will sell readers on the section. Let's see how.

---

[23] Pointing to the dicta and use of merely analogous case law is a good use of rule proof.

[24] This takeaway explains the authors' legal theory in commonsense terms. No expert is needed when everyday folks can detect a substance.

[25] Including these sympathetic details in the heading ensures readers are thinking about them as they start the section.

A Quick Summary

Guide with headings. **Headings break up your writing and provide a map of the forest before the trees. Use more headings to point out what matters in each part of your document. Headings should be understood without reading the section they lead into.**

Prime with headings. **Your headings should grab attention and match the tone of your writing. Avoid drama and stick to persuasive specifics.**

Start sections by guiding and priming again. **After the heading, kick off each section with a brief roadmap that lays out what follows. This preview should provide background and highlight the main points in plain language.**

6.2.1 Guide with Headings

We already covered the most important heading skill in Chapter 2. Your first goal should be to distill the most important ideas from each section into a persuasive package. That way readers have an anchor to what matters as they dive into a section's morass.

But when should you use headings in the first place? The answer is any time they will help your reader—which, for most legal writers, means a lot more. Don't force readers to skim pages of argument or facts, paragraph by paragraph, to figure out what points are made where.

An important heading skill, then, is simply to use them. Don't stop at the generic headings everyone uses. Consider how you can usefully break up sections into smaller pieces and use headings to guide through each. If you see a long section, ask yourself where you can use headings to chop it up so readers have a more manageable path.

You can even use mini-headings to categorize paragraph by paragraph, as this next legal writer did. The case turned on whether AI company ROSS stole copyrighted materials from popular research tool Westlaw. Italicizing the first sentence of each paragraph makes it easy to follow each factor of the relevant test:

1. *There was a contract....*
2. *Ross may have intentionally caused a breach....*
3. *Whether Ross acted without justification is a factual question....*
4. *Thomson Reuters has shown harm....*

Once you've chosen your headings, make sure they'll make sense to a fresh reader. It's frustrating when a brief hosts a list of headings that don't make sense until you read the sections they lead into—either because they are too in the weeds or too in the clouds. That strategy makes no sense. How can your headings persuade if your reader can't understand them until after reading everything that follows?

A few strategies will ensure your headlines will make sense to a new reader. First, keep your headings at a high level—and in a sensical order—so that your readers can understand the basics when they first read the table of contents. That's always a good test: the table-of-contents test. Take this next example. Notice how you need no explanation to follow the story right in the table.

1. **Brandilyn Netz becomes Bradley Roberts.**[26]
2. **[The school district] officially bans Roberts from both the men's and women's bathrooms.**
3. **[The district] circulates an email informing Roberts's coworkers that they should refer to him as a man.**
4. **Roberts files administrative charges and [the district] lifts the bathroom ban.**

Second, to make them hit even harder, set up headings in the prior sections, prior headings, or prior roadmaps. In your introduction, preview the substance of all the top-level headings coming. Then as you enter each section, map out the subheadings and briefly explain why they matter. See how easy it is to pick up on this heading with a setup like this:

Because the plaintiff has **alleged no injury** caused by the cars, there is no **standing** here. But even if there were, the alleged **harm happened after the statute of limitations ran.**

A. **Plaintiff alleges only that he could not use his car for an hour—that is not the sort of injury required to have standing.**
B. **On top of alleging zero facts showing harm,[27] plaintiff fails to allege any relevant facts after 2012—so the four-year statute of limitations has run.**

Finally, to keep headings readable, avoid acronyms, jargon, or technical language in them (unless your reader is sure to understand at first glance). In that last snippet, for example, not one word required a legal dictionary or time spent pulling cases and statutory provisions.

6.2.2 Prime with Headings

Lawyers often focus their headings on bland, generic labels. Or worse, they use headings to channel their frustration at opposing counsel. Just because a heading is not followed by a cite does not mean that your credibility is any less at stake. So please avoid this:

A. Plaintiff's desperate grasping for life by pointing to a new legal theory about statutory remedies utterly fails out of the gate.

Headings are your readers' welcome to sections—they should be *inviting*. Providing curb appeal for your sections will entice readers to come in and read more. In other words, style and tone stand out here. Take this engaging nugget from a motion for summary judgment, complete with snappy verbs and familiar word choice:

[26] The most effective way to make a point is to let the details speak for themselves like this.

[27] Logical transitions like this not only tie the two headings together, but they also provide a chance to reinforce the positive takeaway from the prior heading.

> **A. Marx sidestepped the extra tax penalties by ballooning the fees he raked in from his own customers.**

The pithier your headings, the better they will stick. Try this next heading out for size, and note the word balance, the placement of "buyout" at the end of the first clause to emphasize it, the repeated "b" words to alliterate, and the trio of phrases to tie things up.

> **A. Plaintiffs press for an interpretation where they can breach and buyout—but that has never been the parties' intent; they said so under oath, and their actions confirm it.**

Much of persuading is about highlighting the right point in the right way. Headings are an excellent place to do that. By sifting through your section for the best materials, you will emblazon your best work in neon. See how these next writers flash the key facts and legal points from their sections.

> A. The defendant had no expectation of privacy in his bathroom because he **"called police on the phone"** and **"asked them"** to come inside.

> A. This court has no jurisdiction because **the deadline to file the complaint was June 2017 and plaintiff filed in September of that year.**

> A. The Supreme Court case law requires alleging **the date, time, and means of carrying out the conspiracy—none of which exist here**.

Look at this next clunker from a hefty criminal brief. Not only is it long, but it doesn't capture the section's persuasive points.

> This Court Should Grant Certiorari Pursuant to Rule 39(a)(1)(D) Because the Court of Criminal Appeals' Decision Affirming Summary Dismissal of Mr. Hoffman's Claim That He Received Ineffective Assistance of Appellate Counsel Due to Appellant Counsel's Failure to Argue That Remand Was Necessary to Demonstrate That Mr. Hoffman Is Intellectually Disabled.

Now check out how a rewrite with fewer words can do more work by highlighting favorable specifics.

> Review is warranted because trial counsel never so much as mentioned that **Mr. Hoffman was intellectually disabled—despite that he has an IQ of 50 and this court has held that an IQ of 65 warrants relief.**[28]

Finally, check your headings' design elements. Make sure they aren't too long. Anything longer than three lines and your readers likely will not read it. I don't

[28] This heading is magic because it's specific enough to persuade but simple enough that you understand it without any background knowledge.

know about you, but I would not react kindly if I opened a brief and this heading greeted me:

> **1. This Court Should Grant Certiorari Pursuant to Rule 39(a)(1)(D) Because the Court of Criminal Appeals' Decision Affirming Summary Dismissal of Mr. Marin's Claim That He Received Ineffective Assistance of Appellate Counsel Due to Appellant Counsel's Failure to Argue That Remand Was Necessary to Demonstrate That Mr. Marin Reasonably Relied on the State's Action Is in Conflict with *Moore v. Texas, Montgomery v. Louisiana, Brumfield v. Cain, Hall v. Florida,* and *Smith v. State.***

What a lift. You'll rarely see case names or statutory numbers in good headings (unless the section's focus is about that one perfect decision you don't want readers to miss). Any heading longer than a few lines is begging to get skipped. Look at a version that includes persuasive information but keeps it short and simple:

> **1. Counsel was ineffective because he failed to explain to the lower court that, once free, Rene spent four years building a family and career—all in reliance on the state's mistake in calculating his prison term.**

Weird fonts are hard to read in headings. Don't mix emphasis types and keep typography simple:

> **I. THIS COURT SHOULD GRANT CERTIORARI PURSUANT TO RULE 39(A)(1)(D) BECAUSE THE COURT OF CRIMINAL APPEALS' DECISION AFFIRMING SUMMARY DISMISSAL OF MR. HOFFMAN'S CLAIM . . .**
>
> *becomes*
>
> **I. This Court should grant certiorari pursuant to Rule 39(a)(1)(D) because the Court of Criminal Appeals' decision affirming summary dismissal of Mr. Hoffman's claim . . .**

Now that we've got our heading down, let's move into the section itself.

6.2.3 Start Sections by Guiding and Priming Again

The heading gave your reader a sense of what matters in the section. Now it's time to break the section down so readers are ready to dig in. Start with a brief roadmap explaining what you are analyzing and why—and include some persuasive priming, too.

Good goals for section openers are to explain the context of why you are addressing the issues that you do, dispose of any side matters that you will not be analyzing at length, and guide readers in any other way useful. Maybe some background principles (like burdens) will help set the stage. Perhaps you want to narrow the field and clarify what points are not in dispute. Lists can also help here (as they do anywhere with multiple ideas to march through).

In this next snippet, leading off for several subsections of statutory and regulatory analysis, the legal writers offer two background principles that animate everything coming after: (1) the plain-meaning rule, and (2) that this rule applies to regulations (not just statutes).

> Because the Corp's Savings Clause analysis is a matter of statute, **"[t]he controlling principle in this case is the basic and unexceptional rule that courts must give effect to the clear meaning of statutes as written."** ...
>
> **The same holds true when the court construes agency regulations.** The court "evaluate[s] whether the plain language of the regulation unambiguously answers the question at issue when [it] consider[s] the regulatory language itself, the particular context in which that language appears, and the broader context and purpose of the regulatory scheme as a whole. . . . "

In this next example, a federal appellate judge offers the background law that applies to all the subheadings that follow. He also narrows the universe of law down to the element the section focuses on. Readers are ready to tackle the key copying issue and the three relevant liability theories.

> A copyright-infringement claim has three elements: **ownership of a valid copyright, actual copying, and substantial similarity.**[29] [cites]. Here, all three elements are at least partly disputed. **But the dispute over the second element is legal, so I can decide it now.** And because Ross hired LegalEase to do the copying (if there was any), Thomson Reuters also couches its argument in terms of direct, contributory, and vicarious liability. So . . . I **will consider each of these liability theories as well.**

Here's another example of a section opener done right. The legal writer previews the persuasive point (that the other side's use of a doctrine is unprecedented and omits relevant facts). Then they set up the three subsections: one looking at the doctrine's source, one discussing the underlying purpose of the doctrine, and a final section walking through the precedent.

> Although González never identifies it by name, his argument is premised on []the entry-fiction doctrine[]. By invoking the entry fiction,[30] he proposes to treat Martinez-Agüero as if she had been completely outside U.S. territory when he attacked her. What González does not disclose,[31] however, is that the entry fiction has never been applied to determine legal rights and obligations [regarding] mistreatment of aliens [but only as] to admission or exclusion determinations. Nor does he acknowledge this Court's explicit rejection of the entry-fiction doctrine in such circumstances. **An examination of the doctrine's source, its rationale32 and the cases applying it demonstrates its inapplicability here.**

As with headings, good style matters here. This is your section's welcome mat. Avoid weighing it down with citations, heavy sentences, complex concepts, or anything else that will make your reader dread reading on. The start of your section should promise an engaging and organized read to come, like this next example. You know exactly what's ahead, and you're even told you can skip a nonessential part if you like. How helpful is that?

[29] The judge uses short descriptions of major legal concepts to keep the law accessible.
[30] Labeling the doctrine as a "fiction" subtly undermines its credibility.
[31] Highlighting gaps in an opponent's explanations like this strikes a devastating blow to their credibility.
[32] We won't hold the missing serial comma against this excellent writer.

> In this section[,] I provide background on the source of Congress's and the President's authority to exclude aliens, the Executive Order at issue here, and the proceedings in this case. THE INFORMED READER MAY PROCEED DIRECTLY TO PART II.

These next legal writers manage to map out the section's three parts, use choice quotes from the authority to bolster credibility, and narrow in on the disputed issues to avoid distracting readers.

> Defendants are entitled to removal because (1) Shell is a "person" under the federal-officer removal statute, (2) Shell was "acting under" a federal officer, (3) the suit "relat[es] to" acts Shell took under that federal direction, and (4) Defendants assert a colorable federal defense. . . . **Plaintiffs do not contest the first requirement, and their efforts to dispute the others are unpersuasive.**

Sometimes a section is about only one thing; no roadmap is needed. If so, use the opening paragraph to preview the persuasive takeaway from the section with a little more depth than a quick heading can manage.

> Earley's plan properly treats Triad's claim as unsecured, **but not because *Hunt* controls the issue. It does not. Triad's claim is unsecured because of the nature of Triad's lien and the interplay between [a statute] and the automatic stay under the Bankruptcy Code.**[33]

You've done everything you can to make the beginning of your section welcoming. Now let's make the rest of it easier for readers, too.

6.3 Make Documents Easy to Navigate

Busy readers need usable documents. They need documents they can refer back to and skim for quick answers. This section shares strategies for writing documents like that. You'll learn the importance of grounding abstract legal principles with solid examples, the need to define terms and reiterating key concepts, and how to find opportunities to guide your reader every step of the way.

When Justice Ketanji Brown Jackson wanted to make it easy to dive into her first opinion, she started with one of the most helpful hand-holding devices: A definition of a core legal term in simple language. Many writers would have plunged into the precedent and complexity, but this background makes it easy on readers.

> **"Escheatment" is the power of a State . . . to take custody of property deemed abandoned.** . . . In the context of tangible property, the escheatment rule is straightforward: The State in which the abandoned property is located has the power to take custody of it. . . . But determining which State has the power to escheat intangible property [with] no physical location[] can be complicated[,] as multiple States may have arguable claims.

[33] This last sentence of the section opener tees up the two legal doctrines the writer will walk through.

When walking through her detailed analysis, the Justice offers a brief roadmap to keep it manageable:

> To decide which escheatment rules apply, we must interpret a federal statute that abrogates our precedent. **Thus,[34] we begin with a discussion of this Court's common-law rules for escheatment, followed by a description of the statute that partially displaced those rules.**

Finally, the Justice gives us an example of useful labels. After explaining two distinct lines of cases, she uses shorthand to make it easy for readers to keep them clear as she goes:

> It soon became clear that our **primary** and **secondary escheatment rules** were resulting in inequitable distributions. . . .

Together, hand-holding devices like this won't just make your documents easier to digest; they'll make your arguments more persuasive. Being understood is, after all, the first step to being convincing.

A Quick Summary

Order points purposely. Don't mindlessly stick to the same default order everyone else uses. Order points in a way that makes sense for each document. It's okay to deviate from the norm.

Orient and roadmap. Orienting isn't just for introductions and section starts. Offer readers an overview or framework to guide them through every complex turn.

Strive for the self-explanatory. Good legal writing makes complex topics easy to understand without requiring readers to remember concepts from far earlier in the document. Avoid jargon and give readers all the information they need in each section.

Use examples. Specific examples and hypotheticals can clarify abstract concepts and bring legal points to life.

Craft conclusions. Conclusions should not be a formulaic copy-and-paste summary of your document. This is a final chance to capture your reader's attention and highlight key takeaways.

[34] Shorter transitions like this don't slow down the sentence's action as much.

6.3.1 Order Points Purposefully

At this point, you've done the hard work. You've distilled the value for readers in headings, introductions, and even the starts of paragraphs. You know what readers need and you've made it easy for them to find. Now step back and consider the best order to walk readers through all that great content.

Some research suggests you should go with the foot-in-the-door approach: Begin with the point that you think is strongest (even if it isn't the most important). If your reader agrees with you once, the chances go up they will keep agreeing with you. With the door cracked, you can nudge it open wider and wider.

There are exceptions, though. For one, if you know your reader is most interested in a particular issue and starting with something else will be a distraction, then go with your reader's preference. Or if an opposing attorney makes an unusually powerful argument that could defeat you, maybe go straight there. And if one of your arguments is that a threshold issue disposes of everything else, that might be the best place to start so that readers have a simple path that avoids the harder turns.

At the paragraph level, ordering is not about following some rote rule. It's about remembering what we worked through in Chapter 2. Paragraphs are idea-delivery machines. Each paragraph should deliver a single idea. One thought that every sentence is built around. If you do that distilling first, it's easier to step back and organize your paragraphs.

One of the most helpful strategies on this front is to ask yourself this: Given what I told my reader in the last paragraph, what will be their most burning questions now? Often this imaginary conversation with readers will lead you to the simplest, most effective organization. Figure out where you want to start readers in each section, and then keep asking yourself: Knowing what the reader knows now, what will they ask next? Then deliver the paragraph that answers that question. Keep that exchange moving and readers will stay with you.

At bottom, the secret to persuasive ordering is to organize around each reader and each document. Think about what your reader needs to know at each step and deliver it to them. And that means deviating from the traditional when your message warrants it.

Chronological order is common when relating facts, for example, but sometimes topical organization makes better sense. This next legal writer organized her fact section around a few key documents that underpinned her legal analysis. And it works great.

> **A. Each Document Put Defendants on Notice of the Merger Again and Again.**
>
> 1. **The Financing Document Includes 15 Pages of Details About the Merger.**
> 2. **The 2020 Internal Memo Includes More than 30 Paragraphs About the Merger.**
> 3. ...

Or maybe a scene in your factual story is so pivotal that you want to start or end your section with it (rather than working through events in the order they happened):

> Three months after filing his original grievance that forms the basis of his claim,[35] Smith decided to prepare a special package for the warden. A pipe bomb constructed out of Clorox[36] and other goods that Smith had managed to pilfer from the prison stores....

Rather than starting with the grievance and boring procedural facts, the lawyer gets right to the good stuff. He will have to backtrack later to deliver the earlier events, probably with a good fact heading that keeps the reader from getting lost. But deviating from the norm engaged readers a lot sooner.

Another common change-up great legal writers sometimes use is the fragmented fact section. This approach has you deliver one set of facts, then analyze them. Then deliver another set of facts and analyze those. In other words, instead of a long fact section, then a long analysis section, you deliver a little bit of both at a time. Consider this approach when you have so many facts that readers can't reasonably follow them all in one section—and the legal issues are compartmentalized so that each group of facts is relevant only to one part of the analysis.

Or take our analysis sections. Delivering the rules first is usually most helpful for readers. After all, they can't understand why the facts matter unless they understand the goalposts set by the rules. But sometimes weaving the application and rule discussion together makes sense. In fact, great legal writers sometimes cut the fact section altogether (or include only a brief summary), preferring to deliver the facts in the analysis as they go.

The message here is to adopt a default order for your points, but don't be afraid to deviate.

6.3.3 Orient and Roadmap

As you organize your sections, look for opportunities to do some extra guiding. Roadmaps and orientation aren't just for introductions and section starts. Use both devices throughout your documents whenever readers could use some background before the hard work.

Fresh readers need you to start at the top, without assuming they know or remember much of anything. So constantly orient your readers to the background they need to make sense of anything that is complex or important. Suggest to readers *why* the point matters, or *how* the point fits into the overall case or argument. In short, give readers helpful context to extract what they need from your main points.

This next example illustrates this orientation at work. The legal writers were analyzing a complex procedural issue—protective notices of appeal. These notices preserve a party's appellate rights while some other process is playing out—and they can sometimes annoy courts by creating additional procedural paperwork. So before getting into the weeds, the lawyers offered some context for why, practically, protective notices of appeal are important.

---

[35] Usually long dependent clauses at the start like this weaken sentences. But here, the writer had a reason. They wanted you to understand the background timeline before delivering the thrust in the main clause.
[36] This familiar detail adds realism to the story.

> **Protective notices of appeal play an essential role in preserving appellate rights when a party seeks to appeal a district court order of uncertain appealability.** [L]itigants are not forced to forgo good-faith objections to appealability in order to pursue an appeal on the merits. To the contrary, as officers of the court, would-be appellants are duty-bound to notify the appellate court of potential jurisdictional defects.

Another way to orient is the roadmap. We've looked at these in introductions and the beginning of sections. But roadmaps can be great at the start of a rule pitch, the beginning of a complex set of paragraphs—or anywhere listing categories will help readers.

For example, this next legal writer knew that the *Parel* case packed a lot in and that readers might have trouble following. So she road-mapped her analysis and previewed that the reasoning wasn't obvious, giving readers a framework first:

> ***Parel* foreclosed this species of tort claims, although it requires some digging to see why.**[37] There, the plaintiff brought the same claim that Plaintiff asserts here, along with a host of other claims. The court ended up dismissing the entire complaint largely because of case-terminating sanctions levied on the plaintiff's lawyer. **But in explaining why ending the case was appropriate, the court held that each claim was already statutory foreclosed. In other words, the same claim that Plaintiff asserts here was foreclosed by the statute itself.**[38]

Next is an example of an attorney using more road-mapping to guide readers through a complicated analysis. You get a breakdown of the issues and then each is tackled in turn.

> **The court need only ask two questions about standing here: (1) whether Mr. Jake lived in the home when it caught fire, and (2) did Mr. Jake lose any money because of the fire?** The answer to both questions is no.
>
> **Courts first require that a claimant reside in the damaged home at the time it was damaged.** [Cite.] Mr. Jake admitted that he did not. [Cite.] That alone is enough to reject his claim.
>
> **Courts also require that claimants suffer out of pocket harm.** This element requires evidence of actual out of pocket losses...

6.3.1 Strive for Self-Explanatory Writing

You've ordered your points, oriented readers, and figured out what they need to make the right decisions. Now it's time to ensure that the prose you use delivers all those goods effortlessly.

---

[37] This writer showed off another genius technique we briefly explored earlier: building credibility with an audience by injecting some intellectual honesty into her language. She admits, in an offhand way, that her take on this case requires some thought. Most legal writers wouldn't be so transparent, simply suggesting the case proves their point. But credibility goes a long way toward persuading readers.

[38] These last two sentences show off a rhetorical tool we'll return to in Chapter 9—repeating a point in different language to emphasize it. The writers also smartly link the case's facts to their client's situation.

You've been living and breathing this document for days (or longer). You know it backward and forward. So what often happens? You forget that once you're an expert, it's *really* hard to remember what it was like to be a newbie. This disconnect between lawyers who are experts in their cases—and audiences who are not—is to blame for many major writing fails. Cursed with deep knowledge about the issues, legal writers fill their writing with jargon, forget to offer the basic context new readers need, and abandon audiences to piece everything together on their own.

If you're expecting readers to go back and remember concepts from pages ago, or even paragraphs before, you're setting yourself up for disaster. Busy legal readers skim. Each sentence, paragraph, and section should be as self-contained as you can build it. We've already touched on the power of specifics in Chapter 3, and we'll return to them again when building sentences in Chapter 7. Throughout your documents, though, always ask what supplies you can drop-ship to readers so they jump into your document anywhere—whether it's definitions, lay explanations, hypotheticals and examples, background details, or something else.

Don't refer to the "incident" hoping that readers will remember what "incident" you mean—mention the "fight at the prison." Don't talk about "Section 231," because who can remember what that is about? (Yes, I know you mentioned it three pages ago, but readers can't remember that.) Refer to "the meet-and-confer rule." If your readers will need information you gave them before to make sense of what you are telling them now, remind them about that.

An elite legal team was attacking an expert report in a lawsuit about defective products. The defense attorneys used abstract jargon, talking about "supply-side factors," instead of conveying what they meant in concrete terms readers would instantly understand. Here is what they wrote:

> The plaintiffs' expert report is defective because it ignores **supply-side factors** that are very relevant. The plaintiff ignores this critical defect that proves fatal to their expert report. Excising **supply-side factors** from the analysis is not an effective manner of calculating the damages in this case.

When you read the entire section, eventually (if you were lucky) you might figure out what "supply-side factors" means—the costs to make and distribute the products. To make this jargon self-explanatory, considerate writers would take a moment to explain in simple terms:

> The plaintiffs' expert report is defective because it ignores **supply side costs. That is: The plaintiffs' expert calculates the value of the defendant's product by including only the price that buyers would pay—ignoring that those products cost money to make and distribute. The value of the product is the price buyers would pay minus the cost of making it. The Court doesn't need an expert to figure that out. By leaving out the supply costs, the expert inflates the product's value.**

Now look at what some legal writing pros did in a similar case when they knew readers wouldn't be familiar with esoteric technical-speak. Attorney Liv Kiser and her team broke down some complicated expert methodology so simply that even a distracted judge could follow.

> Plaintiffs . . . sole evidence of "damage" was a "choice-based conjoint analysis" by Stefan Boedeker. **Choice-based conjoint analysis is a marketing research technique that seeks to determine how consumers value the different features (called "attributes"[39]) of a product, and the trade-offs consumers would be willing to make among the different attributes that comprise a product. Put differently, when done correctly, it's a method designed to yield information about what consumers are willing to pay. . . .**

If you're using a term that you aren't *sure* everyone will understand on the first read, explain it. This is true for legal terms as much as it is for factual ones. Jargon, terms of art, or any long or unfamiliar words can use a quick definition. Of course, if you can cut the heavy words altogether, all the better. Here's Justice Kagan being the ever-helpful definer, diagramming some math for readers:

> That is a mouthful[].[40] **So again, in general terms: The numerator is the number of patient days attributable to Medicare patients who are poor. The denominator is the number of patient days attributable to all Medicare patients. Divide[41] the former by the latter to get the fraction "expressed as a percentage."**

You can also explain on the other side of the complexity. When you've forced readers through dense concepts or details, it helps to give them a quick recap. This confirms for readers that they got out of the section what they should have. Take this recap offered by a crafty appellate writer. After explaining a convoluted trademark concept, she quickly sums up a takeaway for readers that puts it into context.

> The fair-use exclusion, though, comes with a caveat. A defendant cannot get its benefit—even if engaging in parody, criticism, or commentary—when using the similar-looking mark "as a designation of source for the [defendant's] own goods." [] **In other words, the exclusion does not apply if the defendant uses the similar mark as a mark.**

Here is Justice Kagan recapping the main point from a series of longer case expositions. The recap isn't random. It summarizes the rule principle—that statutes shouldn't be changed—that readers need to get to their ultimate answer.

> **In each [of the above cases], the Court observed that using a different method required no change in the State's statute, but only a change in an agency's uncodified protocols.** Here, all parties agree that Georgia would have to change its statute to carry out Nance's execution by means of a firing squad. They dispute whether that fact switches Nance's claim to the habeas track.

Quick recaps allow you to reinforce what matters. Look at how an expert appellate writer reinforces his view through a helpful recap.

---

[39] The admirable writers define every term you need to know as they go. No dictionaries needed.

[40] A short sentence opener like this is about the most inviting way to open a paragraph. It promises easy passage ahead. Ending this quick sentence with "mouthful" also highlights the style power in a sentence's final word.

[41] Beginning a sentence with a verb like this is a style tool we return to in Chapter 9.

> Visa uses the FANF structure to drive up the price merchants must pay to process debit transactions, while using its market power to insulate itself from the usual consequences of raising prices. **Simply put, Visa charges merchants an upfront fee for the privilege of accepting Visa products, which merchants cannot refuse, and then uses that upfront fee to keep its per-transaction fees artificially low.**

In sum, be on the lookout for any language that readers won't instantly understand:

- Words that make readers refer to earlier parts of the document or outside the document altogether (like *the issue, the incident, the transaction, the agreement, the error, the finding, the results,* etc.)
- Conclusions or characterizations that don't tell readers why you believe what you do (like *the defendant committed a violation, the plaintiff apparently realizes it has no case*, or *the injury was significant*)
- Industry jargon (from your brief or used by other parties in the case)
- Complicated concepts when it's been a while since you explained them (readers are busy, they can't remember much for long)
- Legal terms of art, statutory references, or any other legalese (even judges don't usually remember what that statutory section or procedural rule stands for)
- Any other time where a new reader will be forced to pause even briefly to remember or refer to something else. Just do the work for them.

6.3.4 Use Examples

Even if you carefully explain every concept in simple terms, your readers might still stumble on the *really* hard stuff. When the abstractions pile up too high, pull out an example. Readers love good examples. Use a hypothetical to make a vague legal principle feel concrete. Use a fact pattern to illustrate how the law works in a way that connects with readers. Or use some examples from your case to illustrate an overarching point—like how much harm your client suffered.

A legal team was pitching readers on why a famous administrative law doctrine should be set aside. Instead of generic criticisms, they marched out examples highlighting the rule's past problems:

> As the *Chevron* two-step began to take hold, criticism mounted. **For example, some argued that *Chevron* is inconsistent with the Constitution's separation of powers; others argued that *Chevron* contradicted the APA; and others expressed skepticism about *Chevron's* workability.**[42]

This next paragraph is from the litigation against Elon Musk about his compensation package at Tesla. The legal writers use a list of examples that come together to convey the writers' argument—that Musk exerted too much control over the company.

> The collection of features characterizing Musk's relationship with Tesla and its directors gave him enormous influence over Tesla. In addition to his **21.9% equity stake, Musk was the paradigmatic**

[42] Check out Chapter 9 to explore several other ways to use examples to amp up your message.

> **"Superstar CEO,"[43] who held some of the most influential corporate positions (CEO, Chair, and founder), enjoyed thick[44] ties with the directors tasked with negotiating on behalf of Tesla, and dominated the process that led to board approval of his compensation plan.[45]**

Hypotheticals and examples aren't as daunting as you think. They do take time to find or create, though. We return to this tool in Chapter 9, as it's one of the most effective in your persuasion arsenal.

6.3.5 Craft Conclusions

That brings us to your document's finale. The conclusion. You'd think that legal writers would finish strong, bringing together the most persuasive threads of their document into a final crescendo. But most treat conclusions as an afterthought, marching out formalities like this:

> Plaintiff's claims fail because they fail to state a claim, and even if they did, there is no jurisdiction here. For the foregoing reasons, the defendant requests that the plaintiff's complaint be entirely dismissed with prejudice, as well as any other relief the court deems proper.

Or perhaps even more common is a copy-and-pasted finisher like this:

> For the foregoing reasons, the defendant motion should be denied.

Don't give up this precious real estate by pasting in nothingness. If you've done your job to this point, readers will listen. Take this moment to say something useful. Use your conclusions to recapture your reader's attention and leave them with a memory they won't forget.

One simple method is to look at your headings and craft a pithy takeaway for each main issue. Another tactic is to remind readers about the most hard-hitting facts that you want burned into their minds. The following legal writer did both, summing up her main points while injecting key facts along the way.

> [T]his Angola-centered dispute must be resolved in Angola. The New York Case precludes relitigation of the forum issue. Were this Court to engage in its own forum non conveniens analysis, it should reach the same conclusion as the New York Case—**this dispute should be resolved in Angola: the place where the parties agreed to arbitrate their disputes; the place where Plaintiff and the Angolan Defendants are located; the place where the contracts between Plaintiff and the Angolan Defendants were executed, performed, and terminated; and the place where the parties are engaged in parallel litigation over the same issues Plaintiff raises here.**... Lastly, Plaintiff failed to adequately state a claim against each Angolan Defendant, **imprecisely lumping all Defendants together in violation of the *Bancec* doctrine.**... [46]

---

[43] Quoting to bring in distinctive language like this is a great persuasive tool.

[44] An example of a useful descriptor: "*thick* ties" evokes the sense of deep ties in an evocative way.

[45] This snippet is from the document's introduction. And notice how deep into the key details the legal writer gets. This isn't about some general conclusions —readers are given a snapshot of what matters.

[46] This is a great example of our collecting details move from Chapter 3. Collecting all these disparate Angola-centered details in one place makes the point finer.

Conclusions are flexible. But make sure you are clear about your main points and what the reader should do next. In this next conclusion, the writer uses their final moment to emphasize the main points while weaving in the most moving policy.

> Even apart from its tendency to spread to other jurisdictions, the decision is important and merits this Court's review. The decision . . . **means that thousands of FDOC inmates will not receive a publication designed to inform them of their legal right and of abuse within the FDOC system. It plainly paves the way for censorship of the First Amendment rights of the many more thousands of individuals currently detained within the confines of the Eleventh Circuit.**

Conclusions are your final shot. Don't miss yours.

Level Up Your Organization with Technology

Organizing is about outlining and planning extensively, keeping track of your main takeaways, being efficient in your drafting process, and ensuring each area of your document is easy to navigate. Technology can help every step of the way.

GAI tools: GAI has the potential to revolutionize legal writing by helping with planning, organizing, and creating compelling content. GAI platforms can generate outlines and offer options for engaging narrative hooks in introductions. Use GAI to:

- Draft initial outlines: Input key themes and facts into the AI, prompting it to generate various outline structures for your document.
- Create roadmaps: The AI can propose synthesized summaries of complex legal issues, to be used as roadmaps guiding the reader through your argument.
- Brainstorm narrative beginnings: Feed the AI with your case's basic facts and legal issues; it will generate multiple options for narrative openings for your documents, which can then be refined for maximum impact.
- Refine structure: Input the main points of your argument and ask the AI to order them persuasively, ensuring that the most potent information takes precedence.

Client relations management tools: These tech tools track client information. Often these will include helpful information like the key contact at the client, client preferences for your work product, and much more. Use them to tailor your documents for clients.

Mind-mapping software: Use mind-mapping applications such as XMind or MindManager to outline the narrative and structural blueprint of your document. These tools help visually plot the logical flow from introductions to later sections, ensuring a coherent progression of ideas and a solid foundation for persuasive beginnings.

Digital note-taking tools: Employ digital note-taking tools like Microsoft OneNote or Notion to gather, categorize, and prioritize ideas and research centrally. Use these platforms to construct an engaging story for your introduction, catalog key points for roadmaps, and keep necessary legal details at hand for reference and insertion into your text.

Collaborative document editors: Platforms such as Google Docs and Microsoft Teams facilitate real-time collaboration. These prove indispensable for crafting and refining document beginnings. Share drafts with colleagues to gather input on your introduction's impact and the document's overall organizational flow, ensuring a unified voice and strategy.

AI legal analytics: Explore legal analytics platforms like Lex Machina, which leverages AI to analyze legal outcomes and behaviors. These analytics help customize the order of argumentation and presentation to suit the predilections of specific judges or legal forums, aligning document structure and introductory narratives with historical data.

Text expansion: Use text expansion tools like PhraseExpress for quicker drafting of repetitive elements that need consistency, such as roadmaps or standard introductory phrases. This not only saves time but also maintains a uniform voice throughout the document.

Document management systems: Implement document management systems like NetDocuments, Worldox, or iManage to handle vast quantities of information. Efficient categorization and search features ensure that during drafting, critical facts and precedent cases are easily woven into the introduction and signposts, bolstering the document's persuasive power.

Practice these techniques and technologies with Write.law's exercises and checklists, plus other resources at www.levelupyourlegalwriting.com

ASPEN PUBLISHING | write.law

7

Level Up Your Style

> Fashions fade. Style is eternal." —Yves Saint Laurent

Building good sentences is like building good rocket ships. What, you don't think legal writing is rocket science? Well, it's not. But the two still share something in common. Poet and writer Ricardo Jaramillo explains:

> "Sometimes we write things that lead us to other, better things, and then we no longer need those original things. But often, we get too attached to our original words and keep them out of some strange sense of loyalty, thereby not giving space for the new, better things to come.
>
> It's like how rockets have pieces of themselves that fall off mid-flight. Those pieces help rockets get up to a certain point, and then, when they become more of a weight than they are useful, the rocket is designed to let them fall away. Sometimes we need to thank a line or section of writing for its service to us, for having gotten us to where we've arrived with our piece, and then: let it fall away."[1]

Good writing is about building something great, and then tearing off anything not helping it be great. It's about getting to the simple, elegant core of your ideas. It's about developing a direct style that delivers points down to the roots.

In this chapter, we explore how to write so that the reading is effortless.

- **Build sentences from the base:** Insert the single most important idea from each sentence in the main independent clause—what we will call the *base*—and build complexity onto the base only with good reason.

[1] Ricardo F. Jaramillo, *Annotated by the Author: 'Why Can't Men Say "I Love You" to Each Other?'*, The New York Times.

- **Fine-tune your sentences:** Keep sentences short, only occasionally incorporating elegantly long sentences. Signal to readers how the ideas in your sentences relate to one another.
- **Choose the right words:** Prefer familiar and specific words over vague and complex ones.
- **Put together paragraphs purposely:** Construct paragraphs with intention by starting them strong and keeping them short and focused.
- **Transition consistently:** Seamlessly connect sentences and paragraphs using logical transitions and anchor words.

Before diving in, let's see what a difference this good style can make. Take verbs. Good legal writers choose verbs like the rest of us buy clothes—they shop through all the options until they find the perfect fit.

Just look at this next example. What could be an enticing piece of legal writing about reality show stars comes off as a dry recitation of details, all because of the stale actions:

> Gunvalson entered into advertising agreements related to the vodka, often with Ayers by her side. She was often at trade shows and conferences, and there are pictures of her with bottles of Vicki's Vodka; she was in photographs with promotional clothes; there were negotiations with her present involving product-placement spots on the Real Housewives television show; she was present for the filming of portions of the show at the vodka-manufacturing facility; and the spirit was used at her backyard parties, which were present in the show's season finale.

Look what happens when we swap those bland verbs for vivid ones, courtesy of federal judge Jennifer Dorsey. Suddenly we see the movie playing.

> Gunvalson promoted the vodka, often with Ayers by her side. She attended trade shows and conferences, where she was photographed clutching bottles of Vicki's Vodka; wore promotional clothes; negotiated product-placement spots on the Real Housewives television show; filmed portions of the show at the vodka-manufacturing facility; and poured the spirit at her backyard parties, which were featured in the show's season finale.

Let's learn simple techniques to hone your foundational style like this.

7.1 Build Sentences from the Base

Razor-sharp prose requires fundamental sentence strategy. Do you think that this next sentence was written by accident?

> **It was a fine cry—loud and long—but had no bottom and it had no top,[2] just circles and circles of sorrow.[3]**

[2] No one expects you to write like Toni Morrison. But you can use deft descriptors ("fine cry"), alliteration ("loud and long"), figurative language ("no bottom and no top"), and echo words ("circles and circles") —all of which we explore in Chapter 9.

[3] Toni Morrison, Sula (Vintage 1998).

The answer is *no*. So how do great writers do it? They learn how to build sentences, word by word, letter by letter. They don't rely on ready-made sentences delivered to them by a lifetime of language osmosis. They learn to strip a sentence to its studs, rework the mortar, saw out some here, weld some supports there—to build a sentence that is all their own.

In other words, you can buy sentences off the shelf and repackage them for your reader. Or you can learn the art of sentence-building for yourself.

Before you can build a good sentence, though, you need a blueprint. A design that you can adjust to fit any situation. The good news is that the best blueprint to start with is a structure you already know well: a simple independent clause. That's right. A subject followed by a verb followed by an object. A character and an action and a result of that action.

I'm going to call this simple independent clause in this simple order our *base* because most good sentences start with it. Legal writers go down wordy paths when they forget the power of the base. The power of a simple character carrying out an action.

Ignore the base at your peril. Because when you start stacking on phrases and complicated structures without keeping track of the base it's all built around, chaos ensues. For example, mediocre writers pack many ideas into a sentence with no sense of which should build on which, like this:

> Private parties may sue "in the name of the government" by bringing a so-called qui tam action that asserts an injury exclusively to the government.

Great legal writers use the base to spoon-feed one idea at a time, layering on more only with a reason. These writers control the flow of ideas into their reader's minds. Like Justice Elena Kagan does with these three bases:

> [P]rivate parties may sue in so-called qui tam actions. Those suits are "brought in the name of the Government." And the injury they assert is exclusively to the Government.

Once you've got the base down, you can start learning when to mix in different sorts of phrases and clauses. Like this sentence by Justice Antonin Scalia, which uses one balanced clause stacked on another to make a poignant point:

> Whatever the general merits of the view that war silences law or modulates its voice, that view has no place in the interpretation and application of a Constitution designed precisely to confront war and, in a manner that accords with democratic principles, to accommodate it.

In this section, we'll uncover the power of the base. We'll learn how to deconstruct our sentences, identify the core message, and then rebuild, adding complexity only where it serves us.

A Quick Summary

Find your sentence's driving idea. Figure out the single, specific idea you are trying to convey with your sentence. If you've already written a sentence and it contains

multiple important ideas, break them out into separate sentences before you start building.

Build from the base. Take the main idea you are trying to convey and turn it into an independent clause—a subject-verb-object sentence. Your *base*. Most of your sentences should deliver the main point in the base. And many sentences require no more than a base.

Build with phrases. Phrases are short groups of words that add color or context to main ideas. Add them to a base to create a more nuanced point.

Build with clauses. Clauses convey bigger ideas and are more taxing when stacked together. Show readers how your clauses relate to the base with logical linking words and use them only when needed.

Build with correlatives. Correlatives are pairs of words that convey related points about two ideas. When helpful, use the right pair for your sentence's goal.

Build complexity sparingly. If most of your sentences are simple, readers can handle the occasional longer, more complex sentence. But craft these so the ideas flow easily.

7.1.1 Find Your Sentence's Driving Idea

On the surface, sentences all look similar. They use the same letters and same words, over and over, just arranged differently. Underneath, though, sentences are sophisticated idea-producing machines. You remove one word from a sentence, plug in another, and a different idea pops into your reader's mind.

Creative writers often craft sentences with some mystery and open spaces—leaving room for imagination to fill in the gaps. Those writers layer idea on idea within a sentence, building a scene or image that takes our breath away.

But as legal writers, we need our idea machines to run more precisely. Our readers are busy and use our writing to get things done. They don't have time to search through a rolodex of ideas in each sentence. And we don't want them to search. If our reader takes the wrong idea from a sentence, that could mean the difference between persuading them and not.

Each legal sentence should deliver a single, specific idea. But most legal writers either overstuff their sentences with details or leave too much to the imagination. In other words, the sentences have a *too-much* problem or a *too-little* problem.

The too-much problem is evident everywhere you look in legal documents. Two, three, four, or more ideas are all pushed together into a sentence, forcing readers to untangle it all:

> Facebook, from time to time, may elect to enforce the provisions of Section 1 herein at any time, but if the time for election has passed, no right to enforce will survive, but Facebook may use other remedies under Section 2, if at the time available.

The lawyers here packed at least four distinct ideas into one sentence:

1. Facebook can enforce Section 1 powers any time.
2. But wait, those Section 1 powers have a deadline.
3. Oh, also, Facebook can use Section 2 to do something.
4. But wait, there is another condition for Section 2 powers (even though we don't know what it is or why it matters).

Which ideas will readers take away? Who knows? Perhaps one. Perhaps none.

As a legal writer, your job is to pick the *one* specific idea that matters most—and spoon feed that idea to readers so they can't miss it. Then feed them another idea, and so on, guiding them from idea to idea until the finish line.

The too-little problem is even more devious. Yes, shorter sentences can be nice. They keep our reader focused. They're easy to follow. But short does not always mean better. Just because a sentence is short does not mean you control the ideas it plants in your reader's mind. We often need to inject some specifics or context into a sentence so the right idea hits home with our reader.

Take this famous sentence:

> I never said she stole my money.[4]

The ideas delivered by this short and unassuming sentence are legion. Will readers leave with the sense that...

- **I** never said she stole my money. (Someone else said it.)
- I **never** said she stole my money. (I didn't say it.)
- I never **said** she stole my money. (I only implied it.)
- I never said **she** stole my money. (Someone did, not her.)
- I never said she **stole** my money. (I considered it borrowed.)
- I never said she stole **my** money. (I said that she stole money—not necessarily mine.)
- I never said she stole my **money**. (She stole something of mine, not my money.)

We need to choose the single, specific idea our readers need. Then we need to build a sentence that instantly plants that idea in readers' minds. If the idea you cared about was who did the stealing, then a few more words would have best delivered that message:

> I never said it was Sam who stole my money; it was Jim.

This next opening paragraph in a high-profile brief conveys one easy idea at a time in simple sentences.

> Finally. Fox has conceded what it knew all along. The charges Fox broadcast[5] against Dominion are false. Fox does not spend a word of its brief arguing the truth of any accused statement.

[4]This sentence has made the rounds on grammar blogs for years, and it's even been the subject of serious research.

[5]This vivid verb is also a play on the theme of the case.

Or take this paragraph of short sentences from a trial court opinion. You get one idea at a time, and straightforward ones at that. These tight sentences make it easy to control what ideas your readers see.

> Courts don't make rules. Courts follow rules. The attorneys ask that we create a new rule out of whole cloth. That should give us pause.

Sentences that convey a single, specific idea can still convey nuanced points. For example, this next sentence is simple and focused but carries a lot of information.

> The American Rule recognizes that each party in litigation must bear its own attorney's fees in the absence of a rule, statute, or contract authorizing an award of fees.

Look at a paragraph penned by Justice Neil Gorsuch. The points conveyed are simple and clear, leaving little room for interpretation—and that precision comes from controlling the number and specificity of ideas in each sentence.

> Andrew Yellowbear will probably spend the rest of his life in prison. Time he must serve for murdering his daughter. So Mr. Yellowbear has found sustenance in his faith. No one doubts the sincerity of his religious beliefs[.] ... Yet the prison refuses to open the doors of [its] sweat lodge to Mr. Yellowbear alone. [A]nd so we have this litigation. [T]hose convicted of crime in our society lawfully forfeit a great many civil liberties. [But] Congress has []instructed that the sincere exercise of religion should not be among them ...

Each sentence supplies a straightforward idea. Yellowbear faces a life in prison. He does so because he murdered his daughter. He turned to his faith. There is very little room for interpretation or confusion.

The first key to great sentences is thus being critical with yourself. What is the exact idea you need to convey to busy readers? You need to develop a deep sensitivity to the ideas lurking behind your sentences and articulate for yourself what readers need to know. Once you have that down, it's time to get building.

7.1.2 Build from the Base

To build great sentences, like anything else, you need to understand your basic tools. In sentence building, these basic tools are groups of words. After all, sentences are made to convey ideas, and we usually need at least a few words to convey an idea.

We have two main ways to group words: Clauses and phrases. As a quick review, a *clause* is a group of words that includes a subject and a verb, like "The lawyer laughed." "The lawyer" is the subject and "laughed" is the verb. Clauses usually convey big ideas. They have both an actor and an action. An *independent* clause is one that can stand alone as its own grammatical sentence. These are the anchors that we build our sentences around (because nearly every sentence needs one).

> The court loves timely filings.[6]

[6] I have it on good authority that this is true.

A *dependent* clause is a group of words with a subject and a verb—but one that includes words that suggests the clause depends on another, independent clause; for example, "after the lawyer laughed. . . ." The main way we connect dependent clauses is with linkers called *subordinates*, which convey that one clause is subordinate to the other. A well-used subordinate for us legal writers is "because."

> **Because** the court loves timely filings, it requires that everyone comply with the two-week deadline.

A phrase, on the other hand, is a group of words with no full subject and verb complement—phrases cannot stand on their own as a sentence, no matter if they have a dependent linker or not:

> Timely filings being loved,

The most important sentence-building principle you need to remember is that—as a default—you should place the sentence's most important point in the main independent clause—your sentence's *base*. Isolating important ideas and putting them in the base makes it more likely our readers will notice them. For example, take this long sentence with lots of ideas packed together:

> While the defendant had a long-standing relationship with the bank, spanning over a decade, and had numerous transactions with various branches, it became evident through a thorough audit, conducted last quarter, that there were discrepancies in the account, amounting to over $100,000, which neither party could adequately explain.

Some of the many ideas crammed in probably matter. Maybe we want readers to focus on that $100,000 figure. Or the many years the defendant had a relationship with the bank. Or that no one could explain the audit discrepancies. By isolating those ideas into the base of new sentences, we focus readers on them.

> **The defendant banked with Wells Fargo for over a decade.** Agents audited his accounts last year, turning up several discrepancies. **Those discrepancies totaled over $100,000. And no party can explain any of them.**

If we put important ideas inside phrases or dependent clauses, readers aren't as likely to see them. And worst of all, when you interject a clause or phrase in the middle of the base, your sentence takes a serious hit. That's because your reader must keep track as you switch back and forth, from one idea, to another, then back to the original:

> **The court loves**, not that it matters or would ever matter, **timely filings**.

We usually want to keep the base together:

> **The court loves timely filings,** not that it matters or would ever matter.

The base sentence should be your go-to sentence. Simple base sentences are storytelling sentences. You meet the character, then see the action play out, and then the result. Base sentences spoon-feed ideas to readers in a way they can keep up with. Look at how this next writer, Judge Stephanos Bibas, has a knack for delivering ideas with base sentences so isolated and clear you can't possibly stumble:

> Free, fair elections are the lifeblood of our democracy. Charges of unfairness are serious. But calling an election unfair does not make it so. Charges require specific allegations and then proof. We have neither here. . . .
>
> In Pennsylvania, each county runs its own elections. [] Counties choose and staff polling places. [] They buy their own ballot boxes and voting booths and machines. []They even count the votes and post the results. . . . In all this, counties must follow Pennsylvania's Election Code and regulations. But counties can, and do, adopt rules and guidance for election officers and electors.

Another bonus of the base: If you're building it in order—actor then action—it's nearly impossible to write in the passive voice. Base sentences are easy on readers because they follow a single stream of events from start to finish.

When getting more complex, have a purpose for every word, and every word you mix it with, and every punctuation mark you include with the words. There are good reasons to combine more ideas in the same sentences: to compare, contrast, build on an idea, or emphasize. But there are also good reasons to isolate points in tight, one-idea sentences. Short base sentences punch.

If you focus on how many groups of words (phrases and clauses) you pack into each sentence, you'll be ahead of the curve. Mediocre legal writers pile groups of words together in sentences indiscriminately. When *good* legal writers pack in more groups of words (and thus more ideas), they have a reason. They are stacking things to make a bigger point, conveying relationships—some goal that requires readers to juggle more ideas at once.

It's all about becoming ultra-sensitive to the ideas lurking behind your sentences—and the ability to identify each group of words embodying those ideas. Punctuation will often signal the distinct ideas because we use commas or other marks to separate phrases and clauses. Look at this next sentence. The words between each pair of commas convey a different idea that readers need to juggle.

> After conducting extensive research and engaging multiple experts, Plaintiff alleges that the Series 7 products, manufactured by the PG Davis Corporation between 2015 and 2020, have inherent design flaws, which have led to multiple explosions, including the widely reported explosion in New York that resulted in severe injuries to multiple users.

If the plaintiff's research and experts matter, then mixing that idea among the rest might not be smart. After all, there are also ideas in here about the defendant's product, the years it was manufactured, indications of design flaws, and that an explosion injured people.

But we need more complex sentences sometimes. Look at this next sentence from a case brought by The New York Times. It connects journalists' tough, risky work with the benefits enjoyed by the public—in a way that two separate sentences wouldn't.

> Times journalists go where the story is, often at great risk and cost,[7] to inform the public about important and pressing issues.

Or check out this next snippet from Justice Kagan.

> **Wooden pleaded guilty to all counts.** The judge sentenced him to eight years' imprisonment for each conviction, with the ten terms to run concurrently. Fast forward now to a cold November morning in 2014, when Wooden responded to a police officer's knock on his door. **The officer asked to speak with Wooden's wife.** And noting the chill in the air, the officer asked if he could step inside, to stay warm. **Wooden agreed. But his good deed did not go unpunished.** Once admitted to the house, the officer spotted several guns.

Most sentences here are so simple they don't need more than a period—a single base. When you find multiple groups of words, it's easy to see the strategy behind the combination:

- The second sentence offers two related ideas (the judge's sentence and that the sentence is concurrent).
- The third sentence is again only two groups of words and is a simple structure (a phrase with some context to set the scene for the officer's visit).
- Then we have another single-clause sentence.
- Then there is a more complex sentence, but once again with crafted complexity: This one is a narrative sentence meant to convey unfolding events.

Good writing uses plenty of complex sentences, but that complexity demands a purpose. Avoid burdening your reader needlessly. To make this easier to put into practice, let's look at common ways the best legal writers build onto the base. We'll start with structures that take the base and add only one more idea for readers to juggle: the two-idea sentence.

7.1.3 Build with Phrases

The first type of two-idea sentence is a base with a phrase added on. Again, phrases are shorter groups of words that usually add context or color to a main clause—they don't have both a subject and a verb of their own.

We name phrases by what they do in reference to other groups of words in a sentence. Here are some common types that can be nice to know when building on to the base:

- Noun phrases: Groups of words acting together as a noun. Long noun phrases can get confusing and you might want to shorten them. "**The award-winning and successful lawyer** received a standing ovation" is not as easy to follow as "The lawyer won three awards and hundreds of cases. The audience gave him a standing ovation."

[7] You'll notice this sentence violates our interjecting phrase principle from earlier. But keep in mind all these tools are just that, tools. Sometimes one tool will take priority over another. Weaving in the "great risk and cost" subtly primes readers without making it the focus of the sentence.

- Verb phrases: A group of words coming together to create an action in a sentence. We can often replace these with a single, targeted verb (as we'll talk about more later in this chapter). "She **has been in the process of writing** her brief for two years" becomes "She **wrote** her brief for two years."
- Modifying phrases: Groups of words that modify a noun (an adjective phrase) or that modify a verb (adverbial phrase). We often want to limit modifying descriptors, particularly wordy ones. Like, "The lawyer with the **horrendously bad attitude** is not going to win."
- Participle phrases: A participle is a verb used as an adjective. Present participles end in *-ing*, and past participles usually end in *-ed*, *-d*, *-t*, *-en*, or *-n*. Participle phrases describe conditions, actions, or experiences related to the nouns they modify; for example, "Running swiftly, the law clerk got to the court on time."
- Appositive phrases: These rename or expand on another noun or pronoun right beside them, adding explanatory or identifying detail. These make your sentences more complicated but can be a neat way to build up a character, which we return to later in this chapter.[8]

Phrases can be used for good, in moderation and with a goal. They add detail, nuance, and complexity to a base point, allowing us to express ideas vividly and precisely.

There are three main ways to tack phrases onto a base: at the start, in the middle, and at the end. To give our readers a bit of context before getting to our base, we use an introductory phrase like this:

> Starving, the dog chewed on the bone.

Introductory phrases usually provide context or prime readers for the main point, which we should be making in the base clause. Like here, we wanted to give readers the context that the dog was starving—which adds color to the idea in the base (the dog chewing on that bone).

To start with our main point in the base, then add some color or qualifcation, we tack on a phrase or series of phrases at the end (usually modifying or participle phrases that modify part or all of the base).

> The dog chewed the bone, breaking it in half.[9]

Generally, you're better off tacking on phrases after your base. That's because sentences that start with the subject (the character in your main base clause) are the most direct, simple sentences. So limit the introductory phrases in your writing and make sure there's a reason to slow down your sentence's start.

[8] Other common phrase types are prepositional phrases, absolute phrases, gerund phrases, and infinitive phrases. You don't need to know them all, but the more you can see what's going on in your sentence, the easier it will be to build them with purpose.

[9] This one is a participle phrase because it's a verb phrase modifying the bone.

Keeping in mind the filing was late, the Court dismissed the case.

becomes

The court dismissed the case, keeping in mind it was filed late.

Finally, phrases can also squish details into the middle of a sentence. These are often the most taxing phrases for readers, so take extra care and have a critical idea to convey, like this appositive phrase:

The dog, **scruffy and having gone without a bath for quite some time**, sauntered over to his water dish.

Like any other group of words, extra phrases add extra work for readers. So most sentences should include only one, along with the base. To give us a rare break from legal examples, up next is a sentence by a journalist for *The Atlantic*. The main idea is in the base sentence (about the author encountering crowds of tourists). The introductory phrase at the start provides context for the base, and the modifying phrase at the end adds descriptive details.

On past visits, I'd always encountered crowds of tourists and school groups, **a space bursting with movement and sound.**[10]

Now let's go up one rung on the complexity ladder: adding on to the base with another clause.

7.1.4 Build with Clauses

Clauses convey a more complex and distinct idea because they have both their own subject and their own verb. Clauses mainly come in two types: the independent clauses that can stand alone (which we usually want to use as our base), and a dependent clause that connects to an independent one with a linking word.[11]

When you attach a full additional clause onto your main base, you're now asking readers to engage with two big ideas: the idea in your base and the idea in this new clause. So use care when adding clauses to more clauses.

The first clause-plus-clause structure is a single dependent clause and a base independent clause. Dependent clauses are created by using a linking word to start or end them, called a *subordinate* or a *relative*. This is often the best way to combine clauses because these linking words tell readers the logical relationship between the two clauses. Common subordinate linkers are words like *after, if, what, although, in order that, when, before, because, even if, even though, even since, whether, unless, until, provided that,* and so on.

The dog chewed on the bone **because** he was hungry.

---

[10] Clint Smith, *Stories of Slavery, From Those Who Survived It*, The Atlantic (Mar. 2021).

[11] Clauses can also act as long nouns or modifiers (like phrases can).

"**The dog chewed on the bone**" and "**he was hungry**" are both full clauses with their own subject and verb—two distinct ideas. The ideas are related and make sense to combine. We insert "because" in that second clause, subordinating it. That shows readers the relationship between the two main ideas: cause-and-effect.

Another way to combine clauses is to use a *relative* linker. Relatives use a word from one clause to connect to a noun in the main clause (this is why relative clauses are often called adjective clauses). Relative clauses start with words like *that, which, who, whose, where,* and *when.*

> I have a bone **that** was chewed on by the dog.

The base is "**I have a bone.**" The other clause is "**that was chewed on by the dog.**" "That" is our relative linker. The relative clause, "**that was chewed on by the dog,**" is describing the bone.

Finally, we have our final clause-combining sentence form: two independent clauses (a compound sentence). To build these, we use either a coordinating conjunction with a comma or a semicolon to attach them in the middle. Coordinating conjunctions are the FANBOYS: *for, and, nor, but, or, yet,* and *so.*

> I have a bone, **but** the dog chewed on the bone.

> I have a **bone; the** dog chewed on the bone.

As you can see, coordinating conjunctions are more generic than our subordinates and relatives. The "and" doesn't tell readers much about the relationship between the two clauses. Other coordinators, like "but," do better, telling readers that there is some contrast. But they still don't make the relationships as clear as linkers like "because," "after," "before" and so on.

7.1.5 Build with Correlatives

Correlative conjunctions are the final common way to join two groups of words. Correlatives work in pairs to join phrases or clauses to convey something about the relationship between the two. Common correlative pairs include *either/or, neither/nor, both/and, not only/but also,* and *whether/or.*

Use correlatives to show readers how two things relate, like by combining two points into one shared conclusion.

> **Both** the court **and** the attorney general agree this case will go nowhere.

Your goal is to use correlatives when it will help readers—not randomly. Each pair emphasizes a different aspect of the relationship between the connected elements. Let's look at the correlatives and when you should consider using each.

- **Both/and:** Combines two things into one affirmative thrust ("**Both** the attorney **and** the client agreed on the necessity of a plea bargain").

- **Either/or:** Emphasizes alternatives ("You can **either file** the claim today **or wait** until the new evidence is collected").
- **Neither/nor:** Combines two things into a negative thrust ("**Neither** the court **nor** the parties can avoid the dismissal rule").
- **Not only/but also:** Emphasizes the two items on a negative point, and often emphasizes the second item ("**Neither the plaintiff nor even the defendant** was willing to settle the dispute out of court").
- **As/as:** Shows similarity or equates two things ("**As many clients as possible** should be informed about the new policy").
- **Just as/so:** Draws comparisons ("**Just as we must** respect the law, **so we must** ensure justice for all").
- **Scarcely/when:** Indicates that one event closely follows another ("**Scarcely** had the meeting started **when** the power went out").
- **As much/as:** Similar to *as/as* but often used for emphasizing quantities ("The firm needs to invest **as much** in training **as** in recruitment").
- **Such/that:** Emphasizes a consequence. ("The case presented **such a complex issue that** it required a bench of five judges").
- **No sooner/than:** Shows that one event quickly follows another ("**No sooner** had the law been passed **than** it was challenged in court").
- **Rather/than:** Expresses a preference or alternative ("The client would **rather** pay a fine **than** spend time in jail").
- **Whether/or:** Presents two possibilities ("The court must decide **whether** the contract is valid **or** void").
- **Not/but:** Expressed contrast or exceptions ("The issue is **not** lack of evidence **but** lack of credibility").

In sum, it's usually best to build either a single-idea base sentence or a two-idea sentence that adds on a phrase or clause to the base with purpose. Stack big ideas together sparingly—whether with phrases, subordinates, relatives, coordinates, or correlatives.

7.1.6 Build Complexity Sparingly

So far, we've talked about using simple base sentences and building on the base with a single structure like a phrase or clause. These structures convey one or two related ideas that are easy to extract. By default, you should strive to keep it that easy.

But it's all about good writing ratios. If most of your sentences are that simple and well structured, your readers will be ready to tackle the occasional long, more complex sentence. You'll build up a bank of complexity. And as a legal writer, you'll need to cash in from time to time.

Long sentences build, unfolding to capture readers in rhythm—they're great for mixing nuance, details, or action. Reserve long sentences for when readers will benefit from overlapping ideas and concepts that build to a greater point.

Just be sure that you still make the ideas (and the relationships between them) easy to follow. For example, a *list sentence* can be fantastic for keeping steps or related items together. That's because the parallel structure and relationship between the items are easy to follow. In this next snippet about Britney Spears's legal fight, the author's base sentence explains that the conservators have controlled Britney's life. The author builds on that base idea with a list that makes that point more compelling:

> **[H]er conservators . . . have controlled her spending, communications, and personal decisions.**[12]

This next example from a federal judge showcases a long sentence—but because it's a list of organized items (bad things an attorney did), it's easy for readers to follow along.

> Stovall got a hacker to send him Ronaldo's attorney-client privileged documents, gave them to his client to review, drafted complaints that relied on the documents in a manner that intentionally obscured the obvious attorney-client nature of the quoted communications in those documents, and waited nine months into this litigation to disclose them.

Another simple long-sentence form is the action-chain sentence. You can think of this as a narrative sentence. The goal is to convey unfolding events or images that you want readers to experience in a chain. You build these sentences by starting with a base and then adding a series of modifying phrases that each follow up on the base. Here is Justice Kagan using one:

> And noting the chill in the air, the officer asked if he could step inside, **to stay warm.**

Another popular longer sentence form is a noun-appositive sentence. This is when you interject a short reference to your starting subject before getting to the action. These can be a helpful structure for setting up more complex actors in sentences.

> Defendant Susie Park, **the current manager,** began firing every employee.[13]

Just don't pile too many on top of each other, like this author did:

> In their written response to defendant's motion, plaintiffs relied, in part, on *Laffoon v. Bell*, where our supreme court held that section 5(a) "confer[s] immunity upon employers only from common law or statutory actions for damages by their immediate employees." Confronted with that legal authority, defendant stated in its reply to plaintiff's response that its prior reference to its "obligations" under section 1(a)(3) was "merely to the fact [that] the Act requires there to be coverage for workers/employees generally and [was] in no means intended to imply that [ENS] was uninsured."

Two heavy sentences here create too much drag. Instead, break up some of the ideas with bases.

> In their written response, plaintiffs partially relied *on Laffoon v. Bell*. There, our Supreme Court held that section 5(a) "confer[s] immunity upon employers only from common law or statutory actions for damages by their immediate employees." Confronted with that legal authority, defendant attempts to sidestep by pointing to language in the statute. But that fails.

---

[12] Ronan Farrow & Jia Tolentino, *Britney Spears's Conservatorship Nightmare*, New Yorker (July 3, 2021).

[13] We saw another form of this sentence type earlier in the New York Times example. There, though, the interjecting description was about the action instead of the actor: "Times journalists go where the story is, **often at great risk and cost,** to inform the public about important and pressing issues."

Once you understand the basics, you can adopt more and more complex sentence forms to write like the greats. And you can find many other complex sentence structures in Chapter 9.

7.2 Fine-Tune Your Sentences

Read good legal writing and you'll see the same sentence patterns: mostly short, a sprinkling of very short, and the occasional long. In other words, shorter to medium sentences with some occasional long ones sprinkled in for flavor. Patterns exist within sentences, too, with important ideas conveyed using specifics and every idea linked easily to the next.

Striking this balance and fine-tuning the structure of each sentence is easier than you think.

A Quick Summary

Keep sentences simple. **Short, simple sentences prevent reader fatigue and reinforce understanding.**

Welcome readers in. **Welcome readers into sentences with simple, recognizable words to engage them.**

Deliver what matters at the end. **Place new, key information at sentence endings for emphasis.**

Before diving into this skill, here is an example of a legal writer ignoring these principles. The entire paragraph is two long, jammed-together sentences:

> Plaintiff Randy Springer defaulted on his home loan and defendant U.S. Bank National Association, the current holder of Springer's mortgage note, began foreclosure proceedings on Springer's home. Springer brought this action, pro se, to stop the foreclosure, and he claims that there is a problem with U.S. Bank's chain of title and that U.S. Bank thus has no basis to foreclose, finally arguing that U.S. Bank and the other defendants committed fraud, that they are violating Nevada foreclosure laws, and that Springer is entitled to a declaration of the parties' rights.

Look at what a difference you can make by optimizing average sentence length, varying sentence structure, and putting the important points in the main clauses (the bases). It's not that every sentence is short. Or that every sentence conveys only one idea. But the sentences are shorter and simpler, and only one sentence packs in more than two ideas at once.

> Plaintiff Randy Springer defaulted on his home loan. So defendant U.S. Bank National Association, the current holder of Springer's mortgage note, began foreclosing on Springer's home. Springer brought this action, pro se, to stop the foreclosure. He claims that there is a problem with U.S. Bank's chain of title and that U.S. Bank thus has no basis to foreclose. He finally argues that U.S.

> Bank and the other defendants committed fraud, that they are violating Nevada foreclosure laws, and that Springer is entitled to a declaration of the parties' rights.

7.2.1 Keep Sentences Simple

Most writing experts suggest keeping sentences to an average of 20 words or less. This often aligns with the best legal writers' briefs. But this is not an exact science; it's a way to give you a sense about when sentences start becoming so long the ideas tend to trail off and readers start getting lost. If 20 sounds like a small number, it's not. You can pack a lot into 20 words. Even 20-word sentences can get clunky, causing your reader to lose their way. Here's a 20-worder:

> The court issued three declaratory rulings that each implicated a different legal doctrine or theory, each in a different way.

That's still a lot of content. We learned about three rulings that each implicated different theories—and in different ways.

To be simple, also keep your language in the positive, present, and singular forms when you can. These are usually easier on readers. So instead of:

> Plaintiffs that have brought a claim must not fail to include each allegation.

Try sticking with the singular, present tense, and positive voice:

> A **plaintiff** who **brings** a claim **must include** each allegation.

Above all, avoid negative constructions, especially multiple negatives in the same sentence or paragraph. Avoid constructions like these:

- "not uncommon"
- "failed to show inability"
- "not insignificant"
- "not uncomplicated"
- "no small part"
- "not incapable"
- "not inappropriate"

Instead, focus on positives:

- "common"
- "showed ability"
- "significant"
- "complicated"
- "large part"
- "capable"
- "appropriate"

Now let's zoom in to the starting of sentences.

7.2.2 Welcome Readers In

As always, the start sets your reader up for everything after. Invite your reader into sentences with familiar words that put them at ease.

- Avoid too many introductory and throat-clearing phrases.
- Begin sentences with short and familiar words.
- Ground most sentences in the subject and action.

First, avoid introductory phrases (a short phrase before your sentence's main subject) and throat-clearing phrases that aren't needed. They waste your reader's attention and slow down the important movement.

> Without any need whatsoever, lawyers continue to open their mouths.
>
> *becomes*
>
> Lawyers needlessly open their mouths.

Even delaying your main clause with a single word can be taxing. These long introductory words are particularly cumbersome:

- **Unfortunately**, Defendant has cited the wrong case.
- **Interestingly**, Plaintiff attaches the wrong case to his pleading.
- **Curiously**, Defendant admits he filed the complaint late.
- **Conveniently**, Plaintiff fails to cite the relevant case law.
- **Namely**, plaintiff's counsel should have known to do their due diligence.
- **Incredibly**, the Appellee contends he should still win.
- **Specifically**, the party never filed the motion.

Popular introductory words like *indeed, notably, critically*, and *specifically* merit special mention. A few hundred years ago, writers typically began with a *whereof* or a *howsobeit*. And writers used lots of conjunctive adverbs, like *moreover, namely*, and *indeed*. These traditions are in retreat. The use of *indeed* in good writing peaked in the eighteenth century and has declined since. The number of *howevers* and *moreovers* has been dropping since the 1840s. But lawyers can't shake these clunky holdovers.

Instead of *indeed* and *notably*, use words that deliver useful information to readers. So avoid this:

> This Court has always applied the one-way test to cases like Plaintiff's. Indeed, it did so just last year.

What is that *indeed* doing for you? It's saying something like "pay attention." But you can do better:

> This Court has always applied the one-way test to cases like Plaintiff's. Just last year the Court used the one-way test to dismiss a plaintiff's complaint.

No slowing down to stumble over the *indeed*—just straight into what matters. Many legal writers also love *specifically*. But again, the weight of great writing is against them. If you can achieve the same narrowing of focus by getting straight to the content you care about, why wouldn't you?

> There is a critical problem with the brief. **Specifically**, no supporting evidence was attached.
>
> *becomes*
>
> The brief has a problem. **No supporting** evidence is attached.

Next, start with short words if you can. Short words want to be read. It was true when you were six and it's true now.

> Being funny is not part of lawyering. **Additionally**, a "funny lawyer" is impossible as a matter of physics.
>
> *becomes*
>
> **Humor** is not part of lawyering. **And** a "funny lawyer" is impossible as a matter of physics.

If you can, start sentences with words your reader knows something about. Familiar words feel comfortable; new words scare them away. And you want your reader to constantly feel invited into your sentences.

> Courts hate word vomit. **Something** you can fix is word vomit.
>
> *becomes*
>
> Courts hate word vomit. But **word vomit** is something you can fix.

Finally, often the most inviting way to start your sentence is to begin with the subject. Who sits in that subject position of your sentence matters more than you might think. Many legal writers simply use whatever subject comes to mind. But if you take control of your subjects, you take control of readers' focus.

> **The search** was conducted several times, but no contraband was revealed.
>
> *becomes*
>
> **Police** searched several times but found no contraband.

At the least, aim to put the subject in the first five or six words of each sentence, lest your reader get lost.

> Making sure their bills were paid first, **the attorneys** filed the motion.
>
> *becomes*
>
> **The attorneys** made sure their bills were paid, then filed a motion.

Grounding most of your sentences in concrete people or entities that your readers can visualize plays the movie. Your readers will see people doing things—parties taking actions. Movement. Progression. Try to focus your sentences on people and concrete nouns, not abstract principles and glue words.

Do you want your reader to see things from the plaintiff's view? The defendant's? Some third party's? Sometimes you want to make things abstract, and that's fine. But make sure you have a reason for choosing the subject you do. Here, the lawyer gives the reader the perspective of . . . a rock.

> **The rocks** were removed repeatedly, without the plaintiff's consent. The rocks had been paid for out of plaintiff's bank account. These payments reached thousands of dollars.

This attorney would probably be better off using his client's perspective:

> **Defendant rented a tractor and removed** Plaintiff's rocks without any permission. **The plaintiff** paid thousands of dollars for these rocks.

Open the door to clear sentences with an inviting welcome.

7.2.3 Deliver What Matters at the End

New, key content you want readers to remember should usually come at the end of sentences. And when helpful, you can use sentence structure and punctuation to emphasize these sentence endings even more.

First, end sentences with concrete, specific words that will leave an impression. Ending a sentence on "the explosion" hits harder than ending on "the incident." Above all, avoid ending on abstracts like a statutory number or legalese no one will remember.

Look how shifting around the ending phrase (especially with a punctuation setoff) changes the ideas imprinted in your mind:

> Steve died in Seattle **two weeks ago**.
>
> Steve died two weeks ago — **in Seattle**.
>
> Two weeks ago, while visiting Seattle, **Steve died**.

Changing the end of the sentences leaves readers with a different impression — and maybe even a completely different idea.

Let's see this technique in another example. To focus readers on how global warming is supported by atmospheric science, we can structure the sentence to end on that point:

> Global warming could raise sea levels to the point that low-lying coastal areas disappear, **according to most atmospheric science**.

To focus instead on the harmful effects of global warming, we can end on that:

> According to atmospheric scientists, **global warming could raise sea levels to the point that low-lying coastal areas disappear.**

In this next example, the lawyers wanted to emphasize that their products worked for their intended use, so they put this idea at the end of each sentence, rather than ending on the less favorable detail of pets dying:

> They allege that their dogs died from different medical conditions (a seizure and lymphoma) after wearing Seresto Collars advertised **to kill and repel fleas and ticks.**
>
> Approved by more than 80 regulatory bodies around the world, some 33 million Seresto Collars have been sold **to protect pets and their owners from serious and potentially fatal disease.**

Imagine what readers would focus on if the sentences ended by emphasizing the collars (that allegedly caused the illness) or the number of collars sold (which represents all the money the defendants raked in).

> They allege that their dogs died from different medical conditions (a seizure and lymphoma) **after wearing Seresto Collars. . . .**
>
> Approved by more than 80 regulatory bodies around the world, some **33 million Seresto Collars have been sold.**

You can also use sentence structure and punctuation to amp up the final emphasis.

> They allege that their dogs died from different medical conditions—**after wearing Seresto Collars.**

Or we could use punctuation to amplify this sentence's end:

> The Court is debating whether to allow this case to go forward, **which is this Court's prime concern.**

Some other ways to focus on the end of sentences include certain word and phrase structures that shift the focus to the end. For example, we can use *not only x, but Y.*

> We must clarify these issues and develop trust.
>
> *becomes*
>
> We must **not only** clarify these issues but develop trust.

Or we can use words like *not, but, yet, or so*).

> The Court should **not** avoid this issue, **but** take it head on.

> There were many witnesses to the attack, **but none of them came to Park's aid.**

Or we can use *of* followed by a key word or phrase.

> The rescue and liberation **of the old.**

Finally, the *what/there* shift is another great device. This is where you go against the normal advice of cutting throat-clearing phrases and use a *what* or *there* at the beginning of your sentence to ensure your reader can't miss the point being emphasized at the end.

> That these collars protected pets **is what matters**.
>
> *becomes*
>
> **What** matters is that these collars **save pets' lives.**

However you do it, shift what matters to the end.

7.3 Choose the Right Words

Words are the tools of the lawyer's trade. But like any tool, their effectiveness hinges on our ability to wield them with precision. Which would you rather read:

> Envision the ramifications of having engendered an unprecedented contrivance, a literary composition, or perhaps an innovative melodic structure. It is an equitable supposition that you should possess the prerogative to delineate who exploits your creation.
>
> *or*
>
> Imagine you make something new—a gadget, a story, or maybe a new song. It's only fair that you get to choose who uses your creation.

Most of us would prefer reading the second version.[14] It takes less work to decrypt. But that doesn't mean it's too simplistic to get the same complexity across. In fact, the more you deliver points using one simple, precise word at a time, the more complexity your readers can handle.

Let's dive in and learn about the language legal readers love. This section is your guide to writing with purpose, where every word earns its place on the page.

A Quick Summary

Use familiar, simple, old words. Pick short, recognizable words with Germanic origins for clarity and simplicity.

Be diverse. Use a wider range of vocabulary and sentence structure for mechanical words that don't deliver important content.

[14] If you like the first version more, this section is particularly for you. Because most of your readers don't agree, and we write for them.

Be precise. **Use precise words instead of vague ones. Don't hedge or be defensive.**

Use labels. **Assign memorable names to complex concepts for easy reference throughout the document.**

Avoid descriptors. **Rely on strong nouns and verbs, using adjectives and adverbs only when they add special value.**

Use visual language. **Transform abstract ideas into tangible images.**

Use verbs that burst. **Select dynamic verbs to activate your writing.**

7.3.1 Use Familiar, Simple, and Old Words

You might be asking, "Legal readers are smart, why worry about using familiar or simple words?" That's how many legal writers think: Why would anyone work to make fancy-sounding words sound like something out of an everyday conversation?

The reason is that, in the words of Leonardo da Vinci, "simplicity is the ultimate sophistication." The best lawyers understand that making writing look easy is the hardest sort of writing there is. Legal readers aren't impressed by long words they need to look up in a dictionary. They are impressed by writing they can understand effortlessly. This next snippet is from a team of legal writers committed to using clunky formalisms rather than words readers enjoy:

> Class action litigation is a procedural mechanism that amalgamates a multitude of individual lawsuits into a singular litigation process, primarily to enhance judicial efficiency and equality among said plaintiffs. The representative plaintiff acts on behalf of an extensive class of similarly situated individuals, who have purportedly experienced comparable harms as a consequence of the defendant's actions. The certification of a class action is contingent upon several intricate criteria, such as numerosity, commonality, typicality, and adequacy of representation, as stipulated by Rule 23 of the Federal Rules of Civil Procedure.

Be honest: Wouldn't you rather read this?

> Class actions are a group suit. Many join hands to fight a wrong in one court case, rather than several small ones. This helps ensure the court treats all equally. One or more people act for the group—and the group must have been hurt in the same way by the same wrong act. To get the green light for a class action, the plaintiff must meet a few key requirements under Federal Rule of Civil Procedure 23.

The difference between the versions is stark: One is written using familiar, everyday words that people use to think and speak—it's written to make the reading easy. The other uses unfamiliar words that academics love and legal writers often fancy—it's written more for the writer than anyone else.

Persuasive writers write like their readers think. That is why President Lincoln's best speeches use the shortest, simplest, and most familiar words. In the Gettysburg Address and Second Inaugural Address (widely considered his two best—and some of the best speeches ever penned), nearly 75 percent of Lincoln's words have only a single syllable. That is no accident.

Here's a snippet from federal Judge Stephanos Bibas explaining a process in a ballot case. He's well known for using the most familiar, simple words he can. And his work pays off.

> Close to the election, the county will mail the voter a mail-in ballot package. [] The package has a ballot and two envelopes. The smaller envelope (also called the secrecy envelope) is stamped "Official Election Ballot." [] The larger envelope is stamped with the county board of election's name and address and bears a printed voter declaration. Id. Next, the voter fills out the ballot. [] He then folds the ballot; puts it into the first, smaller secrecy envelope; and seals it. [] After that, he puts the secrecy envelope inside the larger envelope and seals that too. [] He must also "fill out, date and sign the declaration printed" on the outside of the larger envelope.[]

Why Do Legal Writers Have Two (or More) Versions of Words?

Before digging in more, let's explore some brief language history. Have you ever wondered why we seem to have multiple layers of words in English that often mean the same thing? Why do we have both "pay" and "remunerate"? Or "fire" and "terminate"?

A lot of it goes back to the origins of English—and the old words that still make up much of the language. The nutshell is that Anglo-Saxons conquered early Britain in the fifth century. Before that, folks in the region spoke early forms of modern-day Celtic or Welsh. The Anglo-Saxons brought their Germanic languages, most notably Angles (the namesake of English).

This Germanic origin changed English forever. Words derived from these Germanic roots tend to be short, simple, and direct. They are often a single syllable. For example, words like *ask, tell, see, get, run, eat, drink, house, man, woman*, and *child* are all of Germanic origin. These are everyday words that most English speakers find straightforward and easy to understand.

Now, it's true that English passed through many hands over the years, but that Germanic heritage (for fascinating reasons) took hold deeper than any other. The Vikings conquered Britain next, but their language, Old Norse, was another Germanic language and a close cousin to the Anglo-Saxon language already spoken in the region. Later, when Normandy conquered, English speakers were never able to shake loose the simple Germanic words that formed most of the language.

That isn't to say English hasn't picked up words from other regions and languages. When William the Conqueror took the English throne, the language caught some French-derived words like *arrest* and *mutton*. During the Renaissance, longer, complex words from Latin and Greek were en vogue, and English picked up gems like *chaos* and *physics*.

Often when French, Greek, Latin, and other influences added a longer word, though, it was a synonym for a simple word that already existed in English's Germanic roots. Folks would use these new versions of the same word to sound formal or refined.

These later-added words were often the language of the law, government, and ruling classes in particular.

Fast forward to today, and Germanic words remain the backbone of spoken English. In one recent survey, about half of all words used in English writing were Germanic, with less than 20 percent from Romance languages and the remaining words spread between Latin, Greek, and others.

Now comes the punchline. Legal writers are often in the minority when it comes to words. They prefer the complicated, abstract versions from Latin, Greek, and Romance languages—rather than the simple, direct words that people use to think and speak. So when I say use simple and familiar words, another way of looking at it is using *old* words, or the simple, short, familiar, Germanic words we've been speaking in English for almost 2,000 years.

To achieve this easy reading, prefer words with few syllables, words that will be familiar to most readers, and words that are specific rather than vague. Ask yourself: Is this the shortest word that means what I intend? Would I use this word when speaking? Does nearly everyone know it?

As you start developing a sense of Germanic words versus others, it becomes easy to choose the simpler versions. Here are some examples of Germanic words compared with synonyms from other origins:

- **Buy vs. purchase**
- **About vs. approximately**
- **Give vs. donate**
- **Enough vs. sufficient**
- **Help vs. aid**
- **Make vs. manufacture**
- **Show vs. demonstrate**

This explains why so many people cite this passage from Chief Justice Roberts as among their favorite pieces of legal writing. The words are familiar, simple, and specific.

> Officer Sean Devlin, Narcotics Strike Force, was working the morning shift. Undercover surveillance. The neighborhood? Tough as a three-dollar steak. Devlin knew. Five years on the beat, nine months with the Strike Force. He'd made fifteen, twenty drug busts in the neighborhood.
>
> Devlin spotted him: a lone man on the corner. Another approached. Quick exchange of words. Cash handed over; small objects handed back. Each man then quickly went his own way. Devlin knew the guy wasn't buying bus tokens. He radioed a description and Officer Stein picked up the buyer. Sure enough: three bags of crack in the guy's pocket. Head downtown and book him. Just another day at the office.

This passage is full of the simple and familiar: "a lone man on the corner," and "cash handed over." Chief Justice Roberts chooses specific words over vague ones. So rather than say the officer made "many" drug busts, Roberts says he made "fifteen, twenty" of them.

Take this example of not-so-simple word choice:

> To avert the all-too-common enactment of requirements without regard for their local cost and tax impact, however, the commission recommends that statewide interest should be clearly identified on any proposed mandates, and that the state should partially reimburse local government

for some state-imposed mandates and fully for those involving employee compensation, working conditions and pensions.

By focusing on familiar and simpler words (words with fewer syllables), we get:

New York often passes mandates telling local governments what to do. Often, these laws improve life for everyone in the state. But they come with a cost. Too often, the state doesn't consider the cost to local government, or how much money taxpayers will have to shell out. So we have an idea. The state should pay back local governments for some of these so-called mandates, like those related to employment.

So aim for shorter words—and versions that will be more familiar to your reader (not words that we typically find in judicial opinions).

Here are a few more examples:

- **Pocket** instead of **acquire**
- **About** instead of **regarding** or **with regard to**
- **Say** or **said** instead of **expressed** or **stated**
- **Clone** instead of **create a copy of**
- **After** instead of **subsequent to** or **thereafter**
- **Here** instead of **instant case.**
- **To** instead of **as a means of**
- **Do** instead of **accomplish**
- **Also** instead of **furthermore** or **additionally**
- **Money** or **cash** instead of **funds**
- **Gave** instead of **accorded**
- **Some** or **many** instead of **a number of**
- **Pay** instead of **remunerate**
- **So** instead of **accordingly**
- **Shows** instead of **demonstrates**
- **Next to** instead of **adjacent to**
- **Allow** instead of **afford**
- **Fire** instead of **terminate**

Legal writing should serve the reader, not the writer. Use the same words your readers use when they think and speak.

7.3.2 Be Diverse

Legal writing gurus often talk about how you shouldn't use "elegant variation" in your briefs and motions. Use the same words, consistently, again and again. But this is good advice only for words that need to stay consistent to avoid confusing your reader, like statutory language, a case title, or a party's name. Repeating more mechanical words just distracts readers.

So yes, don't call a case by different names or a legal principle by three different descriptions. Varying either of those in the same document makes readers wonder if you're referring to different things. But for less important words, diversify.

Take dialogue tags. These words signal that someone said something. We lawyers not only use those, but also what you might call argument tags: words that signal what someone *argued*. Our legal writing is full of he "argues" this and she "claims" that. You don't need to stick to these same tags to avoid confusing your readers—and you shouldn't. There are fresh words to use instead.

The best legal writers will vary those attributions, where they are located, and their form—so that readers never get distracted by the plodding repetition. Notice how this next legal writer attributed who said what with parentheses, a refreshing way to maintain a direct, explanatory tone in the sentences. You can avoid repeating the attribution by using linking words that make clear you are continuing what someone said or alleged, with the occasional reminder. No need for "the court held, the court held, the court held. . . . "

> On the court's view, **the First Amendment compels a stringent threshold test when an infringement suit challenges a so-called expressive work—here (so said the court), the Bad Spaniels toy.** And **that test knocked out Jack Daniel's claim, whatever the likelihood of confusion.** Likewise, **Jack's dilution claim failed—though on that issue the problem** was statutory. The trademark law **provides that the "noncommercial" use of a mark cannot count as dilution. 15 U.S.C. §1125(c)(3)(C). The Bad Spaniels marks, the court held, fell within that exemption because the toy communicated a message—a kind of parody—about Jack Daniel's.**

The best legal writers have a diverse toolbox for delivering mechanical information like attribution. Notice how this next legal writer attributes who claimed what by inserting the tags into the middle of a sentence (more like nonlegal writers would):

> It owns trademarks in the distinctive Jack Daniel's bottle and in many of the words and graphics on the label. And it believed Bad Spaniels had both infringed and diluted those trademarks. Bad Spaniels had infringed the marks, **the argument ran,** by leading consumers to think that Jack Daniel's had created, or was otherwise responsible for, the dog toy. And Bad Spaniels had diluted the marks, **the argument went on,** by associating the famed whiskey with, well, dog excrement.

And later in that same document, there are some more examples of varying the attribution tags and structure so readers are never distracted:

> First, VIP **argued** that Jack Daniel's infringement claim failed under a threshold test derived from the First Amendment to protect "expressive works"—like **(VIP said)** the Bad Spaniels toy. When those works are involved, **VIP contended**, the so-called Rogers test requires dismissal of an infringement claim at the outset unless the complainant can show one of two things: that the challenged use of a mark "has no artistic relevance to the underlying work" or that it "explicitly misleads as to the source or the content of the work." [] Because Jack Daniel's could make neither showing, **VIP argued,** the likelihood-of-confusion issue became irrelevant. Second, **VIP urged** that Jack Daniel's could not succeed on a dilution claim because Bad Spaniels was a "parody[]" of Jack Daniel's, and therefore made "fair use" of its famous marks.

Another option for writing about who said what is to simply let your reader know that a few sentences or paragraphs are all an argument or claim made by a particular party or actor:

> **Emily Park's argument is as follows.** She never saw who stole the evidence. The materials just "disappeared." This entitles her to damages, and potentially punitive ones. . . .

Or for a final example, take numbering your points. Watch the problem if we stick to the "no elegant variation" rule here:

> "First, the plaintiff loses on jurisdiction.
> First, the plaintiff alleges no jurisdictional facts . . .
>
> Second, the plaintiff fails to state a claim because . . .
> First, the plaintiff.

You don't need to keep using the word "first" to avoid confusing the reader about what "first" means. Diversify. For example:

> To begin, the plaintiff loses on jurisdiction.
> The plaintiff's first misstep is. . . .

If your reader understands—fluently without any possibility of confusion—vary away.

7.3.3 Be Precise

Lean toward the precise and away from the vague. Precise words are easier to remember and deliver the specific idea you have in mind. Read this sentence full of oblique language:

> He was detained for a significant period and during that time was severely mistreated by his captors, which resulted in the need for medical treatment.

Vague words like "significant," "period," "severely," and "medical treatment" are standing in for the specifics that would give real understanding—like *how* significant, *how* long, *how* severe, and *what* medical treatment.

> He was detained for six days. His masked captors beat him with rubber truncheons. His broken bones and internal bleeding required two surgeries.

This preference for the abstract in mediocre legal writing happens with nouns, too. Instead, use precise nouns instead of vague versions.

- **The brawl** instead of **the incident**
- **Stole $500** instead of **theft of funds**
- **Three broken ribs** instead of **serious injuries**
- **The police's search of the bedroom** instead of **the underlying act**
- **Last year's 30 percent stock price dip** instead of **last year's big drop in the market**

Then we have reference words. Legal writers often use vague words when referring to things they introduced earlier (or things they assume readers already know about from the outside world). For *writers* who know everything about a topic, connecting those dots is easy. But for *readers*, not so much.

Imagine that you tell your reader the scene of an accident was in the parking lot—and then later mention the "scene of the accident." That might be easy for you to put together, but don't expect your reader to remember where the accident was. Also, it's easier to imagine "a parking lot" rather than a "scene of the accident." Just be precise.

Imprecise words paint part of the picture for readers. Some infamous culprits in legal writing are "appear," "seem," and "suggest." "Plaintiff *appears* to" do this and "Defendant *appears* to" do that. Or the cases "*seem* to hold" something.

What do these words mean? Did the Plaintiff do it or not? Did the case hold that or didn't it? Your reader doesn't know what idea to take away when you use imprecise words like these.

These terms might be tempting to use when you're not sure of your position; they can be a shortcut. But this hedging has costs. If you're confident enough to tell an audience something, you're better off telling them with precision. So instead of "The plaintiff apparently disagrees that she's responsible," try this:

> The plaintiff **never once acknowledges that she is responsible for the fire that destroyed two homes**.

Imprecise words are nearly always signals that you are trying to force your reader to read into some fact, but you can't bring yourself to say how. These are some common violators:

- **Indicate**
- **Regarding**
- **Concerning**
- **Seemingly**
- **Apparently**
- **Suggestive**

Each of these can dilute the points you're aiming for. Instead, lean on those specifics.

7.3.4 Use Labels

One of the easiest ways to guide readers is to label complex or critical concepts with intuitive shorthands. That way, after you've explained the concepts once, you can remind readers of all that work by using the label later. You're creating your own document lexicon.

Done right, this is a sleek tool. For example, take many writing techniques we've already explored. Like *base sentences* from earlier in this chapter. I made that up. Not randomly, but as a placeholder to make it easier for you to understand the concept when we talk about it later. I chose the "base" label to convey that this is your default sentence structure—and the one you should be building on. Once I've explained what a base sentence is, and you understand it, we can use that shared vocabulary to return to the idea later. Because it's descriptive, the label helps you remember.

To change it up, let's take a break from the legal stuff and chat about one of my very favorite topics: dogs. This next writer is explaining how dogs can have one of two personality types: those who are more independent and those who are a bit needy. To make it easy to remember these distinctions later, you get a label for each.

> Some dogs are independent, needing little attention or interaction throughout the day. We'll call these the **lone-ranger** dogs. Other dogs crave attention every hour or so, needing to check in with owners and receive at least an ear-scratch. We'll call these the **people-pleaser** dogs. **Lone-rangers** and **people-pleasers** can both make great pets. It all depends on what sort of owner you are. . . .

Labeling is used by nearly every top legal writer. In this next brief in a copyright case, the lawyer first explains a complex legal concept. Basically, when someone wants to use copyright to protect their mere *selection* of publicly available materials, the legal protection is much weaker than that given to folks who create new material from scratch (like a painting). After explaining this weaker type of copyright, the writer gives it a label so they can easily return to it throughout the brief.

> In th[e]se cases, the copyright holder owned only the compilation. In one case cited, the plaintiff had a compilation copyright in the organization and selection of state legal forms. . . . Though the underlying entries were in the public domain, the organizer's exact selection and arrangement were copyrightable. . . . **So in these cases, the plaintiffs owned "thin" copyrights: other than their selection and arrangement choices, none of their compilations' components were protectable.**

Now, later in the document, the writer can trigger all that understanding again by using the "thin" label. The label is also persuasive because it reminds readers that this sort of copyright protection is weak, which is exactly what the lawyer wanted.

> This distinguishes Thomson Reuters's copyright in its headnotes from the **"thin,"** compilation-only copyrights in Ross's examples.

Let's look at another example. The lawyers first explain a novel theory for holding drug makers liable for the drugs they make. The theory had to do with companies that make a drug, market it heavily, and then sell off the rights—and liabilities—to another party at huge profits. The plaintiffs were arguing that the drug companies should be unable to sell their liability and that simply creating the market for the drug should leave them on the hook even after they sell the patents. To make it easy to return to their argument throughout the brief, they gave the theory a label.

> This **"market-creation"** theory of jurisdiction applies with special force in the pharmaceutical context, where companies often develop the demand for a new product; spend millions convincing the public it is safe; and conceal side effects (like cancer) that take decades to be linked back to their drug. GSK did all that here.[15]

You can label any concept you want. But make sure what you label is important so you don't waste readers' time. And make sure you use labels consistently. Readers get confused when you create a naming convention only to change it on them later.

[15] A great final-sentence punch to remind readers who is responsible.

You can name anything that's important. The act of naming it will help your reader trigger the ideas you laid out originally. But here are some common times to think about this tool:

- **A statutory provision.** Repeating lengthy statutory numbering is annoying. Who can remember all those digits? Consider giving key statutory or regulatory sections a short name to refer to: "The statute's **'person-place-and-manner requirement'** was ignored here."
- **A legal principle or concept from cases.** Explain a concept first when explaining your rule and given it a label—then each time you use that same label, your reader instantly remembers your pitch. For example, the "jurisdiction first" approach to considering motions.
- **A case with a long or awkward name.** For example, "*Sliezhelipr Dist. and Fishing Supplies Accoutrements and More, LLC v. State of California*, 314 F. 2d 51 (7th 2019) could become "the Fish Supplies" case. Or you could name the case for a useful legal principle: "The 'no-harm' cases apply here."
- **A factual concept.** When you need to explain something factual that will take heavy lifting from readers, labels can help. "Hoffman's Climbing manufactures its cams by melting down iron and layering it with steel in a proprietary process that combines the molecules in a unique way to make the finished product extremely durable. This **metal-layering process** is what Hoffman is suing the defendant for stealing."
- **A document or exhibit that's important.** If you're relying on a report by a forensic scientist, you could say, "According to the **Forensic Science Report. . . .** " to highlight the document's credibility. You could even use this persuasive label in the citation: "There is no causation evidence." **Forensic Science Report at 3**. That is much better than a vague "expert report."
- **A characterization of any argument or fact or point that is helpful to you.** For example, "In the school's view, the requested **prior restraint** is harmless because it affects only Cooley." Naming the school's demand as a request for "prior restraint" rather than simply "their request" injects a lot of persuasion.
- **Anything else.** You can and should label any concept, fact, principle, or idea that is complicated with an easy-to-remember name that will help persuade readers and remind them of what matters.

This next example features a label for a rule pitch. The lawyer describes his view of the law while distilling it into a compact package for easy carrying throughout the brief:

> The courts have thus created an "any touch is enough" requirement for plaintiffs claiming emotional harm. Literally.[16] A brush in a subway. [cite]. A tap. [cite]. A nudge with a foot in a crowded elevator. [cite.][17]

Now, later in the brief, when the lawyer uses the "any touch is enough" label, the reader will remember all the great work the lawyer did in developing that rule's interpretation. Here's another example:

---

[16] A great example of a sentence fragment drawing readers' attention to a forceful point.
[17] A fantastic use of concrete examples to illustrate a rule pitch.

> But "cost of cure" allegations, where a plaintiff tries to allege [a] loss . . . to remedy the harm . . . only counts as a loss if the underlying injury is, itself, a loss of money or property.[18]

Another benefit of labeling is that it's an easy way to link ideas across different paragraphs or sections. Referring to the same labels links ideas and reinforces your work. Let's say you talked about the "**no search, no violation**" concept a few times in the first section of your brief. In later sections, you should use that same label so your reader instantly connects the two sections.

So label away. Scour your documents for the critical concepts that readers need and might have trouble remembering. Then craft a descriptive label they won't forget.

7.3.5 Avoid Descriptors

Nothing bogs down your writing like too many descriptors. Too many adjectives—and especially adverbs—trigger your readers' skepticism, slow down the pace, and disrupt your flow.

> Your coloring words, particularly adjectives and adverbs, must be used where they will do the most good. . . . Your reader probably has a perfectly serviceable mental picture of a lion; when a lion comes into your [document] you need not burden [them] with adjectives unless it is necessary, for instance, to point out that he is a green lion. . . .[19]

There is a reason that Stephen King and other great writers urge us to kick them. After all, as A. A. Patawaran points out, it's all about letting nouns and verbs, the *things* and *actions*, tell the story:

> A world without adjectives would still have the sun rising and setting, the flowers blooming, the trees bearing fruits, the birds singing, and the bees stinging.

Compare the following generic descriptors on the left with the more targeted nouns on the right. Which would you rather read?

- **Young person** vs. **juvenile, teen, child, five-year-old**
- **Very small house** vs. **cabin, mansion, cottage, villa**
- **The rambunctious crowd** vs. the **horde**

This next example illustrates how descriptors bog down garden-variety legal writing.

> The Government repeatedly and voraciously argues that under the statute there is very broad authority for EEOC to decide precisely how to engage in, and exactly when to give up on, conciliation.

[18] The writers might have had an easier time of it here if they used shorter base sentences to spoon-feed ideas to readers.

[19] Shirley Jackson, Come Along with Me (Viking Press 1968).

Excising the descriptors forces us to focus on the strong nouns and verbs, cutting clutter and honing the points (courtesy of Justice Kagan):

> The Government **highlights** the **broad leeway** the statute gives the EEOC to **decide** how to engage in, and when to **give up on**, conciliation.

Or take this snippet from another federal brief:

> Plaintiffs really offer nothing new here: their **conclusory** and **baseless** allegations that "they alleged defendant's knowledge" is the very epitome of a **quite desperate** ploy.

It is much more effective without the descriptors:

> Plaintiffs argue nothing more than that they "alleged defendant's knowledge." This **legal conclusion** is not the "**specific fact**" Rule 12 requires.

The same is true with these examples, also from federal filings:

> This case is the **absolute** epitome of a big corporation attempting to **insidiously** and **vexatiously** hurt a smaller one.
>
> *becomes*
>
> This is a case of a **corporate giant bullying** a small business.

> The plaintiff sustained **horrible** and **repeated** injuries.
>
> *becomes*
>
> The plaintiff **snapped three bones** in his arm.

> Courts move as **quickly** as possible to review motions.
>
> *becomes*
>
> Courts review motions **within days**.

That's not to say you should never use descriptors. They can be a force for good. For one, descriptors can convey important information that nouns and verbs can't muster by themselves. But on those rare occasions when a descriptor will help, choose carefully. Remember, empty characterizations like "very," "really," and "clearly" rarely add anything worthwhile. Good descriptors convey something useful.

In this next example, the adverb "explicitly" serves a purpose: showing that the court had considered and declined to apply a particular framework.

> [T]his Circuit, almost two months before the district court's ruling in this case, explicitly declined to apply this framework. *Liu v. Amway Corp.*, 347 F.3d 1125, 1136 (9th Cir. 2003).

Sometimes a brilliant descriptor can pack a wallop, used sparingly:

> The wall the court erect[ed] between church and state has become even more warped and twisted than I expected.

Some rhetorical structures put descriptors to good use. As we'll see in Chapter 9, for example, this structure can be an impressive one: [Subject] + [State of being verb] + [Adjective]. For example:

> The ruling is indefensible.

You might also want to use descriptors if they help build an image that nouns or verbs can't. Take some examples from an appellate savant. Each adds nuance and character.

> When the Government starts picking favored speakers, First Amendment values are in grave danger.
>
> The Government also has studiously avoided taking a litigation position here that might bind either FDA or DOJ in the future. The Government never squarely states an official position that FDA's regulations do not prohibit non-promotional speech. . . .
>
> First, the FDCA's "new drug" and misbranding rules trigger First Amendment scrutiny because they are irretrievably content-based. . . .
>
> There is "no hint," however, "that the Government even considered these or any other alternatives" before enacting its draconian regulations suppressing virtually all off-label speech.
>
> It is thus not clear whether FDA ever had a coherent reason for suppressing virtually all off-label speech, or if this approach was less a conscious choice than an inadvertent by-product of regulations aimed at mitigating other harms.

Sometimes descriptors can also help distinguish or contrast.

> Litigants are either prepared or unprepared.

> The testimony is damning; the video is very damning.

> The overbreadth problem posed by the Government's expansive conception of "promotional" speech is particularly problematic because it infringes upon fully-protected speech.

The takeaway: Use descriptors less. Let verbs and nouns do the talking. When descriptors will help, make sure they are unique and build an image, not an afterthought.

7.3.6 Use Visual Language

Legal writing is inherently complex. Abstract ideas and theoretical notions take center stage. Words that can't be seen, touched, or counted can be a necessary part of the lingo. But relying on abstractions too much leads to dense prose.

Concrete words are the words readers can see. Say you write, "A lack of diligence creates problems for clients." Words like "diligence" and "problems" are abstract: What do they look like? How do you imagine them?

Instead, we could say, "When lawyers don't take enough time to explain how clients should act in court, clients can make mistakes like calling the judge by the wrong name or directly addressing a witness." Now we're focused on lawyers doing things (or not doing things), and what it is that's such a "problem."

Read through the abstract nouns and descriptions in this passage:

> The **application** of the statute of limitations is a **nuanced aspect of jurisprudence** that requires the consideration of a **multitude of variables.** This **legislative enactment** prohibits the initiation of **legal proceedings** after the lapse of a **prescribed duration** from **the occurrence** of the alleged offense. The enforcement of this rule fosters **judicial expediency** and circumvents the potential erosion of evidence over time. Moreover, it is the **embodiment of the societal consensus** that legal disputes should attain resolution within a reasonable timeframe.

And now read the same information presented using concrete, tangible nouns and descriptors:

> **Picture a timer that starts** when a **law** is **broken**. That **timer** is the statute of limitations. It puts a hard **end date** on when **courts** can **hear** a case about someone **breaking** the law. **This rule keeps** our courts efficient and makes sure **old facts** don't **go stale**. Most experts agree that we need to resolve disputes within a fair amount of time. This **timer** puts that idea into action.

Search for ways to convert abstracts into real-world people and objects that readers can see. In the next example, most legal writers would have delivered their argument in abstract terms like this:

> The lower court's **opinion impermissibly applied** the **Nonmutual Offensive Collateral Estoppel doctrine** by holding that a small number of trial decisions precludes the MDL.

But these pros put the argument in concrete words that you can envision. No longer are we thinking about "opinion" and abstract doctrines. We see a court acting.

> **The Sixth Circuit decided to allow** the results of a **handful** of early trials to preclude trial on key issues across an entire MDL, misapplying **this Court's decision** in *Parklane* and **splitting with other circuits.**

Abstract nouns lead to abstract verbs, creating sentences that lack force. Consider, "a rise in the unemployment rate." The subject of this sentence, "a rise," is an abstract noun. It's paired with the verb "is," creating an expression that, although technically accurate, feels pedantic.

Contrast that with "more than double the people can't find work to feed their families compared to this time last year." "People" is a concrete noun, and "can't find work" is an action we can all connect with.

So replace the abstract with the concrete when making any point you care about.

- **Workers** is better than **workforce**
- **Pay** is better than **compensation**
- **Sales** is better than **revenue**
- **Rich people** is better than **high-net-worth individuals**
- **Spies** are better than **intelligence community**
- **Scholars** or **teachers** are usually better than **academic community**
- **Fell by half** instead of **50 percent**
- **10 billion** instead of **10 percent increase**

Sometimes you have a goal to keep things abstract for readers. Maybe you don't want them thinking about the 10 billion people harmed by your client's pollution—so a 10 percent increase isn't so bad. Just make sure you're being abstract on purpose.

7.3.7 Use Verbs That Burst

Verbs rev up our sentences. They supply the movement, the action, and the imagery that readers remember. Best of all, verbs add rhetorical kick without annoying readers. A snappy, crunchy verb will stick with readers long after they turn the page.

The power of verbs is twofold. Simply using more active verbs in makes your writing vastly more engaging. But you can also use more targeted verbs to create stunning points.

First, prefer concrete, visual verbs over "state of being" verbs, other non-action verbs, and nominalizations. State of being verbs (*is, are, was, were, been, being, be, am*) deliver little content. The same goes for possessive or linking verbs (like "has" and "have"). So by default, choose verbs that are at least active.

> The statute **has** severe restrictions that only **affect** plaintiff.
>
> *becomes*
>
> The statute **bristles** with severities that **touch** the plaintiff alone.

> Plaintiff's allegations **are** that the odors released from Defendant's factory **have been** noxious.
>
> *becomes*
>
> Plaintiff **alleges** that the defendant's factory **emits** noxious fumes.

> To suddenly constitutionalize this area **is** contradictory to what looks to be a prompt and considered legislative response.

becomes

To suddenly constitutionalize this area **short-circuits** what looks to be a prompt and considered legislative response.

Nominalizations are similarly stale. These are verbs transmogrified into nouns, often called *zombie nouns*. They are *-ion* and *-ent* words that hide simple, clearer verbs.

The court **made a determination** on three of the counts.

becomes

The court **determined** three of the counts.

The cases **are not in agreement** on this point.

becomes

The cases do not **agree** on this point.

Second, select verbs that target the emotions or images you're aiming for. You can't use targeted verbs in every sentence, otherwise you'd spend the rest of your life perusing verbs. But you can choose choice verbs for the most important sentences in your document.

To put these steps into context, here are a few sentences to compare. The last example uses a *targeted* verb, a verb that conveys an emotionally charged point.

State of Being: The plaintiff prefers that this case **is** back in the trial court.

Active: The plaintiff wants to **bring** this case back to the trial court.

Targeted: The plaintiff wants to **plunge** this case back into trial.

State of Being: ConnectU **is** accused of an unauthorized system breach.

Active: Facebook **accused** ConnectU of **entering** the system without authorization.

Targeted: Facebook . . . **accused** ConnectU . . . of **infiltrating** its system.

Because verbs are so important, let's look at some more examples. Let's start with a snippet from Justice Kagan's writing in the *Badgerow* case—but I've replaced the verbs with the sort of stale, state-of-being verbs and nominalizations that plague most legal writing.

This case **is** related to an arbitration of an employment dispute. Petitioner Denise Badgerow **was** employed as a financial advisor for REJ Properties, a firm that **is** operated by respondents Greg Walters, Thomas Meyer, and Ray Trosclair. [] Badgerow's contract **included a requirement** for

> claims arising out of her employment to be brought in arbitration, rather than to court. So when she was (in her view, improperly) terminated, a claim was filed in an arbitration action against Walters, including allegations of unlawful termination under both federal and state law. The arbitrators made a determination in favor of Walters, entering a dismissal of Badgerow's claims.

Now look at the power of verbs in Justice Kagan's writing. What you won't see are empty state-of-being verbs or nominalizations. Instead, you see concrete verbs that readers can visualize.

> This case grows out of the arbitration of an employment dispute. Petitioner Denise Badgerow worked as a financial advisor for REJ Properties, a firm run by respondents Greg Walters, Thomas Meyer, and Ray Trosclair.[] Badgerow's contract required her to bring claims arising out of her employment to arbitration, rather than to court. So when she was (in her view, improperly) fired, she initiated an arbitration action against Walters, alleging unlawful termination under both federal and state law. The arbitrators sided with Walters, dismissing Badgerow's claims.

Here's another snippet with bland verbs swapped out first.

> They do not include an instruction for a court to enter into conjecture about a world without an arbitration agreement, and to consider whether it would then have jurisdiction over the parties' dispute.
>
> Those bedrock principles will not allow us to construct look-through jurisdiction out of thin air—from somehow finding, without textual support, this method may be used to create a resolution as to various state-law-based, non-diverse Section 9 and 10 applications.
>
> The look-through rule is a highly unusual one: It results in jurisdiction not in the action actually before the court, but in another controversy neither there nor ever meant to be.

And here is how Justice Kagan wrote it. We have a couple targeted verbs here that are more charged. For example, Justice Kagan is trying to convey a sense of absurdity, so talks about "pulling" something from thin air.

> They do not instruct a court to imagine a world without an arbitration agreement, and to ask whether it would then have jurisdiction over the parties' dispute.
>
> Those bedrock principles prevent us from pulling look-through jurisdiction out of thin air—from somehow finding, without textual support, that federal courts may use the method to resolve various state-law-based, non-diverse Section 9 and 10 applications.
>
> The look-through rule is a highly unusual one: It locates jurisdiction not in the action actually before the court, but in another controversy neither there nor ever meant to be.

Or take this next passage of verbs from Justice Kagan, which brings to life a dry recitation of background facts:

> This Court first encountered John Sturgeon's lawsuit three Terms ago. As we explained then, Sturgeon hunted moose along the Nation River in Alaska for some 40 years. He traveled by hovercraft, an amphibious vehicle able to glide over land and water alike. To reach his favorite hunting ground, he would pilot the craft over a stretch of the Nation River. . . . By the 1950s, Alaskans hankered for both statehood and land—and Congress decided to give them both. . . . But the State's

> bonanza provoked land claims from Alaska Natives. . . . Yet one more land dispute loomed. . . . That means Sturgeon can again rev up his hovercraft in search of moose.

Being selective about your verbs is a hallmark of the best legal writers. Pick up good legal writing, and the verbs sing. Like in these snippets:

> The law is shot through with other content-based distinctions, demanding special treatment for "journalistic enterprises" and speech "by or about" political candidates.

> Sunbeam played fast and loose to hoodwink Wall Street.

> They are alleged former child slaves of Malian descent, dragooned from their homes and [enslaved] on cocoa plantations.

> Fraud unravels everything.

> But the government attempts to teleport the criminal burden of proof to a very different context. . . .

The verb is the engine of your sentence, so use the highest-performance engines you can and constantly tune them up.

7.4 Put Paragraphs Together Purposefully

Most legal writers don't give much thought to paragraphs. They know they should be neither too long nor too short. And they know that each sentence within one should loosely relate to the same idea. Those are great starting points, but paragraphs are powerful. How you choose to craft them will change not only the readability of your writing, but its persuasiveness, too.

It takes some real inertia to persuade a reader about a point. A word isn't going to do it. Nor is a sentence, no matter how pithy. But string a few sentences together that build on each other just right—a good paragraph—and you can convince someone of something that matters.

Think of each paragraph as a unit: Why is it there? Will readers understand how it connects with the prior paragraph? To the next one? Look at these next two paragraphs. The legal writers use the first sentences to prime readers with favorable details and each is focused on a single goal.

> On the merits, the Government also does not dispute the "dire hardship" its interpretation of Section 6324(a)(2) produces.[] Instead, the Government's defense of the decision below hinges on one thing—a comma. Because Congress placed a comma after the word "receives," the Government maintains that Section 6324(a)(2) unambiguously permits it to recover from trust beneficiaries like Ms. Pickens who receive estate property long after the decedent's death.[20]

[20]This and the following paragraph also offer a balance of sentences in different forms and in different lengths, which makes the flow engaging.

> **The comma cannot bear that weight.** Punctuation is important but "fallible" evidence of congressional intent.[] Here, other evidence overwhelmingly refutes the Government's interpretation—including judicial precedent dating back nearly a century; formal IRS acquiescence to that precedent; congressional ratification of that precedent; statutory context; the fact that the Government's reading would lead to absurd results; and the fact that these results would place "hardship" on beneficiaries who would often be hopelessly unable to bear it.[] In asking the Court to ignore this evidence, the Government advances a sorry facsimile of textualism that elevates one especially fallible measure of congressional intent to the exclusion of all other evidence.

The good news is that we've already covered the most powerful paragraph tool of them all in Chapter 2: distilling your paragraph's takeaway at the start. To finish honing your paragraph skills, you need only a few final tips.

A Quick Summary

Start paragraphs strong. **Craft your paragraph's first sentence to build credibility and showcase your best writing by distilling the paragraph's main takeaway, transitioning smoothly, or engaging readers.**

Keep paragraphs focused and fresh. **Craft cohesive paragraphs centered on a single, definable point. Avoid paragraphs longer than half a page to keep the content digestible. And engage your reader with varied paragraph length and sentence structure.**

7.4.1 Start Paragraphs Strong

Every paragraph is a new beginning for readers. Each delivers its own important idea. And so the beginning of each paragraph is a chance to show off your best writing and build credibility for the rest of the sentences devoted to that thought. Think of it as your paragraph's first impression. Let's break down everything you should consider when developing your paragraph-first-sentence strategy.

Your First Sentence's Style

Your reader might not make it past the first sentence. Their impression of what's valuable and worth paying attention to, paragraph to paragraph, is set by this initial step. Use the style tools we already covered in this chapter—as well as the advanced tools in Chapter 9—to elevate your style with these first words.

Use your style to tap into what makes each paragraph most useful or compelling. In excellent legal prose, there are no unimportant paragraphs. Each has something valuable to offer. Your goal is to capture that unique value in the first sentence.

For example, you can choose key words or phrases from the paragraph—or come up with some new ones that capture the theme you're aiming for. Notice how the word choice or quotes elevate the style in these next first sentences while aiming at a clear persuasive target.

> Plaintiffs ask for a protective order, but what they really want is **secrecy.**

> This **"give relief first ask questions later"** approach is precisely why courts apply this doctrine. . . .

> The word **"solely"** in Section 103(c)'s second sentence does not support that kind of **statute-gutting.**

> In **sketching** those units' boundary lines, Congress made an uncommon choice — to follow **"topographic or natural features,"** rather than enclose only federally owned lands.

Here's another great opening sentence that offers readers specific examples that capture the paragraph's point on a deep level:

> **Touching, tapping, pinching,** and other actions involving limited, non-violent contact do not constitute "physical force" — but **kicking, striking, punching,** and other actions that are associated with violence do constitute "physical force."

And here is another first-sentence powerhouse that leverages specifics aimed at a goal (this time, to shock readers with big numbers):

> Van Buren County took property worth **$206,000 to satisfy a $16,750 debt,** and then refused to refund any of the difference; in some legal precincts that sort of behavior is called theft.

The string of compelling specifics in this next paragraph's first sentence describes the reasons a confession appeared to be coerced. It's a long sentence, but it had a lot of content to capture and uses style to keep you on track:

> Psychological coercion, **questions to which the police furnished the answers,** and ghoulish **games of "20 Questions,"** in which **Brendan Dassey guessed over and over again before he landed on the "correct" story** (i.e., the one the police wanted), led to the "confession" that furnished **the only serious evidence supporting his murder conviction** in the Wisconsin courts.[21]

Choose Your First Sentence's Goal

But good style isn't all you're aiming for. Most good writers use the start of paragraphs for one of only a few reasons. First, and often the most helpful, is to use the first sentence to distill the paragraph's takeaway. That is the work we learned to do in Chapter 2 and what most of the examples we just looked at were crafted to achieve.

As a quick review, readers can't remember all the details in each paragraph. Distilling the takeaway gives readers what they need without the work. Here's an

[21] This is another great example of why having a bank account of complexity is so helpful. Most sentences in this document (which I didn't give you) were simple and kept to a single idea or two. That gives readers enough patience to deal with more layered sentences here and there.

example that starts with the takeaway by highlighting the key case and language from the paragraph:

> []Haywood argues that we should reconsider our holding in *Seifert* **because the definition of "firearm" applied in *Seifert* and by the court of appeals does not take into account the word's plain and ordinary meaning.**

The next option for paragraph openers is transitioning, which we return to in the next section of this chapter. Use this type of paragraph opener when readers might get lost going from the last paragraph's topic to the next. If you are shifting gears, transitioning at the start can help zip paragraphs together.

> **But even if Jones fired Ellie [the topic of the prior paragraph],** that would not matter....

A final option for paragraph starts is to prime. Occasionally, you can tease readers with an enticing first few words. This is the rare instance where distilling or transitioning isn't the goal. Sometimes getting readers invested is your priority because a paragraph matters that much.

There's no one way to prime readers. The goal is to surprise, intrigue, or otherwise engage. In this next example, you can't help but want to keep reading.

> **Have you ever grabbed a live electrical wire?**

Enough said.

7.4.2 Keep Paragraphs Focused and Fresh

Writing gurus offer many opinions about how long a paragraph should be. Suggestions vary from three or four sentences to as many as it takes to explain a point. But based on the bulk of evidence out there, a few yardsticks can guide you.

Break up a paragraph if it goes on for much longer than half a page. Readers could be scared off by the sheer look of a page-long paragraph. And let's be real: If your paragraph is that long, it's probably hiding at least a couple big ideas and needs to be broken up with separate takeaway sentences.

Bryan Garner suggests an average of 150 words, which is a nice aim. As he points out, during the twentieth century paragraphs shrunk in popular writing, and readers are now used to that approach.[22] Not to mention that cognitive science supports smaller, easier-to-digest points (which would suggest that smaller paragraphs are better).

Your best guide is to return to our distilling skills from Chapter 2, though. Use paragraphs to deliver single takeaways for readers. If a paragraph contains two important points, readers need both distilled for them at the outset. That will usually be easiest to do in two separate paragraphs. Read this next paragraph and do some idea work. At least two important points are mixed in.

[22] Bryan Garner, The Elements of Legal Style (2d ed. 2002).

> Despite being informed multiple times about the risks associated with the investment, and being provided with exhaustive documentation which outlined potential pitfalls, the claimant, Mr. Smith, proceeded to invest a substantial amount, totaling $5 million. The documentation was truly exhaustive. Mr. Smith was given more than 40 pages of advisements. He met with a bank representative for three hours. However, now, with the downturn in the market, Mr. Smith lodged a complaint, asserting that he was not properly informed about the volatility of the sector. He claims that he should have been told more about the specific risks in the tech industry his banker invested in, despite that this industry was detailed in no less than six documents he signed when he set up the portfolio, one of which stated he "was aware" of the risks in investing.

It is much better to use those valuable points to anchor your paragraphing. With the anchor of a specific takeaway sentence at the start, you might find that you don't need all the details you have in there, or that they belong in different places—or that you need some more specifics to sell your main points.

> Mr. Smith was given 40 pages of documents and 3 hours of consulting covering the risks of investing in the tech sector. . . .
>
> Mr. Smith chose to invest $5 million after receiving this extensive advice, signing six documents confirming he "was aware" of the risks.

Another tip is to be consistent in point of view, verb tense, and other grammatical structures across your paragraph. If you shift subjects too much within the same paragraph, or use different tenses, like mixing present and past, or shift between plurals and singulars, these can all make your readers stumble.

Keep Paragraphs Fresh

Beyond sticking to shorter, focused paragraphs, consider varying your paragraph structure a bit within each paragraph. Paragraphs create a cadence to your writing, just like sentences do. Varying your paragraph length (mostly shorter, some extra short, some a bit longer) will make your writing pleasing.

To pull this off, vary the sentence structure in your paragraphs here and there. Sprinkling in a semicolon or em dash can increase readability. But don't overdo it. If a paragraph is full of complex constructions, it will make for harder reading.

Most folks agree that the beginning and end of your paragraphs are the most important elements. That is why it's important to craft that first sentence persuasively to prime your reader. But it's also why you should put important points in the last sentences as well. That's what your readers will remember as they leave one major thought and enter the next. So drop a crucial fact or pithy phrase right at the end.

Then there is the short-sentence-punch. You've seen them: extra-compact sentences that stop readers for a moment and emphasize whatever you put in them. You don't want to use these too often. That can be choppy. Like this. But sometimes, when you want your reader to slow down and pay attention, include an extra-short sentence to make a point unmissable. An example is Chief Justice Roberts's famous short-sentence punch here:

> Substituting one decisionmaker for another may yield a different result, but not in any sense a more "correct" one. **So too here.**

Let's look at two final paragraphs that mix sentence length and use short sentences to emphasize.

> Police simply may not perform unrelated investigations that prolong a stop unless they have "independent reasonable suspicion justifying the prolongation." The government concedes that Officer Turley's mission was to investigate a parking violation. **So does Turley.**

> But there is no "irreparable harm" that judicial relief (injunctive or otherwise) could remedy once word is out. *James Cable Partners, L.P. v. City of Jamestown, Tenn.* by Duncan, 107 F.3d 870 (6th Cir. 1997) (explaining that injunctions must be "tailored to remedy the specific harm shown"). **And word is out.**

Finally, the occasional extra-short paragraph can finish a section with a jab or break up a long section by giving readers a breather. Like the legal writers up next did with a two-sentence paragraph:

> [a long section of paragraphs]
>
> **Nobody, not even a former President, is above the law. This Court should affirm.**

Paragraphs are your document's stepping stones. Each should be placed with care to lead readers smoothly to your conclusion.

7.5 Transition Constantly

Transitioning means ensuring that every sentence, every paragraph, and every section leads logically to the next.

There is more than one way to transition. You can use transition words; you can repeat words that signal to readers how sentences fit together; and sometimes the transition is so obvious you don't need a separate transition at all. But make no mistake, even a single break in your flow—a failure to transition from thought to thought—can stymie readers.

The best transitions are those you never notice. They do their guiding work, but they contribute important information as a good citizen of the sentence. The dry and formal transitions many lawyers use aren't all that useful—telling a reader that "something" happened rather than conveying how concepts connect. Take this example:

> **Furthermore**, the defendant's argument fails under governing case law. Such case law includes, among other things, this court's own precedent. Moreover, the defendant raises this argument far into the briefing, in a reply. **Additionally**, this briefing. . . .

Skillful transitioning does not mean sprinkling in the same well-worn *furthermores*. Instead, the best legal writers stitch sentences together with threads. As in this next example, where the first words of most sentences link back to a prior one.

> Thomson Reuters's Westlaw platform compiles[23] judicial opinions according to its Key Number System. That system organizes opinions by the type of law. Westlaw also adds "headnotes": short summaries of points of law that appear in the opinion. Each headnote is tied to a key number. Clicking on the headnote takes the user to the corresponding passage in the opinion. Clicking on the key number takes the user to a list of cases that make the same legal point. Westlaw has a registered copyright on its "original and revised text and compilation of legal material," which includes its headnotes and Key Number System.

Good transitioning like this is about telling readers where the next sentence is going given what they just learned.

A Quick Summary

Use logical linkers. **Use logical linking words to transition by showing readers the relationship between sentences.**

Use echo transitions. **Build bridges between sentences with echo words that signal what in the prior sentence the next sentence will build on.**

The best legal writers mainly rely on two transitioning devices: (1) useful transition phrases that convey the logical relationship between sentences, and (2) echoing words from the prior sentence to convey the relationship. Let's see these two techniques in action. In this next example, as you leave the first sentence and enter the second, you don't know exactly how "monetary harm" relates to what you just read.

> The court issued the ruling the next day. Monetary harm was not addressed in the court's ruling.

To transition better, we could first echo a word from the first sentence as we start the second sentence, making the connection clear:

> The court issued the ruling the next day. This ruling did not address monetary harm.

Our other option is to use a logical transition phrase that tells readers the relationship between the sentences—like whether the second sentence is a contrast, an expansion, or an example of the prior sentence.

[23] This paragraph shows off how powerful base sentences are —and every sentence has style worth paying attention to. Notice how short and targeted each sentence is. Each verb is chosen carefully ("compiles," "organizes," "adds"). Some sentences even dialogue with you, starting with "clicking" things.

> The court issued the ruling the next day. **But absent from** the ruling was the monetary harm factor.

That "but absent from" tells readers the direction that second sentence is going in — that we'll be learning about something absent from the ruling.

Notice in this next example how when we start reading about a "certification" in the second sentence, we can't be sure how that fits into what we learned in the first sentence:

> The agency never filed the correct paperwork. A certification that should have been attached never was.

Our first option is to echo a word to make the transition clear:

> The agency never filed the correct paperwork. **The paperwork** they did file did not even include a certification.

Or we can use a logical transition phrase:

> The agency never filed the correct paperwork. **For example**, the forms did not include a certification.

7.5.1 Use Logical Linkers

When adding extra words to the start of a sentence to transition, just make sure they are conveying useful information about how the sentences or paragraphs relate. You have a long menu of useful transitions that will keep the connections clear. Here are some popular ones (although there are many more):

Introducing examples

- Consider
- A case in point
- This is seen in
- For example
- Take
- Imagine
- As in
- First, second, third . . .
- For one thing
- Like
- Say
- Suppose
- To illustrate

Introducing new topics or contrasts

- Still
- But
- Yet
- Instead
- Nonetheless
- On a different note
- Turning to/moving to
- By contrast
- At its root
- Put another way
- At any rate
- More to the point
- For all that
- Of course
- On the other hand
- That said
- To be sure
- Equally
- In a similar vein

- Distinct from
- Unlike
- As opposed to

Conceding

- While this is true
- Accepting that
- True enough
- All the same
- Although
- At the same time
- Even assuming
- Even if
- Even so
- Granted
- Despite this

Expanding

- Building on this
- To further illustrate
- This also applies to
- In addition to X, Y also
- Extending

Summarizing

- Overall
- Ultimately
- At its core
- At bottom
- The crux
- At heart
- Essentially
- Ultimately
- Central to
- Put simply
- That is
- Stripping away
- To cut through
- After all

Connection

- This leads to
- Thus
- So
- Owing to
- Given that
- Following this
- After that
- Then
- Initially
- To begin
- At the outset
- As in X, Y
- As with X, Y
- By analogy
- By extension
- Here
- In each case
- In the same way
- Just as X, so Y
- Like X, Y
- Likewise
- Similarly
- So too
- To wit

However you transition, avoid the heavy connectors so many lawyers love. They don't make your sentences inviting. Try fresher, shorter versions:

- Accordingly (**thus**)
- Consequently (**thus**)
- Furthermore (**and/further**)
- Moreover (**and**)
- Additionally (**and**)
- Nevertheless (**still, that said . . .**)
- Inasmuch as (**because**)
- Notwithstanding that (**although**)

Look at the clear linking in these next Justice Kagan transitions. Each signals how the next sentence builds on the prior.

> Countless cities and towns across America have adopted ordinances regulating the posting of signs, while exempting certain categories of signs based on their subject matter. **For example**, some municipalities generally prohibit illuminated signs in residential neighborhoods, but lift that ban for signs that identify the address of a home or the name of its owner or occupant.... **In other municipalities**, safety signs such as "Blind Pedestrian Crossing" and "Hidden Driveway" can be posted without a permit, even as other permanent signs require one.... **Elsewhere**, historic site markers—for example, "George Washington Slept Here"—are also exempt from general regulations.... **And similarly,** the federal Highway Beautification Act limits signs along interstate highways unless, for instance, they direct travelers to "scenic and historical attractions" or advertise free coffee.[24]

7.5.2 Use Echo Transitions

Sometimes you won't need an obvious transition because whatever words you're starting with obviously relate to an idea in the prior sentence. And sometimes the best way to link sentences is to begin by echoing a word that creates a bridge to what came before.

This next paragraph doesn't use effective transition devices to stitch the sentences together.

> VMI attracts some applicants because of its reputation as an extraordinarily challenging military school. The math program is a very challenging part of the school and the key to why it is so successful. The plaintiff points out that discriminatory policies exist in the math program, which benefits only males. Plaintiff alleges violations of the Equal Protection Clause of the Fourteenth Amendment.

When we echo words to connect the thoughts, the reading flows:

> VMI attracts some applicants because of its reputation as an extraordinarily **challenging military school. That challenge** largely stems from the school's **math program. This math program** is what the plaintiff alleges **VMI** has used to discriminate against males. **VMI** allegedly violated the Equal Protection Clause by....

Transitioning between paragraphs is just like transitioning between sentences. Bridge the last paragraph into the next with a useful linking phrase or echo. Here is an example with a strong paragraph-to-paragraph transition.

> The questions presented in *Freeman* were whether and when an initial sentence imposed (as here) under a Rule 11(c)(1)(C) plea agreement—an agreement in which the defendant and the prosecutor stipulate to a sentence that the court must impose if it accepts the plea agreement—can be said to be "based on" a guidelines range.
>
> ***Freeman* produced a fractured result.** Four justices, representing a plurality of the court, indicated that they would "permit the district court to revisit a prior sentence to whatever extent

[24] This paragraph shows off the power of examples in analysis. Stacking these examples convinces you that cities need flexibility to regulate everyday signage.

> the sentencing range in question was a relevant part of the analytic framework the judge used to determine the sentence or to approve the agreement."

In this next example, the writer connects the first paragraph's main point (that the business was failing) to the second (that the personal relationships were fraying). This tight connection keeps ideas moving.

> While Nicholson secured final approval for the label from the Alcohol and Tobacco Tax and Trade Bureau, no one managed to nail down distribution channels, retail outlets, or vendors for the vodka. It's also entirely unclear whether they had the necessary state liquor licenses or approvals to sell the product.
>
> **Like the business,** the parties' personal and professional relationships also lacked a solid foundation. . . .

In this example from Justice Kagan, nowhere to be seen are those formal transitions (like *moreover, furthermore,* and *additionally*) that plague legal writing. Instead, you see a blend of logical transition phrases and words echoed from prior sentences.

> Fast forward now to a cold November morning in 2014, when Wooden responded to a police **officer's** knock on his door. **The officer** asked to speak with **Wooden's** wife. And noting the chill in the air, the officer asked if he could step inside, to stay warm. **Wooden** agreed. **But his** good deed did not go unpunished. . . . A jury later convicted him for being a felon in possession of a firearm, **in violation of** 18 U.S.C. §922(g). **The penalty** for that crime varies significantly depending on whether **ACCA** applies. **Putting ACCA aside**, the maximum sentence for violating §922(g) is ten years in prison. **But ACCA** mandates a minimum sentence of fifteen years if the §922(g) offender has three prior convictions for "violent felon[ies]" (like burglary) or "serious drug offense[s]" that were "committed on occasions different from one another."

Finally, transitions can help reinforce persuasive points. As in this next federal appellate brief, where the authors remind readers about the strong legislative record arguments that came before in transitioning to the next point:

> **Here, not only the legislative record**, but Florida's defense of S.B.7072, confirms that the law's speaker distinctions both are "directed at" and "present[] the danger of suppressing, particular ideas."

These next writers use a transition to reemphasize that the opposing party relied on a nonstandard definition (which was the focus of the prior section).

> First, the FCC offers a definition unsupported by every dictionary we pulled from the shelf. . . .
>
> Second, **the non-standard dictionary definitions** of "from" offered by petitioner apply in contexts that are not relevant here.

In the end, building sentences from the words up, choosing the best verbs and nouns, and constructing paragraphs to deliver one undeniable point at a time will all pay off in every document.

Level Up Your Style with Technology

From correcting technical mistakes to brainstorming vibrant language, technology is a great resource for the techniques we've covered in this chapter. With your writing style, focus on technology that can (1) help you generate ideas at the sentence level, (2) edit your writing, and (3) give you feedback or guidance on improving your style.

GAI tools: GAI tools can help you diagnose your basic writing style pitfalls, edit your writing, and offer alternative phrases and sentences that better fit your writing goals. Some useful prompt examples:

- Brainstorm at least five ideas for an active verb that helps convey an unreasonable delay here: [insert your existing writing].
- Provide five examples of a clearer sentence that is more concise: [insert your existing writing].
- Provide feedback about my sentence style in these sentences in terms of clarity and syntax: [insert your existing writing].
- Identify any sentences that a reader might be confused about or that is ambiguous or unclear in this writing: [insert your existing writing].

Writing assistance software: Beyond basic grammar and spell-check, sophisticated software packages like Grammarly and BriefCatch provide an advanced style check that can suggest refinements in word choice and sentence construction, leading to more persuasive legal writing. Their algorithms can detect overused phrases, eliminate redundancy, and suggest alternatives that enhance your text's clarity and flow.

Online thesauruses: Tools like Power Thesaurus or Visual Thesaurus help you refine language to ensure that your takeaways are not only accurate but compelling. These resources offer extensive synonym choices and word relationships that can enhance the clarity and appeal of your takeaways.

Readability analyzers and vocabulary enhancers: Apps like the Hemingway Editor and ProWritingAid encourage brevity and directness, two hallmarks of persuasive legal writing. By highlighting complex and convoluted sentences, these programs prompt legal writers to reformulate their points in a manner that is readily understandable.

Legal drafting software: Platforms like Casetext's Compose offer predrafted arguments that align with legal precedents. These tools are particularly efficient for ensuring that the stylistic choices in a document adhere to best practices while being tailored to the legal matter at hand.

Dictation tools: Voice-to-text software like Dragon NaturallySpeaking allows you to dictate your writing, which can speed up your drafting process and result in simpler prose. These tools can also be particularly helpful in ensuring your documents are coherent.

8

Level Up Your Mechanics and Editing

> My life needs editing."—Mort Sahl

Effective legal writing isn't only about persuasive arguments and pithy prose; it's also about fine-tuning your writing mechanics and sweeping away distracting errors that undermine your message. When your writing is precise and error-proof, your credibility soars.

This chapter is your playbook for rising above the common blunders that even veteran legal writers make. You'll learn to navigate the treacherous waters of grammar and punctuation, and you'll learn how to refine your editing skills to a sharp point.

We'll cover how to:

- **Avoid common legal grammar pitfalls.** Don't fall for the most common grammar pitfalls that appear in everyday legal writing.
- **Write clearly.** Pick up best practices for writing actively, directly, and without distractions.
- **Punctuate perfectly.** Make sure you understand the mechanics and the style choices behind each punctuation mark.
- **Edit efficiently.** Break your editing process into phases so you catch every major improvement and typo.

Let's first see what a difference the technical side of your writing can make. Try making it through this next passage, full of excess and clutter:

> In the instant case[1] concerning the contractual agreement, it is crucial to note that the Contractual Engagement Facilitation Agency (CEFA) is hereby obligated to regularly submit a comprehensive

[1] This is a classic formalism in legal writing. Just say "here."

> report[2] of all transactions. This report, per the stipulations of the agreement,[3] must include details about the provision of financial exchanges, fiscal distributing, and any individual executing a transfer, notwithstanding any unforeseen circumstances or eventualities that may arise.[4] Furthermore, it's imperative for CEFA to ensure that these reports are furnished in a timely fashion, adhering strictly[5] to the bimonthly[6] submission schedule as outlined in the detailed provisions of the contract.

Now what's your reaction to this next version? Who would you be more likely to trust? Who would you be more likely to listen to?

> The Agency must report on all transactions stemming from the party's agreement. These reports must detail who made the transactions, how much cash was exchanged, and who received the money. The Agency must provide these reports every two months.

Fair enough, right? Let's learn how to write as efficiently as this.

8.1 Avoid Common Legal Grammar Pitfalls

Legal writing is a minefield where tiny grammar mishaps can set off big misunderstandings. Read this factual background from a motion:

> The pioneering team, consisting of scientists and engineers, **lead** the industry with its innovative approach and has set a high standard **which** others follow. The **teams** work significantly impacts the market **by** its exceptional products that **offers** an unmatched level of security and efficiency, distinguishing **themselves** from less reliable solutions of the competitors.

It's hard to overlook the pile of grammar mistakes here. If the writer is lazy about checking subject–verb agreement, misplaced modifiers, or possessive punctuation, how can we trust them to get the law right?

Sloppy grammar isn't just embarrassing—it's a weapon your opposition will exploit. Every dangling modifier or misused referent creates an opening. This section equips you to neutralize those distractions.

---

[2] Do readers really need to know it's a "comprehensive" report and not a "report"? Probably not. It's all about focusing on what ideas readers need and cutting words not delivering them.

[3] Giving readers specifics they don't need is a hallmark of poor legal writing. There's no reason to keep referring to the agreement if it's clear we are relating what's required.

[4] Legal writing is full of modifiers —words or phrases that modify other words or phrases. And when we aren't clear about the relationship between modified and modifier, we run into problems. What is notwithstanding the unforeseen circumstances here?

[5] Extra descriptors like this rarely add value for readers. As Stephen King said in his book *On Writing*, "The road to Hell is paved with adverbs."

[6] Opt for simple, familiar language that everyone will instantly understand. Bimonthly can mean either every two months or twice a month. Talk about being ambiguous.

A Quick Summary

Be mindful of modifiers. **Modifiers should usually be placed just before the word or phrase they describe; distant modifiers make sentences unclear.**

Agree subjects with verbs. **Ensure the subject and verb of sentences are consistent with one another.**

Write in parallel. **When listing items or ideas, maintain the same grammatical structure to enhance flow.**

Punctuate possessives. **Correctly use apostrophes to show possession, and remember they are not used for simple plurals.**

Compare correctly. **Use comparative adjectives (*-er*) for two items and superlatives (*-est*) for three or more.**

Describe nouns and verbs grammatically. **Use hyphens with phrasal adjectives and commas with coordinating adjectives.**

Avoid commonly confused words. **Be vigilant about words with similar spellings but different meanings. Don't use the noun *login* when you mean the verb phrase *log in*.**

Capitalize consistently. **Capitalize uniformly and follow the right conventions.**

8.1.1 Be Mindful of Modifiers

We looked at modifiers as persuasive tools back in Chapter 5. As a reminder, these are words or phrases that add detail or descriptions to other words or phrases. Now let's look at some of the mechanical pitfalls legal writers run into here. Take *only*, a notorious troublemaker. When *only* drifts too far from the word or phrase it's meant to modify, sentences turn clumsy. Look at what moving this modifier around does to the meaning of a sentence:

- Joe ate **only the tofu**. (He ate only tofu, not meat.)
- Joe **only ate** the tofu. (He just ate the tofu; he didn't cook with it.)

Or try *almost*:

- Joe **almost failed** every law school class he took. (He nearly failed all his classes but eventually passed.)
- Joe failed **almost every** law school class he took. (He failed most of his classes, but not all of them.)

The two most common types of modifiers are adjectives, which describe nouns, and adverbs, often ending in *-ly*, which modify adjectives, verbs, or other adverbs.

But modifiers cover more ground than that. Even a whole phrase can act as a modifier: "**Responsible for representing lawyers,** the Bar Council plays an important role in campus life."

The goal with modifiers is to keep clear for readers the relationship between modifiers and what each modifies. Avoid two modifier hazards: dangling modifiers and squinting modifiers.

Squinting modifiers make sentences like this next one murky because it's unclear what the modifier is modifying:

> The *Bennett* case involved a lawsuit that was **only permissible** after the repeal of a statute.

Snuggle the modifier up to what it's modifying (we aren't talking about things being "only permissible," we are talking about things being permissible "only after" something else happens):

> The *Bennett* case involved a lawsuit permissible **only after** a statute's repeal.

Dangling modifiers leave you hanging because the modified words are missing. Who or what is ignoring the rules here?

> **Ignoring the rules,** the case wrapped up.

So keep the modifying next to the modified (usually, right before it). Also, modifier problems often hide poor sentence structure generally, giving you the chance to build something better.

> Children **who are abused frequently are** not protected.
>
> *becomes*
>
> Abused children **frequently go unprotected.**

> All vehicles **including saloons, hatchbacks, and MPVs without a permit may not enter.**
>
> *becomes*
>
> All vehicles without a permit—**saloons, hatchbacks, and MPVs**—may not enter.

Modifiers are like rogue punctuation—misplaced, they wreak havoc. Master their placement for legal writing that hits the mark.

8.1.2 Agree Subjects with Verbs

Subject–verb agreement means your verb must harmonize with your subject. If one is plural, the other must be, too. The easy cases stand out. "The company were in breach of contract" likely strikes you as off (even if you didn't pinpoint the subject–verb problem). But legal writers stumble in a few less obvious subject–verb situations.

The first is when a word like "each" turns a plural subject singular:

> Each of the directors have signed the agreement.

That might not sound offputting, given the plural noun near the verb. But "each" refers to individuals, so the verb should follow suit.

> Each of the directors has signed the agreement.

When using correlative pairs, make sure the verb agrees with the subject closest to the verb:

> Neither the manager nor the employees are ready to compromise.

Here, "employees" is closer to the verb, so we use a plural verb ("are") to match.

Speaking of *neither*, both it and *either* take singular verbs, joining the *each* singular club. One exception arises with *either-or* and *neither-nor* constructions; if the second item is plural in these structures, so is the verb.

> Neither the statute nor its implementing regulations apply here.

What happens when a subject includes two nouns that both must agree with the verb? One word to watch for is *and*. *And* creates a plural subject, even if the nouns are singular on their own (because we are talking about both things together).

> The court and the lawyers are late again to the hearing.

An *or* does the opposite, keeping each item singular.

> The lawyer or the paralegal is responsible.

Mass nouns (inanimate objects like *sugar* or *furniture*); and all compound words ending in *one*, *body*, or *thing*, take singular verbs. After all, "sugar **is** wonderful."

Collective nouns refer to a group of things taken as a single entity, like *group*. These default to singular, but they can vary based on the context. So the "jury **is** deliberating" and the "group **is** out for lunch." But it depends on whether you are using the noun to refer to individuals or groups. If you refer to individuals in a group, use a plural verb. If you refer to the group of things as a whole, go singular.

> Families dislike court.

Things get most confusing when a bunch of nouns create a traffic jam in the sentence's subject.

> The quality of the evidence, as well as the court's ability to analyze it, (is/are) crucial for a fair trial.

The verb here should match the primary subject that makes up the main independent clause in the sentence, here, "quality."

> The quality of the evidence, as well as the court's ability to analyze it, is crucial for a fair trial.

A few more tips on agreement:

- When using a to-be verb, the matching subject should follow it: "There **is a bouquet** of flowers." We would not match "flowers" because the subject matches the verb that comes right after the "is."
- Indefinite pronouns like *all*, *any*, *some*, or *none* can be thorny. Their context decides whether they take singular or plural verbs. For example, "**All of the cake is** gone" versus "**All of the cookies are** gone."
- *Half* goes with a singular verb if followed by a singular noun. When followed by a plural noun, it takes a plural verb: "Half the **apple is** rotten, but half the **apples are** rotten."
- *A number of* signifies many, functioning as a plural noun, whereas ***the** number of* refers to a single number, designating singular.
- Institution names, like the United States and Congress, tend to use singular verbs.
- When a subject includes an *of* phrase, match the verb to the noun before the *of*: "**A collection of** cases **lends** credibility to a brief."
- In sentences starting with *here* or *there*, the true subject trails the verb, as in "There **are four hurdles** to jump in this workshop," and "Here **are the keys** to your writing future."
- When an expression of time or measurement is the subject, use a singular verb: "**Ten years is** a long time to wait."

8.1.3 Write in Parallel

Parallelism is the rhythm section of your legal writing. When you craft lists or comparisons in parallel, your writing gains balance. Pulling off parallelism is easy. Just ensure each item's grammatical structure aligns. Like the verb phrases in this next sentence, which are all in the same form.

> The Court knew what it was doing, it cared about its holding, and it carefully documented its findings.[7]

That parallelism packs a punch, doesn't it? Each item stands strong on its own yet builds on its neighbors. Not so much when the items don't grammatically match.

> The Court knew what it was doing, the holding handed down by the Court was critical, and the Court has issued precise findings.

[7] Parallel constructions like that can also help focus storytelling by reinforcing the subject again and again.

Let's look at an example from a brief on intellectual property law:

> The infringing product **mimics** the plaintiff's patented design, **copies** its unique functionality, and **even replicates** its distinctive color scheme.

The parallel verbs ("mimics," "copies," "replicates") emphasize the defendant's infringement on multiple fronts.

Or consider this excerpt from a First Amendment case:

> The law cannot prohibit speech **because it is unpopular**, **because it is controversial**, or **because it offends the majority**.

The repetition of "because it is..." drives home the absolute nature of free speech protections.

Another species of parallelism is those correlatives we talked about in the last chapter. A few pitfalls to watch out for here. First, ensure the items inserted after each correlative are the same grammatical form (e.g., two nouns, two verbs, two phrases).

> Both the **manager agrees** and **the employees are agreeing** on the terms.
>
> *becomes*
>
> **Both the manager and the employees** agree on the terms.

The correlatives should come right before the elements they connect.

> You can **attend either the meeting in person or participate** via video conference.
>
> *becomes*
>
> You can **either attend** the meeting in person **or participate** via video conference.

When using *neither/nor* or *not only/but also*, ensure that negation is correctly placed to avoid double negatives or unintended meanings.

> The policy applies neither to current employees nor to past employees.
>
> *becomes*
>
> The policy doesn't apply neither to current employees nor to past employees.

Don't mix different pairs of correlative conjunctions within the same sentence. This creates density and makes correlation harder to check.

The court both ruled on every claim, either implicitly or explicitly, while also dismissing the pending motions to compel.

becomes

The court ruled on every claim, either implicitly or explicitly. It also dismissed the pending motions to compel.

8.1.4 Punctuate Possessives

Possessives are another snag for legal writers. First, don't be confused about plurals that aren't possessing anything. When making a noun plural, simply add an *-s* or an *-es* (if the word already ends in *s* or an *s* sound). There's no need for an apostrophe in "turtles."

Most singular nouns get an apostrophe and an *s* for possession. "The **attorney's** brief" signifies that the brief belongs to the attorney. For plural nouns that end in *s*, simply add an apostrophe. "The **partners'** agreement" means multiple partners share the agreement.

Beware the possessive versus contraction conundrum. Wherever you see *it's*, you're dealing with a contraction of *it is*, not the possessive form. For possession, use *its* sans apostrophe, as in "**its** contents did not reveal anything suspicious."

When two people jointly possess something, only the last noun needs the possessive form:

Tom and Jane's property indicates the land co-owned by Tom and Jane.

But if we were talking about each person individually, then both would get the possessive apostrophe:

Tom's and Jane's beliefs differ greatly from one another.

Inanimate objects, buildings, and furniture don't require apostrophes to establish possession. "The chair leg," not "the chair's leg," tells us that the leg is part of the chair.

Navigating the possessive minefield becomes tricky with singular nouns that already end in s. There are two schools of thought—the *Chicago Manual of Style* suggests an apostrophe and an extra "s" (Jess's), whereas *The New York Times* prefers an apostrophe only (').

Take "Jones." Following each school, the possessive form of his name would look like this:

Chicago Manual of Style: Jones's car (with an 's).

The New York Times: Jones' car (apostrophe only).

For phrases where you choose whether a noun is plural or singular, just use your preference consistently. So "attorney's fees" (singular possessive) or "attorneys' fees" (plural possessive).

8.1.5 Compare Correctly

Sometimes legal folks run afoul of comparatives and superlatives—words we use when comparing things. Just a few pointers to keep in mind here.

When it comes to *comparatives*—those *-er* words like *smaller*, *better*, and *faster*—the rule is simple. Use them to put two things head-to-head. For example, "As precedent, ***Brandenburg v. Ohio*** is **stronger** than ***Schenck v. United States***."

As we graduate from comparatives to *superlatives*—the realm of *smallest*, *best*, *worst*, and their comrades—we are comparing three or more items or groups. "Among the **plaintiffs**, Jane presents the **strongest** argument for compensation." Here the superlative "strongest" signifies Jane's position relative to multiple plaintiffs.

Then we have *compare with* and *different from*. *Compare with* allows us to convey similarities or differences.

> Compare the precision of a well-crafted contract, which can prevent disputes, With the ambiguity of a handshake agreement, which can foster misunderstandings.

Different from is best suited for comparing people or things.

> The dissenting judge's opinion is different from the majority's reasoning.

For everything else, *different than* is your best bet.

> The ramifications of this statute are different than those of previous legislation.

Finally, we have *like* and *as*. For straightforward comparisons between two nouns, *like* is the ticket.

> The stability of a long-standing legal precedent is like the firmness of an old oak tree.

But when dealing with two actions, qualities, or experiences, as is right.

> A court should weigh the defendant's past actions *as* heavily as it considers the present circumstances.

8.1.6 Describe Nouns and Verbs Grammatically

Nearly everyone forgets when to put a hyphen or comma between two adjectives—those pesky phrasal and coordinating adjectives.

When multiple words together modify or describe a noun, the phrase is ordinarily hyphenated (a phrasal adjective). The key is that the words must work together to describe the noun. If they instead each independently describe the noun, no hyphen is needed.

An easy way to check is to see whether the meaning of the phrase changes when you switch the descriptors around. For example, take "a well-respected attorney."

"Well-respected" is a phrasal adjective modifying "attorney," and the hyphen connects the words to avoid ambiguity. We couldn't flip the descriptors and say "a respected well attorney," so we need the hyphen. Without it, the reader might ponder if the attorney is merely respected and well, or well-respected.

Why is this rule important? Because it clarifies what can often be an ambiguous sentence. Take the phrases "high school kids" and "high-school kids." Is the writer talking about school kids who are high? Or kids who are in high school? The phrasal adjective clarifies that it's the latter.

In an employment dispute, the court might scrutinize "exempt-status employees" (contrasting nonexempt employees) rather than pondering the status of those who are simply employees. A real estate contract could involve "build-to-suit developments," emphasizing buildings tailored to a particular purpose. In an intellectual property case, you might discuss "public-domain works," signifying creative pieces for which copyrights have expired or never existed.

In contrast, coordinating adjectives are separate, distinct descriptors modifying a noun. Ordinarily, they need no hyphenation. Take a phrase like "a thorough, concise brief." Here, "thorough" and "concise" express different qualities of the noun "brief," but neither adjective relies on the other. Each can be reordered or removed without altering the meaning of the remaining adjective. That's why no hyphen is required.

A party involved in business litigation might submit "voluminous, detailed documentation," emphasizing the sheer size and the specificity of the paperwork, independently. A legal memorandum might call for a "swift, decisive resolution," underlining both the need for speed and a definitive decision.

8.1.7 Avoid Commonly Confused Words

English is notoriously difficult for confusing words and spellings. Like using *affect* as a verb and *effect* as a noun. Or swapping "John and I" for "John and me." So let's briefly cover the most common mix-ups (not to be confused with *mix ups*).

First are words or phrases that sound the same but are spelled differently depending on whether they are used as a noun or verb. You *set up* the computer but then it becomes your computer *setup*. You *log in* to your account, but you shouldn't share your account *login*.

Next is *which* versus *that*. These relative pronouns both introduce clauses, but they play distinct roles. *Which* is for nonessential clauses that can be cut without derailing the sentence. *That* is for essential clauses whose removal would distort your sentence's meaning.

> The contract, **which the parties signed last week,** words the arbitration provision in a way **that affects all future disputes.**

Here, removing the "which" clause won't divert our focus from the arbitration clause, but excising the "that" group of words at the end would make the sentence ungrammatical.

Next is *who* versus *whom*. These interrogative pronouns form questions or relative clauses pertaining to people. It can be difficult to determine the right one to use but keeping *who* as the subject (the actor) and *whom* as the object (or recipient of the action) can help.

The judge who presided over the case retired last year.

In this example, "who" is the subject because the judge is performing the action of presiding.

The attorney to whom you spoke recommended filing a motion.

Here, "whom" receives the action of speaking, and thus fits the bill as the object.

And of course, the classic *me* versus *I*. Both are personal pronouns representing the speaker. *I* is the subject pronoun, and *me* is the object pronoun. The best way to conquer this is to consider how the sentence would sound without the other person's name:

The judge met with John and I. (*The judge met with I* isn't right)

becomes

The judge met with John and me. (*The judge met with me* is right)

Here are a few more common culprits seen in legal writing across the nation:

- *Its* versus *it's*: *Its* is a possessive form of *it*; *it's* is a contraction of *it is*. The court upheld **its** decision, but **it's** not the end of the litigation.
- *Lay* versus *lie*: *Lay* is a verb requiring a direct object, whereas *lie* needs no object. "The attorney **lays** the report on the table and then **lies** down for a nap."
- *Excepted* versus *accepted*: *Excepted* means excluded from a group; *accepted* means agreed to or received willingly.
- *Affect* versus *effect*: *Affect* is usually a verb meaning to influence; *effect* is usually a noun meaning result.
- *Fewer* versus *lesser*: *Fewer* is used with countable nouns; *lesser* is used with uncountable nouns and often means smaller in importance.
- *Infer* versus *imply*: *Infer* is to draw a conclusion; *imply* is to suggest something without stating it directly.
- *Principal* versus *principle*: *Principal* can serve as a noun for a key person or the main sum of money, or as an adjective meaning primary. *Principle* is a noun meaning a fundamental truth or rule. "The **principal lawyer** argued the case based on constitutional **principles**."
- *Then* versus *than*: *Then* refers to time; *than* is used to compare.
- *They're* versus *their* versus *there*: Yes, we legal writers even mess these up sometimes. *They're* is the contraction for *they are*, *their* is possessive, and *there* denotes direction.

If you struggle with these word pairs or others, keep a cheat sheet nearby and check for them when editing. Nearly all of us have some commonly confused word pitfalls to watch out for.

8.1.8 Capitalize Consistently

Legal writers struggle with capitalizing references like *plaintiff* and *defendant*, *court*, and common terms like *federal* and *state*. But you don't have to.

Let's start with recurring characters: plaintiff and defendant. They generally should be lowercase, unless we're talking about a specific party in our dispute.[8]

> The Plaintiffs here are like plaintiffs in prior cases: They deserve justice.

How about the often-mentioned *court*? Use lowercase unless addressing the court you're writing to, in which case, it's uppercase:

> This Court previously aligned with other courts in this jurisdiction.[9]

Words like *federal*, *state*, and *commonwealth* sound authoritative, but they remain lowercase unless paired with proper nouns like the *Federal Reserve* or *Commonwealth of Maryland*.

When referencing a document filed in your current matter, capitalize:

> In the Motion to Dismiss, Plaintiff argues. . . .

> Under this Court's August 3, 2022, Order. . . .

Other words to capitalize include names of agencies, government bodies, offices (Social Security Administration, Department of Justice), titles when accompanying names (President Adams, Vice President Perkins), and family relationships used with names (Aunt Amy).

Capitalization in headings is something we all have probably wrangled with. When capitalizing the words in a heading, capitalize all the words except for prepositions of fewer than five letters, conjunctions like *and*, and articles like *a* or *an*. You should capitalize those, though, if they start the heading.

When citing statutes, legislative acts, or regulations, keep the first letter of every word capitalized, except for articles, short prepositions, and conjunctions:

> The Family and Medical Leave Act

> The Freedom of Information Act

But if you're mentioning laws in the abstract, go lowercase:

[8] And what about definite articles? Feel free to omit that pesky "the" when mentioning "the defendant." Or add them in. But whatever you do, be consistent.

[9] Many style guides suggest using *Court* when referring to the U.S. Supreme Court, as well.

federal labor laws

state environmental regulations

Here are a few more common capitalization pitfalls:

- Specific places or areas should be capitalized: "The company is in the Northwest and also has an office in the Big Apple."
- Directions remain lowercase: "The defendant went north on Clarence Street."
- Days of the week are capitalized: "The lawyers waited until the Friday before Christmas to file their motion to compel."
- Capitalize the full names of organizations: "American Bar Association," "United Nations."
- Seasons are lowercase: "Let's schedule that deposition on a Thursday in the summer."

Above all, be consistent. No matter what capitalization preferences you adopt, if you capitalize one term and then use a lowercase version later, all readers will see is a typo.

8.2 Write Clearly

Great! You've locked your grammar down. But even technically correct writing can get bloated and confusing. Archaic jargon, tedious footnotes, and pages littered with acronyms will ruin your writing as fast as a misplaced modifier would.

Take quoting. Legal writers love to splash quotes all over their documents, thinking that a heap of judicial voices will bolster their own credibility. But the best legal writers pluck the useful parts of quotes and place them into better sentences. Lisa Blatt and her team show us how in this next snippet. Every quote is doing work—and it's all delivered in Blatt's telltale voice:

> Under the FSIA, the relevant arbitration agreement is the **"agreement between the parties,"** not the investment treaty writ large.... Courts **"consistently recognize[]"** that investment **"treat[ies] constitute[] a standing offer to arbitrate disputes."** ... The Supreme Court, for example, has described a bilateral arbitration treaty as an **"offer"** to arbitrate—but the private party must then **"consent[] to the arbitration,"** so that the State and private party mutually agree to arbitrate ... Blasket's own expert confirms as much: An investment **"treaty acts as a standing offer by the States party to the treaty to arbitrate disputes covered by the treaty,"** which investors **"can accept ... by commencing an arbitration."**[10]

This chapter is about going clear. Make quotes useful. Shed the weight of passive voice, imprecise words, and passive-aggressive footnotes. Handle gendered language with finesse and banish imprecise words that cloud your arguments. Your readers will thank you.

[10] The longer quote is from an opposing party's expert, which removes any possibility that it was taken out of context.

A Quick Summary

Prefer active voice (usually). **Use an active voice and speak to readers directly. But use passive voice occasionally to focus on the action or when the actor is unknown or irrelevant.**

Use inclusive language. **Eschew gendered terms for inclusive language. Consider using *they* for a singular pronoun or rephrasing sentences to avoid gender altogether.**

Avoid acronyms. **Name parties, people, or entities concrete things that readers will remember.**

Use footnotes sparingly. **Employ footnotes only for nonessential elaboration, because many readers won't read them.**

Use font styles sparingly. **Use underlining, italics, and bold type to emphasize language only when unusually helpful to readers.**

Quote consciously. **Quote with intention to incorporate key outside voices or to highlight critical language.**

8.2.1 Prefer the Active (Usually)

Rather than hide your sentence's action behind weak verbs, make your writing direct and forceful. Or in a word, *active*. It will do wonders for your readability.

So what's the secret weapon of active voice? Putting the doer of the action front and center. Instead of a subject being acted on, the subject is calling the shots. The easiest way to spot the difference is to ask yourself: "Who or what is doing the main action in this sentence?"

Consider these passive sentences:

1. The contract **was signed by** the CEO.
2. The infringement **was committed by** the defendant.
3. The verdict was **upheld by** the appellate court.

Now, let's make them active by putting the actor first:

1. The **CEO signed** the contract.
2. The **defendant infringed. . . .**
3. The appellate **court upheld** the verdict.

Sometimes it can be hard to spot passive constructions hiding in the background. One trick is to look for the word *by*, which often signals a passive construct.

> The ball was dropped by the judge.

> The dog was sued by the Plaintiff.

> Dogs are loved by people.

Here are those sentences back in the active voice.

> The judge dropped the ball.

> The Plaintiff sued the dog.

> People love dogs.

All that said, passive voice gets more hate than it should. Sometimes it's smart to go passive. The passive voice can help:

- Focus on the recipient of the action.
- Minimize the actor (because you don't want them noticed, you don't know who they are, or they would distract readers).
- Highlight the action.
- Smoothly transition by starting with an action or object instead of the subject.

This next sentence purposely focuses on the recipient of the action, rather than the actor:

> The plaintiff was later released from custody and taken by her family to a hospital, where she was treated for several emotional ailments.

Or we can shift the focus to an action and deemphasize the actor:

> When the lights went out, several punches were thrown.

> Mistakes were made in the document drafting process.

Sometimes the actor is trivial and would just be a distraction. We don't need to know who did the chaining in this next example, as the focus is on the victims.

> They were chained up and moved to another facility.

Sometimes you don't know who the actor was.

The Plaintiff's identity was stolen.

Finally, passive voice can sometimes help smoothly transition from other sentences by connecting readers to a concept or word they were introduced to before.

Attorneys can't seem to understand their clients' needs. But these needs should be given priority above all else.

Don't let your writing be acted on; make it the actor.

8.2.2 Use Inclusive Language

Many readers find gendered language distracting, yet traditional fixes like *he/she* tend to be clunky (and not all that inclusive). To craft prose that leaves your audience focused on the substance, employ gender-neutral language.

Three methods can help you be gender-neutral. First, simply cut gendered actors. Sometimes, simplicity is the strongest strategy. By banishing actors from the stage, you put the spotlight on what matters.

Once a plaintiff moves for relief, he/she must file a written memorandum in support.

We can remove the gender and rewrite to avoid requiring a pronoun.

A motion requires a supporting written memorandum.

Second, you can go plural. Convert the subject to be plural so that you can use a plural pronoun.

Once plaintiffs move for relief, they must file a written memorandum.

You can also use the singular *they*. Yes, some might still call it ungrammatical, but Jane Austen and William Shakespeare embraced the singular *they*, and you can, too.

Once a plaintiff moves for relief, they must file a memorandum in support.

Beyond pronouns, many have suggested that a slew of words could have roots or connotations that disrespect readers. Some gendered language is easy to make more inclusive. You lose little by calling the head of a committee the "chairperson" instead of the "chairman." The same goes for making words like *policeman*, *repairman*, and *mankind* more inclusive. *Officers*, *technicians*, and *humanity* are easy replacements.

Ultimately, we write for our readers. If a word might offend them, it isn't doing you any favors.

8.2.3 Avoid Acronyms

Acronyms are another sort of imprecise. Let's be real; they often confuse. Acronyms are a bunch of letters thrown together that your reader must somehow remember ten pages after you mentioned them. Yes, your reader can follow CIA just fine. But not MSFGFDH (a real acronym from a brief).

Use parties' names or self-explanatory descriptions whenever you can. And try to make these labels persuasive. What you name things can change how they look to readers, as we saw in Chapter 7. *Plaintiff* and *defendant* do not engage like *Apple* and *Google* do. Now we're talking about two tech behemoths battling it out in court. So instead of

> The SLM Data Trust and Logistics Company, Inc (hereafter referred to as "SLMDTLC")
>
> *you could write*
>
> The SLM Data Trust and Logistics Company, Inc. ("Data Trust").

Speaking of definitions, question whether you need them. Although defined terms might be needed for technical drafting like in contracts, definitions aren't always needed in legal writing. Unless readers will be confused about who you're referring to, you can often just use a party's name without the fanfare. I promise dropping the "(hereinafter 'plaintiff')" won't bother anyone.

Why don't other writers use defined terms when communicating? Because they ensure readers never need to remember who is doing what. Take this example:

> Hoffman LLP brings this lawsuit against Sampson Services, LLC (hereinafter referred to as "the Company").

First, if there is only one company, the definition isn't helping readers distinguish between anything. And if there is more than one company mentioned in the document, you're asking for confusion by calling one company "Company." Instead, use the full party name once; then use a short form that will be easily recognizable to readers: "**Hoffman sued Sampson. . . .** "

All that said, if you have a reason to define, do. Just ensure it's descriptive so readers remember who or what you're referring to. In this next example, if Aria was alone here, there'd be no need for a definition. But the writer is defining a special term—one that includes several related parties in one conceptual bucket.

> Part-time cocktail server Jodi Tiahrt sues her longtime employer Aria Resort & Casino and several of its employees (collectively, "Aria") for violating company policies by allowing new employees to choose shifts before her and by creating a hostile work environment.

Respect your reader's time; replace confusing acronyms with words they can understand.

8.2.4 Use Footnotes Sparingly

Legal writing has a peculiar language all its own. And one of our favorite devices is the footnote, at times a passing mention, and at others a crucial citation. Lawyers vary in their use of this tool as much as readers vary in their opinions about it. We do know that we can't put important things in footnotes alone. Many readers won't read them. So putting central points in footnotes that you need readers to see is borderline malpractice.

That doesn't mean all footnotes are unhelpful. Footnotes can help demonstrate that a point is well-established without cluttering up your main text. You first explain to readers what matters and that it's well-supported. Then (because it's such an important point) you include that string cite or further support in a footnote.

Another good reason to footnote is because you think readers could benefit from some context or further information, but that material is tangential enough that you don't want to clutter up your main document with it. Readers then get to decide whether to go down the rabbit hole. If you use footnotes like this, still do so sparingly. If your writing is full of detours, readers will ignore them all.

For example, this next legal writer wanted to tell readers that essentially all the relevant contracts called for arbitration in Angola (not in the United States where plaintiffs sued). But there was a single agreement in the bunch that called for arbitration in Portugal. That was a bit of a distraction because it didn't really undermine the writer's point (Portugal was outside the United States as well). So she dropped a footnote to keep her message simple but also ensure readers didn't feel misled.

> These agreements, each in Portuguese, include a clause requiring resolution of disputes exclusively through application of Angolan law in binding arbitration in Luanda, Angola.FN
>
> . . .
>
> FN One contract requires arbitration in Portugal.

Perhaps you need to include a point to preserve it for some other technical reason. Perhaps you know an argument is a nonstarter before a trial judge but want to save it for appeal. Those are respectable reasons to footnote.

> FN Beringer Corp., also maintains its objection based on standing, but this Court has already rejected that argument in a prior Order so it is not argued at length again here.

At bottom, footnotes can bolster your argument or bury it. Choose wisely for your readers' sake.

8.2.5 Emphasize Only Occasionally

Legal writers love using emphasis. Anything that is even moderately important in their documents is bolded, italicized, underlined, in all caps, or sometimes all four.

But read the great legal writers and you'll notice something. They rarely use emphasis like that. Instead, they use verbs, nouns, and sentence structure to more subtly emphasize points so that they don't need to be so obvious. In other words, they *show* readers value rather than forcing it on them with italics. After all, if you constantly hit your readers over the head with emphasis, then how will they know when you *really* mean it? For example, here's an example of lazy emphasis:

> Courts have consistently held as follows: ***The standard for showing harm in defamation cases is strikingly high, and that threshold is not met by a merely circumstantial showing.***

How else can you emphasize these points without the typeface conventions? A surgical quote, stronger verbs, or other rhetorical devices will do more for readers.

> Courts have made clear: Plaintiffs must leap a "strikingly high" hurdle to show harm in defamation cases. "Circumstantial showings" will not cut it.

That doesn't mean that emphasis is never useful. Used sparingly, emphasis can actually do some emphasizing. But you must have a reason beyond yelling, "I think this is important!" Many things are important, and other tools are usually better for communicating that.

When is emphasis helpful? First, when it will help readers distinguish between two concepts by driving home a contrast.

> What the defendant misses[11] in his papers[12] is the difference between domestic discovery requests and foreign requests. This Court has held that foreign requests require an additional showing that the defendant has now admitted he never included—and now can't include given the deadlines for amendment as past.

A second case is when you want to highlight a word or phrase within a larger piece of language.

> The statute imposes both a damages requirement and a procedural process requirement:
>
> Persons filing a claim under this act must suffer actual harm. **Each claim must contain the name, date, and filing status of the person**.

Third, on occasion, a point is so important that you must be sure your readers notice.

> The district court dismissed plaintiff's case with prejudice. That ends the matter: The defendant's entire argument on appeal assumes that dismissal was without prejudice.

> Count I fails for another reason. Plaintiff pressed a claim of commercial appropriation in her complaint, so she cannot maintain a claim of noncommercial appropriation now.

Your readers are smart. They'll notice what matters if you show them in the right way. And that isn't **bold** and *italics*.

8.2.6 Quote Consciously

> *Quotation, n: The act of repeating erroneously the words of another. —Ambrose Bierce*

Quoting is potent. It allows you to invite other trustworthy voices into your writing. If not overused, quoting will help you team up with outsiders to persuade even the toughest

[11] A lighter and more credible way to describe this oversight than the advocacy-laden language most would use —like "the defendant blatantly misrepresents. . . . " No one likes people who talk that way.

[12] A fresher word choice than the same ole' "brief."

audiences. Done badly, though, quoting does more harm than good. Your reader will be bombarded by a cacophony of voices, yours drowned in the process.

Great legal writers make their distinctive voice ring throughout their briefs, even with plenty of quoting involved. I like to think of these writers as the *narrators* of their briefs. You can always tell it's the lawyer telling the story—even when others enter the scene.

To see what I mean, compare these two snippets. First, a legal writer who gave up his voice to the quotes:

> **"The public trust doctrine is an ancient common law principle, from whence[13] several concepts have arisen."** *James v. Platt*, 314 F.3d 524 (7th Cir. 2000). **"The doctrine proceeds in several steps, but it should be noted, that none of these aforementioned steps are dispositive on their accord."** *Id.* Furthermore, **"some have framed this doctrine as one of separation of powers. . . ."**

The lawyer's voice is silent. What voices do we hear? The voices of judges in other cases. Compare that with a quoting pro:

> But as this Court explained in *American Needle*, **"that is not what the statute means."** *Id.* To take an obvious example, **"while the president and a vice president of a firm could (and regularly do) act in combination,"** their joint[14] action generally is not the sort of **"combination"** that §1 is intended to cover. *Id.* at 195. Similarly, when two companies pool[15] their capital to form a joint venture to sell a product, the venture's **"pricing policy may be price fixing in a literal sense,"** but **"it is not price fixing in the antitrust sense."** *Id.*

This paragraph is still heavy on quotes, but the author never gives up control. The quotes are woven into the author's distinctive sentence style, and only the useful portions of the quotes are highlighted.

Quote Only When You Have a Reason

There are many reasons to quote, and if you can articulate one of them, go for it. But please, for the sake of your readers, have a reason before dropping quotes on them. The following are some common valid reasons.

1. You want your reader to hear from someone else directly, like a persuasive judge or a fact witness.
2. The wording matters, like statutory language, language from a case where the wording is disputed, or any other text interpretation.
3. A source says precisely what your reader needs to know about the law or something else.
4. The quoted person's voice—not just the substance of what they are talking about—is helpful to you. When we're talking case law, that means a particular judge in a particular court might be persuasive to your audience, so you want their voice to join yours.

---

[13] Stock quotes from legal sources often bring with them clunky formal language like this.
[14] An example of a descriptor adding useful information.
[15] A great verb that uses storytelling imagery, too.

Check out how this next legal writer uses a surgical quote to make clear what the law requires on a critical point that matters. These sorts of precise, on-off switch rules are a great time to quote because a source is saying exactly what readers need to know.

> Because Tiahrt's claims are preempted by the LMRA, they "must either be treated as [an LMRA] claim or dismissed."

These sorts of quotes are most helpful when a credible source has unusually strong language for your position. Take this quote from a motion for summary judgment:

> As before, this court should agree with the Ninth Circuit that the public trust is "inalienable" — part and parcel of the state's job of being a state.

Or this example, where the identity of the speaker adds credibility:

> The New York Attorney General defends the state's law as one that "falls squarely within the heartland" of straightforward "economic regulation."

Perhaps you want the facts to speak for themselves. Maybe you want your reader to understand the tone or language someone used in a deposition. Take this example from a Susman Godfrey brief filed before the U.S. Supreme Court:

> Martinez-Agüero asked to speak to someone in authority, but González said he was the authority "¡Yo soy la autoridad!"

Another good reason to quote is when you're analyzing the particular words used in the quoted material. If you're parsing statutory or regulatory material, for example, quoting makes sense. When you're arguing about whether the words the defendant used are offensive enough to be defamatory, by all means, quote.

Sometimes you might want to define a term of art (although, if it's become common usage, like *prima facie*, you don't need the quotes). Quoting technical terms is more useful when it's a factual term of art, like industry jargon.

> Initially, cash withdrawals from a foreign ATM involved up to four separate fees. The cardholder might pay a "foreign fee" to her bank (called the "issuing bank"). The issuing bank, in turn, would pay a "switch fee" to the network that processed the transaction, and an "interchange fee" that would ultimately be received by the ATM's operator.

Sometimes, you won't be able to come up with a better way to convey a point than a quote. If you're working hard on your writing, this won't happen often, but sometimes it will. We have some wordsmiths in the courts, and judges can capture points so perfectly that they're worth stealing.

Another good reason to pull out your quoting toolbox is when you want to convey a strong message that your readers will be skeptical about. Bringing guest speakers in to make controversial statements can be strategic. A federal appellate lawyer shows us this technique in the next example. The forceful points are all quotes. It's not the lawyer saying that there are "problems" and that justices have "widely" criticized the doctrine—it's outsiders.

> With the passage of time, the full scale of the **"problems"** with *Chevron* **"have become widely appreciated"** by members of this Court. . . . As a result, **"*Chevron* has been unmentionable"** in this Court for years. . . .

In the end, though, you can usually convey ideas clearer and more persuasively than a quote can. So don't quote to quote. Rather than writing like this:

> That court stated: **"Fraud claims are malum in se and the most deplorable and atrocious of torts given they include requisite elements of falsity and reliance."** *Illiam v. Shack*, 522 F.2d 155 (3rd Cir. 2000).

Write better by paraphrasing like this:

> Fraud is the worst of torts. The defendant must lie to a victim knowing she will rely on that lie. *Illiam v. Shack*, 522 F.2d 155 (3rd Cir. 2000).

Use Your Own Sentence Structure and Narrate Quotes

By maintaining your own sentence structure, you keep your voice. Simple as that. You can usually insert the key phrase or word you want to quote in your better written sentence. Notice in this example how the two short quotes effectively play off one another in a way that long, drawn-out quotes wouldn't.

> Laws that compel speakers to **"alter the content of their speech"** are necessarily **"content based."**

In this next example, from an introduction to a brief, every quote packs a wallop. But more important, each is delivered in the writer's own sentence structure so they keep their voice.

> Ms. [Smith's] counts fail because she has no damages—a requisite element of both causes of action. As she admitted, **"I don't know if they harmed me . . ."** Nor does she have non-speculative evidence of any purported profit attributable to her name and likeness. Though she complains that the organization was **"using [her] name to sell [her] services when [she] wasn't working there,"** she continued, **"I don't know what monetary value that would be."** . . . In fact, she could not identify a single person who joined or renewed memberships with the organization because of any reference to her on the website[]: **"I don't have any names."** . . . She elaborated: **"there was no reason for people to join"** the organization. . . .[16]

[16] This paragraph is an example of introductions done right, too. The writer dished up quotes to persuade readers from the first page (not bland characterizations like "plaintiff admitted there was no damages").

Often all you really want is a pithy quoted word or phrase to make your points, like this next passage in a SCOTUS brief. You pay more attention to the quote when it's an isolated word or phrase.

> All states allow such dual pricing. But a New York statute . . . seeks to control how merchants may communicate the price difference to consumers: It allows merchants to offer **"discounts"** to those who pay in cash, but makes it a crime to impose equivalent **"surcharges"** on those who pay by credit card.

Sometimes you want more of your source's voice to come through, but still, keep control of your sentence structure. Check out how this lawyer maintains control amid a sea of quotes by interjecting at least a word or two to make the sentences smoother.

> **Of course,** "[n]ot every instance of cooperation between two people" **constitutes concerted action within the scope of Section 1. Rather, courts must undertake a** "functional" **analysis of** "how the parties involved in the alleged anti competitive conduct actually operate." **Where** "separate economic actors pursuing separate economic interests" **agree to limit competition among themselves, their conduct is** "concerted" **and subject to Section 1.**

You can maintain your voice even when you are quoting an entire sentence by inserting your voice first, like in this example from an appellate brief.

> The entry-fiction doctrine derives from the recognition that the political branches of government are more appropriately suited to function as gatekeeper of the nation's borders, and thus, **"[w]hatever the procedure authorized by Congress is, it is due process as far as an alien denied entry is concerned."**

Lead Your Reader into Longer Quotes

Don't drop readers into the middle of a long quote without a parachute. Give readers a clear understanding of where the quote is going first. This does wonders for maintaining your voice and making it easier for readers to extract what you want them to. So not:

> The case states in pertinent part. . . .

These examples from trial court motions distill what matters from the long quote first.

> **The *Park* court explained that leaving out allegations about the fraud itself dooms the complaint under Rule 8:** "Without the fraud allegations, the claim must be dismissed entirely."

> Indeed, as the court there explained, **contracts need not be signed by both parties to be enforceable.**

Because the plaintiff had not proved damages beyond those for breach of contract, the court held that the tort claim should have been dismissed.

Block quotes tax readers the most. If you must block quote (and there might be times where it's needed—like when quoting statutory text, longer dialogues from a record, or key language), give your readers enough of a preview so that they can skim the block if they want to. If nothing else, this introduction will make it less scary for readers to dive into the block-quote abyss:

The court drew a line between claims about public trust, which can be brought in federal court, and claims about private nuisance claims, which cannot:

> [Block quote explaining this same point—on principle, I'm not inserting the block quote!]

A final few notes on quoting. Emphasis quotes are not a thing. We can't air-quote in writing. Your argument does not become more persuasive because the other "party 'blatantly' ignores its obligations."

And don't use any other form of *scare quotes.* Scare quotes are quotation marks used around words or phrases that you think are slang or nonstandard, or when you're being sarcastic or offensive. Greil Marcus points out that scare quotes just make us look unsure about our own writing:

> Scare quotes kill narrative. They kill storytelling. And it's not a question of parsing, examining, analyzing, laying bare sacred texts. They are a writer's assault on his or her own words.

So don't do what this attorney did:

Opposing counsel contends that his client has a **"case,"** but that is patently false.[17]

Quote selectively, with purpose and intention, and you'll invite helpful guests into your writing.

8.3 Punctuate Perfectly

Everyday marks like periods and commas are important—but legal writing demands a bigger toolkit. Master the semicolon, the em dash, and the parenthesis to shape the flow of ideas in your sentences even more.

Would this next sentence have delivered the same force without pro punctuation? The lawyers were driving home the danger of a popular drug taken together with everyday foods. By calling out familiar foods with em dashes, the writers ensured you couldn't miss them.

[17] We'll tackle the common grammar pitfalls in quotes in the next section of this chapter.

> Although GSK marketed the drug in th[e] State as a way to treat acid reflux, it knew that taking Zantac with foods high in nitrates—**like tacos and pizza**—is especially dangerous.

Punctuation wields surprising influence in legal writing. But common punctuation errors trip up even experienced lawyers. Let's harness the potential and sidestep the traps.

A Quick Summary

Use commas in the right places. Know the few common ways to use commas and avoid putting them in places they don't belong. Then you'll be ready to use some comma flare, perhaps setting off a final point, like this.

Use semicolons to contrast or expand. Use semicolons to highlight contrasts or contradictions between two main points (that make up a full independent clause on their own). Semicolons can also break up list items when the items have commas of their own.

Use em dashes to emphasize. Em dashes put white space around a word or phrase, ensuring readers notice what's between them. Use em dashes to call out only the important points.

Use colons to explain. Use colons to set up an explanation or expansion. Start with context or a term, then define or build.

Avoid common punctuation pitfalls. For example, don't place commas and periods outside of quotation marks (at least in the U.S.) or use an en dash when an em dash is called for.

Punctuation is part of your writing machinery. And refining this machinery pays off.

8.3.1 Use Commas in the Right Places

We use commas all over our writing, but many legal writers put commas where they aren't needed, confusing readers. Or they snip commas out of phrases or clauses even though they're needed to avoid ambiguities. So learn the simple rules for when you need a comma, and generally avoid inserting them otherwise (unless it's truly needed to avoid confusing readers).

First, use commas to separate two independent clauses (full sentences) with a coordinating conjunction.

> Joe went to Saipan, and he loves reading.

Do not use commas to join two full sentences without a conjunction (also called a *comma splice*).

> Joe went to Saipan, he likes to read.

Use them to set off an introductory phrase:

> Knowing it was warm, Joe brought shorts.

Or use them to set off a dependent clause when the dependent clause comes first, but often a comma isn't needed when the dependent clause comes second.

> Because he was hungry, the judge stepped out for a bite to eat.
>
> *versus*
>
> The judge stepped out for a bite to eat because he was hungry.

If the dependent clause comes after the independent clause and is nonrestrictive, like when using *which*, then use a comma.

> Joe began talking, which he knew wasn't smart.

Use commas when the dependent clause introduces a contrast or an opposition to the main clause. Especially when starting with words like *although*, *though*, or *whereas*, you'll need a comma.

> The team proceeded with the presentation, although they were not fully prepared.

Use them to separate days from years.

> December 12, 2018

Use them to set off a direct address in dialogue or when addressing a court.

> Your Honor, the evidence will show. . . .

Use them to set off a quotation.

> The court held as much repeatedly, "no allegations on that point are required."

Use commas in complex sentences when needed to avoid confusion.

> To win the case, the plaintiff, not just the lawyer, must be prepared.

8.3.2 Use Semicolons to Contrast or Expand

Semicolons separate two independent clauses, but strategically, they emphasize connections between ideas. Use this mark when you want your reader to see two ideas compared, contrasted, linked, or elaborated on.

Here is an example of a contrast semicolon from Justice Elena Kagan:

> The word "applicable" is not necessary to accomplish that **result;** it is necessary only for the different purpose of dividing debtors eligible to make use of the tables from those who are not.

This example is from Chief Justice John Roberts, juxtaposing two words to make a point at the heart of his argument.

> **"Person" is a defined term in the statute; "personal" is not.** When a statute does not define a term, we typically "give the phrase its ordinary meaning."

Here is an example of the semicolon as expander, using the mark to build on an idea.

> Deceit such as tall tales that defendants told about Q-Ray Ionized bracelets will lead some consumers to avoid treatments that cost less and do **more;** the lies will lead others to pay too much for pain relief or otherwise interfere with the matching of remedies to medical conditions.

Here is another example of the expander semicolon, building on the first clause with an expansive second, courtesy of Judge Learned Hand.

> To exclude others from the enjoyment of a chattel is one **thing;** to prevent any imitation of it, to set up a monopoly in the plan of its structure, gives the author a power over his fellows vastly greater. . . .

Use semicolons only when there is some benefit to comparing or building with two ideas—don't use them randomly or they will lose their effect. This isn't helping anyone:

> Judges are great writers; judges usually have extensive legal experience.

Semicolons often go well with a linking word that emphasizes contrast or comparison. Semicolons with linkers slow down the sentence, but they can make the transition more noticeable and convey more about the connection than a simple coordinating conjunction would (like *and* or *but*).

> The defendant had an alibi for the night of the incident**; also,** surveillance footage confirms his presence at another location.

> Negotiations for a settlement are ongoing**; meanwhile,** we continue to prepare for trial.

> The evidence against our client is largely circumstantial; still, we must address each point to cast doubt on the prosecution's case.

These are some common semicolon linkers:

Accordingly
Again
Also
Anyway
Besides
However
Indeed
Instead
Likewise
Meanwhile
Next
Nonetheless
Otherwise
Still
Then

The other common use of a semicolon is to separate list items when the individual items have commas within them. In this example, the commas in the second list item might confuse you without the semicolons.

> The Court should ignore the arguments made by counsel; the evidence submitted, but not received, by plaintiffs; and the certifications filed after the deadline imposed by the Court's order.

8.3.3 Use Em Dashes to Emphasize

Em dashes (which get their name because they are roughly as wide as an *M*) are one of the most flexible marks. You can use them to set off just about any clause or phrase—like this. You can also use them in other ways—like interjecting a key point—so that readers notice whatever you put between them.

Look at how these next authors smartly put within their em dashes the most critical points. Like semicolons, the power of the em dash should not be wasted on the mundane.

> When those words lose their ordinary meaning—**when they become so elastic that they may mean the opposite of what they appear to mean**—we cede our right to be taken seriously.

> A review of the history of alienage jurisprudence, with a particular review of Graham—**both what it said and how it has been applied (and not applied) in the past forty years**—suggests that it is time to rethink the doctrine.

In this next example, the legal writer's entire document turned on the point that someone can't use another's trademark to make money, even if that use is in parody. And that main point sits within the em dashes.

> A defendant cannot get its benefit—**even if engaging in parody, criticism, or commentary**—when using the similar-looking mark "as a designation of source for the [defendant's] own goods."[18]

[18] Another great reason to pull out em dashes is to help readers navigate long, complex sentences. Em dashes are an easy way to gather the subject and verb, or to break up a long group of phrases with white space.

8.3.4 Use Colons to Explain

Colons are a drumroll, setting the stage for an important reveal, whether an explanation, a list, or a quote. Use them to catch the reader's attention and signal that what follows builds on your setup:

> The doctrine of res judicata ensures **finality:** Once a case is decided, it cannot be litigated again.

Colons can be used to build anticipation for a strong, longer quote.

> The court's ruling was final and **explicit:** "The statute of limitations begins to run at the point of discovery."

But like other punctuation, don't use colons randomly. Too many writers insert colons where commas or semicolons should go. Save this mark for when you want to set up a definition or explanation for a concept, word, or phrase.

> The judge filed two **orders:** one dismissing the claim and the other awarding fees.

This next legal writer uses a colon smartly: first to give readers the concept to be defined, then providing the definition.

> The second part of the definition describes every trademark's "primary" **function:** "to identify the origin or ownership of the article to which it is affixed."

Here are two final colon tips. If what follows the colon is a complete sentence, most style guides suggest that you capitalize the first word after the colon.

> Consider the evidence: **The** fingerprints were found on the weapon.

> The case hinged on three factors: **motive**, opportunity, and means.

When a colon is used between two independent clauses, it shows that the second clause fulfills, explains, or summarizes the first.

> The court reached a verdict: **The evidence was incontrovertible.**

You can use colons to introduce a list, too.

> **Joe loves these marks:** commas, em dashes, and semicolons.[19]

[19] Notice that we don't capitalize the items because they aren't a full sentence.

8.3.5 Avoid Common Punctuation Pitfalls

Let's explore a few more often misused marks in legal writing, starting with quotes.

First, **here** is an easy pitfall to avoid: Commas and periods go within quotes (at least in the United States).

> The court explained that the theft of several grocery bags was indeed actionable because "bags are not free here."

Next, use a comma after an introductory phrase that leads into a quote.

> The judge stated, "The evidence is inadmissible."

The same goes for attributive tags:

> According to the witness, "The defendant was present at the scene."

If the quote is integrated into your sentence as if it were part of the sentence itself, no comma is needed.

> The term "reasonable doubt" means that the jury must be sure beyond a reasonable doubt to convict.

In dialogue or when sharing a back-and-forth conversation within text, commas are usually used to separate the spoken sentences from the dialogue tags.

> "I don't agree," the defendant said, "with the prosecution's interpretation."

If you're quoting within a quote, use single quotation marks for the inner quote and place commas according to the usual rules for the outer quote.

> "Did he really say, 'I will not comply'?" the attorney asked.

Let's dash to the *dash*. We've covered the em dash, but its siblings—the en dash and the hyphen—often sow confusion.

The en dash, slightly wider than a hyphen, gets its name from its width: that of the letter *N*. It's largely used to specify ranges: "See pages 30–32 for further discussion," or "The court is in recess from August–October."

En dashes also do something else, although it's rarer: They combine multiple-noun compound phrases instead of hyphens, like "**Pulitzer Prize**–winning journalist," "**Meryl Streep–Robert De Niro** comedy," "a **New York–Chicago** flight," and "a **World War II–era** plane."

Hyphens are mostly used to create compound words and phrases. They help build descriptive compounds like "The **blue-black** haze hung around the room." Whenever you connect two words in an adjective marriage, hyphens are the officiant.

Finally, parentheses whisper. Aside from being used at the end of legal citations, these marks deemphasize whatever you put in them (like this). Use them when you think a brief aside is valuable without drawing too much attention.

> Plaintiff alleges no facts **(nor could he)** to support this claim.

In the end, punctuation isn't just about grammar. Understanding the nuances gives you control over the ideas your sentences deliver.

8.4 Edit Efficiently

Editing is not just about giving your document a quick once-over to check for typos. Editing is when we clip away the excess and elevate our prose to the best it can be. No one writes their best the first time. Editing helps us take our mediocre writing and make it excellent.

Let's start by distinguishing among three concepts: *writing intuition, editing*, and *proofreading*.

Your *writing intuition* is how you write by default. If you sit down and write a paragraph—without any rewriting or serious thought—your writing intuition will guide you. But as we all know, that first draft is not the best you can muster. Because we *understand* more about good writing than we usually *write*.

That is where *editing* comes in. Editing is about improving the mediocre writing our intuition puts on the page. It's about going beyond our normal and finding the excellent writing we want to show our audiences. The good news is that the more we edit to purposely improve our writing, the more we are training our intuition to do it better next time. Indeed, for most of us, purposeful editing ends up being the best writing training we can do and helps us see the biggest changes to our writing over time.

But editing is not just skimming through a document and looking for mistakes. That would be *proofreading*. Proofreading is about catching mistakes that even our quick intuition wouldn't normally make. Look at a quick example of each concept. Perhaps we write this next sentence by intuition with no editing:

> The motion was filed by the lawyer on time.

Hopefully you spotted some improvements we could make. For one, this sentence is written in the passive voice. Let's say we edit for passive voice, spot that we didn't use it here, and improve it:

> The **lawyer filed** the motion on time.

Great! We edited purposely for passive voice and found an improvement.

Later, after we've edited our document and improved it as much as possible, we start proofreading. Let's say we come across this sentence:

> The court issued the ordered quickly.

You probably noticed the typo: It should have been "order," not "ordered." This wasn't about applying some technique to our writing—it was just about looking for obvious mistakes.

Why does understanding the difference among these three concepts matter? Because if what you've done in the past is give documents a passive once-over with a red pen in hand, waiting for things to jump out at you, you've probably been doing something closer to *proofreading* than *editing*.

Real editing is too hard to do passively. And it's too overwhelming to do all at once in a single read-through. Real editing requires strategy and process. Because we humans are horrible multitaskers, and that is especially true when editing our writing.

Passive editing turns us into dogs chasing squirrels. We spot a random thing on the page and focus on it to the exclusion of everything else. So rather than try to improve all the different facets of your writing at the same time (and check for mistakes while you're at it), you need a plan.

Let's work on yours.

A Quick Summary

Use phase editing and checklists. **Our brains are horrible at multitasking, so we need a strategy we can consistently follow to keep the editing and proofreading process manageable.**

Use content-word editing for hard sentences. **Sometimes we write (or need to edit) particularly long, complicated sentences. By focusing on a few content words in a sentence—and rebuilding the sentence from the ground up—you can often find fantastic prose.**

Cut common clutter. **Hundreds of words and phrases have made their way into traditional legal writing but add only clutter, ambiguity, or complexity. By training yourself to look out for these red flags, you can arrive at cleaner prose in no time.**

8.4.1 Use Phase Editing and Checklists

The principle behind *phase editing* is that our minds are easily distracted, and editing is no different. If you try to edit for too much, too quickly, you will miss key improvements. With *phase editing*, you break your editing process up into more manageable chunks, or phases. Each phase comes with a manageable list of related improvements to check for purposefully.

The added benefit is that after you edit for a type of improvement enough, it starts becoming part of your writing intuition. And you probably won't need to keep editing for that point as fiercely in the future. Your editing process should thus evolve, depending on the improvements you currently want to make but aren't deploying in your first drafts. All this is distinct from *proofreading*—which is about those typos or mistakes that you usually don't make intuitively but slip by because you're human.

As you're choosing your phases, make sure each contains only a few improvements to apply to your writing at a time. Three to five points is usually plenty. Your brain can only handle so much. Group similar editing points together so that you can have one major goal at a time as you work through each phase.

These are some phases great legal writers use.

- Phase 1: Fact section. Check for needless details to cut, informative headings, missing facts, and so on.
- Phase 2: Substance. Check for missing arguments or counterarguments, rule or analysis sections to bolster, and the like.
- Phase 3: Organization and flow. Check for transitions at the section and paragraph level, check headings, and so on.
- Phase 4: Sentences. Check for sentence length, structure, and variety.
- Phase 5: Citations. Check for formatting, pin cites, and other details.

Phase editing works well with another editing must: a checklist. You don't need to list every potential edit. But a simple checklist that reminds you about the improvements and pitfalls you care most about can focus your editing attention. Checklists are also an excellent way to remind yourself about new techniques that you want to try or bad habits that you want to break.

To get the most out of your checklists, first prioritize what's on your list. Identify your recurring challenges, the techniques you'd like to incorporate, and the habits you're keen to break. Sort these items by relevance and frequency, and remember, you can only edit for so many things at once.

Next, be specific. Vague phrases like "cut excess words" won't create the laser-focused impact we need. Instead, try something like "cut adverbs like 'clearly.'" Specificity is key to making writing checklists easy to execute.

Update your editing checklist with fresh techniques and tips you come across, remove items that you are not getting value out of, and recalibrate as needed based on feedback from others.

An editing checklist is the bridge between where you are and where you want to be as a legal writer. By embracing the power of checklists, you'll achieve writing so good even Justice Kagan would give a nod in approval.

A Few More General Editing Tips

First, try one-read editing. This is a nifty editing technique both when working on your own writing and when asking others to edit for you. In short, rather than give substantive or style feedback on a document, the editor simply circles every word that they read more than once, puts a check mark next to any sentence they read more than once, and draws a squiggly mark next to any section they must reread.

The idea is that the editor is looking for bumps in the road, not fixing them. This allows the editor to focus on pure fluency and leave the distracting how or why until later. A good one-read edit provides x-ray vision into your document, highlighting all the weak areas. With the readability problems mapped out, you then now tackle one at a time with all your writing tools at the ready.

Editing this way is fast and effective. You are much less likely to get caught up on types of edits or problems to the exclusion of others. Just as important, one-read editing diffuses the awkwardness that comes with editing others' work. Rather than push your own style ideas (and let's be real, many people don't take those suggestions well), you are showing the author where they lost their reader.

All the hurt feelings are avoided. You tripped and had to reread something. Simple as that. So whatever they're doing in the writing, they can probably do it clearer. The other benefit of this approach is that it encourages you and others to not blindly follow edits from better writers, but to instead figure out how to fix what you're doing wrong.

These are a few more editing ideas to consider:

1. Read backwards. This will stop you from skipping things your brain expects to see.
2. As you read, follow along with your finger—or use a ruler to block out sentences below the one you are editing. This can help you stay focused and not skip anything small.
3. Find good writing mentors (to become the best, you need to be around the best).
4. Read your legal writing out loud.
5. Print your final drafts to edit by hand.
6. Practice your editing skills: Try editing other people's writing or your own old writing. It's like going to the gym. The more you edit, the better you get at making improvements.
7. Write separate sections separately so that they are self-sufficient and don't rely too much on other parts.
8. Don't self-edit when drafting. Self-editing tends to shift your focus away from substance. Focus on the substance and get it on the page. Then craft your style through editing.
9. Take time away to get a fresh reader perspective: You cannot get into the right editing mindset unless you build in enough time before your writing deadlines so that you can set your document aside for a while (preferably at least a day) and come back to it.
10. Use others to get a fresh reader perspective: No one can spot errors or improvements like a truly fresh reader (that is, not you!).

Avoiding common errors isn't only about keeping grammar nerds happy: It's essential to building credibility with legal readers. Take control of your editing and ensure every word is doing what it should.

8.4.2 Use Content-Word Editing for Hard Sentences

Sometimes a long, complex sentence is hard to get just right. You might have tried moving words around, replacing verbs, and rethinking the structure—all to no avail. When that happens, consider another editing tool called *content-word editing*. It's a slower process than just skimming through your sentences for quick improvements. But for key sentences, elite legal writers swear by this practice.

This editing strategy is about changing your perspective to focus entirely on which words in your sentences are conveying important *content* and which are *glue* words not doing important work. Start by identifying the content words in your sentences, then scrape out all the glue filling in the gaps, and finally rewrite the sentence using only the valuable content.

Let's look at an example. By forcing ourselves to focus on the words conveying unique, important content, we bypass a lot of the glue that works its way into most legal writing.

> The approach is straightforward but comes wrapped, in many of the decisions applying it, in a formidable doctrinal terminology—the terminology of rational basis, of strict, heightened, and intermediate scrutiny, of narrow tailoring, fundamental rights, and the rest.

Now we can rebuild a sentence from the ground up using those content words: "approach," "wrapped," "terminology," and the examples of terminology.

> The approach comes wrapped in the formidable terminology of rational basis, of strict, heightened, and intermediate scrutiny, of narrow tailoring, fundamental rights, and the rest.

Here's another example from another great legal writer. There is no right or wrong way to choose your content words. Some of the goal is to use your judgment. Which words are standing in for essential content?

> Concluding that the error regarding federal preemption resulted in the admission of evidence on standards of care that was not limited to federally established standards of care and that this evidence was thus prejudicial, the court ordered a new trial.

Now we can rebuild a sentence using those words as inspiration. Our new sentence doesn't need nearly as much glue to convey the same content, and we'll often spot simpler replacements for some of the content words we identified.

> The court concluded that some standard-of-care evidence was wrongly admitted because it was not limited to the federal requirements; so it ordered a new trial.

Forcing yourself to distill your sentences down to a few words—then rewriting from the foundation up—will help you see past your own writing weaknesses.

Let's check out some more content-word editing in action. Take this sentence from a brief:

> The Uniform Trade Secrets Act, *inter alia*, generally provides a definition of trade secret as follows: any piece or collection or grouping of information or documents has intrinsic value such that it derives value from not being known to competitors.

Let's again pick the content words that matter here. Remember you need to use some judgment. What counts as a content word will depend on your other sentences and what readers already know. If your reader already knows from a prior sentence that this case is brought under the Uniform Trade Secrets Act, that idea isn't as important here. But if you hadn't yet told your reader that, maybe it's important enough to choose.

> The Uniform Trade Secrets Act, *inter alia*, generally provides a definition of trade secret as follows: any piece or collection or grouping of information or documents has intrinsic value such that it derives value from not being known.

Those bolded words are probably what matter here. The idea the author is trying to convey is "What is a trade secret?" So we choose the words that convey that content.

We can rewrite the sentence to convey our content words with as little distraction as possible. With only a few words to manage now, it will be easy to build a sentence precisely as we want to. As a reminder, our key words here are "trade secret," "information," "value from," and "not [being] known."

> A **trade secret** is information made valuable by its **secrecy**.
>
> *or*
>
> **Information** that derives **value** from its **secrecy** is a **trade secret**.

Look at some good writing and usually you can tell that the author has already used some kind of content-word editing. Take a sentence Justice Kagan penned:

> Notorious killers, such as Jeffrey Dahmer, Ted Bundy, and David Berkowitz[], all committed acts of violence against animals before moving on to human victims.

We probably can't do much better (Justice Kagan, after all, is one of the best legal writers on any court). But let's try:

> **Notorious killers,** such as Jeffrey Dahmer, Ted Bundy, and David Berkowitz[], all committed acts of **violence** against **animals before** moving on to **human** victims.

These bold words hold important content. Let's try using these to rebuild:

> **Notorious killers** often **abuse** animals **before** moving on to **humans**.

Notice I replaced the phrase "acts of violence against" with a shorter verb, "abuse." Replacing your content words with better ones is often the best way to rebuild your sentence. If we wanted the examples of famous killers (which is probably important enough to include), we could add them back in:

> **Notorious killers** like **Jeffrey Dahmer, Ted Bundy,** and **David Berkowitz abused animals before** moving on to **humans**.

Ultimately, work through these steps when you want to zoom in on the content in a sentence.

- Spot a sentence in your draft that you want to rebuild.
- Underline the few key words that your reader must absorb—the ideas you can't afford for them to miss.
- Jot down these crucial content words.
- You can use the same key words or replace them with new ones that are crisper or more targeted.
- Rebuild the sentence, one word at a time, to deliver those critical content words and little else.

8.4.3 Cut Common Clutter

Another great editing strategy is to train yourself to spot red flags: words or phrases that consistently signal clutter in legal writing. By checking for red flags, you'll often find quick improvements for your draft.

Hundreds of words and phrases have made their way into traditional legal writing that add only clutter, ambiguity, or complexity. By training yourself to look out for these red flags, you can arrive at cleaner prose in no time. For example, here are some of the most common red flags to cut from your legal writing:

- Common throat-clearing words *it is, there is, as such, the fact that, pursuant to, with regard to*, and so on.
- Generic filler words like *thing*.
- Prepositions like *of*.
- *-ion* words, which are often nominalizations that can become juicier verbs.
- *-ing* words, which are often wasted and wordy.
- Words based in Latin, French, or Greek that are often less accessible than their simpler Germanic counterparts.
- Adverbs, but especially intensifiers like *clearly, very*, and *really*.

By focusing on these red flags, you can force yourself to look at your writing through a more objective lens. Look at how a markup of just a few red flags (like excess prepositions and unhelpful descriptors) can signal areas needing good editing.

> Donald Davis, one **of** three law enforcement officers acquitted **in** the drowning deaths **of** three youths **in** Harrisburg, stood **by** his pickup Monday **at** his home **by** the railroad tracks **in** Smithville and said, "It feels good." That morning, he **had** dressed **in** a shirt, tie, and slacks and returned **to** his **old** desk **in** the probation department **on** the **third floor of** the Mitchell County Courthouse.

With some red flag editing, we can focus on simply eliminating the prepositions (a common red flag of clutter) and get much tighter prose.

> A jury found that Donald Davis and three other officers did not drown the Harrisburg children. On Monday, Davis was at home standing near his pickup, and said, "It feels good." After that, Davis was back at his desk. . . .

Let's explore some of the most common categories of red flags to cut or replace.

Cut Common Clutter Words

It's worth being vigilant for a few of the most common villains: *or, of, there*, and *it*.

Often lawyers put useless things after *or*, so it is a red flag to look out for.

> Terminate the employment relationship at any time for any **cause or reason.**

> If you have **questions or need further clarification**, please let me know.

> **At or about** the same time, Samson terminated his agreement with Hoffman.

Unless *it* refers to something like a company or thing, you can either delete all the words from *it* through *that*, delete some of those words, or replace those words with one or two words.

It was not until after the trial that I learned who it was that had made the statement.

becomes

I did not learn until after the trial who made the statement.

It is essential that Plaintiff must plead facts that show wrongful conduct.

becomes

Plaintiff must plead facts that show wrongful conduct.

I had a couple of bad days, and **it dawned on me that** I realized I didn't have to be there anymore.

becomes

I had a couple of bad days, and I realized I didn't have to be there anymore.

More than perhaps any other, the word *of* will flag clutter for you.

In its **discussion of the issue**, Disney recognized the problem.

becomes

In its discussion, Disney recognized the problem.

Employees typically worked ten hours a day and stayed in California during the **pendency of the schedule**.

becomes

Employees typically worked ten hours a day and stayed in California during the schedule.

There is and *there are* (especially at the start of sentences) are clutter signals. Like all the red flag words we've seen, there are good times to use *there is* and *there are*. But this phrase tends to add words without purpose, and you can usually rewrite a better sentence.

There are problems with the lease.

becomes

The lease has problems.

There are several good reasons to delay making this decision.

becomes

We should delay making this decision for several reasons.

There is a natural desire among adolescents to experience freedom from authority.

becomes

Adolescents crave freedom from authority.

Another set of clutter words are past participles. A past participle is the conjugation of a verb we use when we combine it with other verbs, like *have*: *have eaten, have gone, have walked, have talked.* We often follow these with a second preposition. In these pairings, we often do not need the past participle because the preposition does the job for both.

A book **authored by** Hoffman.

becomes

A book **by** Hoffman.

The joy **found within** ourselves

becomes

The joy **within** ourselves

The space **provided** below

becomes

The space **below**

Sometimes we need the past participle to convey important information. The point is to look out for these pairs and question what words are needed to communicate your point to readers.

The terms **stated in** the parties' agreement

Here, perhaps we are distinguishing *stated* terms from *implied* ones, so the past participle is useful (unlike simply saying, "the terms in . . .").

Cut Redundancy, Wordiness, and Obvious Additions

Legal writers love using redundant phrases that repeat for no good reason. They also love wordy phrases that could be replaced with one or two simple words. Finally, folks often add extra words when the point is already obvious.

First, avoid redundant phrases that do nothing but create clutter.

> This agreement is **null and void**, your honor.

"Null and void" means the same thing as just "void," so go with that.

> But plaintiff can't sue here because it was a **free gift**.

This sentence conveys nothing different from "But plaintiff can't sue here because it was a **gift**."

Next, get good at spotting the wordy phrases that legal writers love using. Often they can be replaced by a simple word or two.

> The judge held **with regard to** standing that no showing was needed.

That "with regard to" is a classic wordy phrase that you can replace with *on*.

> The judge held **on** standing that no showing was needed.

Finally, avoid using extra words when the meaning is already obvious without them. *Namely* and *specifically* are common examples..

> The court explained no showing was needed. **Namely**, no money must be alleged in the complaint.

That "namely" is not adding any useful information for your reader.

> The court explained no showing was needed. **No money must** be alleged in the complaint.

Avoid Legalese, Latin, and Clichés

For hundreds of years legal writers have used fancy legal-sounding language that isn't very useful. Avoid this legalese unless the words are terms of art or somehow useful to readers.

Here are some frequent offenders:

- A priori
- Ab initio Vel non
- Above captioned
- Aforementioned

- Arguendo
- Comes now
- Forthwith
- Herein
- Hereof
- Hereto
- Infra Caveat
- Inter alia
- Per se
- Sub judice
- Thereby
- To wit
- Whereas

Cutting overused words doesn't end with strict legalese; clichés and triteness are equally unimpressive. Phrases like "the bottom line," "a diamond in the rough," the "argument misses the mark," and "time will tell" are neither clever nor creative. To get fancy, we'll look at fresh ways to get figurative in the next chapter.

Level Up Your Writing Mechanics and Editing with Technology

This is a place where technology might shine brighter than any other in your legal writing process. Technology tools can consistently catch mechanics and grammar mistakes, formatting errors, and typos. Tools can also help you whip together a fantastic phase-editing and proofreading checklist in no time.

GAI tools: As with our other writing skills, GAI can help here, too. Perhaps the best use is to ask your favorite tool for feedback on your writing, particularly if you're struggling with a mechanics issue and unsure what the right answer is. GAI can also help you brainstorm an editing checklist, revise your checklist to make it more effective, and even give your writing a quick review for grammar and mechanics errors (although other tools like Grammarly and BriefCatch might be more consistent here). For example:

You're a professional copy editor. Review this paragraph of my writing and identify any weaknesses in the mechanics or grammar. For each, explain the concepts for me step-by-step.

I'm not sure what the correct way is to punctuate this sentence. Please explain it to me in simple terms that I can apply in future writing.

Grammar checkers and style editors: Grammar checkers have evolved beyond simple spell-check functions to sophisticated software that analyzes sentence structure, word choice, and overall clarity. Tools like BriefCatch, Grammarly, and ProWritingAid offer real-time suggestions to improve your prose. These AI-driven tools can spot passive voice, adverb overload, and convoluted sentences that content-word editing would look to simplify. They're not infallible, but they serve as an excellent first sweep in the editing process.

Macros, automations, and hotkeys: Your repetitive legal writing tasks (like those during proofreading) lend themselves to simple automations like macros or other simplifying apps and settings. Learn hotkeys for your tools (particularly your word processor) so you can quickly carry out edits. Set up macros (automated tasks) in your word processor and other apps like email to streamline your writing.

Consistency scanners: Legal documents demand consistency, be it in terms of terminology, capitalization, or punctuation usage. Tools like BriefCatch, PerfectIt, and LanguageTool can scan entire documents to ensure uniformity. These scanners review your text for inconsistencies and offer changes to maintain a coherent style throughout your document. Suppose your brief alternates between *advisor* and *adviser*. A consistency scanner will flag this variation, allowing you to choose one spelling for uniformity.

Process and checklist apps: Although checklists bolster efficiency in the editing process, keeping track of each step can be painstaking. Enter editing software with integrated checklist features, like Checkmark or Process Street. These tools enable you to create, manage, and follow a customized editing checklist within the document editing interface, ensuring that you systematically address each editing focus point. You could set up your editing checklist within your document, marking off tasks such as "check for passive voice" or "shorten long sentences," segmenting your editing process into manageable phases.

Citation management software: Legal writing often involves many citations, which can be cumbersome to manage. Clearbrief is a fantastic tool for working on factual citations, automating much of the process. Reference management software like Westlaw Drafting Assistant and Juris-M can also simplify organizing and formatting references for your legal documents. They help maintain a library of sources that you can easily cite in text, and they automatically generate cites.

Personal dictionaries and word expansion tools: Every legal practitioner has their own set of frequently used terms and phrases. Creating a personal dictionary or using word expansion tools like PhraseExpress can save you precious time and mitigate typos. Such tools offer auto-complete suggestions for legal terms, ensuring you maintain accuracy while increasing your writing speed. By adding common legal terms and case names to your personal dictionary, you reduce the likelihood of misspelling *res judicata* or *stare decisis*, and ensure quick insertion of complex terminology.

Proofreading software: Finally, during the last stage of document preparation, proofreading software such as BriefCatch, Word Rake, and Hemingway Editor can prove invaluable. This software highlights hard-to-read sentences and suggests simplifications, ensuring your final document is clear and concise.

Document storage and version control tools: Your organization might require a certain document storage platform to be used, like NetDocuments. These tools will store your working documents so you don't lose them if you have a technical glitch on your device. And they can keep track of different versions of your document, particularly if you are working with others on edits.

Document comparison tools: These applications help manage iterations and revisions during the editing process, identifying changes and differences between document versions. By simplifying review workflows, they enable legal writers to focus on refining their arguments. Examples include Workshare Compare, Draftable, and CompareDocs.

Practice these techniques and technologies with Write.law's exercises and checklists, plus other resources at www.levelupyourlegalwriting.com

ASPEN PUBLISHING | write.law

9

Level Up Your Writing with Even More Style

> Words are free. It's how you use them that may cost you."—Rev. J. Martin

People remember—and treat as more important—words and sentences that stand out from the background noise. In other words, writing penned with exceptional style. So use memorable style to burn major points into readers' minds, like rule pitches, favorable facts, and whatever else matters.

Indeed, it's science (and called the *Van Restorff effect*). People remember what stands out from its surroundings; in a word, *difference*. Cognitive scientists have confirmed what classical rhetoricians have long known: Ideas called out with flair are more memorable than ideas expressed in everyday prose.

Good style also builds credibility. Look at any of the great legal writers who consistently win on the strength of their writing, and you'll see sentences chock full of style. Techniques like alliteration, sentence balance, and parallelism appear in nearly every top lawyer's prose—not in every sentence, but in the places that matter most

When one of my favorite legal writers wants to get readers invested in a case, she dials the style up to maximum. In a case about reality stars fighting over a vodka company, she starts the story with a cluster of fun specifics to engage her readers. She follows with an introduction to the characters who propel the narrative forward.

> **The Kentucky Derby produced more than mint juleps, pastel hats, and a champion thoroughbred in 2012.** Three **friends—**Gunvalson, a long-standing cast member of reality television's "Real Housewives of Orange County"; her then-boyfriend David Brooks Ayers; and **2002 World Series of Poker winner** Williamson—tentatively agreed to start a vodka business. Ayers and Gunvalson had been **toying** with the idea for months. . . .

In this next example, Justice Elena Kagan starts a complicated discussion of trademark concepts with an unusual but compelling figurative structure. "Square 1" is a puzzle game, as distinguished from the phrase "go back to square one." From the opening words, the sentences read like the instructions to a board game. The subject matter might be dense, but the style makes it memorable.

> **Start at square 1, with what a trademark is and does.** The Lanham Act, the core federal trademark statute, defines a trademark as follows: "[A]ny word, name, symbol, or device, or any combination thereof" that a person uses "to identify and distinguish his or her goods . . . from those manufactured or sold by others and to indicate the source of the goods."

Style Structures

I have good news. You can write like the best legal writers by simply adopting the same style structures they use. *Style structures* are repeatable, learnable patterns in writing that achieve a rhetorical or persuasion goal. And you can start using them in no time.

Before diving into the structures, let's work through an example of how you can use them. Let's say you're tweaking a prominent heading in a brief. You want to elevate your style in this key location so that readers take notice. The current heading you're working with is:

> The minors in this case should be permitted to be raised by both parental figures regardless of whether other children are differently situated.

You peruse the style structures and choose the clarification contrast structure and the general echo words structure. Now simply take your original heading and brainstorm.[1] Let's start with clarification contrast. This structure has you first explain the negative of your point so that you can emphasize your affirmative point. Let's do that with our original heading.

> The children have a Constitutional right to be raised **not just by one parent, but by both parents.**

Now we still need to convey the idea that it doesn't matter whether other children outside of this case survive with only one parent. So we can brainstorm a word to echo that relates to our central point, like this:

> The children have a Constitutional right to be raised by not just one parent, but by both parents — that other children are **born** with only one parent, or ***born*** with no parents, changes nothing.

And there we have it: a world-class heading using just two quick style structures, tailored for our goals. Great legal writers use style structure to draw their readers' eyes to the takeaways like this.

[1] Generative AI tools can be a great partner when brainstorming tricky style structures like this. Just provide your favorite GAI tool with an example of the structure you like, type in your original sentence, and get to brainstorming.

Style structures can be organized into five categories:

1. **Use echo structures.** These techniques use a repeated word or phrase to powerfully connect distinct ideas.
2. **Use location structures.** These structures leverage the order or syntax of writing within a sentence or paragraph.
3. **Use word and phrase structures.** These writing structures play with specific words or phrases to achieve a rhetorical effect.
4. **Use sound structures.** These are writing structures that harness the power of sound.
5. **Use concept style structures.** These techniques use rhetorical concepts to shape your sentences.

Peruse these categories, find a structure that interests you, and practice using it. You can use a bit of your old writing, work from a famous sample, or make up the details as you go. Most people can pick up a new style structure with about 20 minutes of practice.

Return to this chapter when you're working on writing projects and want to amp up a particular sentence or paragraph. Choose a structure that fits your goal and insert your content.

Practice incorporating style structure into your own writing, and watch your prose go from everyday to excellent.

9.1 Use Echo Structures

These style structures use a repeated word or phrase to emphasize. Consider them when you want to collect ideas together and build into a final climax for readers.

General Echo Words: Echo a word in similar positions throughout multiple sentences (or multiple phrases or clauses in the same sentence). You can echo any word for rhetorical effect, like prepositions, nouns, modifying words, verbs, or even words that aren't exact echoes but sound similar.

> The place to disagree on important matters of public concern is the **court** of public opinion, not United States District **Court**.

> The defendants' statistics, however, elide the lack of substantive work. Time **spent** only matters when well **spent**.

> He has known her for many years: **before** she went to college, **before** she was a star, **before** she won the Oscar.

> This government is **of the people**, **by the people**, and **for the people**.

> Defendant devoted his life **to those selfish people**, **for their selfish cause**, but **with his own selfish motives**.

> Not every voter can be expected to follow this process perfectly. Some **forget** one of the envelopes. Others **forget** to sign on the dotted line.

> It turns out that, in the area of immigration and naturalization, the '**unthinkable**,' *Bolling*, 347 U.S. at 500, 74 S.Ct. 693, was exactly what the Court had been **thinking** for more than one hundred years.

Starting Line Echo (Anaphora): This is the technique of repeating a word or phrase at the beginning of successive clauses. It can lend a rhythm and emphasis to your writing.

> **Injustice** anywhere is a threat to justice everywhere. **Injustice** in the courtroom undermines the integrity of our judicial system. **Injustice** in our laws creates a society of inequality.

Finish Line Echo (Epistrophe): This is the opposite; it's the repetition of a word or phrase at the end of successive clauses. Like initial-word repeats, this form can create a rhythm and highlight important ideas.

> Where there is a violation of rights, **we will fight**. Where there is an abuse of power, **we will fight**. Where there is corruption, **we will fight**.

Full Circle Echo (Symploce): You can also combine the two prior repeat moves in a group of clauses or sentences by repeating both the start and end of clauses or sentences.

> **In our** country, we strive for **justice**; **in our** courts, we uphold **justice**.

The Switch Back (Antimetabole): Repeat an exact group of words across two clauses or sentences—but reverse the order of the repeat in the second clause or sentence.

> It is not the **evidence that determines the case**, but the **case that determines the evidence**.

> The **law** was made **to serve people**; the **people** were not made **to serve the law**.

Alpha and Omega (Anadiplosis): This technique involves the repetition of the last word of a preceding clause at the beginning of the next one.

> Justice must not merely be done but must also be seen to be **done**. **Done** are the days when justice was arbitrary.

> The law upholds **the truth. The truth,** however, can sometimes be elusive.

The Boomerang (Epanalepsis): Emphasize a concept by repeating it at the start and end of your sentence, encasing related content in between.

> **Without law**, society would crumble, and there can be no justice **without law**.

Bounce-Back Echo (Diacope): Repeat a word or phrase after an intervening word or phrase to create emphasis and rhythm.

> **To serve and protect**, that is our duty, **to serve and protect**.

> **We strive for justice**, day in, day out; **we strive for justice**.

Repeat and Relay (Anadiplosis): Repeat the last word or phrase from the previous line at the beginning of the next. This creates a chain of thought that emphasizes your point.

> Justice demands **honesty**. **Honesty** demands **truth**. **Truth** demands evidence.

> This case is about **trust**. **Trust** that the legal system will hold the guilty **accountable**. **Accountable** for their actions and their consequences.

Echo Chamber: Persistently repeat a phrase or question for emphasis. This helps make your point stick in the reader's mind.

> **How can we ignore** the evidence? **How can we ignore** the testimony? **How can we ignore** the truth?

> This is a matter of **principle**. **Principle** in law, **principle** in justice, **principle** in societal trust.

End Echo: Repeat a word or phrase at the end of successive clauses. This creates emphasis and rhythm and reinforces your point.

> The law must be fair to **all**, justice must be served to **all**, and rights must be upheld for **all**.

9.2 Use Location Structures

These structures play with the order of writing within a sentence or paragraph. Each will change up a familiar word order or syntax in a sentence so that it stands out from the background.

The Embedded Base: Embed a short clause among a string of phrases on both sides. The effect creates movement and then anchors readers in the short base clause in the middle. Consider this structure when sharing a compelling narrative, particularly if timing and pacing matter.

> As the judge began reading from his computer, the courtroom quiet, **I stood,** waiting for the judgment to be rendered.

The Ending Base: Rather than embedding the base in the middle, place it at the end. Use it to build up movement or an event and anchor readers at the end of the sentence on a final moment.

> As the judge began reading from his computer, the courtroom quiet, **I stood.**

Collected Fragments: In this structure, deliver multiple fragment sentences and then tie them together with a final sentence. The result is a rhetorical effect made coherent with the finishing sentence.

> **A highly accomplished litigator. A unique perspective on the legal system. A protector of clients at all costs.** Mr. Smith is all these things and more.

Two-Phrase Flip (Chiasmus): Use two or more clauses balanced against each other by the reversal of their structures to produce an artistic effect. This reversal doesn't necessarily involve exact repetition or the same words, but something close.

> **The law punishes those** who **break** it, but also **breaks those it punishes.**

One Word, Many Hats (Zeugma): Use one word or phrase, typically a verb or adjective, to govern several others in a sentence. Usually the nucleus word should relate to the different words in different ways. This can create interesting and unexpected connections in your sentences.

> The defendant **signed** the **confession** and his **life** away.

> The judge **raised** his **gavel** and the **defendant's hopes.**

Purposefully Unplugged (Parataxis): Place phrases or clauses right next to each other without indicating their relation with any sort of connector. It creates a stark, choppy effect.

> The judge entered the **room. The** defendant rose.

Triple Threat (Tricolon): Use three parallel clauses, phrases, or words in quick succession to emphasize without interruption.

> By the **people**, for the **people**, with the **people.**

> In this courtroom, **we respect the truth, we honor the law, we pursue justice.**

Word Order Wander (Hyperbaton): Rearrange the words or clauses in a sentence in an unexpected order. This disruption in expected flow can create a dramatic effect. But make sure the sentence is still clear.

> Justice must always prevail, **must it not**, even when the scales seem imbalanced?

Tailcoat Adjective (Anastrophe): Position the adjective after the noun, contrary to the standard English sentence structure. This reversal can help create a poetic effect.

> **Evidence, compelling and irrefutable**, was presented by the prosecution.

Descriptive Duo (Apposition): Place a noun or phrase next to another noun to elaborate on the first. This technique can provide additional context or characterization.

> Judge Smith, **a pillar of integrity**, presided over the complex litigation.

Antithesis: Insert two opposite ideas in a sentence to achieve a contrasting effect. This can create a memorable image or concept.

> Though we must adhere to the law's **letter**, we should never neglect its **spirit**.

> While the prosecution builds **walls**, the defense seeks to open **doors**.

Parallelism: Deliver examples or a list of items in consistent grammatical forms. This can create a rhythm and emphasize the relationship between the items. The goal is to keep nouns, verbs, and modifiers parallel.

> **To** seek truth **requires** diligence; **to** speak truth **requires** courage; **to** honor truth **requires** integrity.

> The federal government spends billions of dollars **feeding the hungry, clothing the poor,** and **sheltering the homeless.**

Epithet: Apply a descriptive word or phrase right before a noun to intensify imagery.

> The **infamous thief** was finally caught by Detective Smith.

> The **seasoned prosecutor** took control of the courtroom.

The Appositive Emphasizer: Start with a simple noun, often to identify a key person or thing—then immediately describe the noun in a deep phrase. This structure is great for emphasizing an important noun.

> The defendant, John Smith—**a 35-year-old computer technician renowned for his analytical acumen and previously unblemished legal record**—asserted his innocence today.

The End: Ending a sentence on a concrete detail or verb can emphasize it in readers' minds. So consider choosing that final word with extra care.

> No court has ever held that a claim like the plaintiff's can survive dismissal, **nor should this one**.

> The defendant's actions were not merely negligent, **they were criminal**.

Inverted Sentence Elements: This move stresses the entire sentence, which stands out from everything around it. You simply switch around the subject and predicate.

> "**Not** compelling" is the evidence here. (Instead of "the evidence is not compelling").

> **That kind of trickery** this court will not tolerate.

The Long Modifier Buildup: Modifying phrases have a core clause (the subject and verb that your sentence is built around) with one or more phrases tacked on that end that add flavor to the core. Look at the example and notice how the modifying phrases build on the core clause to create a scene.

> The car burst through the barricade, **plowing through trees, tearing down a neighbor's fence, and settling sideways in a ditch**.

Dependent-Clause-Clusters: Stacking dependent clauses in a sentence, either at the end or beginning of the sentence, can create a striking finishing point.

> **Because it may seem difficult at first, because it may sound awkward or forced, because it often creates lengthy sentences where the thought gets lost,** this pattern seems forbidding to some writers, but it isn't all that hard.

Appositive Clusters: With appositive clusters, you pick a group of appositives (words, usually nouns, in a sentence that are also referred to by another word in the sentence) and deliver them together to create a poignant point.

> **Twitter, Facebook, email**—which is worse for the lawyer?

9.3 Use Word and Phrase Structures

These structures play with specific words or phrases to achieve a rhetorical effect. They often leverage traditional rhetorical moves, pithy phrases, or other structures to create a stylistic impact on readers.

And Avalanche (Polysyndeton): Use several conjunctions in close succession, especially where they might be omitted. This can create a sense of overwhelm or urgency.

> We have facts **and** evidence **and** testimony **and** documents that all point to the same conclusion.

> The legislation could be interpreted this way **or** it could be read in another way **or** it might have a meaning that's somewhere in between.

Junction Jettison (Asyndeton): The opposite of stacking conjunctions; this is the omission of conjunctions between parts of a sentence. This can speed up the rhythm of your text and create a particular tone.

> Justice demands **fairness, impartiality, integrity, courage.**

> The defendant **ran, hid, lied.**

Both Are Great: Great legal writers love using phrases that help emphasize degree. Take "matched only by" or "equaled only by." Both set up a pithy comparison in which two concepts are grouped together to show how extreme each is.

> The state's fault in filing so many documents late **is matched only by** the county's fault in ignoring the mistake for so long.

> The plaintiff's audacity to claim innocence **is equaled only by** his disregard for the law.

True, But: Conceding to set up a powerful counter is a tool of trade for good legal writers. Try the "true . . . but" trick. Concede something minor that won't hurt you and follow it up with the thing that really matters. Juxtaposing a relatively minor concession can make your point hit even harder.

> True, the police officer handled the matter fine in this case. But in 26 other cases there's been documented misconduct.

> **True**, the defendant was present at the crime scene. **But** so were dozens of other potential suspects.

That, Too: Inserting *too* in a sentence can slow readers down and force them to notice another point. Consider using *too* when you want to connect two ideas—especially if you'd like the second point to be emphasized for readers.

> The Supreme Court ruled last year that a prior claim can't be resuscitated when new damages are asserted. This Court recently held that, **too**: holding that a new claim must be asserted when new damages are in play.

Action Opener: When you want readers to focus on an action happening, consider launching right from the verb.

> **Dividing** this court's attention has been the plaintiff's goal all along.

> **Believing** the evidence is true is not the same as it being true.

Double Duty (Zeugma) (Syllepsis when you apply a nucleus word to three or more other words or phrases): Apply a verb or adjective to two or more words in a sentence, but in different ways. It brings an unexpected twist to your statement.

> The jury **held their breath** and **their final decision**.

> The witness colored his testimony and **the opinion of the court**.

> The judge **dismissed the case and the rumors**.

Grandeur to Ground (Bathos): Transition abruptly from a lofty idea or phrase to a trivial or ludicrous one. This can make a stark point about contrasts (as many great advanced style tools do).

> In the **hallowed halls of justice,** where centuries of jurisprudence have been considered, we find ourselves **arguing about missing paperwork**.

Harsh Harmony (Dysphemism): To pull off this technique, contrast a more offensive or critical term with a neutral or positive one. This can add dramatic emphasis.

> The defendant wasn't **mistaken**; he was **deceitful**.

> The lawyer didn't **persuade** the jurors. He **manipulated** them.

Understated Undertone (Meiosis): Use this tool by deliberately downplaying a fact or idea to subtly emphasize its significance. But be careful; it often comes off as sarcastic.

The mistake **resulted in a trivial miscalculation of a few million dollars.**

Our opponent's claim, **a simple misunderstanding**, as he puts it, **asks the Court to rewrite contract law.**

The 500-page contract is **not exactly a light read.**

Vivid Verbs: You can achieve potent effects by selecting one verb over another. When crafting a key sentence, consider choosing among the many verb options to target a specific feeling or image that will resonate with readers.

The defendant **bulldozed** his way through contractual obligations, causing financial havoc.

The plaintiff's accusations **fizzled** under the scrutiny of the facts.

Yes, But No: This is another simple structure to clarify an affirmative and then a negative. Consider using it when you want to concede and then clarify why the negative side is what really matters.

Yes, the statute provides the EEOC with wide latitude over the conciliation process, and that feature becomes significant when we turn to defining the proper scope of judicial review. **But no**, Congress has not left everything to the Commission.

Yes, the defendant has rights. **But no**, those rights do not include endangering the lives of others with reckless behavior.

The Undercut (Paraprosdokian): Craft a sentence where the end delivers an unexpected twist that drastically contrasts or undermines the first part. This can catch your reader off guard and add a touch of wit.

I've had a **wonderful** day in court, **but this wasn't it.**

The defense presented **an incredibly strong case, so strong it crumbled under the barest scrutiny.**

Dual Drama: Dual drama allows you to emphasize two simultaneous points. Use *not only...but, both...and,* and *either...or* to create the structure. It's best used when you're presenting two connected ideas or a choice between alternatives.

Not only must plaintiff plead harm, **but** he **must also** plead the specific actors who carried out that harm.

> The plaintiff must choose: **Either** allege the specifics of the fraud **or** identify the bad actors.

> **Both** the lack of substantial evidence **and** the violation of procedural fairness warrant an appeal.

In Other Words: Explain something one way, then explain it a different way right after to reinforce the point from two perspectives. This allows you to add nuance to a particularly important point. You can use this move by introducing a simple definition to get the reader in the ballpark, then drive home the explanation in a follow-up sentence.

> The rule requires a money loss to be alleged. **In other words:** If the complaint does not specify that the plaintiff made less than he otherwise would have, the claim fails.

> Courts have widely agreed that the First Amendment protects symbolic expressions of any kind, so long as it's expression. **Stated differently:** expression is the touchstone.

Cause Connector: Use *and because* to provide context to a statement, connecting cause and effect. Consider using this structure to add a quick bit of context to set up a powerful final point.

> **And because** this Court was never given the chance to review the original petition, it has no way to discern whether the amendment is proper.

> **And because** the defendant was fully aware of the regulations, his claim of ignorance does not hold up.

In the Same Breath: Great legal writers use this phrase to highlight that someone is inconsistent. Take this example from Justice Neil Gorsuch.

> **In the same breath,** the district court said an Eleventh Amendment objection "is a challenge to a district court's subject matter jurisdiction" and yet "it does not implicate federal subject matter jurisdiction."

Nouning: Turn a noun into a verb. This is a pithy way to get the power of a verb injected into our nouns.

> The plaintiff is merely **papering** this case.

> Mrs. Park knew that **Rule 27ing** this case would end her claim.

Silent Verbs: This flourish creates a pithy sentence that strongly connects two points. Write a sentence with two related points, and structure the second phrase to adopt a silent verb from the first.

> Courts have consistently applied these rules—**litigants, not so much**.

> The plaintiff says the first case is key; **the defendant, the second.**

Without Ado: *Without* can help you make a subtle point about something not crossing a threshold or meeting a definition. Just put the "without" right before the word or phrase you want to emphasize is *not* met.

> The lawyer was smart and articulate **without** being arrogant.

Professes X, Practices Y: Point out a contradiction between what is said and what is done.

> The government **professes** dedication to transparency, yet it **practices** secrecy.

Seems, Yet Isn't: Use this structure to flag something that appears to be one way but is actually not.

> The proposal **seems** fair on its face **yet isn't** because it leaves out the key term the parties negotiated for months.

In Theory, Not in Practice: This structure highlights a discrepancy between conceptual and practical applications.

> The law supports freedom of speech **in theory, not in practice,** as shown by recent restrictions.

Presents as X, Operates as Y: This structure emphasizes a disparity between how something is presented and how it functions or is implemented.

> The new regulation **presents as** a protective measure yet **operates as** a barrier to innovation.

However It Happens: Most legal writers use *however* to link two clauses by suggesting the second sentence is an exception to the first. But *however* can also be used as a pithier version of *whichever.* Notice how this next attorney makes a strong point but then softens it by clarifying that she is not suggesting the outcome.

> The Court needs to rule on this motion, **however** it may come out.

In the Shadow of X, Y Emerges: This structure indicates something is developing or becoming apparent in the context of something else.

In the shadow of conventional law, a new wave of digital rights emerges.

From the Vantage of X, Y Is Seen: This structure offers a perspective-based insight or conclusion.

From the vantage of international law, the treaty's limitations are clear.

Through the Lens of X, Y Comes into Focus: This structure can help explain how viewing a situation from a particular perspective changes the conclusion.

Through the lens of social justice, the policy's implications come into focus.

Part and Parcel: This is a simple structure for sharing elements of something in a compelling way. Just collect the ingredients you want to emphasize and insert "part" before each.

The rule here is part preventative, part corrective, and part practical.

Double As: This is a simple move for comparing two things and suggesting they are equivalent. Just insert an *as* before the first point and one again before the second. The power of this move is in picking the right things to compare. Usually, you'll be equating two good things or two bad things.

Striker Corp. was as diligent as it was careful: sending every detailed notice days before the deadline.

That, Too: Insert *too* before key words to suggest that something is overdone or excessive. This move often works best with adjectives. This judge emphasizes the excessiveness of each point with the well-placed *too*.

The plaintiff was offered a too-expensive vehicle after a too-long delay.

Where X, Y; Less X than Y; More X than Y: Many great style moves are about highlighting the differences between concepts. These particular structures are about comparing two things when you want to emphasize the gap between them. For the first structure, start with one position or status, then emphasize the different perspectives of another. These structures are helpful for shining a light on the differences between two positions.

Where the lower court saw intent, the appellate court saw nothing but coincidence.

This case is less about damages than it is about hurt feelings.

The defamation claim here is more form than substance, offering few specific details.

Fragmentation: Use occasional fragment sentences. A fragment, although ungrammatical, draws your reader's attention. Just ensure it will be obvious you wrote the fragment on purpose for stylistic reasons.

> The defendant beat the plaintiff until her unborn baby died. He then strangled her until she blacked out—and surely would have died, had a Samaritan not stepped in. And now the defendant contends he need not even pay for the medical costs he inflicted because of a technicality in plaintiff's pro-se complaint. The court's answer is simple. **No.**

9.4 Use Sound Structures

These structures harness the power of sound. Either by using the sounds of words, or nearby words, you can create pleasing rhetorical flourishes that make a point stand out.

Alliteration: Repeat the initial consonant sounds, or consonants later in the words, for emphasis or to create a rhythmic link between words.

> That **blow** to the **banks** was **substantially softened** by the later ruling that a presale tender of the full amount of the superpriority lien cures the default....

> Breach of **contract claims** can lead to **bitter battles**.

Vowel Velvet (Assonance): Repeat a vowel sound in nonrhyming words to create an *internal* rhyme, enhancing the musicality of your writing.

> In the **pursuit** of **truth**, we must **scrutinize** each **clue**.

> A just decision can **brighten** the **lives** of many.

Sonic Silk (Euphony): Use phrases or words that inspire melodic sound. This technique makes your prose pleasant to the ear.

> In the soft **murmur** of the courthouse, justice **whispers** its verdict.

> A **ripple** of truth can turn into a **wave** of change.

9.5 Use Concept Style Structures

These structures use rhetorical concepts to shape your sentences. Rather than leverage a particular word or phrase, these structures use relationships or theories to elevate your style.

Mirror Image: Use this construction to illustrate the negatives of a point before presenting your primary point. In other words, clarify what the situation *isn't* before revealing what *it is*. If you show readers the negative of your point, they can more easily grasp the positive.

> **We are not addressing a simple contract dispute here,** but a complex case of corporate espionage.

> The ordinance is unconstitutional, **not because a policeman applied it poorly in a particular case**, but rather because the policeman enjoys too much discretion in all cases.

Clarify and Classify: Give readers a term, new or familiar, and then immediately elaborate on the definition to eliminate any ambiguity or emphasize a point (you can even give a different definition than readers expect for a familiar word; Distinctio).

> When I say **"excessive,"** I mean an amount so large that it exceeds any reasonable limit or standard.

> By **"negligence,"** I refer to the disregard of the duty of care that has led to unnecessary harm.

The Strategic Concession (Epitrope): Give your opponent permission to make their argument but with a heavy dose of irony that will highlight the weaknesses in their point. Just make sure not to take it so far that your tone is disrespectful.

> By all means, **plaintiffs may continue a line of reasoning that sidesteps the incriminating evidence.**

> The defendant is welcome to explain how this **"open and shut" case has lingered for years without resolution.**

The Verbal Wink: Highlight a concept or point by pretending to omit it. This allows you to bring up issues without seeming overly aggressive. Or you can set a point you want to emphasize.

> **Without mentioning the defendant's multiple previous infractions**, let's focus on the current charge.

> We **won't discuss how the other party conveniently lost their files** right before the trial.

The Ask-and-Answered (Hypophora): Raise a question and immediately follow it with an answer to maintain control and direction of the argument.[2]

[2] A related tool, but not as relevant in legal writing, is epanorthosis: Use immediate and emphatic self-correction for rhetorical effect. This can portray passion, show urgency, or intensify meaning; for example, "We have a policy of ensuring fair representation, no, we have an obligation to ensure it."

What is our duty as lawyers? To uphold the law and seek justice.

Why did the defendant flee the scene? It's simple: guilt and the fear of being caught.

The Fractional (Synecdoche): Use a part to represent the whole. This can help to emphasize certain elements over others or add some poetic color to your writing.

After much deliberation, the jury—**12 impartial eyes**—unanimously found the defendant guilty.

Object As Actor (Personification): Give lifelike qualities to an inanimate object or an idea. This technique can make abstract concepts more tangible and relatable.[3]

Justice, **blindfolded and unbiased,** holds the scales that measure our deeds.

The Constitution, **vigilant and enduring,** continues to guide our nation's course.

Rhetorical Questions: Write a question that doesn't require response but rather emphasizes the point you're making. These guide the reader toward your viewpoint by making them ponder the implication of the question.

If we insist on reading "not less than 7 days" to mean "not more than 7 days," why should anyone reading our opinions trust that he understands them correctly? If words are so malleable, might we routinely read our own precedents as saying the opposite of what they clearly say? May one panel simply rewrite another panel's opinion when it thinks the prior opinion is "illogical?"[4] And where might our creativity lead us with provisions of the Constitution that don't make as much sense as we would like? May we amend even the Constitution at will?

Simile: A figure of speech involving the comparison of one thing with another thing of a different kind, using *like* or *as*.

The plaintiff's case fell apart **like a house of cards**, unable to withstand the slightest scrutiny.

Metaphor: With a metaphor, you're simply comparing two things without using *like* or *as*. This is a strong tool for making abstract ideas more concrete and making the reader understand your point more intuitively. But don't be trite.

[3] As we learned in Chapter 3, this tool is particularly useful for telling stories about abstract concepts.

[4] This is a great example of, well, the power of examples—courtesy of Judge Jay Bybee on the Ninth Circuit Court of Appeals.

> The Constitution is the **unshakeable bedrock** on which our society is built.

> The prosecutor's evidence **was a ticking time bomb**, ready to explode the defendant's alibi.

Highlight Gaps to Highlight Differences: A simple way to highlight the difference between two points, or to communicate degree, is to juxtapose two near synonyms or related groups of words. Of course, the comparison must be the right one for the point you're trying to make. So focus on the gap between the phrases or words.

> Filing **nearly on time** is as useless as **filing months late.**

> **Harm** is not met by proving **discomfort**.

> Mr. Davidson has listed the **price** of every hour he spent but the **value** of none of it.

General Beats Specific: A simple structure is to emphasize that a general rule or policy should outweigh narrow readings and exceptions. This is often about emphasizing the core spirit of the rule. Justice Amy Coney Barrett uses this tool to suggest that an exception to the rule is a bridge too far.

> As a **"general rule,"** Congress cannot circumvent state sovereign immunity's limitations through its Article I powers. [E]ven in areas where Article I grants it "complete lawmaking authority," Congress lacks a tool that it could otherwise use to implement its power.

Set It Up, Then Take It Down: Frame an issue favorably, then offer the solution. This can be tricky because it requires you to capture a critical point in a simple sentence that you can then tackle intuitively.

> This case presents the question of whether extending a parking-violation car stop to obtain identifying information from the passengers impermissibly prolongs the stop so as to taint the entire seizure. **Because even a slight extension of a stop is unconstitutional, the answer is yes.**

Adjectives That Add Flavor: Legal writers often rely on descriptors too much, especially adverbs. Descriptors can help, but only to create a point that the nouns and verbs couldn't muster on their own. So ensure that any descriptors in your sentences are adding unique, important information that no noun or verb could capture on its own.

> Many States, especially in the South, suppressed the black vote through a **dizzying** array of methods: literacy tests, poll taxes, registration requirements, and property qualifications.

> The Court is now faced with a **kaleidoscope** of claims, many of which overlap.

Examples and Hypotheticals: When you have a particularly tough concept to explain, in any part of your document, a concrete example or hypothetical can do wonders. Many judges and lawyers are afraid of these, but don't be. With a little practice they are easy to use.[5] These snippets from two different U.S. Supreme Court justices show us how.

> **Suppose a real estate agent promised to find a client "a house, condo, or apartment in New York."** Wouldn't the potential buyer be annoyed if the agent sent him information about condos in Maryland or California?

> Determining the best control technology is like asking different people to pick the best car. **Mario Andretti may select a Ferrari; a college student may choose a Volkswagen Beetle; a family of six a mini-van. A Minnesotan's choice will doubtless have four-wheel drive; a Floridian's might be a convertible. The choice would turn on how the decisionmaker weighed competing priorities. . . .**

Example-Cluster Sentences: You can also use clusters of examples in a sentence to illustrate a concept or point, like this judge did.

> Our country has a long and ignominious history of discriminating against our most vulnerable and powerless. We have an equally long history, however, of brave individuals—**Dred Scott, Fred Korematsu, Linda Brown, Mildred and Richard Loving, Edie Windsor, and Jim Obergefell, to name just a few**—who refused to accept quietly the injustices that were perpetuated against them.

> The basic writing skills (**good vocabulary, knowledge of grammar, sense of style**) can be learned by everyone.

It's a Matter of Degree: A simple tool to show relative degrees of two things—like how one thing compares on a spectrum to another—is to use the *rarely–never* comparison (or similar comparisons, like *sometimes–always*). The idea is to pick two words that convey degree, and by juxtaposing them, you can make an even better point about how extreme something is.

> The truth is something more complicated. **Sometimes** the bits of glass in Sampson's products have caused a lasting medical injury. But **nearly always** these bits of glass have caused short-term injuries: Sending thousands to hospitals around the country.

Riff Off Others: One of the easiest—and most impressive—writing style tools is to riff off other writing. Simply repeat a quote in a different context or use a similar construction to highlight how you're playing with the original words. (When you use this move on an opponent, it's called Syncrisis).

[5] There are a few types of example structures you can use, including specific detail examples and hypotheticals (and lots in between). Choose specific details to convey nuance to your point, spin a quick hypothetical to illustrate a concept, or provide a different example of a concept in different terms or from a different perspective to drive it all home.

> He not-so-subtly threatens **"bedlam"** if he is not on the ballot. But we already saw the **"bedlam"** Trump unleashed when he was on the ballot and lost.

> When the court said that the case was **"unthinkable,"** it left out that it had been **thinking** about it for over two years.

> For a company that prides itself on **"serving customers quickly,"** the only thing Jerricho did **"quickly"** was take Mr. Terry's money.

Figurative Language: Figurative language (words and phrases that you aren't using for their literal meaning) can be impressive, but you can't rely on worn-out platitudes. If you want to use a cliché, change it up into something new. Otherwise, create something all your own with figurative language. Check out these examples of novel clichés and fresh figurative descriptions.

> Still, there is little point in granting rehearing en banc to **move this circuit** from **one side of a conflict to another**. . . .

> Few statutes have proven as enigmatic as 18 U.S.C. §924(c). Everyone knows that, generally speaking, the statute imposes heightened penalties on those who use guns to commit violent crimes or drug offenses. **But the details are full of devils.**

> The penalty provision is merely **the tail** and the mandate is the **proverbial dog**, not vice-versa.

> In the final analysis, Musk launched a **self-driving process**, **recalibrating** the **speed** and **direction along the way** as he saw fit. The process **arrived** at an unfair price. And through this litigation, the plaintiff requests a **recall**.

Speaking Matters: Great writers often tee up important issues or points using dialogue. In other words, they speak directly to readers. This structure is somewhat controversial, as some legal readers don't like it. But you'll find many of the best legal writers using it. For example, Justice Elena Kagan uses this tool in almost everything she writes.

> **Imagine a friend told you** that she hoped to meet "an actor, director, or producer involved with the new *Star Wars* movie." **You would know** immediately that she wanted to meet an actor from the *Star Wars* cast—not an actor in, for example, the latest *Zoolander*.

> **If you need to take a deep breath after all that, you're not alone.** It would be hard to dream up a more round-about way of bifurcating judicial review of the agency's rulings in mixed cases.

Not every style move is for every case. But turn a few key sentences into works of wordsmithing like these writers, and your readers will notice.

10

Level Up
Your Document Design

> Everything is designed. Few things are designed well." — Brian Reed

The pen is mighty — but a well-placed visual can be mightier still. This chapter delves into the often-overlooked arsenal of visual tools at a legal writer's disposal. Images like timelines, charts, and infographics can convey ideas in ways words don't.

When Twitter's[1] lawyers sued Elon Musk for backing out of his purchase of the social media company, Musk's tweets, shown in Figure 10.1, said more than the legal writers could. Musk was gearing up to issue a tender offer, a bid to buy up majority shares by enticing shareholders with a premium price. What would you think of Musk's suggestion that he wasn't aiming for a "tender" offer after you read the tech mogul's own messages — which were embedded right in the complaint?

Figure 10.1. Tweets by Elon Musk Referencing a "Tender" Offer

[1] Now known as X.

Visual appeal also matters in your document's overall design. The choice of fonts, the management of white space, and the balance of text all come together to create the best legal documents. The digital age has also reshaped how we consume information, and legal writing isn't immune.

10.1 Use Vivid Visuals

Visuals are perhaps the most underused tool in legal writing (after technology). Most lawyers are still terrified to use things like charts, graphs, tables, timelines, and images. None of the court cases they read in law school had them; none of the briefs they've read from their mentors had them. There must be some rule against using visuals, right?

Wrong. There is no rule against using visuals, even several of them, in your briefs or memos. Once upon a time, pulling off a visual was tricky. Creating a graph or illustration could require an entire outside team. These days, you can whip up snazzy visuals in seconds. Just using Microsoft PowerPoint's built-in features is enough to achieve impressive visual feats. Tons of other programs can create a vast array of visuals these days. What's more, judges are overwhelmingly using digital devices to read legal documents, so the ease of viewing images has increased tenfold.

I have yet to hear a judge complain when lawyers use the occasional well-made visual. I've heard many judges lament that lawyers never use them. And if you're writing a document for your team or a client, visuals will impress them even more. So this is a set of skills worth investing in. And with tools for creating visuals—including GAI—it's easier than ever.

So consider creating a visual when:

- You have data to present. Graphs nearly always make data easier to swallow than writing about results.
- You have a complex process to discuss, like an agency decision process, or a factual process like how a company handled complaints.
- To show how a statute, regulation, or any other rule operates in many steps.
- Any time you could use a chart to plot out a decision tree for your reader.
- You want to make comparisons, connections, or contrasts among many pieces of evidence of information.
- Any other time that a visual will help emphasize a point or deliver an idea better than words (which is often).

Let's explore some of the visuals most useful to legal readers.

A Quick Summary

Use timelines. **Whenever chronology matters, create a simple timeline that will help readers order events.**

Use tables. **Contrast or compare information or organize points using clear tables.**

Use textual callouts. **Call attention to pivotal language using visual callouts.**

Use charts and graphs. **Share data so readers can visualize. Point out increases, decreases, gaps, and other key insights.**

Use maps. **When space or locations matter, share maps to help readers track.**

Use images. **Capture important information or atmospherics using a well-placed image.**

Use casts of characters. **Help readers keep track of your document's characters.**

Use lists. **Use bullets, numbers, or textual labels to categorize groups of information or points.**

Use flowcharts. **Illustrate processes or relationships using simple flowcharts.**

10.1.1 Use Timelines

Timelines might be the single most helpful visual device for your readers. Timelines give your reader a unique view of how events unfolded—a view that, in some detailed cases, might be impossible to do in mere text.

Any time you have a lengthy series of events, consider building a timeline. Timelines can include factual events that matter to an argument, but you could also build a simple timeline to deliver information like a case's procedural history.

Take the timeline in Figure 10.2, which manages to pack a ton of information about various relevant factual events into a single visual, making clear where each key event lines up next to other critical information in a case.

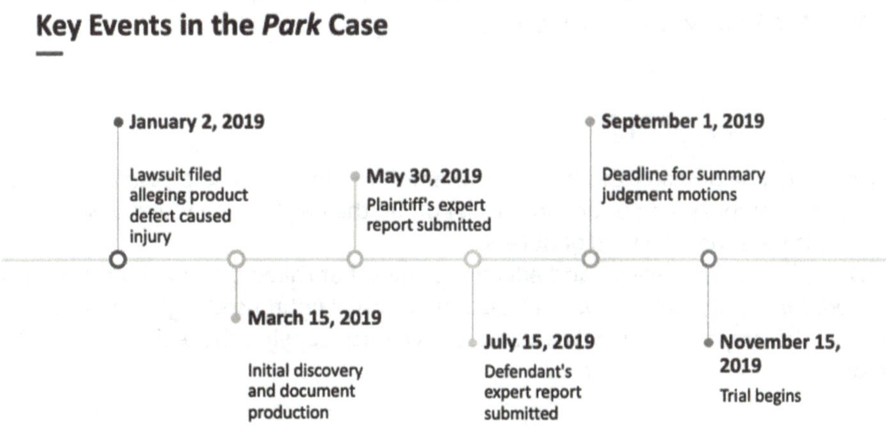

Figure 10.2. Sample Timeline of Filing Dates in a Lawsuit

10.1.2 Use Tables, Charts, and Graphs

Consider using tables, charts, and graphs whenever you want to compare or contrast information or share data. Examples include juxtaposing evidence, juxtaposing allegations, juxtaposing cases, or juxtaposing arguments.

In *The New York Times v. OpenAI*, alleging that the AI maker stole articles from publishers, the plaintiff used the graph displayed in Figure 10.3 to show how many articles were used by the defendant.

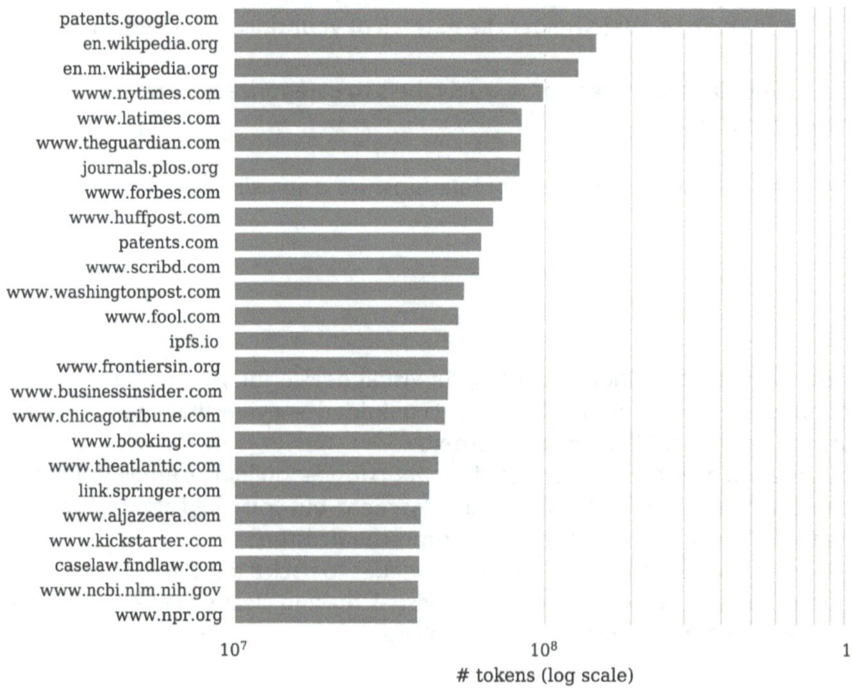

Figure 10.3. Chart Revealing Sources of Data Used in ChatGPT Language Models in *The New York Times v. OpenAI* Lawsuit

10.1.3 Use Text Callouts

Text callouts are perhaps the best of the emphasis tools. These are snippets of the phrases or sentences in your document, set off on the page with a visual of some kind. You can also use them instead of bullets.

One of the most creative and effective visuals that called out text is also from *The New York Times v. OpenAI*, shown in Figure 10.4. The plaintiff used highlighted text in a side-by-side comparison to make clear just how much copying the tech company's tool had done.

A callout like this can highlight what's important. But don't overdo it. Too many callouts can become distracting. And because this is such a new sort of tool, tread with care. Most judges and other legal readers end up appreciating visual cues. But if you have reason to believe your legal reader won't appreciate it, don't take the risk.

Output from GPT-4:
exempted it from regulations, subsidized its operations and promoted its practices, records and interviews showed.
Their actions turned one of the best-known symbols of New York — its yellow cabs — into a financial trap for thousands of immigrant drivers. More than 950 have filed for bankruptcy, according to a Times analysis of court records, and many more struggle to stay afloat.
"Nobody wanted to upset the industry," said David Klahr, who from 2007 to 2016 held several management posts at the Taxi and Limousine Commission, the city agency that oversees **medallions**. "Nobody wanted to kill the golden goose."
New York City in particular failed the taxi industry, The Times found. Two former mayors, Rudolph W. Giuliani and Michael R. Bloomberg, placed political allies inside the Taxi and Limousine Commission and directed it to sell medallions to help them balance budgets and fund **key initiatives.**
During that period, much like in the mortgage lending crisis, a group of industry leaders enriched themselves by artificially inflating medallion prices. They encouraged medallion buyers to borrow as much as possible and ensnared them in interest-only loans and other one-sided deals that often required **borrowers** to pay hefty fees, forfeit their legal rights and give up most of their monthly incomes.
When the market collapsed, the government largely abandoned the drivers who bore the brunt of the crisis. Officials did not bail out borrowers or persuade banks to soften loan

Actual text from NYTimes:
exempted it from regulations, subsidized its operations and promoted its practices, records and interviews showed.
Their actions turned one of the best-known symbols of New York — its **signature** yellow cabs — into a financial trap for thousands of immigrant drivers. More than 950 have filed for bankruptcy, according to a Times analysis of court records, and many more struggle to stay afloat.
"Nobody wanted to upset the industry," said David Klahr, who from 2007 to 2016 held several management posts at the Taxi and Limousine Commission, the city agency that oversees **cabs**. "Nobody wanted to kill the golden goose."
New York City in particular failed the taxi industry, The Times found. Two former mayors, Rudolph W. Giuliani and Michael R. Bloomberg, placed political allies inside the Taxi and Limousine Commission and directed it to sell medallions to help them balance budgets and fund **priorities. Mayor Bill de Blasio continued the policies.**
Under Mr. Bloomberg and Mr. de Blasio, the city made more than $855 million by selling taxi medallions and collecting taxes on private sales, according to the city.
But during that period, much like in the mortgage lending crisis, a group of industry leaders enriched themselves by artificially inflating medallion prices. They encouraged medallion buyers to borrow as much as possible and ensnared them in interest-only loans and other one-sided deals that often required **them** to pay hefty fees, forfeit their legal rights and give up most of their monthly incomes.

Figure 10.4. Image Comparing Text in *The New York Times v. OpenAI* Lawsuit

10.1.4 Use Maps

Maps are great for making any sort of spatial or location points pop for readers. You can annotate a map to show where a company's offices are or where important events happened. Or use a map any other time space and location matters.

Judge Posner used the map shown in Figure 10.5 to illustrate locations of buildings relevant to a defendant's testimony—which is much clearer with visual reference.

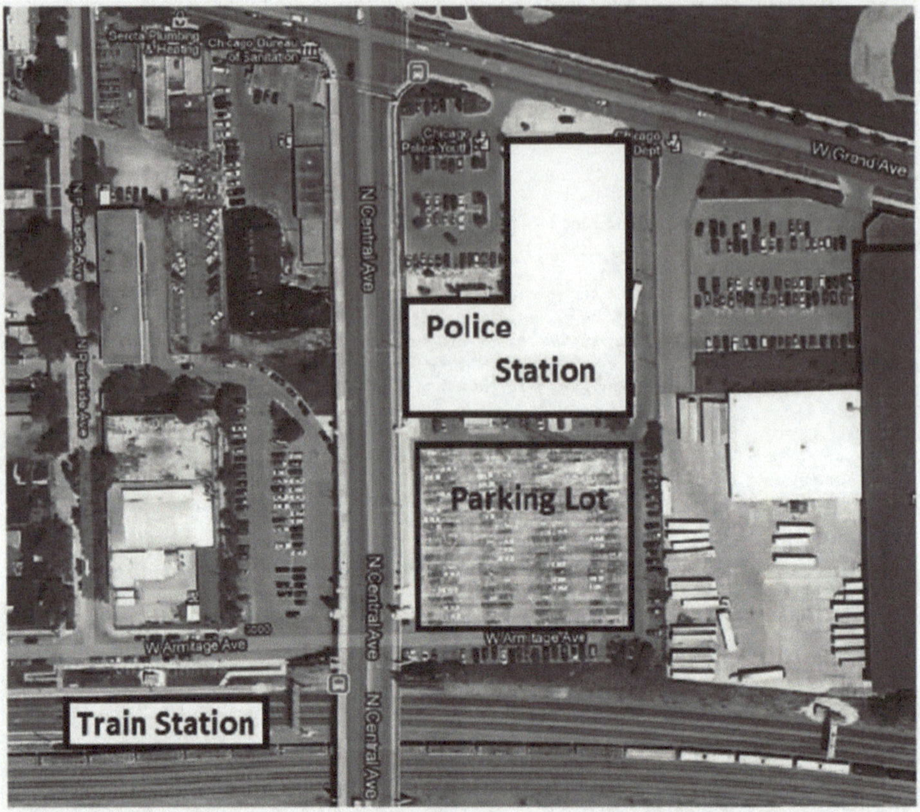

Figure 10.5. Labeled Photograph from a Judicial Opinion Illustrating Locations Relevant to the Lawsuit

10.1.5 Use Images

Images are useful in briefs for many reasons. Perhaps you want to shock readers with the damage suffered by your client, like showing an image of the accident scene.

The Federal Trade Commission used the image in Figure 10.6 in a complaint to illustrate how Apple was marketing to young children in its apps.

Any other time that a location or look of something could matter to your argument, visuals are a great option. Good intellectual property attorneys, for example, often use these to make important points about how products look similar or different. Like the lawyers for Apple did when illustrating how similar another company's logo was to Apple's recognizable trademark, as displayed in Figure 10.7.

Figure 10.6. Image Contrast from an Appellate Brief Used to Illustrate a Company's Intentional Marketing to Children

Figure 10.7. Image Contrast from a Brief to Show Trademark Similarity

10.1.6 Use Casts of Characters

When your case has a lot of characters, and it will be tricky for your reader to keep track of who is who, consider creating a legend at the outset of your brief (or as an appendix) with a cast of the characters. Include their name, their role, and any other helpful information.

Ralph Gilbert	Chief Executive Officer
Lester Start	Chief Financial Officer
Graydon Treat	Chief Investment Officer
Justin Bister	Board Director
Mark Sholes	Board Director
Harvey Flexer	Board Director

Or use an image-based organizational chart, similar to the one shown in Figure 10.8.

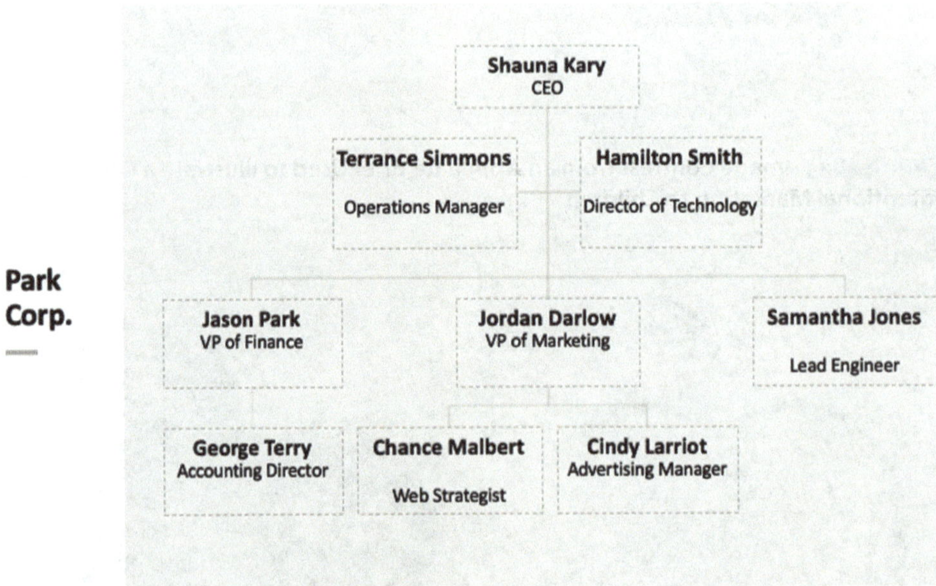

Figure 10.8. Sample Company Organizational Chart

10.1.7 Use Lists

If you have a list of points, reasons, or related facts, consider using bullets to summarize them instead of prose. Bullets are a powerful emphasizing tool, making it easy for your reader to see the list visually set off from the bulk of the text.

Judge Diane Wood uses this device in one of her opinions, adding bullets to make her readers take stock of the many reasons supporting her view that a confession was coerced.

The video recording of the police interrogation of Dassey, however, tells another story—one that is diametrically opposed to the state's tidy and selective summary. Among the many red flags are the following:

- **Dassey's answers to questions frequently changed at the detectives' prodding.**
- **The officers laid a trail of crumbs (indeed, large signposts) to the confession they sought.**
- **Whenever Dassey went off-course, the investigators would shepherd him back in the desired direction—at times with the use of fatherly assurances and gestures, and frequently by questioning his honesty.**
- **The detectives misleadingly conveyed to Dassey, whose ability to think abstractly was minimal, that his honesty was the only thing that will set [him] free.**
- **Through subsequent questioning it became clear that honesty meant what the investigators wanted to hear.**

Other than bullets and numbers, you can also create visual lists using short words or phrases that act as labels for each category of information. Look how the legal writers in a copyright case use bolded phrases to group information:

Groundbreaking, In-Depth Journalism and Breaking News at Great Cost

To produce world-class journalism, The Times invests an enormous amount of time, money, expertise, and talent, both in its newsroom and product, technology, and other supporting teams. Core areas of focus include:

Investigative Reporting. The Times does deep investigations—which usually take months and sometimes years to report and produce—into complex and important areas of public interest . . .

Breaking News Reporting. The Times is equally committed to quickly and accurately reporting breaking news . . .

Beat Reporting: The Times invests significantly in its beat reporting by giving its beat reporters the time and space to go deep on a single topic . . .

Reviews and Analysis. The Times is a trusted source for reviews and analysis of arts and culture, including food, books, art, film, theater, television, music, fashion, and travel. . . .

10.1.8 Use Flowcharts

Flowcharts are amazing at showing how processes work. Or you can use flowcharts and infographics, like Figure 10.9, to show relationships between parties or entities.

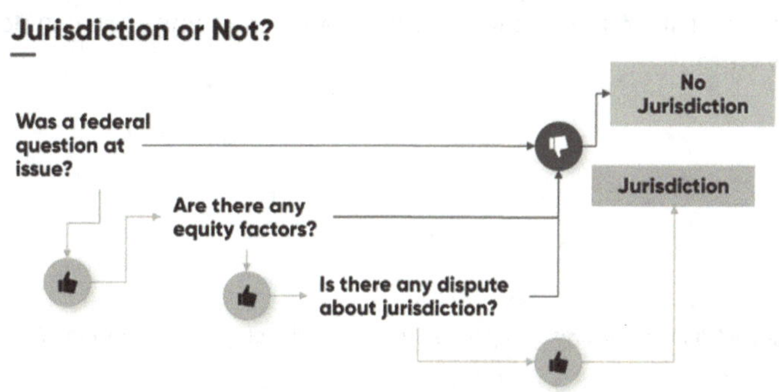

Figure 10.9. Sample Flowchart Illustrating a Legal Process

Here are some final tips for making your legal visuals look snazzy.

1. Always explain the visual well beforehand, and do so in detail. You should never force your readers to use a visual, lest they resent you for it.
2. Consider whether it will be less risky, and easier, to include a visual as an attachment rather than inserting it into a brief. Usually, if it's important, it can be inserted into your brief and formatted well. But if you have any sense that your reader will balk at the visual, put it at the back.
3. Use colors to show contrasts, similarities, and groupings.
4. Label everything clearly, with legends that are as simple and stylistic as your regular prose.
5. Keep it simple. Complex visuals can be harder to decipher than writing.

10.2 Design Your Documents

With the words written, it's time for the final design. From using white space to hyperlinking exhibits so they are easily within reach, there's a lot you can do to take your document to the next level.

A Quick Summary

Digitize your documents. **Use simple tools to make it easy for readers on digital devices, like tablets and computers, to navigate your documents and find useful sources.**

Design your fonts, spacing, and negative space. **Use white space and the look of your words and pages to make the best impression.**

10.2.1 Digitize Your Documents

The days of drafting dead documents are done. Legal audiences like judges and clients consistently report that they now read legal documents on digital devices. And reading digital is not like reading paper.[2] There are several things you can do to draft like a modern-day writer.

[2] Mary Beth Beazley, *Writing (and Reading) Appellate Briefs in the Digital Age*, 15 J. App. Prac. & Process 47 (2014).

First, use more headings so readers can navigate quicker. There's no need to pretend folks will be flipping through pages to get around. Make your headings self-explanatory so readers can decide where they want to go right from the table of contents.

Most legal writers file and send documents as PDFs. If that's what you'll be using, do two things: (1) make sure all the headings are hyperlinked in the table of contents, and (2) insert a *Return to TOC* hyperlink next to each heading in your document. That way readers can easily jump back to the table of contents anytime.[3]

Next, link your document up generally. This means adding links to every related document or external source that your readers might want to check out while reading your document.

There are three main links that matter: internal cross-references, exhibits, and URLs. First, like headings, you can insert internal links to any relevant part of your document. Say that you are explaining a battery claim and that one relevant point is whether the plaintiff suffered harm—and you already addressed this same point in another section covering a different claim.

You can insert an internal link (a cross-reference) in your battery section so that readers can jump back to the harm section if they want a refresher on that relevant point.

You can also link to any documents attached to your main document as an exhibit or appendix. Let's say you are writing a memo about the same battery claim and plan to attach some pictures of the medical bills to support your harm analysis. You can insert links that will bring your reader directly to those other documents.[4]

Finally, you should link your readers to any external web addresses you refer to. This is especially useful when linking to court decisions, websites, or anything else on the Internet. This way, readers can jump right to a court decision or other resource wherever you cite it in your document.[5]

10.2.2 Design Your Fonts, Spacing, and Negative Space

How the text appears on your reader's page or screen matters. Document design, white space, and typography can all reflect on your credibility. These are the silent persuaders.

Choosing the Right Fonts

When it comes to fonts, the choices you make can impact both the readability and professional appearance of your document. Your goal should be to choose fonts that make your text easy to read while reflecting the serious nature of the material.

There's a reason why some fonts are called "book-friendly"—they're easy on the eyes, especially when read over prolonged periods. This is an essential consideration when your audience is using e-readers. Fonts like Book Antiqua, Century, Garamond,

[3] If you prepare your document in Microsoft Word and set each of your headings using the Styles feature, the table of contents will automatically be hyperlinked when you export the document to PDF. Specialized document creation tools can also automate this process for you.

[4] AI-powered tools like Clearbrief even make it easy to link straight to the specific page or a highlighted portion of the exhibit. This is easiest to do by preparing all your documents or images as PDFs —because PDF editors typically offer a feature that allows you to easily link between different PDFs.

[5] Make sure to include links to free open sources (or at least to both of the two major research databases, Lexis and Westlaw).

and New Baskerville have stood the test of time and remain popular choices because of their readability and elegance.

Styling and Emphasizing Text

Italics often serve as a better tool for emphasizing case names and other critical details in your text. Unlike underlining, italics do not interfere with any descenders in the letters, ensuring that the text remains clean and clear.

Use smart quotes and apostrophes, also known as curly cues. Unlike straight quotes and apostrophes, these have a curved shape, and they enhance your text's professional look. Remember, it's often the small details that count when building credibility with readers.

A word about using all caps. Generally avoid them because it can make text more difficult to read and could give the impression of shouting. But if you need to emphasize something strongly, limit your use of all caps to a single line of text (and better yet, a single word of phrase).

Punctuation and Text Spacing

Consider joining the one-space crew if you aren't a member already. In our digital age, there's no need to use two spaces after a period, a practice inherited from the typewriter era. Modern fonts provide sufficient space after a period already. Especially when using the ones recommended above.

Kerning, the process of adjusting the spacing between characters in a proportional font, is another key aspect of document design. Turning kerning on can improve the visual harmony of your text, leading to a more polished look.

Mastering White Space

White space, or negative space, refers to the unmarked portions of a page. It's not empty space, it's a tool that can enhance your document in several ways. White space gives readers visual breaks. Consider the humble paragraph break: a single line of white space that provides a visual cue of a new thought or idea. The use of bullet points and numbered lists can also create valuable white space, breaking up long, complex passages into more manageable chunks. Likewise, headings and subheadings not only introduce white space but also provide signposts to guide the reader through your argument.

When writing for smaller digital screens, white space takes on a larger role. Limited screen space makes text denser. So use more headings, more section breaks, and more paragraph breaks.

Layout and Alignment

The layout of your document, including margins, alignment, and line length, can also affect readability. Left-aligned text is typically the easiest to read, as it maintains a consistent starting point for each line. Ensure you have ample margins. Not only do they frame your text and help guide the reader's eye, but they also provide space for readers to make notes.

On line length, keep in mind that shorter lines are generally easier to read. A good rule of thumb is to aim for 60 to 70 characters per line, including spaces. This will keep your reader's eye movement consistent. Finally, whatever design choices you make, be consistent. Random changes in font, style, or layout will be distracting.

Some More Considerations in Visual Selection

Using visuals ethically, particularly stock images and copyrighted material, is also important.

- **Avoiding misrepresentation:** Legal writers must ensure that images do not mislead or misrepresent facts or concepts. The images should be relevant and used in a context that accurately reflects the legal argument or information being presented. Manipulating graphs, charts, or images to mislead or exaggerate can not only undermine the argument but also breach ethical standards.
- **Alt text for images:** When using digital documents, provide alternative text (alt text) for images. This text should concisely describe the image's content or purpose, enabling screen readers to convey the information to visually impaired users.
- **Colorblind-friendly design:** Use color schemes in charts and graphs that are distinguishable to individuals with color vision deficiencies. Tools are available to test visuals for colorblind accessibility.

Designing your documents requires some work outside of the normal words and sentences legal writers most often focus on. But form can affect function. So your document's design is worth investing in.

Level Up Your Document Design with Technology

In constructing visuals and optimizing document design, technology is everything. Many tech tools will streamline the creation of compelling visuals, improve document navigation, and enhance readability.

GAI tools: Harness the power of GAI to enhance your document design and visualization.

- **Visual brainstorming:** Need ideas for turning data into a persuasive chart? Ask your AI tool this: "Generate five potential chart types to visualize the growth of case law citations related to [your topic]." Include sample data for even more tailored results.
- **Accessibility review:** Ensure your visuals are truly inclusive. Use prompts like "Describe this image for a visually impaired reader, focusing on elements essential to legal understanding" help you identify areas for improvement.
- **Design critique:** Get AI-powered feedback! Try this: "Analyze the typography in this brief. Suggest improvements for professionalism and readability, citing specific legal design principles."

Charts and diagrams: Gone are the days of wrestling with spreadsheets. Programs like Microsoft Excel and Google Sheets offer intuitive charting options, transforming numbers into pie charts, bar graphs, and more. Explain legal trends, damages calculations, or resource allocation with striking visuals that stick in the mind long after the words fade.

Timelines: Case chronologies can overwhelm even the most attentive judge. Specialized software like Office Timeline and Precedent bring order to chaos, creating clean, visually appealing timelines. Emphasize key dates, highlight gaps, and draw attention to key moments.

Data storytelling: Distill masses of research or statistics into infographics with platforms like Tableau. Heat maps, network diagrams, and even interactive visualizations break down complex data into easily digestible chunks, revealing patterns and insights that simple tables cannot.

Image generators: Struggling to find the perfect stock photo to illustrate a concept? AI image generators take the guesswork out of the equation. Provide descriptive text prompts and watch as these tools conjure up custom images that align perfectly with your argument's tone and message.

Infographic makers: Turn key takeaways, summaries, or processes into engaging infographics with AI assistance. These tools offer templates and design suggestions, allowing you to focus on content while the technology handles the aesthetics.

Document assembly: Streamline production of frequently used documents with platforms like HotDocs. These tools automate template creation and insertion of case-specific information, ensuring consistency while saving valuable drafting time.

Typography and layout: Take charge of your document's visual impact with Adobe InDesign. This software provides precise control over font selection, spacing, and layout, allowing you to create truly professional-looking materials for both print and digital presentations.

E-briefing software: Cases increasingly involve multimedia evidence. Tools like CaseMap and TrialDirector seamlessly integrate such evidence with your legal briefs, creating a cohesive and dynamic presentation that immerses the judge in your case.

PDF editors: Adobe Acrobat and Foxit empower you to optimize navigation within digital documents. Linking, bookmarking, and proper tagging with screen readers ensure that visually impaired readers have equal access to your persuasive arguments.

Responsive design tools: Today's legal documents must work flawlessly across devices. Adobe Dreamweaver or frameworks like Bootstrap help format text and images for optimal display, whether on a desktop monitor or a smartphone screen.

Practice these techniques and technologies with Write.law's exercises and checklists, plus other resources at www.levelupyourlegalwriting.com

11

Level Up Your Legal Documents

> “The discipline of the written word punishes both stupidity and dishonesty.” — John Steinbeck

We've covered a lot of legal writing ground: from distilling what matters to crafting the major sections of a document to elevating your style. But so far, we've explored writing techniques in isolation—in other words, we've learned about techniques on their own and not as part of a real legal document with the many moving parts they require. It's great to learn how to choose great verbs and build great sentences, but at some point, we must bring all that together into a cohesive final product. To help connect the dots, let's explore a sample legal document, section by section, with some concrete tips for incorporating the many tools we've worked through so far.

But before we do, keep in mind that although we are reviewing a specific type of litigation document here, most every legal document that analyzes legal issues is structured the same way. Each has an introduction, a fact section, a legal analysis section, and a conclusion. Whether you're writing an objective memo predicting the outcome of a lawsuit, a motion for summary judgment seeking to defeat a claim, a demand letter to an opposing party asking for a settlement, or something in between, legal analysis documents should usually proceed through the same four steps:

1. An introduction or executive summary (discussed in Chapter 6)
2. A fact section (discussed in Chapter 3)
3. A legal analysis section (discussed in Chapter 4)
4. A conclusion (discussed in Chapter 6)

Legal analysis documents tell readers everything they need to know about how the law applies to a factual situation—does a set of facts satisfy the relevant law? To get readers to that answer, legal writers provide an introduction, or executive summary; a factual background section that delivers the key factual details; a legal analysis section, where we teach readers the law and apply the law to our facts; and a conclusion that wraps it all up. So everything you learn in this chapter can be applied to any form of legal analysis document you're working on.

Following each section of our sample legal analysis, you'll find a simple list of questions that you, as a legal writer, should ask yourself as you draft. Use these or make your own to create one more powerful tool to add to your belt: a *drafting checklist*.

We talked about *editing checklists* in Chapter 8; they help you refine your prose after you've written a draft. A *drafting checklist* helps you get that draft together in the first place. Your drafting checklist should contain questions that will keep you focused on what the reader needs to know, and on your major goals for writing each section of your analysis.

These questions should be specific but straightforward. And they should focus on your reader's needs at each juncture of your document, from introduction to conclusion. Because good legal writing is usually that simple. Answer the burning questions your readers will have as they read through the document, and they will have all the answers they need to reach a decision.

The sample document we use in this chapter is a motion to dismiss. Motions to dismiss are the most common type of analysis document filed in the civil court system because they seek to dismiss a case at the initial complaint stage—before the costly process of discovery begins.

This motion was filed by lawyers representing a blood-testing laboratory in a case about unfair debt collection practices.[1] The defendant lab was sued for sending notices to consumers about unpaid bills for lab work—notices that the plaintiffs contended were illegal debt collection "threats" under the governing law. With that background, let's dive in.

11.1 Answer Readers' Questions in Introductions

We start with the all-important introduction, the linchpin of your legal writing. This is where you trot out key details that get your readers primed, win your readers' trust, and highlight the important takeaways that readers need to understand to reach a favorable decision.

[1] Technically, in some jurisdictions, the "motion" and the "legal memorandum in support of the motion" are two distinct documents. But in other jurisdictions, the terms are used interchangeably. I'm referring to a "motion" throughout this chapter, but in your court, the convention may be to call it something like a "supporting legal memoranda" or a "memorandum of points and authorities."

MEMORANDUM IN SUPPORT OF DEFENDANT PARK HEALTHCARE'S MOTION TO DISMISS

...

Introduction

The plaintiff failed to pay her bill for blood tests she received at one of Park Healthcare's labs.[2] Instead of pestering the plaintiff with collection calls,[3] Park sent a few invoices asking that she please pay.[4] In one of them, Park included a general advisory notice[5] that "if permitted by law"[6] a consumer "may also be liable for additional expenses and costs," which could "substantially increase the amount you owe." The plaintiff claims that by including this general notice in an invoice, Park "willfully" threatened her with illegal fees, a violation of the Illinois Consumer Collection Practices Act (ICCPA).

The plaintiff's claim fails for three reasons.[7] First, Illinois courts have been clear that a defendant cannot be liable under the ICCPA for informing a consumer about a valid cost.[8] And valid means what it says: That the cost can be legally charged to someone—whether a company intended to or does make the charge doesn't matter.[9] Here, the costs mentioned in the invoice were valid ones. For example, the plaintiff would be liable for court costs and interest if she continued to ignore her bill and a judgment was entered against her.[10]

But even if the Court assumes the invoice somehow misrepresented a cost,[11] the statement is not a "threat" under the ICCPA. The statute targets companies using illicit means to scare[12] consumers into paying bills; it doesn't penalize com-

[2] Orient readers from the first sentence: What led to this dispute? Why is your reader reading this document?
[3] Although it's important to open credibly, that doesn't mean you can't frame the dispute favorably. The writers insert a short context phrase here to prime readers before delivering the main point about sending invoices.
[4] Notice the simple, familiar words to build a good first impression with readers. Words like "sent" and "asking" are direct and easy, signaling a document that will be a breeze to read.
[5] This is powerful labeling: The disputed term can be called many things, but a "general advisory notice" is about as innocent-sounding as you can get. Labels can change how readers view a fact.
[6] Using surgical quotes builds credibility because they reassure readers that you are not misrepresenting the key language that forms the crux of this case.
[7] Roadmaps help readers by giving them expectations and making dense writing manageable.
[8] This introduction maps the document, offering takeaways for each of the three main arguments, spoon-feeding one at a time.
[9] Distilling what matters from the rules is often the hardest but most important content for your introduction. Because if readers view the rules in the right light, a favorable answer becomes obvious. Notice how specific this rule pitch is.
[10] After the rule pitch, the key facts will help readers see the full picture: We understand now that the costs merely need to be lawful and possible. And there are lawful costs possible here.
[11] Useful transitions tell readers how paragraphs or sentences relate to what came before.
[12] Targeted verbs persuade more than characterizations or conclusions. Framing the law as about "scaring consumers" gives you a flavor of how the law works in a way favorable to the writers.

panies for notifying someone about possible future costs (valid or not).[13] Examples of actionable threats include informing someone they "will be arrested" if they don't pay, or warning someone they "must pay or you will lose their home."[14] Park worded its invoice[15] to ensure that no reasonable consumer would feel threatened by it. Park told the plaintiff that she "may" be liable for costs and only if "permitted by law." This language is worlds away from the kinds of threats the ICCPA prohibits.

If the court disagrees on both fronts, the plaintiff also fails to meet the ICCPA's knowledge prong. Plaintiffs must allege specific facts showing that the defendant knew that the cost it threatened to impose was illegal. This means pointing to concrete facts showing that the defendant was informed that a charge was illegal—either in writing or through direct testimony.[16] When a plaintiff merely alleges that a defendant "knew" a fact, this Court routinely dismisses the claim.[17] And the plaintiff here did just that: merely alleging that Park "knew" the cost was illegal. She offers no specific facts supporting that conclusory allegation.

At bottom, the plaintiff's Complaint alleges that Park sent her invoices about an unpaid bill and accurately advised her of possible costs she could face if she ignored her bill. Park did everything it could to communicate with the plaintiff fairly.[18] The complaint should be dismissed and with prejudice.

Drafting Questions

Have I given readers enough context to welcome them in and frame the dispute favorably?

Assume your readers have no idea what this document or case is about: How can you cue readers about why this matter exists and frame the dispute favorably for your client? Here, the legal writers use a narrative opener, telling a story that makes the plaintiff sound unreasonable—she used a service, didn't pay, and is now complaining about getting an invoice that mentions everyday costs we've all probably received before.

[13] Drawing a line in the sand is a powerful persuasion tool. Here, the legal writers are saying, even invalid costs are not actionable when mentioned —without some sort of harmful threat attached. The parentheses, though, deemphasize this fact —after all, it's not a favorable one.

[14] These specific examples are the magic: They give readers a deep understanding of the concepts in a way that can convince on their face.

[15] After the key legal takeaways are laid out for this issue, the writers supported their point with the emotional: Park purposely tried to avoid alarming consumers like the plaintiff.

[16] Another nuanced takeaway on the rule that gives readers enough specifics that lead to true understanding —and thus persuasion.

[17] The writers allude to the authority confidently without drowning readers in case citations. There's plenty of time for the drudgery later. Good introductions are about making your points.

[18] Finishing with the emotional pull ensured legal-focused readers aren't turned off. The writers have already made all the legal points, so finishing with a value-based point is welcome.

Have I given readers enough information so that they have a deep sense of what matters in my document?

As you turn to the legal questions your document answers—and most important, the answers—give readers a quick but deep summary of what they need to know. That means first signposting the overarching questions your document will answer.

Have I taught readers the rules that will answer each question?

Teach your reader about the specific parts of the rule that matter so they can get to answers now without waiting to read your whole document. Be specific enough so that readers can easily discern the conclusion once they read the facts. Here, you can see the legal writers take one legal question at a time and follow a truncated version of the PPP: You're prepared for the pitch with some quick background, you're given a specific pitch for how each rule works, and the proof (the supporting authority) is weaved in by referring to the "courts" and "Illinois law."

Have I given readers the specific facts that answer their questions?

The writers dish up the key facts that satisfy (or don't satisfy) the rules, one at a time. They use specific quotes and facts so readers can trust them. What you don't see are any bare conclusions or subjective opinions. Every factual point is backed up with details.

Have I weaved in themes, policies, and values to start persuading?

If there are other policy, value, or emotional points you'd like to make, start weaving them in here at the start. And then finish with a concrete bottom line for readers. Here, the legal writers persuasively summarize the narrative again, inserting some details that make the defendant sound like it was simply trying to help the plaintiff by notifying her of a valid bill.

11.2 Answer Readers' Questions in the Fact Section

As we explored in Chapter 3, the fact section houses four main types of facts: analysis facts, context facts, emotional facts, and character facts.

The *analysis facts* are the facts that readers need to navigate the legal analysis later in the document. The *context facts* are those background details that readers need for the analysis facts to easily flow. The *emotional facts* are details you weave in for purely persuasive appeal. And *character facts* help readers get a deeper sense of the key players—the heroes and the villains and everyone in between.

Good legal writers weave these facts into a compelling narrative[19] to win the reader's empathy and capture the essential factual points they will need to make sense of the legal analysis that comes later.

[19] For a refresh on your entire menu of storytelling techniques, refer to Chapter 3.

Factual Background

Park is a healthcare company and the largest medical laboratory in the United States, with facilities nationwide.[20] The plaintiff lives in Hodor, Illinois, and received services from one of Park's Illinois labs in late January of 2017. Compl. ¶ 6. She[21] failed to pay her bill, so Park sent her invoices asking that she please pay—and that if she did not, she could incur fees for not paying her bills.[22] The fourth invoice Park received is attached to the plaintiff's complaint and forms the crux of her claim. *See* Compl. Ex. A.

A. The plaintiff received her fourth invoice, letting her know that if she didn't pay, she could face more fees and costs—which was true.[23]

The plaintiff received a fourth "Laboratory Invoice" several months after she received her lab services—which included a general notice that unpaid bills can incur additional fees. *Id.* The notice informed the plaintiff of what she owed on her bill, $229.30,[24] as well as other details like payment options and the date of service. *Id.* The notice then included a general advisory notice that if she ignored her bill, she "may also be liable for additional expenses and costs, as permitted by law, which can substantially increase the amount you owe." *Id.*

According to the plaintiff,[25] this last sentence constitutes "willful" "harass[-ment]" and "abuse" under the ICCPA, because it "claim[ed], attempt[ed], or threaten[ed] to enforce a debt when" Park knew "that the debt [was] not legitimate." *Id.* at ¶ 37. In other words, by letting plaintiff know that an unpaid bill "may" make her liable for additional expenses "if permitted by law," Park "blatantly ignore[d]" Illinois law by "threatening her" with illicit fees. *Id.* at ¶ 16.

B. The plaintiff alleges that informing her of unpaid invoices and that she could face more costs if she failed to pay them is harassment.[26]

The plaintiff's complaint alleges that Park was not "permitted by state law to charge additional expenses or costs" to collect on the plaintiff's debt. *Id.* ¶ 15. So

[20] Leading with these reputational character-building details positions Park as the hero in the story.

[21] Notice the writers choosing who should be in the subject position, the actor, based on whether the details are good or bad.

[22] Style tools control readers' attention —this em dash highlights the key factual information the legal writers wanted to focus on. She is suing over being told she could owe more if she ignored her bills.

[23] This heading not only highlights the persuasive facts, but it captures the takeaway of this group of facts.

[24] As always, specifics sell when the idea you're conveying is a favorable one. Using the modest number (a couple hundred dollars) rather than a generalization like "a modest bill" confirms for readers that this plaintiff is suing over a little more than $200 that she refused to pay.

[25] This is another great example of having a reason to slow down the main base sentence —the writers wanted to make clear what comes after is plaintiff's version of events.

[26] A great example of purposeful word location. Ending on "harassment" is forceful and focuses readers (here, on how absurd the claim sounds).

> when Park included a general notice that she may incur additional expenses if permitted by law, Plaintiff says Park was threatening her that it would charge her an illegal fee. *Id.* at ¶¶ 17, 37. But as explained next, the plaintiff was subject to a variety of lawful expenses and costs if she ignored bills that she admits were valid bills — as is true for every other lawful bill anyone receives and refuses to pay.

Drafting Questions

Have I given readers a movie trailer version of the story at the start?

Give readers your story's major scenes — the big-picture version that will make it easier for them to follow the details coming. That way readers will have a framework for all the major events and following along will be easy. And include facts that will prime readers favorably. Here, the legal writers share some reputational character details about their client — a lab offering helpful medical care across the country. Then you get the major scenes. The plaintiff received lab services, she never paid for them, and she simply received a bill.

Have I selected all the analysis, context, emotional, and storytelling facts readers need for a persuasive story?

Readers want the whole story: the setting, the characters, the buildup to key scenes, the plot. Build your storyline and work through each fact type. This document is about a simple story, but you still get to know the characters (particularly the defendant, whose reputation is bolstered). And events unfold in chronological order.

Have I leveraged the facts' details to craft a narrative?

Good legal storytellers use details to paint a picture — using tools like location, quantity, and specifics. The writers here use storytelling language (like "months later" instead of the dates), active verbs, and perspective to make the facts feel like a narrative.

Have I used headings to distill each big factual takeaway I want readers to leave the fact section with?

What are the manageable set of factual points readers need to know to tackle your analysis later? Use specific, concrete headings to distill those main takeaways for readers so they can't miss them. Here, each of the fact headings captures a snapshot of a group of facts, with persuasive details weaved in (like emphasizing that the plaintiff did not pay her bills).

Have I distilled what matters from each fact paragraph?

At the paragraph level, capture the takeaway for readers so they can quickly grasp what factual points matter without working through the paragraph for them. Here the legal writers do that well, for example, in the first paragraph: "The plaintiff received a fourth 'Laboratory Invoice' several months after she received her lab services — which included a general notice that unpaid bills can incur additional fees," captures the key specifics from the paragraph as a whole. Readers could skip the details and still get the key takeaway.

11.3 Answer Readers' Questions in the Legal Analysis Section

Now to the legal analysis section. This is where we answer the questions that brought our readers to us in the first place. In legal memos, this section is often called the "Discussion" or "Legal Analysis." In documents meant to persuade readers to reach a favorable conclusion—like motions, appellate briefs, demand letters, mediation statements, and so on—lawyers often label this section the "Argument."[27]

Whatever you call it, and whatever the document, your legal analysis should usually unfold in a similar way. Begin by deciding what major legal issues your document should focus on and the order in which to tackle those issues (as we explored in Chapters 2 and 6).

As a reminder, a legal issue can be framed as a simple question: Does a set of facts meet the requirements set by the law?

- Does a party's complaint satisfy Federal Rule of Civil Procedure 8? That is an issue.
- Does a party's failure to send a shipment on time constitute a breach of contract? That is an issue, too.

Analyze one issue at a time to keep things manageable for readers. Spoon-feed issues to readers by breaking up the legal analysis section into subsections. Generally, you should use one section or subsection for each important issue. If your document tackles three elements of a key legal doctrine, and each element is important, then you can break the analysis up into three sections.

Now for the fun part. Each section or subsection begins with a heading. We explored tactics for distilling the takeaway from each section of your analysis in Chapter 2, and we learned techniques for crafting those takeaways into effective analysis headings in Chapter 6. Strong headings convey the gist of each section while priming readers with persuasive details.

Following the heading, give readers a quick, persuasive roadmap (as we learned in Chapter 6). Then, as you dig into each section in earnest, teach the rules to your readers using the PPP framework (from Chapter 4). And then apply those rules to the relevant facts in the case (as we learned in Chapter 4 as well).

All these techniques come together to give readers a clear, organized journey through the law so that they can agree with you effortlessly.

Let's dig into the legal analysis section now (which the attorneys here label as their "Argument"). The goal with the opening sentences of our analysis section should be to orient readers to the legal issues and persuasively map out the substance of our analysis.

[27] Some legal writers use a modest label like "Analysis" even in persuasive documents such as appellate briefs —to strike a more credible tone.

Argument

The plaintiff raises a single claim in her complaint: that Park intentionally threatened to impose costs on the plaintiff that Park knew it had no legal right to collect. This claim is governed by Ill. Stat. §559.72(9), which requires that a person not "[c]laim, attempt, or threaten to enforce a debt when such person knows that the debt is not legitimate . . ." (the Intentional Threat Rule). In short, this rule prevents companies from scaring consumers into paying their bill by threatening them with illegitimate fees.[28]

A few legal principles help at the outset.[29] When evaluating ICCPA violations, courts view a defendant's statements "from the perspective of the least sophisticated consumer"—which is less forgiving than it sounds.[30] *Crawford v. LVNV Funding, LLC*, 758 F.3d 1254, 1258–59 (11th Cir. 2014). The least sophisticated consumer "possess[es] a rudimentary amount of information about the world and a willingness to read a collection notice with some care." *LeBlanc v. Unifund CCR Partners*, 601 F.3d 1185, 1194 (11th Cir. 2010). This standard "prevents liability for bizarre or idiosyncratic interpretations of collections notices by preserving a quotient of reasonableness."[31] *Id.*

All that said, Illinois courts make clear that an intentional threat claim requires the plaintiff to make several affirmative showings.

1. First, the plaintiff must show that the costs threatened were legally invalid—that there was no possible way the cost could exist.
2. Second, she must plausibly allege that the defendant made a "threat," not merely an advisement.
3. Third, she must allege specific facts plausibly showing that when the defendant made the statement, it knew that what it said was a lie.[32]

The plaintiff's Complaint fails at each step.[33]

The writers provide a roadmap of the main legal issues covered in their analysis. They share this roadmap by highlighting persuasive details that will start priming readers, too. The three numbered issues are each framed persuasively to advance the writers' goals: suggesting the notices listed only "valid" costs, that the notices didn't contain any "threats," and that the plaintiff provides no "specific facts" to support the claims.

[28] After providing readers with dense legalese, it can be helpful to reframe in simpler terms so readers don't get tripped up.

[29] Direct, simple dialogue with readers makes it easy to follow along—and engages readers.

[30] The introduction to general sections is a great housekeeping area: Address background principles, discard side issues that aren't worth your readers' time, or offer insights that will apply to everything that comes below.

[31] This sort of intellectual honesty—conceding unhelpful points but putting them into context right away—is the right approach for the unfavorable. Don't avoid the bad, but steal its power.

[32] Lists make the points easy to navigate—and easy to return to.

[33] Short sentences pack a punch. As do occasional single-sentence paragraphs like this.

Now let's move on to section A., the analysis of the first issue, beginning with the section heading, followed by the rule and application.

A. The plaintiff cannot allege that the costs mentioned in her unpaid bill were unlawful because when people fail to pay their bills in Illinois, they may owe additional fees and costs.[34]

To state a claim under Section 9, the plaintiff must allege that Park threatened a cost that was legally impossible to exist. This means the "legal status of the debt" is unlawful—and has nothing to do with the defendant's intent or whether charges were actually imposed. *Malowney v. Bush*, 2009 WL 3806161, at *6 (M.D. Ill. Nov. 12, 2009) (holding that §559.72(9) "relies on the legal status of the [threatened] debt. . . . Unlike the FDCPA, this section of the ICCPA does not address a person asserting a debt or other legal right that he does not intend to pursue").[35] Illinois law thus contrasts with the FDCPA, which allows plaintiffs to state a claim by merely alleging that a defendant threatened a charge that it did not intend to collect. *Id.*[36]

In other words, telling a consumer that they may be liable for a cost that is legally possible cannot be actionable, period. *Bentley v. Bank of America*, N.A., 773 F. Supp. 2d 1367, 1372–73 (S.D. Ill. 2011) ("To establish a violation under section 559.72(9) of the ICCPA, it must be shown that a legal right that did not exist was asserted."); *Pollock v. Bay Area Credit Serv.*, LLC, 2009 WL 2475167, at *9 (S.D. Ill. Aug. 13, 2009) (same). For example, a defendant told a homeowner that he was liable for attorney's fees and collection costs, so the homeowner sued him under Section 9.[37] *Malowney*, 2009 WL 3806161, at *6. The Southern District of Illinois dismissed the claim, pointing out that there was a legal basis for making the plaintiff liable for these costs in the future—which is all that mattered. *Id.*[38]

Even telling a consumer her employer would be contacted and her wages would be garnished is not enough.[39] A defendant sent a letter to a consumer stating that if she did not pay a bill her wages could be garnished. *Jelencovich v. Dodge Enterprises, Inc.*, 2009 WL 4899405, at *3–4 (S.D. Ill. Dec. 14, 2009). The Southern District again dismissed the plaintiff's ICCPA claim because "the correspondence [wa]s an accurate portrayal of well-established Illinois law." *Id.*

[34] Headings are a place of emphasis —words every reader will read. Framing the law as about the public weaves policy into the argument subtly.

[35] This is a great use of a parenthetical. It says nothing new, but it provides support for a key point —the rule standard that governs this first issue.

[36] Explaining contrasts and lines in the sand like this helps make the affirmative point clearer. Some states do penalize intent —but not this one.

[37] Not all the precedent's facts are marshaled out. Only the ones that help prove the rule pitch —that costs must be invalid as a matter of law to create liabilities.

[38] The legal writers continue to convey most points by building sentences around actors carrying out actions, using concrete verbs.

[39] This is an effective rule pitch because it positions the line even higher than what the writer knows his own case offers.

The plaintiff's claim thus hinges on whether she could incur additional lawful costs in the future if she failed to pay her bill. And there is no question that she could incur those costs: Illinois law imposes costs on people who owe a debt and get a judgment entered against them. There is no disputing that if the plaintiff continued to ignore her bill, she could have a judgment entered against her. As a matter of law, then, the potential costs mentioned in the invoice were accurate and the plaintiff's claim must fail.

True, the plaintiff's bill was not for much, but that does not change that she faced additional collection costs if she ignored her debt.[40] Illinois law imposes weighty[41] court costs on parties who have a judgment entered against them. Ill. Stat. §57.041. If Park recovers a judgment against the plaintiff, the company "shall recover all . . . legal costs and charges" from Park. *Id.* These taxable costs include all sorts of expenses, like filing fees, witness fees, transcript costs, and the price of a deposition.[42] Those costs could easily run up a bill exceeding what the plaintiff owed Park in the first place. Not to mention that the plaintiff would be liable for interest accruing on her unpaid debt. See Ill. State. 687.01 (discussing the rate of interest on unpaid judgments).

Park took care to tell the plaintiff that she could become liable for additional costs only if permitted under Illinois law, which was true, not that it would seek to impose illicit fees on her if she failed to pay her bill. Companies are routinely held liable under the federal law for not notifying consumers that their unpaid bills can expose them to additional liabilities. So in effect, Park could advise the plaintiff that she "may" become liable for substantial costs and expenses if she ignored her debt, or it could keep quiet at its own peril.[43]

The analysis is where all the pieces come together: You frame the issues, explain the rules that matter, and apply those rules to your case's facts.

Drafting Questions

Do my headings capture specific takeaways from each section of the analysis while being accessible enough for fresh readers?

The best headings balance priming details with self-explanatory writing.[44] Headings do no good if new readers can't make sense of them on their face. But generic conclusions won't help persuade them, either. Here, the legal writers convey the thrust of the

[40] The advanced style structure (true, but) allows the writer to concede a point to gain credibility —but immediately put it into context with better facts.

[41] Descriptors often add needless words to sentences. But occasionally they can help add nuance to a noun or verb.

[42] Stacking all these examples together in the same sentence makes them collectively feel more expansive.

[43] This is a powerful policy finisher that suggests if the legal writer's argument is denied, companies will be in an impossible position of being penalized for telling consumers about costs —and perhaps also for not telling them about costs.

[44] We dug into headings specifically in Chapters 2 and 6. But all of our good writing style techniques—from base sentences to the power of specifics—will all help you write strong headings.

section's point (that the plaintiff was merely informed of lawful costs, which are not actionable) in a single sentence. Headings are also a place of emphasis: The legal writers knew that well, using simple, familiar words and a clear base sentence to deliver the section's point.

Does the beginning of each section guide and prime readers, too?

Follow your useful headings with a welcome into the section that guides readers through what's coming, highlighting persuasive details and mapping out any complexity. Here, the writers start with some background principles and a clear explanation of the single issue tackled in this section.

Have I taught readers the rule with the PPP?

Perhaps the most challenging stage is explaining all the dense legal concepts to readers. Remember from Chapter 4 that we want to be methodical here, because rules are complicated. Prepare readers with background legal principles, pitch readers on your winning view of the rules, and then strategically prove your pitch with the authority. The rule section here starts by preparing readers for the key rule pitch with some background: "To state a claim under Section 9, the plaintiff must allege that Park threatened a cost that was legally impossible to exist." Then the legal writers deliver a few pitches, clearly articulated at the beginning of the following paragraphs.

These pitches are specific and concrete—guiding readers to the conclusions the writer is aiming at: (1) In other words, telling a consumer that they may be liable for a cost that is legally possible cannot be actionable, period. (2) Even telling a consumer her employer would be contacted and her wages would be garnished is not enough.

The second pitch is particularly powerful because it sets the rule's standard at a much higher level than the writer's own case, which will make it easy for readers to favorably apply later. Finally, the legal writers provide an array of facts, quotes, and other evidence from the supporting authority to confirm those concrete rule pitches.

Have I logically linked rules to facts?

After the rules are taught, we need to link them to our case's facts.[45] The legal writers here offer a master class in applying the rules. They start by clearly linking the rule pitches to the facts using similar language (like focusing on the "lawful" requirement). And then linking the facts to the rules—with devices like quotes from authority—so that the application seems a foregone conclusion.

Have I woven in persuasive tools like values, policies, and emotions?

Finally, these legal writers leverage the power of policy by giving readers a final nonlegal reason to agree with the analysis. This is a critical step. Give readers a reason to *want* to rule for you.[46] Here, that reason is that companies can be liable for not telling consumers about possible future costs—putting defendants and others in the hard situation of facing liability in two directions.

---

[45] We dived deep into this skill in Chapter 4.

[46] Refer to Chapter 5 if you need a refresh on persuasive devices like these.

Now let's continue with the legal analysis by looking at another section that tackles a distinct issue: whether the invoice was a "threat" under the governing rules.

B. Illinois law says a "threat" means a harassing and malicious statement — and plaintiff's invoice stating that she may owe more "if permitted by law" is not that.

Even if the plaintiff could not be liable for additional costs, the statement is still not actionable given that Park worded it to ensure that no reasonable consumer would take it as a threat.

Advising a consumer of a possible cost (even an invalid one) is not actionable — the plaintiff must allege that a reasonable consumer would perceive the statement as an actual "threat" to enforce that cost against her. *LeBlanc*, 601 F.3d at 1193 (explaining that a plaintiff must show that the defendant "actually threatened" the plaintiff).

Courts have also noted that when companies advise consumers that costs will be charged only "if permitted by law," a reasonable consumer would understand that illicit fees are not being threatened.[47] For example, a plaintiff alleged that a defendant threatened to charge her "collection costs for paying with a credit card," thus violating the FDCPA. *Bryant v. Aargon Collection Agency, Inc.*, 2017 WL 2955532, at *7–8 (S.D. Ill. June 30, 2017). But the court pointed out that what the defendant actually said was that the fee might be charged "if authorized by law." *Id.* The court concluded that the letter on its face thus did not claim to charge an illicit fee. *Id.*

Park was careful to word its invoice advisory[48] by telling consumers that they may face additional costs only "if permitted by law," ensuring that no reasonable consumer would worry that the company was threatening an illicit charge.

The plaintiff asks the Court to infer that by notifying the plaintiff that she may be liable for a cost in the future if *permitted by law*, Park was threatening that it would charge her fees in *violation of the law*.[49] That is not a reasonable interpretation for a consumer willing "to read [the] collection notice with some care." No Illinois court has ever come close to holding a company liable under Section 9 for an advisement like this.[50]

[47] This is perhaps the best rule pitch, and takeaway, in the motion. The writer suggests that including these magic words in an invoice prevents it from being a threat. That's why this point is highlighted in the first sentence and other places of emphasis.

[48] Another great example of labeling a concept persuasively — here, the portion of the invoice that is being sued over. Calling the disputed provision an "advisory" suggests it's helpful to consumers and far from a threat.

[49] Usually formatting emphasis like this isn't needed. But the one time it can help is when you want to point out a true contrast or useful comparison like this.

[50] For brevity, the final analysis subsection (analyzing the third issue road mapped earlier about the plaintiff's failure to allege specific facts) has been removed.

Drafting Questions

Have I put the information in the best real estate?

Introductions, headings, and paragraph beginnings are all places where readers pay attention.[51] So these are the places to highlight details and craft your style to make the best impressions. The legal writers here knew that well, and you'll notice their best writing is saved for these key locations. For example, the heading for this section uses surgical quotes and a well-placed em dash to hit readers with the point.

Have I distilled the takeaways for paragraphs, transitioned, and built my sentences from the base?

In the analysis, readers are trying to follow complicated legal concepts, archaic authorities, and hard-to-parse statutory language. Make it all easy by distilling each distinct takeaway for readers in the beginning of your paragraphs—as we learned in Chapter 2.

Also be mindful of transitioning as readers try to juggle everything in the analysis. Here you can see the legal writers linking the sentences with logical linking phrases like "for an example" and "but" to keep clear how each distinct point fits together. And the sentence structures are purposeful, built around the bases, which makes the writing easy to follow even at the smallest level.

Have I concluded each issue concretely?

As you wrap up each issue in your analysis, end strong. What is the clear conclusion readers should reach on the issue? Has the rule been satisfied, or not? Why?

The legal writers here emphasize the absurd-sounding theory behind the plaintiff's claim—telling someone they will be charged if "permitted by law" is somehow threatening a cost "not permitted by law." A final quote to wrap up this analysis subsection leaves readers with the impression that the plaintiff's theory clearly misses the mark.

With the analysis section done, readers have all the pieces they need to assemble the puzzle. But you have one final chance to persuade them: the document conclusion.

The document conclusion is your last chance to reiterate the specific takeaways that will help readers agree with you. As we learned in Chapter 6, many legal writers rely on formal copy-and-paste conclusions like "For the foregoing reasons, the Court should grant the motion." Don't be like those writers and throw away your final shot. Use your last moments to strike a chord.

> **Conclusion**
>
> Park's invoice to the plaintiff states the truth: Ignore a bill, face possible lawful costs.[52] These are facts, not threats.[53] Plaintiff's claim lacks concrete evidence of any intent to mislead or intimidate, as Illinois law requires.

[51] We explored tactics for crafting the beginnings in Chapter 6.
[52] This style structure is one of many that plays off the location of key words and contrasts between words to create a rhetorical effect.
[53] Short sentences make forceful points.

> Dismissal is thus required. Park's message was legal, appropriate, and devoid of coercion. Without a credible claim of wrongdoing, this case should end where it stands.

Drafting Questions

Have I left readers with a final impression of my most important points?

Finish with specific final takeaways and your best writing. Capture policy points, emotional details, and any final ideas that will leave readers with the right closing impression.

The writers here smartly curated their style, using techniques like moving strong words to the sentence ends, parallelism, and targeted verbs (all simple style techniques that we learned in Chapters 7 and 9). And they managed to capture each of the three main takeaways the document shared: (1) the costs in the notice were valid, (2) the language in the notices were not "threats," and (3) the plaintiff failed to provide the specifics that the law requires for their claim.

11.4 Design Effective Emails to Answer Legal Questions Even Faster

All of this has been great advice for long documents like memos, motions, briefs, and demand letters. But there's one final sort of writing worth mentioning: email. In today's fast-paced environment, the quality of quick written communication can be a game changer.

Effective emails go beyond conveying information; they reflect a lawyer's ability to simplify complex ideas and guide clients and colleagues to what they need. Let's look at some things you should do differently here.

A Quick Summary

Front-load your emails. **Make key components like subject lines and introductions useful. Craft your writing style so that your emails make the best impressions on readers.**

Design emails for easy navigation. **Use white space, headings, and lists to make digesting your emails easy.**

11.4.1 Front-Load Your Emails

Good emails begin with the subject line. These should offer enough information for recipients to triage and decide when to read the email (if at all). Is this an urgent task? An important one? Craft subject lines that include the matter your email relates to, how urgent it is, and a sense of what information you're conveying. A precise subject line sets the tone and expectations, like this next example does.

> Need a response by tomorrow for *Smith* case discovery deadline.

Your opening paragraph then plays a crucial role. Good email openers are a compass, guiding the reader to the heart of the message. For example, "I'm writing to update you on the latest developments in the *Smith* case, which may impact our strategy moving forward." Make sure your reader knows why you are emailing and what it's about.

When you get to the email's body, start with a quick summary of the most important takeaways. As always, leading with the most key points will do the work for readers and free them up to decide if they need to keep reading. So don't do what this next lawyer did, which is to merely share a general topics and conclusions from a long email without focusing readers on what they need to know:

> The EU has enacted a number of advertising-related laws in the past four years. These new laws address a wide variety of issues, including the format, manner, timing, and other aspects of online marketing efforts that occur within the EU. Among these are several laws regulating advertising through email. It appears that the proposed marketing program could violate several of these provisions.

Instead, deliver a few manageable takeaways for readers that will sum up the most useful information they need from the email:

> The marketing team wants to send advertising emails to potential clients in the EU and asked our team for advice about how to do so lawfully.[54]
>
> **EU law requires us to only email people who have somehow interacted with our company before, like answering a nonmarketing email, emailing or calling someone at our company, or some other communication. So we will need to ensure our advertisement emails only go to people that meet this criterion. All emails should also include a simple link or message making it easy to opt out of future emails.[55]**

Above all, remember how helpful distilling takeaways for readers is, even at the paragraph level. Don't expect readers to do all the work, like this lawyer did:

> The team has reviewed over 100,000 documents related to the Galadrial deal for our client Terry Corp. We were looking for documents that could create financial risk, specifically lawsuits and federal compliance issues. Critically, we did find a particular batch of documents suggesting that Terry Corp. was sued for failing to disclose to shareholders that one of its manufacturing centers burned down. Although that lawsuit, it turns out, is still ongoing, Terry had a slew of lawyers and firms do an analysis, and it's almost certain that the omission was not material and that Terry will succeed in defending the claim. So we don't think this lawsuit will create any risk that would jeopardize the deal.

[54] This version opens by orienting readers to what this email is about and why it's useful.

[55] Better yet if you can give readers a concrete example to make the takeaways even clearer.

Instead, do the work at the outset, distilling what they need to know first:

> **In reviewing documents for Terry's Galadrial deal, we discovered an undisclosed lawsuit—but multiple outside reviewers suggest the omission at the heart of the suit is minor and that there is no real risk to the overall deal. . . .**

11.4.2 Design Emails for Easy Navigation

Perhaps the most important email skill, though, is to use structure and white space to make your message easy to navigate on the small screens readers usually use. Use bullet points, numbered lists, and headings to break down complex information. Use shorter paragraphs and white space to help readers easily jump around.

For example, take this email sharing some research about statutes of limitations in three jurisdictions:

> I looked into the regulations in Jurisdiction A, B, and C. In Jurisdiction A, the statute of limitations is three years. Relevant here is that we may not be able to toll the limitations period, as we have been planning to do, because financial fraud cases like ours do not qualify for tolling. Jurisdiction B has a five-year statute, but it can be extended under certain conditions. There's a landmark case from 2018 that might be relevant because it required a different tolling standard going forward, and we are arguing the limitations period is tolled. Jurisdiction C doesn't have a fixed statute; it's based on the discretion of the court. We have found some similar cases to ours where the limitations period was set at five years, which is the best guidance we have.

Give some thought to how you can label or categorize dense information like this. Here, perhaps we can take one jurisdiction at a time and use headings and white space to make it easy for readers to find the different categories of useful information:

> Here is what I've found for the three jurisdictions:
>
> **Jurisdiction A:**
>
> *Statute of Limitations:* Three years.
>
> *What to know:* Financial fraud cases like ours trigger an exception that prevents tolling.
>
> *Implications:* Given our case's nature, the exception could be relevant and we may not be able to toll the period.
>
> **Jurisdiction B:**
>
> *Statute of Limitations:* Five years, with potential extensions.
>
> *What to know:* There's a landmark case from 2018 that might be relevant because it required a different tolling standard going forward, and we are arguing the limitations period is tolled.
>
> *Implications:* We need to explore the conditions for extending the statute.
>
> **Jurisdiction C:**
>
> *Statute of Limitations*: Discretionary, determined by the court.
>
> *What to know:* We have found some similar cases to ours where the limitation period was set at five years, which is the best guidance we have.

> *Implications:* We won't know for sure what limitations period applies here, although five years is most likely.

A bit easier to digest, right?

Also make sure that any outside references are easy for your recipients to find. Attach relevant cases or documents directly to your messages. And why just mention a case? Highlight the golden nugget within that 50-page opinion. At least give readers those handy page and paragraph numbers so they can instantly zero in.

Taking the extra time to organize and make your points more digestible in quick emails will make a big impression on readers.

Level Up Your Documents with Technology

Bringing together all your writing techniques into a single, cohesive document means wrangling a whole lot of techniques into a polished final product. Let's look at some simple technology tools that can level up your writing at the document level.

GAI tools: GAI can help you brainstorm and organize each section of your document, it can assist with drafting the text in each section, and then it can help you wordsmith the final product. But keep in mind that—as we discuss more in Chapter 13—the more you throw at GAI at the same time, the harder time it will have keeping up.

So avoid asking a GAI tool to do too much all at once in your document. Work on one goal at a time. After that goal is complete, use the results of your collaboration with the GAI tool on another task. For example:

- "Here are my notes for a motion to dismiss I'm working on. Review them and propose the most effective order of main points for my analysis section."
- "Now that I've outlined the order of my main points, let's take the first one and work on crafting a persuasive heading. Here are my notes from this particular section. . . ."
- "Now that we've written this section's heading, let's work on turning my notes into coherent paragraphs."

Another great use of GAI at the document level is critical feedback. Ask your favorite GAI product to take on the role of an opposing attorney and critique your arguments, your factual story, or any other part of your document:

"You're federal appellate judge in the Second Circuit. Review my argument below and critique it. What questions would you still have after reading my argument? What are the strongest counterpoints?"

Finally, when you've got your document mostly drafted, use GAI tools to help make your writing more cohesive so that the sections and points all work together better: "Review my motion for summary judgment below. Provide at least five examples of places I could work in my theme better."

Document template tools: These tools help you create and organize document templates so that you can easily reuse your prior work in the future. Microsoft Word, for example, offers a feature to save any document in a template format, making it easy to apply your preferred formatting and other aspects to a new document with a single click.

Checklist apps: There's a lot to keep track of when drafting and refining each section of your document. Consider using a digital checklist app to keep track of each question you want to answer in each section of your document.

Process and workflow apps: These tools make it easy to not only create checklists, but also to keep handy different resources or references at each stage of your writing process. Process Street is a popular general workflow tool. And several workflow tools have also been recently launched for legal work specifically.

Practice these techniques and technologies with Write.law's exercises and checklists, plus other resources at www.levelupyourlegalwriting.com

ASPEN PUBLISHING | write.law

12

Level Up Your Writing Process

> "Excellence is a continuous process and not an accident."—A. P. J. Abdul Kalam

Sure, if you had years to write your legal documents, they would all be amazing. But we legal writers don't have years to write documents. We have weeks. Or days. Or hours.

To juggle all your writing goals, take a note from other industries that must balance quality with limited resources: Use process improvement. *Process improvement* means keeping track of the steps you use to tackle complex tasks like legal writing and reflecting on how to improve those steps. If you're familiar with process-improvement methods like lean, agile, Six Sigma, or design thinking,[1] they are what this is about: breaking down a process into steps and regularly improving those steps for better results.

If you're thinking "I'm not a process person," think again. You already use processes to research the law, assemble the components of your drafts, and much more. But the question is whether you are in control of that process—and whether it works as well as it could. If you leave your writing process to chance, you'll likely skip important steps, skirt important goals, and end up with a lot of inefficiency.

To see why legal writing requires a purposeful process, consider one small task: Managing legal citations in a trial motion. To do this right, you must:

- Check citation formatting.
- Check that citations cite the correct sources.
- Check that the citation truly serves your goals: Is it in your jurisdiction? Does anything in it hurt your client's position? Is it still good law?

[1] If you're unfamiliar with these process methodologies, they are excellent frameworks for legal writers, too. Use your favorite GAI tool to explore how these different approaches can help you rethink your processes. *See Six Sigma, Lean, and Agile: Understanding the Connection and Benefitting from It*, ISSP, https://isssp.org/six-sigma-lean-and-agile-understanding-the-connection-and-benefitting-from-it.

This list is just a fraction of what a real citation checklist might look like. Depending on your practice, the steps for a citation process can span a page or more. And each of them matter. What happens if you forget to check a citation's accuracy? Perhaps your judge chooses that citation to look up, and you lose the motion.

Invest in your processes by taking stock of the steps you need to take for each writing task, and then explore ways to improve each of those steps. This is particularly important when it comes to legal writing technology, because these tools can be more hassle than they are worth if not used at the right time and in the right ways.

As we dig into improving your process in this chapter, keep in mind that no process is perfect, because you should constantly adjust for different types of writing projects and your individual goals. But rest assured, any time spent improving your process will pay off.

To develop your own purposeful writing process, it helps to start with a model process that great legal writers use.[2] That is the focus of this chapter. In working through this model process, consider which steps you think are most useful to adopt yourself. Take what you believe is useful and weave in additional steps that you think are more appropriate for the type of writing you do. Because let's be clear, your process is your own. Don't feel like you must adopt every aspect of this model just because it works for other great legal writers.

Let's review the major steps of this model process before we dive in.

A Quick Summary

Make a plan. Ask questions, gather resources, and ensure you know precisely what answers your document must provide.

Take stock of the facts. Get a handle on the key facts to guide you as research.

Develop your rule pitch. Research the best authorities to plot a winning journey through the law.

Think through your draft. Spend time thinking and planning to ensure you develop your ideas before writing too much.

Get words on the page. Start drafting the substance. Avoid self-editing so you can focus on the big takeaways.

Edit, proofread, and finalize. Edit with purpose, in phases, and with a checklist in hand. Spend separate time searching for mistakes and finalizing your document.

[2] I developed this process after interviewing hundreds of great legal writers over the last decade. It's an amalgamation of the common steps legal writers use to thoughtfully break down their process.

As we work through each step, remember that there is no perfect process. There's only a perfect process for you. So adjust to your taste.

12.1 Make a Plan

As with many important tasks, the first step may be the most important. This is where you make sure you understand what questions you need to answer in the first place. If you invest time upfront to ask questions and set goals, your research and writing will be exponentially easier.

12.1.1. Gather Your Starting Resources

Gather all the information you can before diving into the research. Review any relevant documents (Were you emailed some facts? References? Notes?). Make sure to ask lots of questions to whoever gave you the project. Here's a list of some you might want to consider.

- **What will your audience do with this information?** For example, is this for an email update to the client? Will your document be incorporated into a filing before the court? The difference matters because your writing style and what information you include may change depending on what your work product will ultimately be used for.
- **How much time should you spend on this project?** Sometimes colleagues or clients want you to spend 40 hours and dive down every hole; other times they want you to spend two hours turning up only the obvious rules and cases.
- **How much information do they want?** This can be a critical question. If you write a 50-page treatise, but your audience only wants a few-page summary, you could be in trouble.
- **When do they want it?** This is important to know because research and writing can take a long time. And you must be sure you plan your time to account for any deadlines.
- **What, exactly, are the questions you should answer?** The more specific, the better. We will talk more about these questions in a moment, but these questions will guide every aspect of your research and writing.
- **Are there any helpful places to start or any resources to get started?** Maybe someone else has already researched this topic or a similar one. If you've prepared this sort of document before, is there a template you can start with to jumpstart formatting and organization? Have you ever researched similar issues, so that your prior notes may help? Does your organization have a knowledge management system that organizes work product from others that you can use as templates or starting resources? If so, those resources could save valuable time. So don't hesitate to ask or look.

Along with getting those answers, ensure you have key information about the matter that could affect how and what you write, like:

- Who are the parties?
- What do you already know about the law?
- What relief is being asked for?

- What jurisdiction's law will be primary authority for this issue?
- Are there any other jurisdictions that may be particularly persuasive?

12.1.2 Focus on Precise Writing Goals

In this initial phase, one of the best steps to consider is writing out the specific questions your legal document needs to answer. This will ensure you won't waste hours researching and writing about issues that aren't valuable to readers.

Say your client's child was injured in a car accident caused by a negligent driver. The claim is for negligence and hinges on whether the other driver was paying attention when he slammed into your client's car. A colleague on the case with you is meeting with the client and needs to know which statute of limitations applies—in other words, what the deadline is to file a case after the original accident.

In writing out the questions you need to answer, be careful to limit yourself to the *statute of limitations*. If you start researching and writing about negligence in general, you'll waste everyone's time. This might sound simple, but even experienced attorneys get off course like this.

So your writing plan could start with this question: *What statute of limitations applies to a negligence claim in this state?* We'll build on this question later after we've gathered some initial facts and research.

12.2 Take Stock of the Facts

You've asked all the right questions and set goals for your document. You're ready to start mastering the facts.

Facts come in many forms. You might be given notes from an initial client meeting. Or you might be given a quick oral rundown from a colleague. Be careful to track all these facts, whatever the source. If you misunderstand a fact at this initial stage, it can taint the research process you're about to embark on.

There's no wrong way to gather and parse the facts, but here are two tips that work for any legal document.

First, write down the key facts that you think matter most. Use common sense at this stage. What facts seem unusual or important? What facts did others on your team highlight? Don't eliminate your other facts—because you haven't dived into the research yet, you can't be sure which facts matter. But inventorying your key facts now will help guide your initial research.

Second, draw a timeline of key events. Getting a high-level view of the chronology can help you wrap your head around a fact scenario. So if it makes sense for your document, plot out a timeline.

In the end, you're looking to make a workable list of the crucial facts so that you can find the most relevant cases and authorities. If you rush into the research, you'll likely miss quite a bit of useful things that this prework with the facts would have prevented.

12.3 Develop Your Rule Pitch

Now it's time to find all the authority you need to teach the rules to your readers effectively. We'll start with those first research steps then move on to developing the final rule pitches that will win the day.

Don't start scouring cases yet. Take the time to write down key search terms for your research first. Search terms are the words or phrases you think will be most helpful when searching through digital repositories like those offered by Westlaw or Lexis. With new GAI tools and algorithms, you might be tempted to skip search terms. The truth is, it's up to you. But you'll usually find that time spent coming up with search terms serves you either way, because search terms help you narrow in on what exactly you're looking for and how to tell when you find it.

Here are ideas for creating an initial search term list.

- Review everything you already know about the issue. Go back through all your notes from the first two steps. Think about the parties, where things happened, who else was involved, and anything you know about the law that might apply to your case's facts. Useful search terms could include potential claims and defenses and relief sought.
- Peek at secondary sources. If you don't know a lot about the area of law you need to research, check a secondary source. This can be helpful in learning the terms used to describe your research topic. Try a legal dictionary if you come across language you don't understand.
- Find a first statute or case that is on point. You might learn key terms by finding a good case or statute at the outset that addresses your legal question.

With the preliminary work done, you're ready to start finding the authority you need. But legal research can quickly become overwhelming, so let's break down this task into more steps.

First, it can help to sketch out the basic law at this point—to help you more efficiently dive into the deep research. Take the facts and general rules you've gathered and your initial research—then sketch out the key rules. Doing this visually can help. Let's start with your first question: Did the statute of limitations run on the negligence claim here?

Write out the rules that, at this point, you think will govern this question:

> The statute of limitations in Nevada is two years. It starts when the plaintiff knew or should have known the claim existed. Whether the person knew or should have known turns on the circumstances of the case.

This is probably about as deep as you can get at this stage. You will need to dive deeply into the research to get the specific answers you need: "What does it mean to 'know or should have known that a claim existed?'" And more important, "Do the facts in your case meet this standard?"

After you've created your high-level map of the law, you might find that some of your earlier assumptions were wrong and that facts you thought were important are not. At the same time, you might discover that facts you thought were unimportant actually matter.

So return to your facts and update your notes after you've completed an initial foray into the legal research. Ask yourself:

- Are there more key facts to add to your list?
- Does the law suggest any missing facts are important? If so, you might need to track more down.
- Can you make your research questions more specific now that you understand how the relevant law works?

Now that you've refined your research questions and gathered any other facts you need, you're ready to dive into the legal research again.

But now the excitement begins. You've equipped yourself to be surgical and find precisely what you need to develop your rule pitch. Now you'll want to use all your research resources, like citators and AI-fueled research features, to find the authorities you need to convince readers. Above all, your goal here is to find authority (cases, statutes, or regulations) that will allow you to answer the legal questions you fleshed out in the prior steps.

Remember that you might not find that perfect answer. If it were that easy, we wouldn't need lawyers. Instead, you'll be absorbing the facts, language, and details from similar cases and authorities—and drawing on them to interpret the law and predict how it will apply to your facts. Then, you'll package that understanding up in your rule prep, pitch, and proof like we worked through in Chapter 4.

A common struggle here is "How do I know when to stop researching?" You will never know that you've found every helpful piece of authority. Two yardsticks can help, though. First, the traditional advice is that if you keep coming across the same authority, over and over, and from different search paths, you've probably done a good job finding the best authority.

Second, consider whether the legal issue you're pinning down is an important one. If it's a smaller or tangential issue, you might want to spend less time there so you can prioritize the biggest issues. In practice, we often only have so much time to spend researching, so focus that time where it counts. In fact, it might help to give yourself a specific amount of time to research—and then cut yourself off once you hit that threshold.

When you make it this far, you have the understanding to write a winning document. Now it's time to put the pieces together.

12.4 Think Through Your Draft

We've all been there, staring at that blank page. We've got something to say and now we just need to say it! It's not your fault. There's a lot of psychology behind the terror of the blank page. But there's good news, too.

Most important, know that embracing that delay often leads to better writing. That is, assuming you're using that time to think through your draft. Studies show that folks who noodle longer about what they want to write produce stronger work product. So rather than beat yourself up over not getting more words on the page, spend time thinking more. You'll end up with something better.

Let's explore ways to use that prewriting time productively and develop better content, organization, and refinement. Each approach has been developed after working with attorneys trying to stare down that empty page.

12.4.1. The Brass Tacks

One of the simplest ways to outline is to condense your entire document into your takeaways, the brass tacks.[3] What are the one, two, or three essential points you want your

[3] No one knows exactly where this old term comes from, although theories abound. But it's probably stuck around so long because the consonance (both *brass* and *tacks* end in an *s* and have the same *a* sound) and balance.

reader to grasp? You should aim for a few paragraphs at most. With these anchoring sentences in front of you, you'll find it easier to assemble the supporting pieces.

Another advantage of the brass tacks is you can give some thought to organization while things are still simple. What order will make it easiest for readers to take in these three to four main takeaways?

12.4.2. The Sales Pitch

Another way to get writing is to come up with a sales pitch. Aim to create one—yes just one—paragraph that sells the most sizzling parts of your document. Think of it as your elevator pitch. Bonus points if you talk it out with a friend before writing your paragraph.

If you had to explain to your friend what the purpose of this document is, what would you say? It turns out that forcing ourselves to explain to someone else can help clear the clouds. Speaking it out is more natural than writing it out. You'll find yourself focusing on the most moving points, which your readers will want, too.

12.4.3. The Reconnaissance

Another easy way to start outlining is to read similar work that others have done. Writing a brief to exclude an expert witness in a copyright case? Spend a few hours reading briefs others have written on the same topic. Make sure you have a notepad handy. You'll be amazed at how the ideas start taking shape. After all, in writing, nothing is new.

12.4.4. Embrace Your Brain

Brainstorming and outlining are personal. Plenty of folks have studied this stuff, and there is no perfect way to formulate your thoughts. Great writers do it in all the ways already mentioned, and other ways, too. What you must do, though, is give yourself time to think and outline so that you explore different ideas before you commit to them.

Love whiteboards? Sticky notes? Free writing? Long conversations on a walk? Planning what will go in each paragraph? Relating all your points to your dog? All can work if they work for you.

12.5 Get Words on the Page

With your outline complete, it's time to start on the dreaded first draft. But don't fear, you can learn to love them.

I recommend trying the "extra-rough" draft technique; that is, vomit the words on the page with no regrets. Cognitive science tells us we cannot juggle much at once. So better to focus on your message and return later to fine-tune the style. This will ensure you produce the highest quality content you can, rather than dividing your attention. Remind yourself: The first time is about getting good ideas on the page—not writing perfect prose.

When drafting, the key is to have a starting strategy for each piece of real estate. What are your concrete goals for your introduction? For your fact section? Your analysis? Your conclusion? What should be your starting goals for crafting a good heading? Or first sentences of sections?

Most legal writers agonize about these decisions in every brief. They vacillate about what should go where and how to get the foundations of each section built.

But you won't have that problem. Because several chapters of this book are entirely about what to include in these major pieces of your document, and Chapter 11 offered a detailed walkthrough of each section. To make it easy, again, make a checklist of what you want to hit in each part of your document. Better yet, include the questions you should answer for readers at each juncture. You'll find that the drafting process goes quicker with a reminder of what should be in each section, and, most important, you'll stay focused on your readers. And that is gold.[4]

This strategy has worked for some of the most successful legal writers in the world. Take introductions, perhaps the most important section. This might be your checklist of questions to answer when writing:

- Why was there even a lawsuit and who are the parties?
- What is a persuasive way readers can view the dispute at a high level?
- What are the main issues (legal questions the court must answer to get to your conclusion) that matter in this document?
- Take one key issue at a time and answer: How does the rule work for this issue (in a way that will make sense and drive readers to the goal you want)?
- How do the specific facts here align with your rule pitch on the first issue?
- Why should your reader agree with you emotionally or pragmatically?
- What is the ultimate conclusion your reader should reach?

By giving yourself a list of concrete questions to answer in each section of your document, you can focus on answering them (which is all readers want). Fill in the information and you're nearly to the finish line.[5]

12.6 Edit, Proofread, and Finalize

Next you must edit with purpose. We explored tactics for editing earlier in this book—most important, the power of using phase editing and checklists to take control over how you hone your prose. So get a process and stick to it.

As a reminder from Chapter 8, your editing checklist should incorporate the specific improvements you want to see in your writing—broken up into categories so that you can focus on a few related goals during each editing round.

Finally, don't shirk your postwriting process. First up is proofreading. Again, this is not editing. Editing is about improving your writing decisions after you've churned out a draft—cutting clutter, replacing poor word choice, and shoring up weaknesses. Proofreading should be your final step and is about looking for mistakes like misspellings, formatting errors, problematic citations, grammar mishaps, and so on.

Like editing, you should have a proofreading checklist to work through. Customize your checklist over time based on the common mistakes in your writing. Legal writers can be sunk by typos, which can damage credibility and result in big client problems.

Next, as part of your proofreading step or otherwise, ensure that your document adheres to any required formatting or preferences from your audience. For litigation

[4] Check out the example document in Chapter 11 for key questions to ask yourself in each major section.

[5] Of course, you'll want a different drafting checklist for each type of document you write. Opinion emails to clients will have different components than a motion for summary judgment.

documents, this means checking local rules, your judge's standing orders, and any other requirements like word limits, page limits, required certifications, formatting requirements like typeface and size, and so on. When writing for clients or others, you should focus on whether your audience has any formatting or other preferences you can adhere to (like the format of the opening page of a memo).

If you're preparing a document with attachments, like exhibits or supporting declarations, set aside a lot of time for this part of the process. Ensure you attach the right documents, clearly label each of them, and that any references in your main document (like a motion, memo, or brief) have clear and correct citations to the attachments.

Finally, when you've proofed your document, checked any formatting or other requirements and preferences, and prepared accompanying documents like exhibits and declarations—make sure to file or store your document smartly. You'll often want to reuse documents, or portions of documents, so make sure you file away your projects using a system that will make them easy to find later.

12.7 Improving Your Process Over Time

We've now worked through a model process, so how do you start improving your own? You might want to begin by mapping out your own existing writing workflow and then decide which parts of the model you want to incorporate.

Chart every step of your writing process, from when you first start planning and researching your writing projects to completion.[6] Do this for each type of document you produce—a motion won't follow the same path as a demand letter. To make it easy, there are apps that will track your work each day—even breaking down which tools you were using and when.[7] These tools can give you insights into what you actually do when you sit down and write (because most legal writers don't know).

Once you have the steps down, identify which ones you might want to expand or swap with parts of the model process we just worked through. Adjust your process using the model as a template. And you'll want to write this all down into a process checklist to make it easy to refer to when you're working on writing projects in the future.

With your process checklist in front of you, it's time to improve. Because the model process we looked at earlier isn't built for your precise habits and practices. So consider how you can improve any steps in your new process.

Focus on what matters. What steps do you dread? What steps are slowing you down? Then you can start exploring improvements for each.

- Are there technology tools that could help automate annoying repetitive tasks?
- Are there steps you should delegate to others or at least have someone else review?
- Are there better ways to organize your templates or source materials to be more efficient in the future?

[6] For example, Process Street can easily keep track of even the most complicated processes as you map yours out. Other process or workflow apps can help as well.

[7] For example, Rescue Time keeps track of every app you use on your devices and how long you work on each. It even gathers data about what you're doing on each. Similar time-tracking apps are becoming more popular every day.

Say you write a lot of summary judgment motions. You realize that the factual citations to "undisputed facts" take a long time in every case, and you often end up with mistakes even after checking them several times. Most folks would just keep doing it the same way. But if you break down your process, you can ask, "Is there a better way?"

A quick online search reveals tools that automatically link citations from supporting documents. They even update when content is moved around.[8] Worth the investment, right? So you spend a little time learning the tool, perhaps using a GAI product to help explain it to you, or the product's documentation. And you write down in your process checklist some reminders to use the tool when you get to this step in your next summary judgment project. Process improvement can be that simple.

Again, there is no perfect writing process. Track the steps you take to complete your writing projects. Invest some time in improving these steps. Then regularly revisit and keep improving your process, so you never stop getting better.

Level Up Your Process with Technology

The final step to creating the perfect writing process is to use technology to streamline each previous step. Don't think about technology as something separate you need to use or manage. Instead, consider how you can team up with technology at each step. We've already covered a slew of tech tools in this book, so this list mentions some tools you should consider at each stage. When gathering information and resources and researching, useful tools include:

- Knowledge management apps.
- Client relations management tools.
- Project management apps.
- Process management and task apps.
- Collaboration tools.
- GAI.

When working on your fact section, consider:

- Factual research tools.
- Timeline apps.
- Case, project, and information management tools to organize all your facts and documents.
- GAI.

When diving into the hard legal research, consider:

- Document analyzers.
- AI-powered search tools.
- Litigation analytics tools.

[8] For example, Clearbrief creates auto-updating factual citations and even proposes new citations from your sources.

- Internal legal research libraries.
- Other legal research tools like visual research providers.
- GAI.

When outlining your draft, consider:

- Brainstorming apps.
- Visual planning apps.
- Outlining apps.
- Project management tools.
- GAI.

When you're writing your draft, consider:

- Checklist apps.
- Process apps.
- Project management apps.
- GAI.

When editing, consider:

- Style editing apps.
- Research linking and citation apps.
- Document comparison tools.
- Collaboration tools.
- AI-enhanced editing apps.
- GAI.

Practice these techniques and technologies with Write.law's exercises and checklists, plus other resources at www.levelupyourlegalwriting.com

13

Level Up with Generative AI

> Any sufficiently advanced technology is indistinguishable from magic."—Arthur C. Clarke

Legal writing is evolving. What used to take hours of manual research, drafting, and editing now takes moments with the right technology. And at the heart of this transformation is an innovation shaping the future of legal practice altogether: generative AI (GAI).

GAI tools like ChatGPT, Claude, and Gemini mark a new era in legal technology. The brain behind OpenAI's groundbreaking ChatGPT contained 175 billion artificial neurons when it launched widely to the public. That brain was trained on 500 billion pieces of text gathered on the web. All that data and computing power makes for the smartest publicly available AI ever before. And this technology will keep getting smarter now that the GAI arms race has begun.

GAI opens exciting new possibilities for legal writers. And this is no longer a story about what to expect in five or ten years. The technology is *here*. You can use GAI to refine a legal sentence in dozens of ways. You can use it to credibly summarize pages of legal text in seconds. In other words, GAI can do many useful things that will save you time and help you do better work for clients and colleagues.

In this chapter, we'll cover:

- **Understanding how GAI tools work and their strengths and weaknesses.** GAI tools are not for every writing project or every step in your process. But used for the right purposes at the right times, this technology can transform how you do legal writing.
- **Navigating the ethical and practical pitfalls.** This is cutting-edge technology that evolves nearly every day. If you plan to use it, you must keep up on the minefield of ethical and practical pitfalls.

- **Learning prompt engineering.** Using best practices when working with GAI tools will transform the quality of your results. The skill of working with GAI—instructing, guiding, and providing feedback—will pay off for years to come.

Before we dive in, let me share an example of what a powerful legal writing collaborator GAI can be. My team at Write.law has used GAI on thousands of documents written by some of the world's best lawyers. In nearly every one, GAI suggested useful improvements.

You know what I think of Justice Elena Kagan's writing. She has been with us on this writing journey from the first chapter. And I asked GAI to see what it thought of her writing. With some gentle guidance you'll learn how to do in this chapter, GAI had a lot to say about the Justice's excellent opinion in *Badgerow v. Walters*. We gave GAI the introduction:

> This case grows out of the arbitration of an employment dispute. Petitioner Denise Badgerow worked as a financial advisor for REJ Properties, a firm run by respondents Greg Walters, Thomas Meyer, and Ray Trosclair.[] Badgerow's contract required her to bring claims arising out of her employment to arbitration, rather than to court. So when she was (in her view, improperly) fired, she initiated an arbitration action against Walters, alleging unlawful termination under both federal and state law. The arbitrators sided with Walters, dismissing Badgerow's claims.
>
> Believing that fraud had tainted the arbitration proceeding, Badgerow sued Walters in Louisiana state court to vacate the arbitral decision. Walters responded by removing the case to Federal District Court—and, once there, applying to confirm the arbitral award.

GAI offered some pointed suggestions:

- Replace: "This case **grows out of the arbitration of an employment dispute**" with the more concise "This case **stems from an employment arbitration**."
- Replace: "Badgerow's contract required her to **bring claims arising out of her employment** to arbitration, **rather than to court**" with the snappier "Badgerow's contract required her to **arbitrate employment claims, not file lawsuits.**"
- Replace: "So when she **was (in her view, improperly) fired**, she initiated an arbitration **action** against Walters" with the tighter "So when she **felt she was wrongly fired**, she initiated an **arbitration against** Walters."
- Replace: "**Believing that** fraud had tainted the **arbitration proceeding**, Badgerow sued Walters in Louisiana state court to **vacate** the arbitral decision" with the more concise and targeted: "**Convinced that** fraud tainted the **arbitration**, Badgerow sued Walters in Louisiana state court to **undo** the arbitral decision."

Whether you agree with all these suggestions or not, at least a couple were probably improvements. And if GAI can offer even tiny ideas for the best legal writers in the world, it's a tool worth understanding.

13.1 Understand How GAI Works

Modern GAI relies on large language models and natural language processing. These AI advancements allow technology to understand and generate human-like text. The main GAI models, known as foundation models, are created by various companies and organizations. OpenAI, for example, developed the GPT models that power the popular ChatGPT tool. The GAI landscape is complex, as companies often license these foundation models for use in a wide range of products.

Imagine a GAI foundation model as a prodigy who has devoured libraries of text. Give it a task, a bit of your writing, and it will generate answers, rewrite your work, and complete a wide range of language-based tasks.

The way you usually interact with GAI is by providing instructions or text for the tool to work with. This is called *prompt engineering*: The "prompt" is your instructions and the "engineering" means you are tweaking those instructions to get the best results. But there's a lot more to know about GAI, so let's dive in.

A Quick Summary

Understand GAI's mind. **The first step to using GAI is getting a sense for how it works under the hood. Learn the basics so you're in the driver's seat.**

Understand what's possible. **Understand what GAI tools can do for your legal writing and practice, and what they can't do.**

Understand GAI's strengths and weaknesses. **GAI is not good at everything. It has strengths and weaknesses, like any tool.**

13.1.1. Understand GAI's Mind

Groundbreaking foundation models like OpenAI's GPT rely on the recent innovation of *transformer* architecture.[1] First introduced in 2017, transformers revolutionized how language models process human language, enabling GAI to generate its own remarkably human-like text. The key lies in a concept called "self-attention," which allows GAI to grasp the relationships between words much like we do. These models further hone their skills by training on massive data sets, mastering grammar, writing styles, and even problem solving.

GAI models work by coming up with *probabilities* for the best words to put into a response. It's easiest to understand if we walk through a quick example. Let's say you type into a GAI tool:

> What are the consequences of copyright infringement?

First, the GAI "tokenizes" the text you type in, which means it chops up your text into smaller pieces, or tokens, that are easier for the technology to work with. For example,

[1] Partha Pratim Ray, *ChatGPT: A comprehensive review on background, applications, key challenges, bias, ethics, limitations and future scope*, in Internet of Things and Cyber-Physical Systems, Volume 3 (2023).

the GAI might break this sentence up into: ["What" "are" "the" "consequences" "of" "copy" "right" "infringement" "?"].[2]

Next, the text we typed in (now tokenized) enters the transformer. The text passes through layers of analysis, and each layer refines the GAI's understanding of the text's meaning and word relationships. These layers give GAI a sense of which words in your input are most important and the relationship between them.

One layer might highlight the importance of the word "consequences." Another might recognize a strong connection between that word and "copyright infringement," signaling the core topic of the text.

As the transformer analyzes your input, the decoder (the response-generating part of the GAI) begins predicting the best words to form an answer. The decoder draws on the transformer's insights and its own vast knowledge of language to calculate these probabilities.

Based on everything it's learned, the GAI starts crafting its text, selecting words with the highest likelihood of forming a good response. These probabilities are based on what the GAI learned in digesting the billions and billions of sentences it was trained on. In our example, words like "penalties," "fines," and "damages" would likely rank high due to their association with "consequences" in a legal setting.

Now the model is ready to give us its response. The GAI selects each word in its response based on the probabilities it generated. Let's say it chooses "The" first because it had a 60 percent probability of being the most relevant way to start a sentence, which was a much higher probability than any other token.

The chosen token is added to the response: ["The"]. The GAI repeats the process to predict the next word in its response. Now, words like "consequences" or "penalties" could have higher probabilities, as they logically follow "The" within the context of our original question.

As the response develops, the GAI continually refines its word choices. It analyzes the growing response alongside your input to guide its predictions. For example, after generating ["The consequences of copyright infringement may include . . ."], the GAI might prioritize words like "fines," "damages," "injunctions," or "criminal."

We now have our final response:

> The consequences of copyright infringement may include fines, damages, injunctions, and even criminal charges in some cases.

GAI models are commonly used in two distinct ways. First, there's the chatbot experience. Think of tools like ChatGPT, Claude, Gemini, Microsoft CoPilot, or Westlaw AI: You directly interact with the model, submitting a question or some text, and these tools generate a response.

Second, GAI can power other software behind the scenes, automating tasks, enhancing searches, and much more. So you might not even realize you are using GAI when you use it.

This chapter focuses on GAI chatbots, but there's another key distinction to make. Nonspecialized chatbots (like ChatGPT) draw from broad, general knowledge. They're

[2] Technically, the tokens are converted into digital data, called embeddings, which capture their meanings and relationships in a way that computers can process faster.

versatile but might not always be accurate for specialized tasks like legal research. Specialized chatbots (like Westlaw AI) work with particular data and are designed for specific uses. These tend to be more reliable for their designed purpose.

Finally, GAI tools can be either cloud-based, meaning your instructions and responses are processed on remote servers, or local, with everything processed on a device owned by you or your organization.

13.1.2. Understand What's Possible

The possibilities unlocked by GAI are mind-boggling, and they're only expanding. It's almost silly to document the possibilities in a book because new ones emerge every day. But beyond directly editing or drafting your legal writing (our focus in this chapter), GAI-powered tools can:

- Enhance your existing legal tech. Nearly all popular platforms are integrating GAI. Think of Westlaw's tool that drafts case summaries for you.
- Analyze data for insights. Upload a spreadsheet and ask, "What trends might help my case?" Extract key takeaways or writing preferences from a court decision.
- Automate everyday tasks. Seamlessly connect email, spreadsheets, cloud storage, and more.
- Provide tech support. Get quick explanations of how something works or setup assistance.
- Build new tech. Describe the app you want, and GAI can collaborate with you to develop it.

The possibilities for GAI on its own or along with other tools are nearly limitless. This is even more reason to practice with these tools as much as you can—and stay abreast of new developments that may impact your practice.

13.1.3. Understand GAI's Strengths and Weaknesses

GAI sometimes gets legal questions wrong—but that often stems from misunderstanding how these AI tools think. Language models use thinking processes that don't always line up with how we humans think. So to get the best results, we need to adjust our approach.

GAI tools excel at creativity, like devising stories or a poem about your dog. GAI doesn't always understand that you want it to tell the truth. Or that it should tell you if it doesn't know an answer. But this shouldn't be a surprise. Tools like ChatGPT are designed to do a lot of things, so left to their own devices, who knows what answers you'll get?

Using a GAI to help with your legal writing is about understanding what the tools are good at by default—and then learning how to guide the GAI's brain so that it understands what you want from it. What's amazing is that you can guide a GAI tool almost like a human, using natural language and simple instructions—and having a conversation about what it's getting right or not so right.

GAI tools can best enhance your legal writing, often without much guidance, in the following ways

- Improve your writing style. This is one of the easiest ways to start using GAI. You don't need GAI to know the right answer or perform complex analysis. You're leveraging something it's great at: Using its language insights to come up with different ways to approach your writing. Have GAI rewrite legalese into readable plain language. Or use it to brainstorm different ways to write a sentence that subtly primes readers.

- Summarize defined text. Quickly grasp the main points of cases, briefs, motions, or other passages by having GAI summarize them. This is something other tech tools can do well, but GAI is often faster and more cost-effective.
- Brainstorm creative ideas. Tap into GAI's vast knowledge base for inspiration. Generate themes, storylines, or catchy headlines for your briefs.
- Draft starter text. Overcome blank-page syndrome with GAI-generated outlines, headings, or templates. Although you shouldn't blindly trust its legal accuracy, GAI can kickstart your writing process.
- Extract and organize information. GAI is great at working with defined text. Have it pull specific details from a brief or classify data into tables for you.
- Get quick answers. Use GAI for initial research on simple factual or legal questions. It can be a good starting point, especially for focused inquiries, but don't rely on it for specific cases or information you need to rely on. Domain-specific tools like Westlaw AI are better for that.
- Translate or explain text. GAI is a powerful translator and can help you understand complex terminology or concepts, making it ideal for explaining things to others.
- Content generation. GAI can be used to draft content for legal blogs, websites, or newsletters, which can help you reach a wider audience.
- General reference information. You can teach yourself about a client's matter, technology, a business concept, or nearly anything else.
- Note taking. Multi-modal models that can see and hear, like GPT's latest versions, can listen to you and take notes from your conversations or do quick research and tasks from voice commands. I often have a tool like ChatGPT listening in and have it look up things while I'm working on projects so I don't have to pause and do it myself.
- Other tasks that involve text, facts, or data that you can easily identify for GAI. The great thing about GAI is that if you work with it enough, you'll constantly find new uses. You simply need a sense of its limitations and the writing tasks it can help with.

GAI can fundamentally alter how we interact with language, opening doors to creative solutions and unprecedented efficiency. But understanding its strengths and limitations is everything.

13.2 Avoid Ethical and Practical Pitfalls

GAI has the potential to change the legal writing landscape, but you can't ignore the ethical and practical pitfalls. Because "with great power comes great responsibility."[3] And there may be no greater power in the coming years than the GAI-equipped lawyer.

[3] Spiderman made this phrase popular, originally in 1943 when he appeared in a comic for the first time. Brian Cronin, *When We First Met—When Did Uncle Ben First Say "With Great Power Comes Great Responsibility?,"* Comic Book Resources (July 15, 2015).

The first step is ensuring that your organization (your law school, your client, your law firm, or whoever else is relevant) allows you to use GAI as part of your writing process. For example, under guidelines issued by the California Bar, lawyers should get a client's approval before using GAI on their matters.[4] It is equally important to understand any legal requirements you might need to follow in using GAI. Some courts require lawyers to publicly disclose if they used GAI in their briefing. You'll also need to ensure your use of GAI doesn't risk disclosing sensitive client information to the public.

Even if you are allowed to use this technology on a task, there are as many pitfalls as possibilities. Let's explore key concerns to consider.

A Quick Summary

Don't overly rely on GAI. **GAI is a great tool for some things. It's a bad tool for others. Use your judgment and make sure GAI makes sense for your task.**

Stay competent and confidential. **GAI tools are changing fast. Stay up to date, make sure you understand how the particular tool you're using works, and pay particular attention to how your information is protected.**

Don't trust and always verify. **Accuracy in these tools could be a challenge for many years to come. Create a process of verifying anything you want to use from GAI.**

13.2.1. Don't Overly Rely on GAI

GAI works so well at first glance that it can lead folks to become too reliant on it. You might be wondering, "Should I be all that worried about this legal writing stuff? After all, if the technology is already smart enough to write a passing first draft of a motion or memo, why invest in my writing skills at all?"

Although GAI might sound like it knows what it's talking about, you can't effectively use this (or any tech tool) if you don't know what you want the final product to look like. So don't put your pen down yet. You still need to know how to produce good analysis, reasoning, research, and writing. You might be able to *pilot* GAI to create those things faster and better. But if you aren't in the driver's seat, then you'll be beholden to GAI in the years to come. Because our robot overlords will get smarter, and you might find yourself assisting the technology instead of it assisting you. Make the decision now about what sort of GAI relationship you want.

More of what lawyers do is being automated. That means it gets easier to skip learning how to research, learning how to put together a sentence, and soon, perhaps, learning how to think. This isn't an entirely new problem. If you fall for that trap, then you won't know when technology is providing you with a *good* answer, and when it's

[4]The State Bar of California Standing Committee on Professional Responsibility and Conduct, Practical Guidance for the Use of Generative Artificial Intelligence in the Practice of Law (2023).

providing you with a *great* answer. You certainly won't know how to guide the technology to come up with an *excellent* answer.

This is all why the new era we are entering is often referred to as the "pilot" era of lawyering: more of the small details in legal practice getting done by technology, with lawyers at the helm, controlling the levers of tools like GAI. So yes, maybe soon you'll even get a first draft of a motion or memo drafted by GAI. But you'll still be the pilot, adjusting, steering, and generally making the ride as smooth as possible.

That's too complicated for me; I like the analogy of bread machines. I make a lot of bread these days, and my bread machine makes it so much easier. I don't have to knead the dough by hand for an hour. I don't need to wait for the dough to rise. It's amazing. But the thing is, when the bread comes out bad (and it sometimes does), adjustments must be made. It could be that the flour I'm using should be kneaded a little less. Or that factors like humidity are putting a wrench in the works. When those challenges arise, I know how to adjust. Because although the bread machine is doing the heavy lifting, I know what it takes to make amazing bread.

If I didn't know what good bread looks like—and I didn't understand making bread myself—I couldn't make anything special happen with that bread machine. Every time, I would get the same bread, good or bad. Because at that point, I am working for the bread machine. It tells me what to put in it, and I do, and I get what I get.

So in the end, do you want to be a bread machine assistant, or do you want the bread machine to assist you? (If you don't like bread, I'm sorry and you can replace this analogy with something else.)

13.2.2 Stay Competent and Confidential

Lawyers owe an ethical duty of competence and diligence to their clients—as well as a duty of candor to courts and others. This means legal writers are on the hook for knowing how their tools work, how to use them, and what pitfalls to avoid. That certainly includes GAI. If a lawyer uses GAI to draft a paragraph or rewrite a sentence, it's their responsibility to ensure that the results are as effective as if the lawyer penned it themselves.

Being competent with GAI requires that you know some basics about how the technology works—and that you stay reasonably up to date as the technology evolves.[5] These tools are changing so quickly, and being used in so many other products, that it might soon be malpractice to *not* stay up to date, regardless of whether you're using GAI yourself.

When learning your GAI tools, pay particular attention to how your data are protected. Lawyers must consider confidentiality and data privacy duties when using GAI tools. We have an ethical obligation to maintain the confidentiality of our clients' information, which could be compromised if a GAI tool stores or shares your inputs with others.

Keep in mind there are two main ways your data could be compromised in GAI products: transmission and storage, on the one hand, and training data, on the other.

Like any cloud-based technology, GAI must stream your data from your device using some sort of service, store your data while being processed, and then transmit data back to you in a response. If your data are snatched in one of those streams, your information could be compromised. So it's always important to check on the data security practices your GAI product is using.

[5] Commentary to the ABA's Model Rules of Professional Conduct instructs that lawyers must continuously stay apprised of the "benefits and risks associated with technology." ABA Model Rule 1.1, Cmt. 8.

But GAI then poses unique data privacy challenge. Your inputs (and the responses you receive back) are gold to GAI companies. Indeed, these companies pay humans to do exactly what you do: work with GAI again and again as part of the human-training element of large language model creation. So you must also ensure your information won't be used in the GAI's training model.

One other issue to keep on your radar: bias. GAI tools so far have demonstrated bias in their responses. This bias stems from the data used to train these models, as well as the data we input while using them. GAI models learn from vast data sets, inevitably including some discriminatory content. As the saying goes, "Garbage in, garbage out." If a GAI's training data set is racist or prejudiced or hateful, those dark parts can leak into the GAI's responses. For instance, if ChatGPT encounters biased case law, it might subtly perpetuate harmful stereotypes in legal writing—something no ethical lawyer would knowingly do.

To ensure fairness in GAI-generated legal writing, developers and users must actively fight bias. This involves using bias detection tools, but also developing a critical eye to spot and adjust any harmful language in the writing that these models produce.

13.2.3. Don't Trust, but Verify

GAI-generated content might not always be entirely accurate or nuanced, particularly when dealing with complex legal concepts. Legal writers must be critical when using GAI tools, exercising their judgment and expertise to supplement the GAI's output.

Although GAI tools can generate content based on patterns in their training data, it might not have a comprehensive understanding of complex legal concepts. This limitation could lead to GAI-generated content that lacks depth or misinterprets legal principles. When drafting a brief on a novel legal issue, GAI could struggle to fully grasp the intricacies of the arguments, leading to a less coherent final product.

Legal writing also often requires adherence to jurisdiction-specific laws, regulations, and formatting standards. GAI's ability to adapt to these nuances might be limited, requiring legal writers to invest more time in tailoring the GAI-generated content to their audience's needs.

GAI-generated legal writing, although perhaps technically proficient, could also lack the intuition and emotional intelligence that human writers bring to our work. It might fail to effectively convey empathy, respond to client concerns, or adapt to unique situations. Again, this is a tool, not a wand.

GAI is transforming legal writing, but it cannot (yet) replace the critical thinking, ethical judgment, and client-centered approach that define a good lawyer. Remember, you should still be making the bread.

13.3 Learn Prompt Engineering

Now let's get in the GAI pilot seat. When you enter a question or some instructions into a GAI tool, you're *prompting* it for a response. At least that's what folks call it.[6] As anyone who has played around with GAI tools might have realized, different prompts result

[6] Query whether we'll keep calling it prompt engineering in the future. That's not the most exciting way to describe this collaboration.

in different outputs—some of which are closer to what you want than others. *Prompt engineering* aims at creating ideal instructions to get as close as possible to that perfect response.

And prompt engineering works. The results of your collaboration with GAI will greatly depend on your prompting skills. Even GAI experts don't always understand why prompting is so important. But it is. Shifting how you ask the question changes the results you'll get. Indeed, in the latest research, even tiny differences in a prompt produced dramatically improved results.[7] There are few skills more useful right now than prompt engineering, because this skill will unlock your ability to get GAI to do amazing things.

Let's start with the elephant in the room: Is there a magic "best prompt" for whatever legal task you are trying to accomplish? Sorry, but not yet. Despite the clickbait online suggesting the author has the "only five prompts you'll ever need," those one-size-fits-all prompts are rarely the best (or even close).[8] You often need to customize your prompts for your tasks and taste, particularly with legal writing. The good news is you can reuse your best prompts again and again—and keep improving them.

If you've tried a generic GAI chatbot like ChatGPT, you know it's easy. You type in some instructions, hit Enter, and get a response. But to unlock the legal-writing power of GAI, you need to go further to guide the AI. The more you guide it, the better it will know what sort of help you need.

A Quick Summary

Use organized and precise instructions. Although more information can help guide GAI, inconsistent or vague instructions create confusion. Organize your instructions and be specific.

Use roles. Give GAI a role so that it better understands how and what you want it to accomplish.

Use reasoning. Trigger step-by-step reasoning for complex questions.

Use parameters. Give GAI structure for its responses to get the results you're aiming for.

Use examples. Give GAI examples of what good responses (and bad responses) look like.

[7] Dina Genkina, AI Prompt Engineering Is Dead: Long Live AI prompt Engineering, IEEE Spectrum (Mar. 6, 2024) (sharing research about prompt optimization). This research also suggests that, over time, technology itself might help us optimize our prompts so that we need to work less to find the best instructions for our GAI tools. But this skill will still help you understand how and when to use GAI tools effectively.

[8] Again, emerging research suggests that someday there could be tools to help us optimize our prompts. But for now, we need to build them ourselves. Although we will see that GAI tools can help us brainstorm ways for improving our prompts already.

Use context and hints. Provide background context, priorities, and focuses to keep the GAI on task.

Iterate with follow-ups. Collaborate with GAI tools. You'll rarely get the best results the first time.

Consider emerging best practices. Research is suggesting that certain approaches and wording can dramatically improve your prompts. So experiment and keep up on the latest best practices.

Consider some writing use cases. GAI can collaborate on many different writing projects and tasks. Learn the possibilities and keep your mind open.

13.3.1. Use Organized and Precise Instructions

Prompts that are specific and narrow get better results. Your prompts should also deliver one point at a time. And, organize your prompt using headings, delimiters, and other tools that prevent the GAI from getting lost.

When you're first drafting your prompt, consider how you can precisely instruct GAI, given your goals. GAI struggles if you give it the whole world to parse, like "draft a contract." So go narrow and specific. Start with a concrete verb to let the GAI know what you want it to do, like "summarize," "brainstorm," "rewrite," extract," "create" and so on.

Instead of "Draft a confidentiality agreement," deliver one key piece of information at a time and keep the task narrow. We can then use this initial outline of the contract to dig deeper—perhaps working with GAI to craft each section with more guidance:

> Let's work on drafting a confidentiality agreement together. The agreement is between Acme and Widgets. Let's start by drafting the headings for the contract. Craft each heading to summarize the key terms of that section. Include an exhaustive list of possible terms for now.

Clear writing is key. That means proper punctuation, headings to break up information, and something unique to GAI called *delimiters*. This simply means separating portions of your prompt so that it's easy for GAI to understand what parts of your prompt are doing what. For the best results, use delimiters to separate text you want the GAI to work on from the rest of your instructions (so it doesn't confuse the text you want it to edit with your instructions for editing it). You should also use delimiters to separate examples from your general instructions.

Delimiters can be anything consistent so long as it won't confuse the GAI because it looks like a word. "***" works very well, according to the research. For example:

> As a renowned legal writer, please edit the following text. . . .
>
> ***
>
> For context, here is an example of excellent writing . . .
>
> ***
>
> Here is the text I'd like you to edit: "The court here has done a terrible thing. . . ."

Let's cover a few more preliminary principles for crafting the clearest prompts. First, understand that weights and priorities are key for these language models. So reinforcing the most critical goals for your task and being clear about the most important priorities helps:

> Above all, ensure that you do not change the substance of my writing at all. This is the most important limitation to keep in mind.

This power of priorities is likely why emerging research suggests that using strong emotional language gets better results. Powerful verbs, like "*transform* my writing into a very clear bulleted list" might get better results than a bland version of the same request. As might "You are doing a great job!" added onto your prompt.

Second, use GAI tools to give you feedback on how to better organize, simplify, and clarify your prompts. Experts often call this self-improvement prompting:

> You're a generative AI prompting expert.[9] Review my prompt below and revise it to be as effective, clear, and unambiguous as possible. Take it step by step and explain your reasoning at each stage.

Finally, the most effective prompts are often ones that break down tasks into smaller steps for the GAI and then ask it to do one thing at a time. This is often called "Skeleton of Thought" prompting.

The idea is that you first have the GAI tool create an outline of its response, or only the first step of its response. Then you give it feedback or guidance for carrying out the next step. So you might first ask the tool to provide ten ideas for a better verb in a sentence. Then once you pick your favorite, ask it to rewrite the sentence using the verb (as opposed to asking it to both pick the better verb and rewrite the sentence all at once). You don't always need to break tasks out like that, but doing so will help keep instructions more manageable for the AI brain.

13.3.2 Use Roles

Roles refer to giving GAI context and direction for how it should tackle a task—and how to prepare its answer—by having the AI take on the role of a person or entity. In legal writing, you can have GAI take on certain writing styles (like famous lawyers or publications) or take on the role of the sort of person you would normally be working with on that task, like a research librarian or judge.

The role you assign the GAI can influence the tone, style, and focus of its response. For example, assigning a research role might yield a neutral, factual response, while an attorney role could generate persuasive arguments. A judge role could help you test out a theory to see what the pushback might be to an argument.

There are few tasks that won't benefit from a role. So when crafting your prompts, consider this: What sort of person or job should the GAI emulate?

For writing style, I've had great success mixing some of my favorite legal and nonlegal writers and sources. Experiment until you find the right role for each task.

---

[9] This part of the instruction is giving the GAI tool a role. We'll revisit this concept later in the next section.

When using a role, it's often best to start your prompt with a concise phrase that sets the role—and add a helpful adjective to encourage GAI to use only high-quality sources when taking on the role (like mentioning a "well regarded lawyer" or "renowned legal writer"). For example:

> As an excellent legal research assistant, summarize the main points of the U.S. Supreme Court case "Brown v. Board of Education" in a neutral tone, suitable for a legal memo.

> As a highly skilled attorney representing the plaintiff, draft a persuasive opening statement for a medical malpractice case, highlighting the defendant's negligence.

> As a law professor, explain the concept of "res ipsa loquitur" in a clear and concise manner, providing a hypothetical example to illustrate the principle.

Consider a few final tips when it comes to roles. First, you can give GAI tools multiple roles. You might want to give your GAI the role of both a researcher and a judge to trigger both of those perspectives. Second, you can give GAI diverging roles. For example, you can have the GAI take on the perspective of different judges with different perspectives:

> Take on the role of 10 judges with different ideological perspectives about Constitutional law. Then analyze my brief from different perspectives to explore weaknesses from different angles.

13.3.3. Use Reasoning

For a legal writer, it's essential to understand how to harness the power of GAI's reasoning abilities to generate accurate and high-quality results.

GAI can be thought of as operating in two modes: a *reasoning* mode and a *nonreasoning* mode. In reasoning mode, GAI carries out discrete steps, like retrieving information first—and then a second step of using that information to carry out another task, like analyzing a question. In nonreasoning mode, GAI quickly generates answers based on its general knowledge.

Chain-of-thought (COT) prompting is used to trigger GAI's reasoning capabilities.[10] And there are a few ways to pull it off.

First, the easiest way to trigger reasoning is to use some magic words in your prompt. Research suggests that including language like "Let's think step-by-step" can instantly improve response quality. The following language has performed even better in the research: "Let's work this out step by step to be sure we have the right answer."

Second, you can trigger COT reasoning by breaking down the steps you'd like GAI to follow. This might take some time (and some trial and error), but you can generally think about the tasks you'd carry out—and then tell GAI to do the same thing. For example:

[10] Zhipeng Chen, *ChatCoT: Tool-Augmented Chain-of-Thought Reasoning on Chat-Based Large Language Models*, ar5iv (Jan. 9, 2024).

> First, find relevant legal provisions.
>
> Second, analyze the applicability of those provisions to the case.
>
> Third, provide a conclusion based on the analysis.

Next, you can ask GAI to explain its reasoning as it provides your answer. This forces GAI to come up with the steps it will take to reach a conclusion—and identify potential pitfalls to avoid.

For example, if you want GAI to check an answer to a question, you can tell it to first come up with its own answer—and then to check yours. This forces GAI to take at least two general steps before rushing to the answer, all without requiring you to provide every individual reasoning step.

> Your task is to determine if a solution is correct or not. To solve the problem, do the following.
>
> First, work out your own solution to the problem.
>
> Second, compare your solution to my solution and evaluate if my solution is correct. Don't decide if my solution is correct until you have done the problem yourself.
>
> Third, provide your feedback.

Or, again, ask GAI to give you the steps it will use to complete a task.

> Specify the steps you'll use to carry out this task.

A more advanced type of COT prompt is called a self-asking prompt. With this prompt tactic, you again have the GAI tool work in steps, but this time, you have it ask *itself* clarifying questions at each step. This encourages the model to do even more careful reasoning work as it reaches an answer:

> Improve the writing in the following paragraph. Take it step by step. **After each step, start a self-asking process where you ask yourself a series of relevant, critical questions about your approach and your answers from the prior step and ensure you've reached the best answer possible. Use any insights from this self-asking process to inform the next step.**

A final form of COT prompting is to ask the GAI tool to evaluate its responses using different criteria, then to redo its entire reasoning based on any insights it comes up with:

> Once you've completed your task, thoroughly review your answer and ensure it completely and fully answers the questions I provided you. Use whatever insights you find during this final review to produce a new response using what you learned.

A few final tips on reasoning prompts:

- Incorporate *if–then* statements to guide GAI's reasoning and focus on specific conditions. For example, "if you cannot find a source to support my statement, then respond 'no source found.'"

- Instruct GAI to compare and contrast ideas or concepts to provide a deeper understanding.
- Instruct GAI to provide citations or references for the information it uses in its response, ensuring accuracy and credibility. For example "Provide a citation to a support source for every statement you make."
- Use explicit reasoning constraints. For example, you could instruct GAI to "consider only the relevant case law and statutes from the jurisdiction of X."
- Specify which aspects of the task are more important than others to help GAI focus on what's important.
- Ask GAI to summarize your instructions to ensure it understands what you want.
- Ask GAI to reflect on its own thinking process, assumptions, or biases while generating a response.
- Consider using "certainty" prompting. This tactic instructs the GAI to provide a statement about how certain it is in the accuracy of its statements. This can help reduce accuracy issues and flag responses that you might want to triple check (rather than the double check you do on everything GAI provides you).

13.3.4. Set Parameters

GAI will follow nearly any guiding parameters you give it. The more information you provide about the structure and format of the response you're looking for, the better.

First, you can control how much depth you'd like GAI to provide. By default, GAI will often give you concise, superficial answers. Be granular and tell GAI what level of detail you'd like.

For example, let's say you're trying to improve the verb in a sentence. Rather than telling GAI to simply improve the verb, ask it to generate ten different examples, each using a different verb. If you're asking for GAI to explain a legal concept, tell it what its answer should look like. The more specific you can be—like by telling GAI how many examples you want, how many reasons you'd like, and so on—the better.

> Your explanation should be at least five paragraphs long and offer specific quotes from relevant cases. Your explanation should also include at least five specific examples of this legal doctrine.

On the flip side, when GAI is giving you too much information, confine its response by telling it how many lines, paragraphs, reasons, details, or other parameters to stay within.

You can also give GAI ground truths to overwrite what it might otherwise think. This is a different sort of parameter, as you are giving GAI some guidance about the universe within which it should provide its answer. For example, you can tell GAI to ignore certain things. Let's say you want GAI to edit some of your legal writing but ignore anything in quotation marks:

> All text within quotation marks is accurate and should not be modified.

You can also tell GAI the format you'd like its response in. Perhaps you want a table with labels. Or you'd like a list set up a certain way. Or you'd like bullet points. GAI is exceptionally good at identifying patterns like this.

Provide a list of every citation in this brief. List each citation in Bluebook format. Organize the citations by court decisions, statutes, and other sources:

Court Decisions:

Statutes:

Other Sources:

Here are a few more parameter tips:

- Instruct GAI to generate multiple, independent answers or ideas to increase the chances of obtaining a great response.
- Use keywords like *summary* or *detailed* to help guide the preferred response depth.
- Give GAI a reading grade or specific audience to write to, which will help refine its response.
- There are nearly endless ways to set parameters for detail or depth GAI will provide. For example, some experts suggest the five Ws: asking GAI for the who, what, when, where, and why of a topic.
- You can even ask many GAI tools for a format that will optimize your ability to paste its results into a spreadsheet, or instead, a format optimized to paste into a Word document.

13.3.5. Provide Examples

Examples are often called *few-shot* prompts in the GAI world. This means you're giving GAI a few exemplar prompts and responses that have the characteristics you're looking for. These examples are even more powerful than other parameters because you're showing GAI exactly what you want it to do—and it can learn a ton from even a single example. Keep the following guidelines in mind:

- Diversify your examples. Ensure that your examples cover a wide range of scenarios to achieve diverse results.
- Randomize the order. Arrange your examples randomly unless you are specifically looking for a pattern.
- Provide at least four examples, although the research suggests using as many as possible to maximize effectiveness.

Let's say you want GAI to help you come up with better verbs for key sentences in your brief, such as headings. Provide GAI with examples of headings containing weak verbs followed by sample responses with improved verbs. GAI is highly adept at recognizing and following patterns, so it will also learn from your labels and formatting.

Weak sentence: The court issued a ruling on the motion.
Better sentence: The court ruled on the motion.

Weak sentence: The deadline was not met by the lawyers.
Better sentence: The lawyers missed the deadline.

Then you can include the sentence you actually want GAI to improve, following the same pattern:

Weak sentence: The court's ruling is not released.

(GAI's response): Better sentence: The court has not ruled yet.

Here are some more few-shot tips and tricks.

- While providing several examples is helpful, ensure that each is of high-quality and relevant to your desired outcome. Poor examples can inject confusion.
- Try to use situations from actual legal cases or documents to provide GAI with a more accurate understanding of real-world scenarios.
- Structure your examples as prompt–answer pairs, presenting a problem and its solution, to help GAI identify patterns and learn to generate good responses.
- Mix both long and short examples to help GAI learn how to handle different levels of complexity and verbosity in responses.
- Show GAI examples of both correct and incorrect answers for a given problem, so it can learn to differentiate between the two.

13.3.6. Provide Context and Hints

Context plays a crucial role in guiding GAI toward generating your desired output. By supplying background information about the topic or the type of response you want, you improve the model's understanding of your task. To indicate that the provided text is context, make it explicit by stating, "The following information is context." And use delimiters like *** to keep your context clear from the rest of your prompt.

For example, let's say you want to be sure GAI uses the right case for some task you've given it:

Summarize the *Palsgraf v. Long Island Railroad Co.* case.

***

The following information is context. In the legal case I'm looking for, the plaintiff, Mrs. Palsgraf, sued the railroad company for injuries sustained because of the negligence of its employees.

You can use a word like *hint* to signal to GAI that certain keywords are critical to your desired result. In recent studies, using hints significantly increased the quality of responses.

For example, if you instruct GAI to summarize the *Palsgraf* case, you could provide some hint words to help GAI focus on what you care about most:

Summarize the *Palsgraf v. Long Island Railroad Co.* case.

***

Hint: Reasonably foreseeable, causation, negligence, proximate cause

These are some additional tips for using context:

- Provide GAI with any background information that could be helpful for your legal task, like your jurisdiction, the most important cases, key legal concepts, and so on.
- Provide the GAI with analogies to help it understand complex concepts or relationships more easily.
- Provide bullet points or content from your writing project to get GAI started. The more context you provide, the better.
- Keep in mind different GAI tools have different "context windows"—meaning they can only handle so much text in your prompts.

13.3.7. Iterate with Follow-ups

GAI tools remember your previous prompts within a conversation—at least to some extent and depending on what type of GAI tool you are using. And one of the easiest ways to improve results is to give GAI feedback, telling it what it did right and what it did wrong. By using a few follow-ups and iterating (you'll get much better answers, as well as improved prompts you can use in the future).

This makes working with GAI much easier than prior tools. If the GAI tool doesn't give you a good answer, tell it that and it will do better the next time. If it gives you a partially good answer, tell it so and it will try again.

Let's consider a few other principles when iterating with follow-ups, then we'll look at an example.

- When providing feedback to a GAI, be as clear and specific as possible. This helps the GAI understand your expectations and refine its response accordingly.
- Provide the GAI with examples based on its response—what did it do well and what didn't it? Quotes from a GAI's response work great.
- When following up, address the GAI directly, and explicitly state that you are asking a follow-up question. This can help GAI understand the context and provide an appropriate response.
- If the GAI seems unsure about your prompt or the desired outcome, encourage it to ask clarifying questions. This can help improve its understanding of your requirements and lead to better results.
- If you're not satisfied with the GAI's response, ask it to provide alternative answers or approaches. This can help you explore different perspectives and solutions.
- Start with simpler prompts and examples to familiarize the GAI with the task, then progressively introduce more complex scenarios.

For example:

> Improve the two verbs in this sentence: "The garbage is removed by John, and Susie is taking a walk to the park."
>
> (GAI's response): John took out the garbage, and Susie walked to the park.

Pretty good, but let's say you want a more descriptive verb in the second clause about Susie. Follow up with this:

The first clause is great but choose a better verb for Susie that describes walking quickly.

(GAI's response): John took out the garbage, and Susie ran to the park.

Consider some final prompt engineering tips.

- Ask the GAI tool to generate potentially useful information about a given question before generating a final response. This is a kind of follow-up. The idea is that you can often get better results by first getting some starting information or data from GAI. Then use that response to craft a more detailed second prompt.
- Affirmative instructions work better than negative ones. Avoid saying *not* to do something, instead specify what to *do*. For example, it's better to get more specific with "provide only a single line of text in your answer" as opposed to "do not provide lengthy text."
- Repeat instructions at the end. The research suggests that GAI tools can be susceptible to recency bias, meaning that information at the end of the prompt might have more significant influence over the output than information at the beginning. So try including a reminder of the key instructions at the end of your prompt.
- Consider giving the GAI a path if it can't find a good answer. Say you are asking the GAI to edit your writing. What if your writing is already perfect? Don't make GAI make stuff up: Tell it that if it has no improvements to simply respond with "This is already great!" Tell the GAI tool if it can't find a source to respond with "I cannot find an answer." These sorts of parameters will help encourage the tool to be accurate.
- Use diverse prompting. The idea here is that you create multiple versions of an important prompt you want to perfect. Five is the best target number from the research. To make this easy, you can ask the GAI tool to create the versions for you: "Please create five different versions of the following prompt. Make each version unique and from a different perspective." Then run each prompt and compare results. Remember that you can save prompts and portions of prompts that work well for future projects. So your investments are not wasted.
- Come at difficult tasks from different angles. GAI is unlike any other tech tool you've worked with before. But it might take some creativity or trial and error. For example, researchers have confirmed better results on certain tasks by having the GAI explain its thinking process (for example, when asking the GAI to choose between options, have the GAI explain the reasoning or strengths and weaknesses of each option).
- Stack prompts of different types. Provide a role, instructions, parameters, context and hints, and examples all together: "Act as a federal judge. Explain how defamation works. Provide two paragraphs or less. Hints: intent, defamatory, falsity." Prompts with more structured guidance like this will get you the best results.
- Don't get discouraged with poor results at first. Working with GAI is a skill set, albeit one you need no technical background for. Give yourself time to experiment. There is no one right way to work with these AI tools (at least, not yet).
- Finally, invest in your work. When you find good prompts (or a good structure for certain types of prompts), save them so you can reuse them later. You can also

use GAI to help you revise your prompts, improve them, organize them, compress them into fewer words, and more.

13.3.8. Get Creative

GAI is great at giving you averages: the average structure for a brief, the average approach for a motion, the average writing of lawyers. And those averages can be a great place to start on your writing projects. Because getting to average takes time. With GAI's help, you can spend more of that time getting to excellent, which is what this book has been all about.

But GAI can help you on this last part of your journey, too. You just need to push its limits. When you're looking for help on tasks where average won't cut it, encourage your GAI tool to get creative.

Some simple prompt language will get you a long way here. Indeed, in a recent study, references to the popular sci-fi show *Star Trek* dramatically improved certain prompts. So experiment and come at your prompting from different angles.

> Come up with three unique angles to approach this sentence in an unusual way most lawyers wouldn't.

> Provide the contrarian view on this topic.

> Brainstorm the most unique, unusual approach for the verb in this sentence.

Creativity prompts like this won't usually get you a finished product. But they will often get you ideas, inspiration that will spark a truly fantastic improvement that you might have struggled to find on your own.

You can also try triggering different thinking styles, design approaches, and other parameters to get GAI to think outside the box. For example:

- "Use an outline format"
- "Use a mind map format"
- "Use the structure: (1) What, (2) Why, (3) How"
- "Use lean thinking"
- "Think like an artist"
- And so on.

In the end, the breadth of GAI's powers is easy to miss among the averages. If you're working on a task that requires the unusual, then use an unusual prompt. Let me hit it home with a real-life example. I was consulting with an elite appellate team in a pro bono case. The matter was an important one, impact litigation, and the lawyers knew that they needed to curate every word.

The team was struggling to get the wording in a heading just right. They'd tried dozens of ideas and none was perfect. They asked me for some help. If I can find the time, I'm always happy to throw around ideas in pro bono matters. This time it was easy. I asked them, "Have you tried brainstorming with a GAI tool?"

They hadn't, so we did. We tried a couple of generic prompts, like "help me improve this heading" and "provide five versions of this heading that use better style."

But the results still weren't there. The case was about parody, and just for fun, with the team watching on the Zoom, I tried something random: "Try rewriting this heading in the form of a Haiku."

Silly, right? But the GAI started giving us verses and, incredibly, one of the lines had a turn of phrase that we all knew immediately was the seed of the perfect heading. With a bit more refining, we had a winner.

I'm not suggesting you have GAI tools write poems about all your writing projects (although you could try that). But I am suggesting that you unleash your creativity and have fun when working on GAI tasks that require out-of-the-box thinking. You never know what prompt will be needed to get the perfect response.

13.3.9. Consider Common Writing Use Cases

Let's finish our GAI journey by considering some examples of the most common legal writing use cases.

First, we can clearly use GAI to help us with writing style. GAI is amazing at generating ideas to improve your prose. This might be the most helpful way to use GAI in legal writing. Because you aren't looking for accurate facts or complex reasoning. You're looking for writing ideas—and GAI has access to more syntax and style than you can imagine. So we can have GAI help us with things like this:

> Pick better verbs in this sentence to convey [insert emotion or imagery you're aiming for in the sentence].

You can also ask GAI more open-ended questions to improve sentence style—but as always, the more guidance you give it about what you want to improve, the better.

> What could be better about this sentence: "The boy cried and whined."
>
> (GAI's response): This sentence is a bit repetitive. The word "cried" implies the action of whining, so the word "whined" isn't necessary. Try something like, "The boy sobbed. . . .

Work with GAI to improve the style of key sentences like headings, introductions, or an important email opening. Ask GAI to emulate a writing style that you prefer (like a popular lawyer or publication) or break down exactly what style improvements you would like some inspiration on.

> I am trying to improve the verb in this sentence. I want to use a verb that makes the action sound worse: "The plaintiff is not filing the appropriate paperwork."
>
> (GAI's response): How about "The plaintiff is disregarding the appropriate paperwork"?
>
> Can you come up with another verb instead of disregard?
>
> (GAI's response): "The plaintiff ignored the appropriate paperwork"?

Second, GAI can help with our grammar and mechanics. Existing tools can't check for a fraction of the pitfalls that GAI can. Mechanics and grammar are well-defined topics GAI can tackle. For example:

> Correct the punctuation in this page: . . .

Or use GAI for help identifying (or explaining) writing mechanics that you aren't sure of:

> What is wrong with this sentence: "The lawyers was wrong once again."
>
> (GAI's response): This sentence should be "The lawyers were wrong once again." "Lawyers" is plural, so it should be "were" instead of "was."

Third, summarize text and extract information. Summarizing text that you want to use or quickly understand is another GAI superpower, because you're giving the GAI tool a defined set of information to work with. We can make our reading easier:

> Summarize this text for a third grader:
>
> Summarize the statute and keep it to one paragraph.

GAI is also great for paraphrasing or revising quotes. This is another task that focuses on defined text, so the technology excels at it.

> Paraphrase this quote:

Fourth, use GAI to draft documents or sections of documents. GAI is great for giving you some starter text for a common procedural section, a template for a contract or rote motion, or a kernel to start writing a bigger document so you can get something on the page with a rough structure. Of course, you will always need to customize, edit, and verify anything you draft with a GAI tool.

Fifth, brainstorm writing ideas. This is a great way to use GAI. But realize that the more it's being creative, the less you can trust any facts or data it gives you. Consider GAI here a muse rather than a writer. For example:

> Brainstorm interview questions for a witness involved in [insert facts].

> Write a theme for two people fighting over a retirement account.

Sixth, classify, format, or get help with other technical work. If you need to organize information from your case's facts, or case law and holdings; format parts of a document; or any other easily identified task with text and data, GAI has you covered. And if the task is too difficult for your GAI tool, you can always ask it for help using another tool like Microsoft Excel.

> List these cases in alphabetical order:

> Help me create an Excel formula to organize my deposition data.

Another fantastic use of GAI is to help with editing others' work and writing collaboration generally. Use GAI to help you explain your writing feedback to a colleague in a clearer way that they can understand. Or have a GAI help you create a style guide to help others on your team in their writing projects.

> Below is a sample of my writing. Create a style guide providing 20 items exemplified by my writing with examples of each.

You'll need to do some follow-up prompting to get your guide tweaked, but there's no easier way to create a writing playbook for yourself or others.

Beyond simple brief drafting and style improvement, you can do more. Run a presentation by GAI for feedback, ask for the biggest weaknesses in your oral argument, or get help with mundane tasks like labeling exhibits. In the end, GAI can be a fantastic legal writing partner. It can help you brainstorm. It can prod you to look at a sentence or paragraph or topic in a new way. It can help you organize or extract information from nearly any text.

But getting good results will require you to be the pilot, not the passenger. You will need to be the one questioning, guiding, editing, and verifying. GAI is a tool, and it likely will be for many years to come. So remember what GAI is good at, and what it will need some help to figure out. And know what things it isn't helpful for at all.

Practice these techniques and technologies with Write.law's exercises and checklists, plus other resources at www.levelupyourlegalwriting.com

ASPEN PUBLISHING | write.law

14

Level Up Today and Tomorrow

> Success isn't always about greatness. It's about consistency. Consistent hard work leads to success. Greatness will come."—Dwayne Johnson

Hopefully you feel like you've learned a lot by now. But don't confuse *learning* and *improving*. Studies show that we humans love the *feeling* of learning—that emotion you get when you're reading something and the light bulb blinks on.

Maybe it's a book like this one. "Wow!" you think. "This is fascinating!" You read voraciously, close the cover, and go about your day. Science suggests that you just got a learning high. You felt like you learned something. You felt like you got smarter. And that felt good. But really, not much changed in your brain. You probably won't even remember what you read a few days later.

For legal writing, like any skill, learning isn't enough. You need to take what you learn and put it into action. And that can be the hardest part. But there are tools that can help you see real writing improvement in short order.

In this chapter, we cover:

- How to leverage habit science.
- Making a writing practice plan.
- Making it fun.

14.1 Leverage Habit Science

The first tool is *habit*. That word triggers many of us. It means going to the gym daily and always doing your homework early. But habit science is exciting, because it offers proven ways to develop not only personally, but professionally, too. Let's explore some of the simplest methods for building new writing habits.

Experts often talk about the habit cycle.[1] This is a framework for creating new habits, bad or good. The cycle has four parts:

- The cue
- The craving
- The response
- The reward

Every habit is powered by these four underlying steps. Some cue in our environment (or our own mind) triggers a craving. We respond to that craving with action. And then we receive a reward that reinforces the entire cycle. Each step is always present (in some form), or we wouldn't be in the habit in the first place.

Eliminate one step and the habit breaks. Put each in place and a new habit forms. Here's a simple example of how this cycle can work to create a bad habit.

- The cue: You hit a stumbling block in drafting your motion.
- The craving: You feel frustrated and overwhelmed and want to distract yourself from those feelings.
- The response: You pull out your phone and scroll through social media.
- The reward: You forgot about your frustrations for a few minutes and feel better.

You've now created a habit cycle with an enticing reward. When you hit the hard stuff, you go right to the phone and relieve the negative feelings.

To exploit this insight, use the cycle to your advantage. Let's say you want to create a habit of working on your writing a little bit each day. Simply build each of these steps for yourself and stick to it for a while. Habit made.

- The cue: Set an alarm to remind yourself to write at 2:00 p.m.
- The craving: Be concrete with yourself about why you want to write better. Perhaps to win more cases.
- The response: Spend ten minutes working on your writing.
- The reward: Don't shirk this step. Give yourself some sort of reward and make it concrete. Maybe it's some smartphone time or something else entirely. But make sure you enjoy it.

Other habit tricks out there might work wonders for you, too. For example, *habit stacking* has you take an existing habit and link up a new habit that you want to start. It's much easier to piggyback off an existing habit than it is to create a new one out of whole cloth.

Another habit tool is temptation bundling. You take something you enjoy and bundle it with a habit you want to build. It gets at that reward step in the cycle. Maybe you review your emails each day while having your favorite coffee.

In the end, you can use habit cycles to adopt better writing practice and to break the practices that make your writing worse.

[1] James Clear, Atomic Habits: An Easy & Proven Way to Build Good Habits & Break Bad Ones (2018).

14.2 Make a Writing Practice Plan

With the basics down, let's get into the details: your writing practice plan. There are a few insights from training experts that will help you stick to your writing training over the long run.

First, start really small. This is the most proven method for building new skills. And it's easy. We humans love instant gratification, and that's true even when we are *imagining* the results we want. But going big at the outset will nearly always fail because we fall off the wagon and get discouraged. Or we are so overwhelmed we never hop on in the first place.

So start your legal writing training with small commitments. Try working on your writing every week for ten minutes. Trust the science here. By creating that small habit, you'll start to see payoffs. And it's much easier to build on existing habits. Even if you only stick with that ten minutes, you'll start improving in big ways and faster than you'd think.

In the same start-small vein, focus on a single skill at a time. The more you try to pile on, the harder it is to create strong new writing habits. So pick one writing technique, or one set of techniques, to develop and focus on. When you have it down, add another. Be specific and concrete with each new writing tool you want to practice.

Maybe you want to work on your sentence style. Great. Jump to that chapter now, pick up a few techniques, and start practicing them. Perhaps you take 30 minutes to draft an email to a friend—but actively build each sentence, questioning every writing choice. Maybe you pull out some of your old writing and rework the sentences in the first few pages.

Next, you've got to stay accountable. Training is more likely to succeed if you don't go it alone. By finding one other person to train with (or to at least check in with) you'll multiply your chances of success. So find someone who wants to hone their skills, too, and buddy up.

You can also leverage self-accountability—giving yourself deadlines and other rules to stick to your training. It's too easy to devote some time to your skills today and fall behind tomorrow. Regularly check in with yourself and see where you're going.

As part of that check-in, work hard to find your pain points. When you struggle in your writing, always stop and ask *why*. Most of us avoid peering too closely when we struggle with skills like writing. Because focusing on that struggle requires us to reflect on failure or what we aren't good at. And who likes doing that?

But if you make yourself give a little thought to why you're avoiding or procrastinating—or simply why you're stressed about a writing project—you will often discover insights that will unlock your writing in new ways. This gets back to your process. Figuring out what you hate about your writing is the best insight for getting better. Your pain points steer you toward the best improvements.

We've already covered perhaps the most useful way to develop your writing skills: using editing checklists. By taking control over your editing time, you're training your brain to use new writing techniques with purpose. By focusing on, say, using better verbs or crafting better headings, you're going to the writing gym with every project.

You can be more active with your editing time, too. Try picking up a draft that you've been working on and edit it for a single new writing technique that you're interested in. If you want to take it to the next level, mark each time that you already used the technique or any time that you should have—you'll be doing some benchmarking. You're training yourself to spot these moves and wiring your brain to recognize when the technique is helpful.

Don't passively check off boxes; force yourself to find at least five or ten examples of each technique whenever you work on a project. That way, you can be sure to practice the techniques, even if it's only because you're looking for places to use them. There are few techniques that you can't incorporate at least once or twice into a meaty legal document.

You can also work to get more sensitive in noticing what techniques are being used by the authors you are reading everyday—both legal and nonlegal. Why did the author use that phrase? That structure? What works better for you? One of the best ways to pick up new techniques is to read writing that uses them. Everyone from Stephen King to Brian Garner recommends this approach, and for good reason. There is no better way to reprogram your writing intuition.

So identify some legal writers you admire and read them voraciously. Even better, mark each time you spot one of the moves you happen to be working on at the time.

I offer a few final tips to keep in mind, cultivated from years of coaching top practitioners.

- **Get feedback on your weaknesses.** Ask for feedback regularly and with purpose. Set expectations with your feedback giver ahead of time. Schedule feedback meetings well in advance. Ask your feedback giver for specifics and take careful notes. And of course, set aside time to track your weaknesses for yourself.
- **Keep track of what writing muscles you want to work out.** Keep a running list of specific writing improvements you want to work on so that your training is manageable and easy to remember when busy.
- **Schedule writing time (not working time).** Be consistent; be reasonable. Scheduling more frequent shorter sessions is more likely to build habits. Remember to forgive yourself for falling off the wagon and reward yourself for work well done.
- **Benchmark so you know if you're improving.** Ask for mentors and peers to plot out improvements and stagnancies. Ask for specific examples in your writing. Better yet, ask for feedback on goals you're working on at the time. Tell your feedback giver your expectations before their review. You can also benchmark yourself. An easy way is to pull out a piece you've written recently and edit for the items in your working list.
- **Write your training plans down.** Regularly revisit your writing plan. How can you expose yourself to different types of legal writing? How can you work on different types of legal matters to stretch your writing muscles? How can you get feedback from different legal writers?

Now let's get to some concrete ideas for going to the writing gym.

14.3 Make It Fun

Let's finish with some final ideas to start you on your writing workouts. Keep in mind, though, that the key is to experiment and only adopt the practices you enjoy. This will never work if you hate the process.

- **Practice your legal writing on a platform like Write.law.** Online learning tools—particularly those powered by AI, like Write.law—can make learning new techniques a breeze. Just log in and start practicing the structure or style you're most interested in.
- **Re-edit old work.** Pull out a piece that you wrote in the past (preferably at least a few months old) and scrupulously edit it for 15 minutes. Focus on incorporating your running list of new moves.
- **Edit someone else's work.** Grab a brief or article—doesn't matter what it is; something that you didn't write—and meticulously edit it. Again, focus on incorporating your running list of new moves. You could add transitions throughout the document. Or any other writing techniques that you need some practice with. By focusing on a single move for an entire edit, you get results. But also notice any new writing techniques that you think are working as you read. You're developing your reading sensitivity.
- **Use one-read editing to focus on bumps in the writing road.** Use the one-read editing techniques we looked at in Chapter 8 on some writing to gain insight into what slows readers down. As a reminder, one-read editing has you mark a page every time you need to reread a sentence, paragraph, or section to extract the key ideas. You can use one-read editing to practice on one of your documents or someone else's. A few pages are enough. Now go back and try to figure out how to smooth over the bumps. How could the author have written so that the one-read rule was met?
- **Try journaling.** There are a million ways to journal. If you want to go very modest, try one-sentence journaling. This has you write down one good sentence you found each day. Or a paragraph. The point is to force yourself to find *something* writing-related, and new, to add to your journal each day. Soon you will have a compendium of excellent writing ideas tailored to your preferences.
- **Stretch your writing muscles with writing parameters.** Explain some broad or complex subject you know a lot about in 100 words, or using only single-syllable words, or only active verbs. These parameters force you to look at your writing differently.
- **Write an introduction for one of your favorite judicial opinions.** Try to capture the persuasive points and themes even better than the judge did. Or try the same tactic on a brief by a writer you admire.
- **Explain a complicated legal doctrine that you are familiar with without looking at any resources.** The point is to write as clearly and conversationally as you can. Compare this version with an introduction you wrote traditionally. See what you learn.

These are by no means the only way to go to the writing gym. But they're a good start. If you are spending time working on writing, there's no going wrong.

Level Up with Technology

Technology can also help you hone your legal writing skills. As we've already explored, technology can assist you in creating an editing checklist, which is an easy way to keep track of your skills and practice techniques in your projects. Scheduling apps, calendaring apps, and other tools we've covered can also help here, as can education tech tools. For example, Write.law offers dozens of legal writing courses, full of interactive practice and examples. We make it easy to improve your legal writing in minutes a day.

GAI is once again a fantastic legal writing practice companion. Sit down with your favorite GAI chatbot (or use one of Write.law's training apps powered by AI) and start learning. Perhaps:

Can you explain what is wrong with this sentence grammatically? Break it down step by step for me and provide a corrected version with an explanation.

I want to practice writing more concisely. Please provide me with a confusing piece of legal writing so that I can edit it. Make sure there are realistic but wordy phrases and sentences for me to practice on.

I want to elevate my writing style. Can you give me a few examples of [insert a technique you want to learn] from legal writing?

I want to create a schedule to practice my legal writing. I only have an hour or so a week to devote to my writing improvement. What are some ideas to make my learning time the most effective it can be?

Conclusion

Lawyers come in many varieties, and we all bring something unique to our craft. Some love the courtroom. Some wouldn't be caught in court if you paid them. Some love working with clients. Some prefer to lock themselves in their office, untangling complex questions in silence. Some love geeking out on the latest technology. Some wish they could lose their smartphone and never find it again.

You don't need to lawyer like everyone else to love this job. And you don't need to be good at everything to succeed.

But there is one thing we all must do, and do well. And that is write. Because there is no lawyering without writing. Whether it's to clients, to colleagues, to judges, to companies, or to ourselves. We write to share our expertise and our ideas. We write to persuade and we write to educate. There is no skill that will serve you more, every day, than your writing.

My hope for you is that wherever you are on your writing journey, the techniques in this book help you reach the next level. But there is no end to getting better. So build on these techniques with your own. And never stop leveling up your legal writing.

Practice these techniques and technologies with Write.law's exercises and checklists, plus other resources at www.levelupyourlegalwriting.com

ASPEN PUBLISHING | write.law

INDEX